CANADIAN SOCIAL POLICY

Edited by Shankar A.Yelaja

HN
107
.C354

Canadian Cataloguing in Publication Data

Main entry under title:

Canadian social policy

Bibliography: p.
Includes index.
ISBN 0-88920-049-1 bd.   ISBN 0-88920-050-5 pa.

1. Canada - Social policy - Addresses, essays,
lectures.   I. Yelaja, Shankar A., 1926-

HN107.C35   309.2'12'0971   C77-001818-1

Copyright © 1978

Wilfrid Laurier University Press
Waterloo, Ontario, Canada
N2L 3C5

Cover design by Michael Baldwin MSIAD

Dedication

To fulfill the social work profession's original commitment to its ideals and simultaneously to foster that passion of inquiry which is the essence of scholarship.

For that passion, in the end, determines what social workers truly know and therefore how they will act, if they act well.

Acknowledgements

Writing a book can be a lonely venture but in this case the undertaking has been greatly lightened—and at times even made a decided pleasure—through the help, encouragement and support from several persons. I am grateful to those scholars whose collaborative efforts have been crucial in creating this volume. The contributing scholars drawn from different social science disciplines were patient in working with me throughout the project.

Through its appraisal process, the Social Science Research Council of Canada has offered valuable suggestions for revisions and improvements in the manuscript. The feedback from the Social Science Research Council appraisers has reinforced my conviction that scholarly peer review provides a necessary service to academic writers. The book has been published with the help of a grant from the Social Science Research Council of Canada, using funds provided by the Canada Council. Naturally, I am grateful to SSRC for its subvention.

My colleagues at Wilfrid Laurier University have offered moral support and consultation. In particular, I am indebted to Professors John Redekop, Francis Turner and John Weir, whose encouragement and guidance helped keep up my spirits. The editorial assistance I received from Sue Crowne in improving the overall quality of the manuscript is gratefully acknowledged. Finally, the continued support of Wilfrid Laurier University and its many resources, including Wilfrid Laurier University Press, was indispensable in the completion of this project.

To all my deepest gratitude!

Faculty of Social Work   SHANKAR A. YELAJA
Wilfrid Laurier University

Contributing Authors

GRACE M. ANDERSON
Professor of Sociology
Wilfrid Laurier University
Waterloo, Ontario

ROBIN F. BADGLEY
Professor of Sociology
University of Toronto
Toronto, Ontario

DANIEL BURNS
Program Manager
City of Toronto Planning Board
Toronto, Ontario

CATHERINE A. CHARLES
Doctoral Student in Sociology
Columbia University
New York, New York

MARGRIT EICHLER
Associate Professor of Sociology
Ontario Institute for Studies
  in Education
Toronto, Ontario

MAURICE KELLY
Associate Professor of Social Work
Wilfrid Laurier University
Waterloo, Ontario

JOHN MELICHERCIK
Professor of Social Work
Wilfrid Laurier University
Waterloo, Ontario

E. PALMER PATTERSON II
Associate Professor of History
University of Waterloo
Waterloo, Ontario

JOHN REDEKOP
Professor of Political Science
Wilfrid Laurier University
Waterloo, Ontario

DAVID ROSS
Principal Administrator
Manpower Policies
Organization for Economic
  Cooperation and Development
Paris, France

MAX SALTSMAN
Member of Parliament
House of Commons
Ottawa

RICHARD SPLANE
Professor of Social Work
University of British Columbia
Vancouver, British Columbia

FRANCIS J. TURNER
Professor of Social Work
Wilfrid Laurier University
Waterloo, Ontario

JOHN WEIR
Professor of Economics
Wilfrid Laurier University
Waterloo, Ontario

BRIAN WHARF
Professor of Social Work
University of Victoria
Victoria, British Columbia

SHANKAR A. YELAJA
Professor of Social Work
Wilfrid Laurier University
Waterloo, Ontario

Preface

During my past ten years of teaching social policy at the Wilfrid Laurier University Faculty of Social Work, I have been appalled by the lack of Canadian literature on social policy. It has been necessary to sift through many diverse sources such as government documents, Hansard reports, unpublished reports and documents of social agencies to assemble comprehensive teaching materials. The lack of Canadian literature on social policy forces reliance on British and American literature. Although there are several excellent books written on the analysis of social policy and social welfare institutions, it is clear that these books do not provide an adequate frame of reference for the assessment and analysis of Canadian social welfare institutions, social policies and social services. While non-Canadian books can be used to gain a universal perspective of social policy, texts which interpret Canadian social policy as it has developed from Canadian socio-cultural and economic institutions are required to give our students an appropriate background.

In assembling this volume, I have attempted to fill this need by including original articles on some of the facets of social policy in Canada. While my primary purpose is, of course, pedagogical, I have tried to organize the book so that it can be maximally useful to several disciplines. Therefore, the first section is devoted to conceptual and theoretical aspects of social policy. The second section is composed of nine studies on specific issues of interest to students of social policy. The third section incorporates five studies which deal with the process of social policy development. The fourth and final section is devoted to one essay on the evaluation of social policies.

This book is a modest attempt to make a contribution to the Canadian literature on social policy. The central objectives of this collection of essays are: (1) to help students of Canadian social policy begin to understand social welfare concepts, ideology, the process of social policy formulation, and the substantive issues of social policy from a Canadian perspective, and (2) to stimulate discussion and debate on major social policy issues confronting Canadian society today.

These two objectives are perhaps easier to state than to realize in practice. When the project began in 1972, it became obvious that it would not be easy to combine the two objectives in a single book because of the varying demands of students and others wishing to follow social policy debate and its implications. An attempt was made to reconcile the two objectives by means of a common outline that was made available, at the beginning, to each essay author and also by specifying expectations for the individual author's contribution. To what extent both of these objectives are realized is, of course, left open to the judgment of the reader. Some readers will have the impression that some topics are lightly touched upon and could be explored in greater depth. These readers may wish to follow the topic further with the help of the bibliographies at the end of the specific chapters.

The editor of any volume that has such a broad scope is beset by many problems of choice. In selecting the studies and writers for this book, I approached the task well aware that it would not be possible to include all the issues involved in the development of social policy in Canada. Indeed, it is often difficult, if not impossible, to identify issues that will remain timely and pertinent without becoming dated. The articles and their authors have been chosen, then, because they seem to me to represent the most current and challenging ideas in social policy.

In Canada today, we are experiencing a period of great social tension and turbulence. Manifestations of the social turbulence are evident everywhere. The poor people have stopped marching with placards in front of Parliament Hill. They have organized and are demanding an end to the inequality of their income and opportunities. The native people have seen the smoke signals of the devastating social and economic effects of northern development. They are united in their assertion of claims for their native and territorial rights. The arrival of new immigrants from distant lands with differing cultural backgrounds, particularly the visible minority groups from Third World countries, has put the multicultural policy to a test. Demands from the elderly, physically handicapped, prisoners, mentally retarded, rural poor, women, and many other groups for social services have become volatile. The interest groups have progressed from rhetoric to an organized voice for participation in the decision-making on policies and programmes that affect their lives. And finally, the election of the Parti Québécois in Quebec on November 15, 1976 has shaken the nation's political structure, thus creating a crisis around national unity. All of these societal conditions have profound implications for Canadian social policy.

These conditions force us to identify and deal with elements of conflict apparent in Canadian society. Conflicts around the sharing of national wealth, distribution of resources, regional disparities, linguistic rights, and the role of government in welfare have become more intense. As the gap between rich and poor, powerful and powerless, government and people, bureaucrats and recipients of their services widens, the stark reality of these conflicts becomes apparent. Failure to deal with these conflicts will only help to escalate social tensions leading perhaps to more violent forms of expression.

What Canada needs more than ever before is a commitment to social goals expressed in the form of more just, humane and well-thought-out social policies and programmes. The gross national product as an economic goal has its place but not as the centrepiece of Canadian social development. A proper balance between the economic and social goals which emphasize normative values respecting the "quality of life" for everyone is to be sought. If all of this can be accomplished within our democratic framework and philosophy, Canada could well become the beacon light for other industrialized nations. The northern star will shine or fade depending upon how we as a nation pursue this commitment.

It is my hope that this collection will be useful to the student of Canadian social policy as a springboard to further study—to the teacher of Canadian social policy as a basic reference which incorporates a variety of readings—and to the Canadian policy-maker as a guide for action.

Waterloo, Ontario   SHANKAR A. YELAJA

Contents

Part I

The Nature of
Social Policy

This introductory section attempts to explore the varying theoretical bases upon which a definition and concept of social policy may be constructed.

While the principal aim of this chapter is to set the stage for the specific studies which follow, it also contributes a preliminary survey of the prevalent values and attitudes toward social policy in our modern society.

1

What Is Social Policy? Its Assumptions, Definitions and Uses

SHANKAR A. YELAJA

Numerous views prevail on the precise meaning of "social policy." In order to arrive at some conceptual clarity, it will be useful to examine the assumptions underlying the definitions and ideological perspectives of social policy. Such an examination should help us to extract the "threads of commonality" for advancing our understanding of what social policy is.

There are four key assumptions implicit in social policy: (1) the government has a responsibility to meet the needs of less fortunate members of society; (2) the state has a right to intervene in areas of individual freedom and economic liberty; (3) governmental and/or public intervention is necessary when existing social institutions fail to fulfill their obligations; (4) public policies create social impacts, the consequences of which become the moral obligation of some group to act upon.

Social policies are formulated through governmental interventions and measures in order to provide for a wide range of human needs for a segment of the population that is dependent on the society. The reasons for dependency may arise either due to personal misfortune or societal conditions. Physical and mental illness, death of a wage earner, accidents resulting in loss of income, ethnic or cultural factors, breakup of family, lack of skills, low education, and old age are some of the factors that adversely affect the abilities of individuals to be self-sufficient in all respects. Societal conditions often cause and contribute to personal troubles and dependency. Unemployment due to automation, regional disparities in income distribution, relocation of industries, lack of equal opportunities for self-betterment, sudden and unanticipated social or economic changes threaten the abilities and capacities of individual human beings and groups to plan and act for their own well-being. Personal response to accelerated social change often results in withdrawal and reassessment of one's life goals. Thus, the social policies which are formulated to deal with certain exigencies of personal misfortune and societal conditions are best summarized in Sir William Beveridge's 1942 analysis of the "five evil giants" of modern society: idleness or unemployment and underemployment; ignorance or inadequate education; disease including ill health and physical or mental disability; squalor or poor living conditions; and lack of sufficient income to maintain an acceptable standard of living.

Sir William Beveridge, writing in the report on social security,[1] observed that the objective of government in peace and war is not the glory of rulers or of races, but the happiness of the common man. F. Gustav Möller, one of the architects of Sweden's welfare state,[2] argued that the civilized state has a moral obligation to fulfill the three goals of social welfare:

(1) it should guarantee a basic minimum standard of living for every citizen;

(2) it should provide for social welfare as an inherent right of everyone regardless of income;

(3) it should meet these goals through equality of income and social justice.

Möller, in his capacity as a Minister of Welfare in the Social Democratic Party, led Sweden to its zenith in social welfare.

Governments as representatives of people assume moral and legal administrative responsibility for providing leadership and formulating social programmes. Governments at all levels are called upon to assume this responsibility because they control the public finances and are presumed to have the technical expertise dealing with these problems and, in democratic countries, receive the mandate of voters for legislative action. The aims of social legislation, generally speaking, are the promotion of individual well-being and also the protection of societal interests. Furthermore, the formulation and development of social policy involves moral choices. It is fundamentally desirable that such policies, programmes and their administration are accountable to the society. Since governments are accountable to people, their intervention in social policy is also accountable.

The second key assumption prevalent in all social policies has to do with the right of the state vis-à-vis individual freedom. In the formulation and development of social policies, it is assumed that the state has a right and a

---

1 Sir William Beveridge, *Social Insurance and Allied Services*, The American Edition (New York: The Macmillan Company, 1942); Sir William Beveridge, *The Pillars of Security* (New York: The Macmillan Company, 1943); Asa J. Briggs, "The Welfare State in Historical Perspective," in *Social Welfare Institutions*, ed. Zald (New York: John Wiley & Sons, 1965).

2 For a detailed explanation and analysis of the Swedish welfare state, see M. Childs, *Sweden, The Middle Way* (New Haven: Yale University Press, 1947); Ronald Huntford, *The New Totalitarians* (New York: Stein and Day, Publishers, 1972); E. Michanek, *For and Against the Welfare State—Swedish Experiences* (Stockholm: Swedish Institute, 1962); Gunnar Myrdal, *Beyond the Welfare State* (New Haven: Yale University Press, 1960).

moral obligation to interfere with individual freedom and intervene in its social, economic and political institutions. Such an intervention is called for in order to promote the well-being of those who are directly affected by some adverse condition and, at the same time, to promote the welfare of all members in the society. For example, the history and development of the welfare state in the industrialized nations of the world clearly reflects the doctrine of the state's right to intervene in the free play of the economy to protect and thereby enhance the well-being of disadvantaged members. Although, as we shall see later, the extent of such intervention continues to be a central concern and basis for debate; social policies cannot be formulated without the state exercising this right. In the so-called "laissez-faire" state, intervention is considered unnecessary.

Third, the assumption is made that governmental intervention is justified because the existing societal institutions such as family, community and the market economy either do not or cannot meet the needs and problems arising from individual misfortune and social conditions. When personal troubles become social issues, they no longer remain within the realm of individual responsibility for their resolution. Because social issues have ramifications and consequences beyond the scope of individual action, governments and social agencies are called upon to intervene. In these days of rising expectations, governments are not only asked to govern (law and order) but also to make delivery on the promise of a good life for every citizen.

Finally, almost all public policies by virtue of their purpose and goals create a social impact. The consequences of this impact may be known or unknown, but some group in the society is expected to take action in dealing with those consequences. Here again, as we shall see later, the debate is around the central questions: whose responsibility is it to act, and what are the criteria against which we measure the positive or negative consequences?

Definitions of social policy are influenced by the above implicit and explicit assumptions. With the key assumptions spelled out, let us now examine a number of definitions from the literature in our attempts to clarify the concept.

Professor Richard Titmuss,[3] an outstanding and respected British scholar of social policy, has defined social policy in this way:

> The social services or social welfare, the labels we have long attached to describe certain areas of public intervention such as income maintenance and public health, are seen as the main ingredients of social policy. They are obvious, direct and measurable acts of government, undertaken for a variety of political reasons, to provide for a range of needs, material and social, and predominantly dependent needs, which the market does not or cannot satisfy for certain designated sections of the population.

T. H. Marshall, another British social scientist, essentially provides the same distinction in conceptualizing social policy as a "policy of government with regard to action having a direct impact on the welfare of the citizens by

3 Richard M. Titmuss, *Commitment to Welfare,* 2nd ed. (London: George Allen & Unwin Ltd., 1976), p. 188.

providing them with services or income."[4] Professor F. Lafitte, in a lecture published by the University of Birmingham in 1962, states:

> ... social policy is not essentially interested in economic relations but is very much concerned with the extent to which economic relations and aspirations should be allowed to dominate other aspects of life; more specifically that social policy addresses itself to a whole range of needs—material, cultural, emotional—outside the wide realm of satisfaction which can conveniently be left to the market.[5]

He further defines social policy as a function or activity which steers society in a direction other than that which it would normally go on its own.

Peter Townsend, another British scholar, has defined social policy from a broader sociological perspective including objectives and means. He writes:

> Social policy is best conceived as a kind of blueprint for the management of society towards social ends: it can be defined as the underlying as well as the professed rationale by which social institutions and groups are used or brought into being to ensure social preservation or development. Social policy is, in other words, the institutionalized control of services, agencies and organizations to maintain or change social structure and values. Sometimes this control may be utterly conscious, and consciously expressed by government spokesmen and others. Sometimes it may be unspoken and even unrecognized.[6]

Further definitions of social policy by such American writers as Nathan Glazer and Howard Freeman are useful to consider because they illuminate the concept. Glazer recognizes that the term "social policy" is very elastic. He has attempted an operational definition of the concept:

> ... all those public policies which have been developed in the past hundred years to protect families and individuals from the accidents of industrial and urban life, and which try to maintain a decent minimum of living conditions for all. The heart of social policy is the relief of the condition of the poor.[7]

Freeman and Sherwood add a further dimension to the definition by stating that social policy is:

> ... the fundamental process by which enduring organizations maintain an element of stability and at the same time seek to improve conditions for their members. Existing social policies are usually never fully developed; they are continually modified in the face of changing conditions and values.[8]

Rein[9] has defined social policy as the examination of the social objectives of social welfare policies as well as the social purposes of economic policies. He further states that social policies are designed to plan for social externalities, redistribution and the equitable distribution of social ser-

---

4 T. H. Marshall, *Social Policy* (London: Hutchinson University Library, 1965), p. 7.
5 Francois Lafitte, "Social Policy in a Free Society," an inaugural lecture delivered at the University of Birmingham, Birmingham, England, May 18, 1962, pp. 8-9.
6 Peter Townsend, *Sociology and Social Policy* (London: Penguin Books Ltd., 1975), p. 6.
7 Nathan Glazer, "The Limits of Social Policy," *Commentary* 52, no. 3 (September 1971): 51.
8 Howard Freeman and Clarence Sherwood, *Social Research and Social Policy* (Englewood Cliffs, N.J.: Prentice-Hall, Inc., 1970), p. 3.
9 Martin Rein, *Social Policy: Issues of Choice and Change* (New York: Random House, 1970).

vices. Drover,[10] a Canadian writer, reaffirms the notion that social policies are aspects of public policy (authorized collective intervention) concerned with distribution of goods, services, and rights, guided by principles of equality and justice.

From these definitions, the following concept of social policy begins to emerge: Social policy is concerned with the public administration of welfare services, that is, the formulation, development, and management of specific services of government at all levels, such as health, education, income maintenance, and welfare services. Social policy is formulated not only by government but also by other institutions such as voluntary organizations, business, labour, industry, professional groups, public interest groups, and churches. Furthermore, social policy is to be understood within the framework of societal ends or objectives and means. The ends and means of social policy are inseparable because of their direct and indirect effect on each other.

This writer tends to view social policy in a broad perspective. He would distinguish between "social welfare policy" and social policy. Social welfare policy is the expression of the philosophy and programmes concerning the poor, dependent, handicapped (physically and mentally), and other members of society who for a variety of reasons need support (economic, social and psychological) for their well-being. Social welfare policy concerns itself with a restricted segment of societal functioning. Social policy, on the other hand, is an area of public policy-making of which social welfare policy is one facet. Prominent among other social policy dimensions are those diverse sectors of public concern that focus on human resource development, either directly or indirectly. For example, health policy is a social policy in that it defines the principles and conditions under which health care can be made available on a universal basis for all segments of the population. In this sense, it is directly concerned with human resource development. However, indirectly, it also deals with such allied public concerns as the availability of family planning services, nutrition, health education and recreation which affect the health of the entire population.

Why is it essential to define social policy from such a broad perspective? The principal justification for a broader social policy definition lies in the essential interaction among several modes of socio-economic intervention. For example, social welfare policies for the poor cannot be adequately explained without understanding and analyzing a number of related public policies concerning taxation, minimum wages, work incentive, full employment, opportunities for work, manpower retraining policies and programmes, and regional disparities in income and work opportunities. Of course, it is not implied that all public policies, in and of themselves, are social policies. Nevertheless, by virtue of the *social impact* created by public policies, they must be considered part and parcel of a conglomerate of diverse policy components which constitute a national social policy. Consequently, social policies principally are concerned with a broad range

10   Glen Drover, "Social Policy Teaching Project," Canadian Association of Schools of Social Work, Ottawa, 1975.

of public policy issues and the *social impact* arising out of the interaction among the diverse social, economic, political and cultural factors.

It is impossible to explain adequately the nature and functions of social policy without an analysis of dominant social values and ideologies prevalent in a society. Ideology, as defined in Webster's *Third New International Dictionary,* is "the integrated assertions, the theories, and aims that constitute a socio-political programme."[11] Further, ideology is the pattern of beliefs and concepts (both factual and normative) which purport to explain complex social phenomena with a view to directing and simplifying socio-political choices facing individuals and groups. Social values form the core of a given ideology. Because social values transcend objects and situations, ideologies remain firm and are less susceptible to dynamic change. Although ideology provides a non-empirical perspective, it is not a hypothesis for empirical verification but a thesis; its strength lies in the socio-economic support of its followers. Ideology is one of the moving forces of a time or age—a justification for social action or inaction, a rationalization for social justice or injustice, and an explanation for state intervention or lack thereof in social welfare.

Because social policies and social welfare programmes are influenced by ideologies and in turn affect social values, it is worthwhile to analyze some divergent ideologies in order to extend our understanding of the relationship between the two. We will restrict our analysis to four major ideologies: conservative, liberal, radical and Marxist.

The conservative ideology is essentially based on a philosophy of individualism and a concept of an evolutionary society with emphasis upon preservation of traditional values, norms and social institutions. Consequently, from a conservative point of view governmental interference with individual liberty, societal institutions, market economy and traditional values must be minimal and are justified as a last resort when all other measures fail. Conservative ideology is dedicated to the preservation of the work ethic, self-help and moderation in all things. Emphasis is placed upon gradual social development rather than abrupt social change. The implications of conservative ideology for social welfare and social policy are noteworthy.

Those who argue for the preservation and promotion of individualism as the *sine qua non* of societal welfare would suggest that the individual must be self-reliant: he must rely upon his own resources and must indeed pull himself up by his "boot straps." The North American doctrine of individualism has even suggested that public subsidization to the poor stifles their initiative, robs them of their sense of self-responsibility, helps create parasites and destroys the moral fibre of society. Whenever social policy measures to increase government intervention are brought into the arena of public discussion and debate, the crusaders of individualism oppose the policies because they view these as counter to their value systems and beliefs. They argue for less governmental intervention, curtailment of public expenditure on social programmes, preservation of old values (thrift,

11   *Webster's Third New International Dictionary,* p. 413.

moderation, initiative and prudence), and safeguards for social institutions such as the family and the community. A segment of conservative opinion argues for punitive and restrictive measures so that the "welfare poor" will find their dependency uncomfortable. It is no coincidence then that in the heat of controversy over rising local expenditures for support to unemployed, able-bodied, single men and one-parent families, local government councillors advocate work measures such as shovelling snow and cutting dead elm trees along provincial highways in order to teach the poor a lesson in the Protestant work ethic and morality.

However, those who argue that society and government are responsible for helping the needy, poor, dependent and unfortunate victims of our socio-economic system support more government intervention. The philosophic base for their support exists in the 1948 United Nations *Declaration of Human Rights.* Articles 22 and 25 spell out the basis for justifying state intervention on behalf of the individual:

> Article 22 Everyone as a member of society, has the right to social security, and is entitled to realization, through national effort and international co-operation, and in accordance with the organization and resources of each State of the economic social and cultural rights indispensable for his dignity and the free development of his personality.

> Article 25 Everyone has the right to a standard of living adequate for the health and well-being of himself and of his family, including food, clothing, housing, and medical care and necessary social services, and the right to security in the event of unemployment, sickness, disability, widowhood, old age, or other lack of livelihood in circumstances beyond his control.[12]

These two articles emphasize social rights which must be distinguished from the civil and political rights guaranteed by legislation in most democratic countries. However, the increasing complexity of modern society and the rapidity with which social, technological and economic changes are occurring in Western societies requires that recognition be given to social rights as a protection against those profound changes which threaten the well-being of man. Social rights tend to have a relative character gradually changing as the society's attitudes, values, mores and resources change.

The statement on social policy by the Canadian Council on Social Development clearly reflects the viewpoint that both the individual and the society are responsible for human well-being. Thus, the Council states:

> The objective of social policy is human well-being. This has two aspects. On the one hand, the individual must be guaranteed the freedom and opportunity to carry responsibility, so far as he is able, for meeting his own needs and aspirations. On the other, the achievement of human well-being, especially under today's conditions, is as much a social as an individual responsibility. Only through collective planning and action [social policies] can the conditions be established that will enable all people to realize their potential and contribute creatively to society.[13]

12 Quoted from Canadian Welfare Council, *Social Policies for Canada,* Part I (Ottawa: Canadian Welfare Council, 1969), p. 1.
13 Ibid., p. 2.

Such a viewpoint can be interpreted as a liberal ideology emphasizing the dual responsibility to be shared by both the individual and the society for one's well-being.

While the conservative viewpoint of social policy leans toward the preservation of established societal values, morality and responsibility of individual members of society to help themselves, the liberal viewpoint recognizes the need for change and reform in established social values. The liberal viewpoint of social policy argues for changes and reform in those aspects of society that hinder opportunities for maximum individual freedom from oppressive conditions. It advocates individual responsibility but not entirely without government support. A conservative viewpoint opposes radical changes through social policy but supports moderate cautious courses of action for the preservation of established societal values, whereas a liberal viewpoint considers social policy as one of the potent and powerful instruments of change in society for the support of individual well-being.

There is still another viewpoint that argues for a radical perspective of social policy. Within this perspective, individual problems are interpreted as the direct consequences of societal problems. Poverty, for example, is not due to the inability of people to work for their own economic well-being but rather as a consequence of the exploitative economic system that has trapped people in a cycle of poverty and does not allow them to escape from it.

A radical perspective of social policy emphasizes the societal responsibility for amelioration, correction and elimination of individual problems. The basic values and assumptions of the society are called to account for their contribution to individual well-being and welfare. Government intervention in social policies is seen as justified because society holds government responsible and accountable. Naturally, public expenditures on all types of social policy measures to increase the government's responsibility would be increasingly sought. The aim of social policy is also seen as changing those conditions within the socio-economic and political systems that cause individual problems. Thus, a radical viewpoint advocates fundamental social, economic and political reforms or changes and the aim of social policy is seen as contributing to those changes. By the use of direct and uncompromising methods, radicals go to the root or origin of social problems to seek fundamental solutions.

Finally, there is a Marxist perspective on social policy. Using conflict theory as a point of departure, the Marxist postulates a basic and inherent conflict between the individual and the society. Social policies in a democratic system are interpreted by Marxist analysts as a ploy to exercise control over the *definition, emphasis* and *direction* of social welfare. These policies are seen as supportive of the capitalistic economy whose power is controlled by the elite. An example of a Marxist interpretation of social policy may help to explain this viewpoint.

Galper in his book, *The Politics of Social Services*,[14] offers a useful critique of social services in America. His main intention is to analyze the

14   Jeffry M. Galper, *The Politics of Social Services* (Englewood Cliffs, N.J.: Prentice-Hall, Inc., 1975).

purpose, values, assumptions and functions of social services and to consider the role they play in supporting or challenging the values, institutions,
and behaviours of the present social order. He begins his analysis with the
existing contradiction in social services: the positive social concerns and
the efforts to meet human needs representing the better impulses of the
social services are undermined by the forces which the social services
sustain and reinforce in the society at large. At the same time that they are
concerned about the promotion of human welfare, the social services
buttress values, institutions, and procedures that are destructive to that
welfare.

Galper's analysis of social services in the United States is leftist, strongly
rooted in Marxist theory and clearly, often brilliantly, radical in perspective,
argument and intended resolution.

According to Galper, most of the political debate about the social services has been conducted within a liberal-conservative framework which
has defined the boundaries of the argument. Galper contends that the
liberal position rests on an assumption that social services are essentially a
"good thing" and if we can increase the services we can solve the problems.
Consumer participation is basic to evolving a social service structure that is
humane and responsive to people's needs. The ineffectiveness of social
services can be made more effective by reordering the priorities in social
spending. The conservative position, on the other hand, maintains that
"less is better." For Galper, the liberal-conservative debate on social services is unproductive in getting to the issues that must be addressed.
Furthermore, these two positions are more alike than they are unalike in
their basic assumptions about *human nature* and the *social order*. The
Marxist can identify the ideological commonalities in the two positions and
criticize them on similar grounds.

It is argued that the social services are products of, and responsive to, a
social order that values economic growth and political stability above
human well-being. Furthermore, the present social order uses social services and the helping professions to preserve and strengthen the
ideologies, behaviours, and structures of the status quo. Galper postulates
that the failure of social services is rooted not in their particular shortcomings or specific limitations, but in the fact that they operate in conjunction
with and in support of the same anti-social forces that they theoretically are
organized to mitigate.

Galper states that the problems in the welfare state and in the social
services are inherently related to the larger issues (socio-economic and
political structure and function) and are not *ad hoc*, temporal or idiosyn-
cratic. The inadequacies of the social services are rooted in the logic of the
society as a whole, endemic to the society in its present form and even
functional for the maintenance of current socio-economic and political
arrangements. He concludes his analysis by way of the following solution:

> As we interpret the dilemmas of social services and the social service profes-
> sions in systematic terms, we suggest that the solutions to these dilemmas
> must also be systematic. If we accept the premise that the problems of the
> social services reflect the conservative role of the welfare state in a larger
> society that is not organized primarily for the sake of human maximization,

then we will find no solution in either modest reform within the social services or in expansion of existing services by whatever degree. Solutions will be found only through basic or radical change in the whole society.[15]

The book calls on the social services to engage people in a collective struggle to eradicate the causes of oppressive conditions in order to achieve a decent, socialistic type of society.

Galper's analysis of social services is penetrating but it is weak in terms of resolutions or an agenda for specific change. As one critic, Stumpf, of his book observes: "The proposals are flimsy; the strategic changes that are explored do little to advance our professional thinking, our options, and instrumental capabilities for change."[16]

While the Marxist analysis provides a useful perspective for social policy analysis and its strength lies in its theoretical rigour, it suffers from a major drawback. The Marxists seldom provide concrete solutions to social welfare problems other than the ultimate reckoning of all problems in terms of societal revolution. Concrete, specific and sharply-defined agendas for change that form a part and parcel of systematic designs for social policy change cannot be expected within the framework of Marxian tradition. Thus, its usefulness to social policy development still represents an unfulfilled promise.

Marxian analysis of social policy is based on the assumption that the present social, economic and political system in a democratic country such as Canada exploits the poor and benefits the affluent. Stressing the doctrines of dialectic materialism, class struggle, the labour theory of value and the inevitable decay of capitalism leading to the goal of a classless society, the Marxian views social policy as one of several means to bring about a social revolution.

It is important to distinguish between radical and Marxian social policy perspectives. The essential distinction appears to be centred around the goals at which social policy is aimed. A radical argues for fundamental change through social policy measures, but the end results or goals are left to the judgment of the society which, in a democratic system of government, is represented by a majority. A radical will tend to support change through democratic means whereas the Marxian will leave both the means and ends to the definition of those seeking to bring about revolutionary change.

Thus, the various ideological stances toward social policy are antagonistic. They reflect differing philosophies concerning man, his relationship to society and the nature of human conditions which require governmental intervention. Social policy, through governmental intervention, can be justified to support man's adjustment to the ever-increasing complexities and problems of societies. On the other hand, social policy can be instrumental in conceiving and implementing major social, economic and political changes. Social policy, because it raises the fundamental questions of freedom for man and control by government, often creates a tension in the differing values of society.

15   Ibid., pp. 6-7.
16   Jack Stumpf, review of *The Politics of Social Services*, by Jeffry M. Galper, in *Social Work* 21, no. 4 (July 1976): 333.

To summarize the discussion of social policy so far: key assumptions underlying the concept of social policy were examined; several definitions were considered and divergent ideologies influencing social policy were analyzed. In our discussion, we have only outlined the complex issues inherent in defining social policy. However, we can conclude from this discussion that social policy is concerned with values, facts, social needs and problems and how to address them. Social policy reflects the morality and political ideology of a society. Admittedly this is a very broad concept of social policy, but it provides a degree of intellectual freedom for those who are interested in its theory as well as practice.

Let us now explore the practical uses of social policy. Social policy is not just an academic discipline but also a field which emphasizes the practical application of social policy concepts to a wide range of human problems. Social policy is used in planning welfare services, in setting priorities and goals for government spending, in distributing the benefits and rewards of an economic system, in directing the socio-economic system toward certain desired ends, and in justifying the lack of action for meeting social needs. Four common perspectives on the uses of social policy will be explored:

(1) unlimited use in gauging the social impacts of public policies;
(2) planning of welfare services and programmes;
(3) functional use in evaluating the effects of social policy;
(4) comparative analysis of social policy.

In a highly complex, modern industrial society such as Canada's, public policies generally affect, directly or indirectly, the life, work and values of all citizens. Because public policies have such pervasive and diverse effects on people, it is necessary to study them as complex phenomena. A distinction between public and social policies is useful to delineate the effects. When the social effects of public policies adversely affect the "quality of life" of a particular group, community or sector in a society, it is essential to examine the public policies from a social policy perspective. Such a perspective helps us to provide insight into *how* and *why* policies have been enacted and put into effect and *why* certain policy decisions occur under particular conditions.

This "unlimited" use of social policy helps to examine many policy choices and decisions from a critical stance in terms of their social effects. As such, its usefulness in social planning and action is unlimited. Indeed, questions of purposes and values are left to the discretion of those seeking to use social policy as an instrument for change.

The welfare function and use of social policy can simply be summarized as meeting the objectives of social security. The term "social security" covers such programmes as public health insurance, income security (income insurance and income support measures), as well as social welfare services provided to meet personal and social problems. Within a broad range of social policies, social welfare policies are measures that are limited in their scope and specific in their objectives. However, the objectives of social welfare policy are open to further debate. Three conceptualizations of the objectives of social welfare policy can be identified as residual, redistributive and developmental.

The residual conception of social welfare is based on the assumption that economic growth and development takes precedence over welfare. An industrial society must concentrate its energy on economic growth, that is, the accumulation of the gross national product. In fact, the state of industrial development is measured in terms of its performance on the barometer of the G.N.P. Welfare services are identified with those unmet human needs which cannot be met by existing social institutions. Welfare services essentially are provided with a view to support the economic aims of the society. Wilensky and Lebeaux label this concept of social policy as a "residual" conception of social welfare. They state, "residual view holds that social welfare institutions should come into play only when the normal structure of supply, the family and the market break down."[17]

Redistributive concepts of social welfare policy are based on the assumption that there are inherent inequities in the present Western industrial society. Inequities in the distribution of power, income, goods and services have created a disadvantaged social class in North American society. This social class, identified as "the Other America" in Michael Harrington's[18] study of poverty in the United States and as "the underside of Toronto" in W. E. Mann's[19] work, refers to people who are victims of society. They are untouched by the affluence of the capitalistic economy and have failed to realize the North American dream. Their condition is characterized by lack of opportunity, apathy, hopelessness and despair. It is argued that social welfare policy must aim at the redistribution of societal benefits in order to help the disadvantaged members of society.

A third concept of social welfare policy is based on the assumption that economic and social welfare development are interdependent. One without the other would result in a lopsided society. Whereas the economic aspects of public policy contribute to the G.N.P., social aspects of policy help us implement the normative values for quality of life.

Where economic development and social welfare are conceived to be interdependent functions, social policy emerges as a necessary and viable function of a modern urban industrial society. Wilensky and Lebeaux use the term "institutional" to refer to this concept of social welfare:

> ... [which] implies no stigma, no emergency, no abnormality. Social welfare becomes accepted as a proper, legitimate function of modern industrial society in helping individuals achieve self-fulfillment. The complexity of modern life is recognized. The inability of the individual to provide fully for himself, or to meet all his needs in family and work settings is considered a "normal condition"; and the helping agencies achieve "regular" institutional status.[20]

Other writers have refined this institutional concept of social policy. Alfred Kahn[21] has identified this concept as "a social planning phase of the welfare state" whereby various social services are accepted as "social

17 Harold Wilensky and Charles Lebeaux, *Industrial Society and Social Welfare* (New York: Free Press, 1965), p. 138.
18 Michael Harrington, *The Other America* (New York: Macmillan, 1960).
19 W. Mann, *The Underside of Toronto* (Toronto: McClelland and Stewart Ltd., 1970).
20 Wilensky and Lebeaux, *Industrial Society*, p. 140.
21 Alfred Kahn, *Social Policy and Social Services* (New York: Random House, 1974), p. 78.

utilities" by communities on similar lines to public utilities whose provision of service is a public responsibility for meeting the essential needs of local communities. John Romanyshyn has redefined this concept as "social development,"

[which] recognizes the dynamic quality of urban industrial society and the consequent need to adapt to change and to new aspirations for human fulfillment. It goes beyond the welfare state to a continuing renewal of its institution to promote the fullest development of man.[22]

When the Canadian Welfare Council adopted a new name, the Canadian Council on Social Development, the debate over the ideology of welfare versus development was both lively and stimulating. To sum up the entire debate in a few words would obviously do injustice to many complex issues. But if one were to recall the heart of the debate, it was clearly over the issue of whether the Council as a policy institution should principally concern itself with the effects of welfare or address itself to those social policy issues which create welfare problems. As an independent, autonomous organization with the support of informed public opinion and citizen participation, the council decided to opt for social development. Thus, one of the basic objectives of the C.C.S.D. is to give leadership in Canada on matters of social policy and to direct attention to changes which may be required in existing social policies and provisions, and to ways of developing desirable new policies and programmes, and, to this end, to further co-operative efforts by all bodies.

Few concepts in modern social science history have generated as much discussion as those of structure and function and the type of analysis associated with them. Structural-functional analysis[23] is not new in either the social or natural sciences; it has a pedigree stretching back in both disciplines. What is relatively recent, however, is the use of structural-functional approach in the analysis of social policy. Simply speaking, the application of structural-functional concepts to social policy analysis consists of articulating and conceptualizing empirical questions in one of the following forms or some combination of them: (1) What observable uniformities or patterns can be discovered or alleged to exist in the phenomena studied? (2) What conditions (empirical states of affairs) resultant from previous operations can be discovered or alleged to exist in the phenomena studied? (3) What process (or action, i.e., changes in the patterns, conditions or both, depending upon one's point of view) are discernible between any two or more points in time) can be discovered (or alleged) to take place in terms of observable uniformities, what resultant conditions can be discovered? In short, the first question asks, "What structures are involved?" The second asks, "What functions have resulted?" And the third asks, "What functions take place in terms of given structures?" The term "function" is any condition, any state of affairs, resultant from the operation of a

---

22 John Romanyshyn, *Social Welfare: Charity to Justice* (New York: Random House, 1971), p. 380.
23 Marion J. Levy, "Functional Analysis: Structural-Functional Analysis," in *International Encyclopaedia of Social Sciences,* vol. 6 (New York: The Macmillan and the Free Press, 1968), pp. 22-23.

structure, and the term "structure" is a pattern, i.e., an observable uniformity in terms of which action takes place.

The functional approach to social policy analysis raises the questions: Who benefits from social policy measures? What are the *manifest* objectives of the stated policy? What are the *latent* objectives of the programmes and the manner in which the policy is implemented? What are the *unanticipated consequences* of a social policy? Why did they occur? What are the *side-effects* of the social policy? In the formulation and development of social policies, multiple interests converge. Various interest groups with their own vested interests and concerns want to claim a "share of the pie." If this is so, how are these decisions made? Who gets a piece and who doesn't? And what are the criteria governing the decision-making? The question of priorities in social policy formulation is also crucial. A functional approach to social policy analysis necessarily raises questions of policy outcome and consideration of the assumptions on which policies are based.

Robert Merton,[24] one of the proponents of functional analysis, argued that it is essential in examining the functions of social institutions to distinguish between the purposes or reasons which are conventionally given for their existence and the objective consequences which flow from them. Original purpose and result need not and, in most cases, probably do not always coincide. A distinction, therefore, must be made between *manifest* and *latent* functions of social policy. Manifest functions are those objective consequences of social policy which are "intended and recognized" by those who formulated them. Latent functions are those consequences which are "neither intended nor recognized." The line between manifest and latent functions is not fixed or inevitable. In some social policies, latent consequences may become apparent only after policies are implemented; in others, these may come to light after a long period of time.

Herbert J. Gans[25] analyzed the problem of poverty in the United States. The analysis started with a thesis that the poor perform certain functions in society that are both indispensable and contributory to the maintenance of poverty. Three categories of functions were identified: economic, social and political. The analysis also identified several policy alternatives and examined them in realistic terms. Gans concluded that poverty in the U.S. is a very complex problem and therefore its solution lies in both structural and functional changes within the society.

Frances Piven and Richard Cloward, in their book *Regulating the Poor: The Functions of Public Welfare,*[26] have argued that the key to an understanding of relief-giving is in the function it serves for the larger economic and political order. Relief policies are cyclical, liberal or restrictive depending on the problems of regulation in the larger society with which govern-

24 Robert K. Merton, *Social Theory and Social Structure* (New York: Free Press, 1957).
25 Herbert J. Gans, "The Uses of Poverty: The Poor Pay All," *Social Policy* 2, no. 2 (July/August 1971): 20-24.
26 Frances Fox Piven and Richard Cloward, *Regulating the Poor: The Functions of Public Welfare* (New York: Free Press, 1971).

ment must contend. When economic conditions create widespread unemployment and resulting turmoil, relief has been extended to control disorder. When order is restored and conditions stabilized, relief is withdrawn and an increased number of persons must compete for jobs in the labour force. The authors attack the supposition that government social policies, including relief policies, are becoming more responsible, humane, and generous. They conclude that governmental regulation of the poor was the factor primarily responsible for the dramatic increase in the welfare rolls during the 1960s. Critics of this thesis, however, point to the fallacy of using a single variable (increase or decrease in welfare rolls) for analysis. Using a multi-variant analysis, one of the critics[27] argues that Piven and Cloward fail to deal broadly with welfare as a complex social institution interacting with other social institutions and with demographic trends which are important factors in influencing welfare growth.

One of the significant contributions of functional analysis in social policy is that it uncovers the unanticipated or unintended consequences of social policies and programmes. An example to illustrate the point is a pilot programme developed and applied in the small community of Yarmouth, Nova Scotia, focussed on a "strategy to facilitate the increased participation of disadvantaged citizens in community efforts to find solutions to their socio-economic problems."[28] It was found that the main benefits of the programme went to those who were not seen as target populations for change by the project staff. Although the study made cautious note of the degree of success in involving the disadvantaged in the planning and decision-making process, it concluded with a question: What actual benefits accrue from such a project to the disadvantaged sector and to the community at large?

David Gil[29] identified four social policy functions:
(1) to develop life-sustaining and life-enhancing resources, goods and services;
(2) to allocate to individuals their statuses, roles and prerogatives;
(3) to distribute entitlements, rewards and constraints;
(4) to regulate the relationship of these rights and statutes in society.

These social policy functions help us understand both the latent and manifest purposes of social policy.

Given the tremendous diversity of social welfare programmes (public and private), it is helpful to have a framework to use in analyzing a particular programme. An analytic framework helps to isolate the essential characteristics of the programme, to explain its social impact and to evaluate the extent to which the programme is meeting the stated objectives. Bell[30]

27 E. Durham, "Have the Poor Been Regulated? Toward a Multivariate Understanding of Welfare Growth," *Social Service Review* 47, no. 3 (1973): 339-59.
28 Edward Newell and Leonard Denton, "From the Bottom Up: A Strategy to Facilitate Participation of Low-Income Groups in Solving their Problems of Disadvantage," Canada, New Start Program; A Nova Scotia Project, 1971.
29 David G. Gil, "A Systematic Approach to Social Policy Analysis," *Social Service Review* 44, no. 4 (December 1970): 411-26; David G. Gil, *Unravelling Social Policy: Theory, Analysis, and Political Action Towards Social Equality* (Cambridge, Mass.: Schenkman Publishing, 1973).
30 Winnifred Bell, "Obstacles to Shifting from Descriptive to the Analytic Approach to Teaching Social Services," *Journal of Education for Social Work* 5 (Spring 1969): 5-13.

suggests a conceptual framework which is helpful in evaluating both the structure and outcome of social policy. This framework takes into account the seven criteria guiding social policy development. These are: objectives (stated and unanticipated), legislative authorization, source of funding, administrative structure, eligibility requirements, coverage, adequacy and equity. Although the major utility of this framework is for public social security programmes, its potential application to other social policies and social services deserves to be explored. From a functional consideration of social policy, the framework has strong merits because it introduces analytic thinking and rigour in social policy development.

One of the key contributors to the structural-functional school of thought is Talcott Parsons[31] who identified four functional problems that must be solved by every social system. These are:

Adaptation: Systems must produce the resources and facilities to permit adjustment to the environment and create new adaptive techniques.

Goal Attainment: Systems must set goals and establish priorities, mobilize the means of attaining them, and reward the successful.

Integration: Systems must develop agencies of social control that ensure the adjustment of parts to one another and to the whole system.

Latency: Systems must maintain institutions and manage tensions within them to ease strains.

In recent years, attempts have been made to relate Parsons' analytic paradigm, known as A.G.I.L., to social welfare problems and social policy analysis. Parsons argues that the adaptive problem is handled by the economy; the goal attainment problem by politics; the integrative problem by religion, courts, police, hospitals and the profession (social welfare institutions); and the problems of pattern maintenance and tension management by the family, the educational system and social policy network. Clearly, Parsons' analytic framework has much use in social policy.

The functional approach to the analysis of social welfare problems, institutions and social policy concerns is fruitful since it helps to view these as problem-solving mechanisms. However, functional analysis can also lead to preoccupation with adjustment and continuity, thereby failing to account satisfactorily for social change.

Comparative social policy review and analysis[32] has emerged as one of the useful conceptual tools in the field of social policy. The comparative method is rapidly becoming a busy crossroads in the social sciences. It has been a result of two interrelated factors. Collaboration among the social sciences has gained increasing momentum. The traditional discipline boundaries are crossed and there is a growing recognition that social

---

31   Talcott Parsons, *The Social System* (Glencoe, Ill.: Free Press, 1951).

32   For a detailed discussion of the rationale, methods and problems in comparative research the following references are useful: Adam Przeworski and Henry Teune, *The Logic of Comparative Social Inquiry* (New York: John Wiley and Sons, 1970); Richard Merritt and Stein Rokkan, eds., *Comparing Nations: The Use of Quantitative Data in Cross-National Research* (New Haven, Conn.: Yale University Press, 1966); Reinhard Bendix, "Concepts and Generalizations in Comparative Sociological Studies," *American Sociological Review* 28 (1963): 532-39; Stein Rokkan ed., *Comparative Research Across Cultures and Nations*, Round Table Conference on Comparative Research, Paris, 1965 (Paris: Mouton, 1968).

sciences must develop a "holistic perspective" on the social reality. At the same time, social policy has no longer remained the legitimate concern of a single discipline. Quite the contrary, it has become the domain of social scientists as they reaffirm their liberal-humanitarian traditions.

Comparative social policy is aimed at several analytic levels. It may begin with a simple codification and description of social welfare programmes including their objectives, scope of operation, financial outlays, administrative structure, etc. in two or more countries. The primary focus here is on "programme" description with a view to identify and document similarities and differences that exist between the countries under study. Such a comparison serves a limited purpose in that it helps identify how different countries are responding to socio-economic needs through social welfare policies and programmes. Further, it may inform us of innovative or new ideas emerging in social policy. For example, Bismarck's innovative social insurance plans enacted in the 1880s in Germany were studied throughout Europe and America and copied by some countries. The British social security report under the leadership of Sir William Beveridge in 1942 has been a similar standard by which many nations have formulated philosophies and programmes for social security legislation. More recently, Americans have taken a great deal of interest in Canadian health policies and programmes and Canadians have adopted social welfare programmes tried in the United States. Such searching and borrowing has been so significant that many Western nations have institutionalized the comparative social policy intelligence gathering within the government bureaucracy. Specialized bodies within the United Nations have gathered a wealth of information on comparative social policy and make it available for use in national and international social planning.

Comparative social policy analysis also aims at explaining why certain policy patterns emerged under certain societal conditions and what results they have had. In order to answer these questions it would be necessary to research the social and political origins of the policies and programmes, their development over time, their operational dynamics, interactions with their social and cultural environments and their societal consequences. A study may begin with a focus on a single nation and then compare the results across two or more nations. Here the objective is to state and explain the rationale for similarities and differences in policy but not necessarily to test the hypothesis by means of empirical findings. An example of this type of comparative research is the Wendt study[33] on housing policy in which he compared policies and programmes in the United Kingdom, Sweden, West Germany and the United States since World War II.

The next level of comparative analysis goes beyond the descriptive search and the explanatory rationale. It is aimed at the analysis of those social, economic, political, cultural and other factors which influence the development of social policies. A set of empirically formed propositions regarding characteristic patterns and processes in policy formulation and

---

33 Paul F. Wendt, *Housing Policy—The Search for Solutions: A Comparison of the U.K., Sweden, West Germany, and the U.S. since World War II* (Berkeley: University of California Press, 1963).

their interactions with national factors guides the formation of hypotheses. The comparative policy analysis is aimed at testing such hypotheses about uniformities or divergencies of policy in different nations. To formulate these hypotheses, comparative analysts must devise a framework and also state a *priori* criteria for designating those aspects of policy which are comparable in two or more contexts. Hypotheses are then stated within a designated framework and empirical evidence is gathered.

The comparative social policy analysis is therefore aimed at knowing, understanding and examining similarities and differences in social policies and programmes across nations. Furthermore, it seeks to find answers and provide insight into *how and why national policies have been enacted* and put into effect and *why certain policy outcomes occur under particular conditions.*

However, we must note some difficulties that limit the effective use of the comparative method of policy analysis. The first and foremost conceptual problem arises out of the "middle range" theory and the concomitant difficulties in using this theory as a base for predictive purposes. The comparative method must, out of necessity, rely on "middle range" abstractions of social policy. Further, devising a framework for comparative analysis is fraught with problems. One cannot separate the imposition of values in any analytic framework. The very nature of the questions or problems posed for analysis tend to reflect a value bias. Conversely, the analyst may unwittingly bias the information and data being analyzed from a certain value perspective. For example, in any comparative study of social policies between democratic and totalitarian societies, personal values associated with individual freedom and its consequences for self-esteem and dignity tend to colour the analytic perspective. And yet it is clear that the operational meaning of these values varies enormously in all societies. At the same time, locating, tracking, and documenting adequate information and data are probably the foremost hurdles. Comparative policy analysts must use information available in government agencies and departments which produce and keep records for their own purposes. Access to information also poses further problems because in only a very few countries of the world is relatively free access to information on social policies and programmes available. There is a continuing debate on the use and abuse of such information: under what circumstances it should be made available and who should have the access to it, and what, if any, conditions, qualifications, etc. should limit accessibility.

We have discussed the variety of uses of social policy. There are a number of analytic approaches with varying theoretical bases. The scientific validity of all these analytic approaches is beyond the scope of our consideration. Some analytic approaches are more useful than others. Some of the approaches are based on objective empirical evidence while others are simply at a level of hypothesis formation for further research and correlational testing. Still others are theoretical. However, it is noted that social policy continues to face the lack of an adequate social theory base resulting in challenge and frustration for academicians as well as practitioners.

BIBLIOGRAPHY

Aaron, Henry. "Social Security: International Comparisons." In *Studies in the Economics of Income Maintenance,* pp. 13-48. Edited by Otto Eckstein. Washington, D.C.: The Brookings Institution, 1967.

Adams; Cameron; Hill; and Penz. *The Real Poverty Report.* Edmonton: M. G. Hurtig Ltd., 1971.

Armitage, Andrew. *Social Welfare in Canada: Ideals and Realities.* Toronto: McClelland and Stewart Ltd., 1975.

Bryden, Kenneth. *Old Age Pensions and Policy-Making in Canada.* Montreal: McGill Queen's University Press, 1976.

Canada. Department of National Health and Welfare. *Social Security in Canada.* Ottawa: Information Canada, 1974.

Canadian Council on Social Development. *Social Development,* occasional newsletter, vol. 5, no. 1 (January 1976).

Donnison, David. *Social Policy and Social Administration.* London: Allen & Unwin, 1965.

Economic Council of Canada. *Eighth Annual Review.* Ottawa: Queen's Printer, 1971.

Fraser, Derek. *The Evolution of the British Welfare State: A History of Social Policy Since the Industrial Revolution.* London: Macmillan, 1973.

Friedman, Milton. *Capitalism and Freedom.* Chicago: University of Chicago Press, 1962.

George, Vic, and Wilding, Paul. *Ideology and Social Welfare.* London: Routledge and Kegan Paul Ltd., 1976.

Gruber, Murray. "Policy Planning Models: Heuristics for Education." *Education for Social Work* 8, no. 3 (1972): 30-39.

Hall, Phoebe; Land, Hilary; Parker, Roy; and Webb, Adrian. *Change, Choice and Conflict in Social Policy.* London: Heinemann Educational Books, Ltd., 1975.

Harris, Robert. "Policy Analysis and Policy Development." *Social Service Review* 47, no. 3 (September 1973): 360-72.

Helco, Hugh. "Politics and Social Policy." Ph.D. dissertation, Department of Political Science, Yale University, 1970.

_____. *Modern Social Politics in Britain and Sweden.* New Haven: Yale University Press, 1974.

Horowitz, Gad. "Conservatism, Liberalism, and Socialism in Canada." *The Canadian Journal of Economics and Political Science* 32, no. 2 (May 1966): 143-71.

Horrowitz, Irving Louis. *The Use & Abuse of Social Science.* New Brunswick, N.J.: Transaction Books, 1971.

Janowitz, Morris. *Social Control of the Welfare State.* New York: Elsevier Scientific Publishing Company, Inc., 1976.

Jenkins, Shirley, ed. *Social Security in International Perspective.* New York: Columbia University Press, 1969.

Kaim-Caudle, P. R. *Comparative Social Policy and Social Security: A Ten Country Study.* London: Martin Robertson and Company, 1973.

Kallen, David, and Miller, Dorothy. "Public Attitude Toward Welfare." *Social Work* 16 (July 1971): 83-90.

L. T. Hobhouse Memorial Trust Lecture No. 27. London: Oxford University Press, 1957.

Lalonde, Marc. *Working Paper on Social Security in Canada.* Ottawa: National Health and Welfare, 1973.

Lindblom, Charles. *The Policy-Making Process.* Englewood Cliffs, N.J.: Prentice-Hall, 1968.

Lund, Michael S. "Comparing the Social Policies of Nations: A Report on Issues, Methods, and Resources." Centre for the Study of Welfare Policy, University of Chicago, 1972.

Mannheim, Karl. *Man and Society in an Age of Reconstruction.* London: Routledge and Kegan Paul Ltd., 1940.

Marris, Peter. *Loss and Change.* New York: Random House, 1975.

Marshall, T. H. "Value Problems of Welfare Capitalism." *Journal of Social Policy* 1, no. 1 (1972): 15-32.

Marx, Karl. *Capital: A Critique of Political Economy.* New York: The Modern Library, 1936.

Miliband, R. *The State in Capitalist Society.* London: Weidenfeld & Nicolson, 1969.

Miller, S. M., and Reissman, Frank. *Social Class and Social Policy.* New York: Basic Books, Inc., 1968.

Mills, C. W. *The Power Elite.* London: Oxford University Press, 1956.

Mitchell, M., and Mitchell, Joyce. *Political Analysis and Public Policy.* Chicago: Rand McNally, 1969.

National Anti-Poverty Organization. *Occasional Reports and Documents.* Ottawa, 1976 and 1977.

Newbauer, Dale. *Ideology and Society.* Morristown, N.J.: General Learning Press, 1975.

Pinker, Robert. *Social Theory and Social Policy.* London: Heinemann Educational Books, Ltd., 1971.

Prefontaine, Norbert. "What I Think I See: Reflections on the Foundations of Social Policy." *Canadian Public Administration* 16, no. 2 (Spring 1973): 298-306.

Research Committee of the League for Social Reform. *Social Planning for Canada.* Toronto: University of Toronto Press, 1975.

Rimlinger, G. *Welfare Policy and Industrialization in Europe, America and Russia.* New York: John Wiley and Sons, 1971.

Ritchie, Ronald S. "Policy-Making for the Long Term: The Need to Do More." *Canadian Public Administration* 16, no. 1 (Spring 1973): 73-82.

Rivlin, Alice M. *Systematic Thinking in Social Action.* Washington, D.C.: Brookings Institute, 1971.

Rodgers, Barbara N., ed. *Comparative Social Administration.* New York: Atherton Press, 1968.

Rys, Vladimir. "Comparative Studies of Social Security: Problems and Perspectives." *Bulletin of International Social Security Association* 19, no. 7-8 (July-August 1966): 242-68.

Schorr, Alvin L., and Baumheier, Edward C. "Social Policy." *Encyclopedia of Social Work* 16, pt. 2, 1361-76. New York: National Association of Social Workers, 1971.

Special Senate Committee on Poverty. *Poverty in Canada.* Ottawa: Queen's Printer, 1971.

Stein, Herman D. "Issues in the Contribution of Social Welfare Research to National Development." Paper prepared for International Symposium on Social Welfare Research, The Brookings Institution, Washington, D.C., May 23-June 9, 1971.

Steiner, Gilbert. *Social Insecurity: The Politics of Welfare.* Chicago: Rand McNally, 1966.

Stuart, B. C. "Who Gains from Public Health Programs?" *Annals of American Academy of Political and Social Science* 399 (January 1972): 145-50.

Tawney, R. H. *The Acquisitive Society.* First published in 1921; reprint ed., London: Fontana, 1961.

_____ . *Equality.* First published in 1931; reprint ed. (with a new introduction by Richard M. Titmuss), London: Allen & Unwin Ltd., 1964.

Titmuss, Richard M. "The Relationship Between Income Maintenance and Social Service Benefits: An Overview." *International Social Security Administration Review* 20, no. 1 (1967).

_____. *Essays on the Welfare State.* London: Allen & Unwin, 1958.

_____. *The Gift Relationship.* London: Allen & Unwin, 1970.

_____. *Social Policy.* London: Allen & Unwin, 1974.

Verba, Sidney. "Some Dilemmas in Comparative Research." *World Politics* 20, no. 1 (October 1967): 111-27.

Wedderburn, D., ed. *Poverty, Inequality and Class Structure.* Cambridge: Cambridge University Press, 1974.

Wilensky, Harold L. *The Welfare State and Equality: Structural and Ideological Roots of Public Expenditures.* Berkeley, Calif.: University of California Press, 1975.

Williams, Walter. *Social Policy Research and Analysis.* New York: American Elsevier Publishing Company Inc., 1971.

Zald, Mayer N., ed. *Social Welfare Institutions.* New York: John Wiley & Sons, 1965.

Part II

Selected Issues in Canadian Social Policy Development

The nine chapters in this section have been selected as representative of the major concerns of social policy today. Each author has attempted to trace the history of the development of Canadian policies which influence a specific sector of our society. An assessment of how adequately the policies fill the needs for which they were developed is followed by suggestions for change or reform.

The studies are designed to give the reader an overview of the development of policies in relation to the frame of reference within which they were constructed. Many of our social policies were born out of a crisis-type concern over a social problem that arose at some point in time. Other policies have grown "like Topsy" in many unplanned directions until we are almost unaware of their scope and dimensions. As one reads through the series of studies, one is struck by the necessity of understanding the circumstances under which these policies were constructed.

The use of this unit can be quite varied. Certainly each study can be used as a starting point for a more in-depth review of social policy in a discrete area—and, for this purpose, broad bibliographies have been included. The section also lends itself to the general search for the trends and patterns to be found in the development of social policy. The expression of recognized needs for comprehensive reform of existing social policy is presented not as a panacea but as a stimulus to discussion and debate over the identified issues.

Part II

Selected Issues in Canadian Social Policy Development

Inflation and Unemployment*

JOHN A. WEIR

One often hears that inflation must be stopped because it crucifies the poor. It is intuitively appealing to assume that when prices—especially of food and housing—increase, those on low incomes are the least able to defend themselves. This paper examines the plight of various groups during inflation and tries to determine the consequences for these groups of measures designed to stop the inflation.

The first section deals with inflation and unemployment as alternatives, and discusses how government can reduce one only by allowing an increase in the other. Canadian experience during the period 1960 to 1976 is examined in an effort to determine the posture of governments over those years with respect to unemployment and inflation. The section also attempts to detect whether or not fundamental changes have occurred with respect to unemployment and inflation in recent years.

The second section studies income distribution in Canada, and how it has changed in response to recent economic conditions. Using definitions of poverty established by Statistics Canada, the section identifies the poor and discusses characteristics which would tend to make them more or less vulnerable to unemployment or to inflation.

Section three discusses how governments have attempted to ease the burden of inflation by means of indexing, i.e., the linking of fixed contracts such as wages, transfer payments, and income taxes to the rate of inflation.

* I would like to thank Miss Jacqueline Klink for research assistance and Professor O. Ralph Blackmore for helpful suggestions.

This section cites experiences with indexing in both Brazil and Canada, and attempts to determine whether any one index is appropriate for all income groups.

The fourth section is a rather theoretical treatment of wage and price controls. It attempts to explain why certain groups, especially labour, resist the imposition of such controls, and deals with some experiences with controls in Canada and other countries.

Finally, the conclusion gives a brief summary of the findings and makes some general observations about the issues discussed throughout the paper.

INFLATION AND UNEMPLOYMENT

Inflation can best be defined as the process of generally rising prices. Some other definitions such as "too many dollars chasing too few goods" imply a relationship between the quantity of money and prices which many economists believe to be the only real cause of inflation. While few economists would deny that there is some connection between changes in the money supply and changes in prices, there is considerable debate about the preciseness of the relationship. It is therefore convenient to differentiate between what is known as "demand pull" and "cost push" inflation.

Types of Inflation

Demand pull inflations are those in which prices are pulled up by increases in total demand in the economy. This is felt to be the easiest type to cope with, and the cure lies in having the government reduce aggregate demand by decreasing its own spending, increasing taxes, or making money both expensive and difficult to obtain. The danger in such a policy is that a reduction in total spending causes a contraction in output and consequently an increase in unemployment. Economists refer to this relationship between inflation and unemployment as a "trade-off." It is felt that when inflation is due to excess demand the trade-off is rather precise, and policy-makers merely have to decide whether they would prefer more unemployment or still higher prices.

Cost push inflation, on the other hand, exists when prices are being pushed up by increased costs, such as wages or import prices. This type of inflation is much more resistant to decreases in aggregate demand. To put it another way, the amount of increased unemployment that will accompany a given reduction in the rate of inflation is much higher, or the trade-off is more costly in terms of jobs. Some would even go so far as to argue that under certain conditions of cost push, particularly those originating outside the country, there is no trade-off at all even at fairly high rates of inflation. That is to say that all reductions in demand will simply contract output and price increases will not respond at all to monetary and fiscal policies. It is under these conditions that some look for entirely new solutions and advocate wage and price controls, while others suggest that we ought to "inflation-proof" the economy through indexing and learn to live with the inflation rather than suffer the consequences of much higher unemployment as we attempt to cure it. More will be said later about wage and price controls and indexing.

It is much easier to categorize the types of inflation from a theoretical point of view than to identify them in practice. One type can meld into the other, and indeed a particular inflation might contain elements of both. Consequently it is difficult to determine the exact policy mix that is appropriate in particular circumstances.

Inflation and Unemployment in Canada

Table 1 shows the annual rates of inflation and unemployment in Canada for the period 1960 to 1976. The data show that up to and including 1966, declining rates of unemployment were associated with higher rates of price increases. For the remainder of the sixties, however, price increases accelerated but so did the rate of unemployment.

TABLE 1

UNEMPLOYMENT AND INFLATION, CANADA, 1961-1976

	Percentage Rise in C.P.I.	Unemployment Rate
1961	.91	7.1
1962	1.2	5.9
1963	1.8	5.5
1964	1.7	4.7
1965	2.5	3.9
1966	3.7	3.6
1967	3.6	4.1
1968	4.1	4.8
1969	4.5	4.7
1970	3.3	5.9
1971	2.9	6.4
1972	4.8	6.3
1973	7.6	5.6
1974	10.9	5.4
1975	10.8	6.9
1976	7.5	7.2

Source: Calculated from *Bank of Canada Review* (Ottawa), various issues.

During the earliest years shown in the table, monetary and fiscal policy were quite restrictive, and authorities appeared to be more concerned about inflation than unemployment. From 1963 to 1968 monetary and fiscal policy were expansionary.[1] It was during this period that Canada had a total

---

1 For discussions of monetary and fiscal policy in Canada see Grant L. Reuber and Ronald G. Bodkin, "Stagflation: The Canadian Experience," in *Issues in Canadian Economics,* ed.

of three minority governments, and it might well be that since the appropriate policies of reduced government spending and increased taxes are unpopular it is more difficult for weak governments to cope with inflation.

In 1968 the Trudeau government was elected with a majority. On December 23, 1969, the *Globe and Mail* quoted the Prime Minister as having said, "The Government will not let rising unemployment—even if it reaches six per cent—deter it from tough anti-inflation measures next year."[2] As Table 1 shows inflation did subside, and unemployment just about hit the predicted 6 per cent in 1970. During the period 1969 to 1971 monetary and fiscal policy were much tighter than they had been from 1963 to 1968.

The years 1970 and 1971 are particularly interesting, since they follow Mr. Trudeau's declaration of war on inflation. During those years Canada's price performance was the envy of the Western world, but this country paid dearly in terms of increased unemployment. It was largely because Canada allowed the international value of her currency to increase by about 7 per cent during this period that her performance was different from that of her trading partners. The change in the exchange rate reduced the price of imports in Canada and increased the price foreigners had to pay for Canadian exports, thereby reducing production, employment, and price pressures in Canada. The experience of the period suggests that changing the exchange rate does not completely insulate a country such as Canada from inflationary pressures in the rest of the world; such action merely changes the way in which the external pressures become manifest. That is to say, Canada can either accept the foreign inflation or, by changing the exchange rate, can convert the external pressure into domestic unemployment.

The trade-off relationship in the period 1971 to 1975 was much different from what it had been previously. In 1963 when the rate of unemployment was almost identical to that of 1974, the rate of inflation was below 2 per cent compared with a level of 11 per cent in 1974. As will be discussed below this changed relationship between the rate of inflation and the rate of unemployment is in part due to a change in the rate of inflation in the rest of the world, particularly in the United States, our major trading partner.

It is important to note though that there is good reason to believe that unemployment rates in recent years do not serve as an index of misery to the same extent that they once did. For example, while the unemployment rate in 1961 and in 1975 was around 7 per cent, unemployment was relatively a much more serious problem in the former year. In 1961 approximately 55 per cent of the unemployed in Canada were family heads, whereas in 1974 only 35 per cent of the jobless were the main breadwinners in their families.[3] This implies that any current rate of unemployment is less of a social problem than that same rate would have been in an earlier time.

    Officer and Smith (Toronto: McGraw-Hill Ryerson Limited, 1974), pp. 25-37; and Thomas J. Courchene, "Stabilization Policy: A Monetarist Interpretation," in *Issues in Canadian Economics*, ed. Officer and Smith, pp. 38-54.

2 *Globe and Mail* (Toronto), December 23, 1969.

3 *Financial Post* (Toronto), August 16, 1975.

Despite the fact that inflation in Canada increased from 3 per cent to 11 per cent between 1971 and 1975, both monetary and fiscal policies were highly expansionary. Federal government deficits, resulting largely from unprecedented increases in transfer payments and increased pay to civil servants were at an all-time high during the period.[4] In each of 1974 and 1975 Canada's money supply grew at an annual rate of approximately 20 per cent.[5] This rapid expansion in the money supply was to some extent necessitated by the government's need for cash to finance its huge deficits. These expansionary policies during a period of rapidly-increasing price levels suggest that the government was, if not the prime mover, at least a reluctant accomplice in the inflationary spiral of 1971 to 1975.

In October of 1975 the federal government introduced a programme of wage and price controls. During 1976 the rate of inflation declined to 7.5 per cent and the jobless rate increased slightly to 7.2 per cent, but much of the improvement in price performance was in components of the index not subject to controls. For example, between October 1974 and October 1975 food prices increased by 11 per cent, whereas in the twelve months following controls food prices actually declined by 2 per cent. For the same period other items in the index increased by 10.9 per cent and 9 per cent respectively, a much less dramatic improvement.[6]

Concomitant with the controls programme the federal government attempted to bring its spending and monetary expansion under control. Among other things, the government placed a one-year moratorium on price index-linked increases in family allowance payments, and attempted to reduce the rate of increase in the expansion of the civil service. During 1976 the money supply increased by 16 per cent, down from approximately 20 per cent in the previous year. During the fourth quarter of 1976, the annual rate was down to 10 per cent from 13.5 per cent and 26.5 per cent in the corresponding quarters of 1974 and 1975.

Table 2 shows the extent to which inflation has increased in twenty-one selected countries during the period 1961 to 1974. Under such circumstances it would have been impossible for Canada to suppress inflation without paying dearly in terms of increased unemployment. That is, had Canada not accepted some of the world-wide inflation, unemployment would have been much higher than 5.4 per cent in 1974.

The trade-off relationship has also been affected by the fact that inflation has persisted for some time and is expected to continue. While experts generally agree that Canada ought not to attempt to decrease inflation below world levels, it is important that we do not allow our rate to go above the world rate, and that our rate go down when and if the world rate declines. It is therefore necessary that internal conditions, especially expectations about inflation, adjust in step with changing conditions outside the country. It was a recognition of the need to change expectations that finally persuaded the Trudeau government to implement wage and price controls in October of 1975. A later section of this paper discusses this programme in more detail.

4 *Bank of Canada Review* (Ottawa), May 1976.
5 Ibid., Table 1.
6 Calculated from *Bank of Canada Review* (Ottawa), May 1977, Table 62.

TABLE 2

CHANGE IN THE CONSUMER PRICE LEVEL OF TWENTY-ONE SELECTED
COUNTRIES, 1961-1974 (PERCENTAGE)

Country	Annual Rate of Increase		
	1961-1962	1973	1974
Argentina	20.7	60.7	23.3
Canada	2.6	7.6	10.9
Chile	25.9	351.6	585.1
China	2.6	13.1	48.2
Denmark	6.0	9.3	15.3
Ecuador	4.8	13.0	23.4
France	4.1	7.3	13.6
Germany	2.6	6.9	7.0
India	6.4	17.4	28.5
Iran	1.8	9.8	14.1
Italy	4.2	10.8	19.1
Japan	5.7	11.8	22.7
Mexico	3.5	12.1	32.5
Netherlands	4.4	8.0	9.6
Norway	4.7	7.5	9.5
Syria	0.9	19.8	—
United Kingdom	4.1	9.1	15.9
United States	3.1	6.2	11.0
Uruguay	38.8	97.0	—
Vietnam	21.0	46.4	56.4
Yugoslavia	11.9	20.0	21.5

Source: IMF, *International Financial Statistics* (1974, 1975).

INCOME DISTRIBUTION

Both unemployment and inflation change a country's income distribution. In the case of unemployment some who are willing and able to work cannot find employment and as a result either lose all their income or have it reduced to the level provided by unemployment compensation plans. These people are highly visible and it is relatively easy to devise schemes to compensate them, but the loss from unemployment in terms of the goods and services not produced is not recoverable. It is generally agreed that unemployment compensation plans must therefore not fully compensate the individuals thrown out of work or there will be little incentive to return to work when the opportunity arises, and society will continue to be denied the output which could be used to solve still other social problems. This naturally enough is one of the reasons why governments sometimes prefer to employ people on public works projects rather than simply pay them for doing nothing. While they were never billed as such, the Opportunities For

Youth Programme and Local Initiatives Programme were in many respects "make work" projects.

The distributional effects of inflation are far more subtle and difficult to identify.[7] During periods of rising prices it is possible for income to transfer between the public and private sector, inasmuch as progressive taxes increase the percentage of income that goes to government. Governments, therefore, are able to finance increasing expenditures without raising tax rates and find themselves ambivalent in their fight against inflation in much the same way that a boxer who has bet on his opponent has an incentive to lead with his chin. As will be discussed later, indexing the tax system can prevent this type of transfer.

Other types of transfers can take place between wage earners and profit earners, between low-income groups and high-income groups, and between creditors and debtors. It is difficult to precisely identify the winners and losers in this process, and difficult also to design systems to compensate the losers if indeed the transfers are undesirable.

TABLE 3

INCOME SHARES OF LABOUR AND CAPITAL, 1965-1976

Year	Wages, Salaries and Supplementary Labour Income as a Percentage of G.N.P.	Corporate Profits before Taxes as a Percentage of G.N.P.
1965	50.93	11.41
1966	51.56	10.85
1967	53.16	10.28
1968	52.96	10.67
1969	53.97	10.39
1970	54.49	8.98
1971	54.75	9.22
1972	55.00	10.32
1973	54.13	12.26
1974	54.29	12.98
1975	56.21	11.53
1976	56.54	10.07

Source: Calculated from Bank of Canada Review (May 1977), Table 52.

Labour vs. Capital

Table 3 shows that between 1965 and 1972 wages and salaries increased rather steadily from 51 per cent to 55 per cent of the G.N.P. This increase took place despite the fact that during that period unemployment increased

7   For a theoretical discussion of income redistribution under conditions of inflation, see Ruben A. Kessel and Armen C. Alchian, "Effects of Inflation," The Journal of Political Economy 70, no. 6 (December 1962): 521-37.

from just under 4 per cent to slightly over 6 per cent. Inflation during the period was relatively mild, but persistent, with the largest change in the rate occurring in 1972, when it rose from 2.9 to 4.8 per cent.

In 1973 and 1974 labour's share dropped to just over 54 per cent, but it recovered to slightly more than 56 per cent in 1975, and in 1976 hit 56.5 per cent, a record for the period shown in Table 3. The decline in labour's share during 1973 and 1974 was accompanied by an increased share for corporate profits. The most plausible explanation for these shifts is that the dramatic upswing in the rate of price level increases in 1973 and 1974 was largely unanticipated by labour and therefore not fully included as a factor in wage negotiations. It would appear that by 1975 after price increases had been accelerating rapidly for three years, high inflation was expected to continue and appropriate compensation was included in wage increases.

It is interesting to note that during 1976, the first year of the controls programme, wages and salaries as a percentage of the G.N.P. continued to increase. Part of this increase was at the expense of corporate profits which declined from 11.5 to just over 10 per cent of the G.N.P. While this evidence is not conclusive, it does suggest that the controls programme did not have a relatively adverse effect on wages and salaries during its first year of operation.

Income Shares by Quintiles

Unemployment and inflation also affect the shares of income received by groups at different ends of the income spectrum. Between 1951 and 1969 the lowest 20 per cent of all family units in Canada received between 4.2 and 4.4 per cent of total income, a rather consistent ratio. In 1971 this percentage dropped to 3.9 per cent but had recovered to 3.8 per cent by 1973. Between 1951 and 1969 the share of the top 20 per cent of all families fluctuated between 41.1 and 42.8 per cent and was 42.7 per cent in 1973.[8]

The decline in the bottom group's share in the early 1970s could have been due to a dependence on transfer payments, which did not keep pace with inflation while other incomes rose. The decline might also be due to weak labour markets preventing the working poor from raising their incomes in line with those of other workers, perhaps because of a higher incidence of unemployment or shorter work weeks. The improvement by 1973 is likely in part at least attributable to the linking of transfer payments to the cost of living. It should be noted that these figures do not indicate that the low group was worse off in an absolute sense than it was before; the data only suggest that they were relatively worse off with respect to other groups.

Incidence of Poverty

If one defines poverty as some percentage at the lower end of the income distribution, say the bottom 20 per cent, then there will always be poverty unless all incomes are exactly equal. Since 1967 Statistics Canada has defined low-income or poor families as those family units or individuals that

8   *Globe and Mail* (Toronto), May 7, 1975.

spend 70 per cent of their incomes on food, shelter and clothing. The percentage of families poor by this definition declined steadily from 18 per cent in 1967 to 12 per cent in 1973, and during the same period individuals classified as being poor dropped from 39 to 31.6 per cent.[9] The relatively high percentage of individuals in the poor category is likely due to the large percentage of single young people who are unemployed and the large number of old people who live alone, supported only by low pensions. It could well be that the automatic increases in transfer payments that now occur in Canada helped to reduce poverty in recent years.

Brief Profile of the Poor

According to data published by Statistics Canada for 1973,[10] over 50 per cent of the poor lived in Ontario and Quebec. Close to 40 per cent of poor families lived in rural areas, and a high percentage of the working poor were farmers. About 60 per cent of poor families, compared with 71 per cent of other families, owned their own homes, making a higher percentage of poor families renters. Old and young heads, as opposed to middle-aged heads, accounted for a disproportionately large percentage of poor families. This characteristic was most pronounced in the case of old individuals, where 42 per cent as opposed to 23 per cent were over sixty-five. A striking percentage of poor individuals were females, probably because women live longer than men and many, no doubt, were widows living on pensions.

Over 50 per cent of the heads of poor families were in the work force, that is to say, either working or actively seeking employment, but only about half worked full-time. Wages and salaries were the major source of income for 31 per cent of the heads of poor families, compared with 85 per cent for other families. Transfer payments were listed as the major source of income for 50 per cent of poor heads compared with 5 per cent for the non-poor heads.

Private pensions were the major source of income for only 1 per cent of the poor heads, and were just slightly more important to the non-poor heads. It has been noted elsewhere that in the United States,[11] and it probably holds even more true in Canada, about 90 per cent of those presently retired receive no income from private pensions, because widespread coverage of private pension plans is a relatively new phenomenon in North America. This implies that in Canada many retired people rely almost entirely on government pensions for their income, a fact which is substantiated by the large percentage of poor people who list transfer payments as their major source of income. Since government pensions are a policy variable, it ought to be easy from an administrative point of view to assist the aged and to keep their incomes in line with the cost of living as will be discussed later. To some extent this has been attempted in Canada by linking government pensions to the consumer price index.

9   Ibid.
10 Statistics Canada, *Income Distributions by Size in Canada, 1973* (Ottawa, August 1975).
11 John L. Palmer, *Inflation, Unemployment, and Poverty* (Toronto: D. C. Heath and Company, 1973), p. 73.

Unemployment or Inflation?

While it is difficult to quantify the harm done to the poor by unemployment versus inflation, increasingly economists have been opting in favour of increasing aggregate demand to keep labour markets tight even at the risk of considerable inflation. Harry Johnson has argued that high levels of employment are usually of greatest benefit to the poor.[12] Noting that a high percentage of the unemployed and of the poor are the very young and the very old, he points out that during periods of slack the young find it difficult to gain the experience necessary to get them better jobs, whereas when labour is relatively scarce employers find it profitable to invest in training programmes to provide the skills they need. Older workers benefit by being allowed to work beyond normal retirement age, rather than being forced into early retirement because labour markets are slack.

Since the data referred to above indicate that a high percentage of the poor are quite old or quite young, tight labour markets would help reduce poverty in Canada. Tight labour markets, besides employing older and younger members of the work force, would also assist other members of the working poor by helping to keep their incomes in line with the cost of living. Since it is a well-known fact that migration increases as the rate of employment in the receiving areas improves, an added advantage of tight labour markets is that the rural and regional poor would be more likely and more able to migrate to areas where jobs become available.

Professor R. Blauer has studied the impact of inflation in Canada on fixed income and asset groups for the period 1950 to 1967. Her general conclusions were:

> During the period of study, inflation was not accompanied by any major changes in income distribution over broad socio-economic categories that did not also occur during periods of price stability. While it was certainly true that the elderly, the poor, and the recipients of transfer income and retirement pensions all found their relative income positions deteriorating during periods of rising prices, it was true that this also occurred during periods of price stability. The problem is clearly not that of inflation but of society's grossly inadequate treatment of the elderly and the poor. To a certain extent these groups were worse off in an absolute sense during periods of inflation in that they experienced declines in real income not fully matched by increases in real wealth. To the extent that inflation induced legislative action to counter such declines in real income, these households were better off than they would have been had prices not risen, as such action generally increased their share of total income.[13]

Professor Blauer's findings are almost identical to those of a number of researchers in the United States covering a similar period.[14] It does not

---

12   Harry G. Johnson, "Unemployment and Poverty," in *Poverty and Affluence*, ed. Leo Fishman (New Haven: Yale University Press, 1966), pp. 182-211. See also Palmer, *Inflation, Unemployment, and Poverty*, p. 57, and R. Blauer, "Fixed Income and Asset Groups in Canada," in *Inflation and the Canadian Experience*, ed. N. Swan and D. Wilton (Kingston: Industrial Relations Centre, Queen's University, 1971), p. 147.

13   Blauer, "Fixed Income and Asset Groups in Canada," p. 146.

14   Robert G. Hollister and John L. Palmer, "Impact on Inflation on the Poor," in *Redistribution to the Rich and the Poor*, ed. K. E. Boulding and M. Plaff (Belmont: Wadsworth, 1972), pp. 240-70; and Thad W. Mirer, "The Distributive Impact on Purchasing Power of Inflation

necessarily follow though that the results will hold for conditions of double digit inflation presently being experienced throughout the world. In Canada, however, transfer payments are now indexed to the cost of living and as long as that remains the case a large percentage of the poor in this country will at least stay even with inflation. The working poor present more of a problem because their major source of income, wages and salaries, is not a policy variable. In the absence of some sort of a guaranteed annual income, this portion of the poor must rely on the market to keep them in step with the cost of living.

The Economic Council of Canada has recently compiled estimates of the effects of inflation on income distribution in Canada for the period 1969 to 1975. These estimates are displayed in Table 4. The data suggest that recent inflation has worked to the disadvantage of high-income households. On the average, the highest-income group realized the lowest relative gain in income and suffered the highest losses in assets. This group received a high proportion of its income from investment and self-employment, particularly in the professions. While the lowest group also sustained a loss in assets, this was partly offset by real income gains, particularly from enriched transfer payments. This group included many widows, students, farmers and fishermen. Wages and salaries accounted for 40 per cent and transfer payments for 38 per cent of their family incomes. Middle-income groups benefited from increased income and job opportunities, and gained further by a reduction in the real value of their fixed debts. In this group wages and salaries accounted for over 80 per cent of household income. With respect to age, the Council notes that the earnings of pensioners have generally managed to keep pace with the income of others in the economy.

TABLE 4

ESTIMATED IMPACT OF INFLATION ON THE RELATIVE POSITIONS OF HOUSEHOLDS, BY INCOME GROUP, 1969-1975

	Income Group			
	Less than $4,000	$4,000-7,999	$8,000-14,999	$15,000 and over
Increase in income	107.1	74.5	69.3	54.2
Increase in expenditures	48.6	47.3	46.5	45.8
Increase or decrease in value of net assets	-10.8	5.1	10.9	-10.0

Source: Economic Council of Canada, *Thirteenth Annual Review* (Ottawa: Information Canada, 1976), p. 22.

The Council's findings suggest that the various indexing schemes have managed to prevent a deterioration in the relative position of certain low-income groups, despite a fairly severe inflation. The middle-income group,

during Price Controls," *Quarterly Review of Economics and Business* 15, no. 2 (Summer 1975): 93-96.

which relies more heavily on wages and salaries, would seem to depend to a greater degree on expanding employment opportunities and higher wages in their battle for relative income during inflation.[15]

INDEXING

As inflation has become embedded in the world and as experts believe it is likely to persist, governments are becoming increasingly involved in trying to devise schemes to "inflation-proof" their economies so that price increases will not lead to massive redistributions of income. A completely indexed economy would have the money values of all contracts changing in proportion to the price level.

Measuring Inflation

Governments use a variety of measures to estimate price changes. The three most commonly employed are the Gross National Product Deflator, the Wholesale Price Index, and the Consumer Price Index. The G.N.P. Deflator measures the prices of all goods and services including those in the government sector. The Wholesale Price Index includes only goods at the wholesale level. The Consumer Price Index (C.P.I.) includes goods and services purchased at the retail level. The C.P.I. is the one generally used to measure the impact of inflation on the purchasing power of individuals. Like all indexes, the C.P.I. employs weighted averages and reflects changes with respect to a base year.[16] In this particular index a basket of goods and services is priced in 1961 dollars and the value is set at 100 points. If the basket cost the equivalent of 162 points in 1974, prices have increased a total of 62 per cent in the years between 1961 and 1974.

While attempts are made to allow for price increases due to quality improvements, it is generally believed that the index overstates price increases, since goods and services generally increase in quality to a greater extent than the index is adjusted for such improvements. It is estimated that this bias is around 2 per cent per year. However, when the index is increasing at a high rate the importance of this problem becomes less significant. Another upward bias is associated with the fact that as items in the index become relatively more expensive, people change their purchases towards cheaper items, such as less expensive cuts of meat, which could make the weights used in the index inappropriate. A more serious problem has to do with the expenditure patterns used in the calculation of the index. The quantities used in the consumer price index reflect the buying habits of a middle-income urban family which spends roughly 55 per cent of its total on

15   The Economic Council of Canada, *Thirteenth Annual Review* (Ottawa: Information Canada, 1976), pp. 5-24. This paper was originally written prior to the publication of the Council's *Thirteenth Annual Review.* Many of the topics covered in this paper are dealt with extensively in the *Review,* but time and space precluded the inclusion in this paper of many of the Council's findings.

16   For discussions of some of the problems of the C.P.I. see Statistics Canada, *The Consumer Price Index* (Ottawa: Information Canada, June 1973); and Denis S. Karnosky, *A Primer on the Consumer Price Index* 56, no. 7 (St. Louis: Federal Reserve Bank of St. Louis, July 1974): 2-7.

food and housing. This is not representative of expenditures of poor families which spend higher percentages of their total on these two items.

Indexes and the Poor

Extensive work has been done in the United States and to a lesser extent in Canada to construct price indexes which apply to the expenditure patterns of varying income groups. In the United States, Hollister and Palmer[17] have constructed a Poor Man's Price Index for the 1960s and discovered that inflation during that period was more adverse to the rich than to the poor, when viewed solely from the expenditures side. Thad Mirer extended the above study to 1973 and found that the more recent inflation has fallen more heavily on the poor than the rich.

The Economic Council of Canada has constructed similar indexes for Canada[18] and, as Table 5 shows, the impact of inflation on the rich and on the poor has been quite similar to the experience in the United States. Note that for every year up to and including 1973 the highest income group suffered more from inflation than did the lowest. For the last two periods the situation is reversed, the very poor being hit harder than the rich. According to the figures in Table 5, however, the impact of inflation on the expenditure patterns of all groups has been amazingly consistent, the highest figure being 162.7 and the lowest being 159.9, with both using 1961 as a base year of 100. The recent deterioration in the relative position of the poor in both Canada and the United States is no doubt due to greater than average increases in the prices of food and shelter. As governments more and more attempt to compensate the poor for inflation, it may become necessary to use special indexes which are appropriate to the deterioration of purchasing power of low-income families, as opposed to the C.P.I. which is more representative of middle-class purchasing patterns.

Canada: Partial Indexing

While Canada has stopped short of indexing financial securities, this country has been more daring and innovative than most in trying to soften the redistributional impact of inflation.[19] Canada has fully indexed practically all federal government transfer payments to individuals, and has linked income tax payments to the C.P.I. in such a way as to reduce these taxes to the level they would have been in the absence of inflation. The federal Department of Labour has been pushing for the inclusion of cost of living clauses in labour agreements in the private sector. While only about 10 per cent of the agreements existing in 1974 had such clauses, they are becoming increasingly popular with labour.

The federal government's pension scheme for civil servants and Members of Parliament is fully indexed to the C.P.I., but very few private pension

---

17 Hollister and Palmer, "Impact on Inflation on the Poor"; Mirer, "Distributive Impact on Purchasing Power."

18 The Economic Council of Canada, *Eleventh Annual Review* (Ottawa: Information Canada, 1974), pp. 171-74.

19 Ibid., pp. 169-71; "A Look at Indexing for Price Changes," *Bank of Nova Scotia Monthly Review* (August-September 1974); and *Financial Post* (Toronto), September 29, 1975.

TABLE 5

CONSUMER PRICE INDEX, BY INCOME CLASS, ALL FAMILIES OF TWO OR MORE PERSONS, 1969-1974

Income Class ($)

(1961 = 100)

Year Ending	Under 3,000	3,000-3,999	4,000-4,999	5,000-5,999	6,000-6,999	7,000-7,999	8,000-8,999	9,000-9,999	10,000-10,999	11,000-11,999	12,000-14,999	15,000 or over	C.P.I.
January 1969	121.8	121.7	121.4	121.5	121.5	124.4	121.7	122.2	122.0	122.0	122.0	122.6	122.6
January 1970	127.1	126.9	126.6	126.6	126.7	129.8	127.0	127.6	127.3	127.4	127.4	128.1	128.2
January 1971	128.9	128.5	128.3	128.4	128.5	131.9	129.1	129.9	129.7	129.7	129.8	130.8	130.3
January 1972	135.6	135.0	134.8	134.7	134.9	138.3	135.5	136.3	136.0	136.0	136.0	137.0	136.7
January 1973	143.8	142.8	142.4	142.1	142.2	145.8	142.7	143.7	143.1	143.1	143.0	144.1	144.5
January 1974	158.2	156.8	156.2	155.7	155.6	159.3	156.0	157.1	156.3	156.2	156.0	157.1	157.6
April 1974	162.7	161.2	160.6	160.0	159.9	163.8	160.3	161.4	160.6	160.5	160.3	161.4	161.9

Note: There may be no weighted combination of the price indexes for the income groups between $4,000 and $12,000 that will produce the published C.P.I. This is due to the use of different weighting schemes. The price indexes for the income classes use 1969 expenditure weights, and the published C.P.I. uses 1957 expenditure weights prior to May 1973 and a combination of 1967 and 1969 expenditure weights for May 1973 onwards.

Source: Economic Council of Canada, *Eleventh Annual Review* (Ottawa: Information Canada, 1974), Table 7-4, p. 172.

schemes make any provision whatever for the decreasing purchasing power of pensioners. This is understandable since the stock of financial assets held by insurance companies does not automatically produce increased revenues as prices go up. A system of indexing securities would be necessary if private carriers were expected to guarantee indexed pensions. The few private plans that do contain provisions for inflation compensation usually limit an increase in any one year to around 2 per cent, and in these cases it is extra contributions by the employer that provides the necessary funds. The Canadian tax laws, however, make it extremely awkward to finance these since the additional contributions are not tax deductible.

Brazil: Complete Indexing

Brazil has come closer to complete indexing than has any other country.[20] In Brazil the money value of such things as wages, bank loans and deposits, government bonds, and private securities is index-linked to the country's Consumer Price Index. Wages, however, were only partially linked: that is, the workers were compensated only for a portion of the inflation and this caused a redistribution of income. The indexing was accompanied by strictly enforced wage and price controls and a tightening of the money supply. Under these policies, inflation was brought down considerably from its rate of 144 per cent per year.

Side Effects

As well as preventing undesired redistributions of income, Brazil's system of complete indexing was probably anti-inflationary. Since the value of bank accounts was indexed, people found it less necessary to spend money before it deteriorated in purchasing power; this meant that money that would have been chasing after all sorts of goods thereby forcing up prices was being saved instead. Some writers have noted that the system was enforced by a military dictatorship, and expressed doubt that such extreme measures would be tolerated by a democracy. The critics of the system also insist that the improved price performance was due almost entirely to tight monetary policy that accompanied the indexing and controls.

It is likely that Canada's present system of indexing is inflationary. While from an equity point of view it is desirable to increase transfer payments and reduce tax collections to compensate for erosion due to inflation, both of these schemes increase purchasing power when prices are already rising. Between 1973 and 1975 the federal government's deficit increased almost five-hundredfold from $10 million to $4.7 billion.[21] As has been suggested above, the resulting increased need for cash encouraged the government to allow the money supply to increase at an annual rate of about 20 per cent so that the deficit could be financed without overloading the bond markets. Since the usual prescription calls for a reduction in purchasing power in an inflationary environment, the Canadian system will probably require an

20 Albert Fishlaw, "Indexing Brazilian Style: Inflation without Tears," *Brookings Papers on Economic Activity* 1 (1974): 261-82; and Ronald A. Krieger, "Inflation and the Brazilian Solution," *Challenge* 17, no. 4 (September-October 1974): 43-52.
21 *Bank of Canada Review* (Ottawa), May 1976, Table 2.

increase in general tax levels or a reduction in certain government expenditures to offset the automatic stimulation price levels received from the indexation of transfer payments and tax revenues.

One general fear often expressed by economists is that by taking the sting out of inflation, the practice of indexing removes much of the political pressure on governments to reduce the rate of inflation. Their fear is that inflation feeds on itself, gets worse and worse, eventually exploding into the type of hyperinflation experienced by Germany in the 1920s. Others, most notably University of Chicago's Milton Friedman, argue that by reducing the inequities usually associated with inflation, indexing provides governments with time to ease the economy down without throwing it into massive unemployment by a sudden application of the brakes.[22]

WAGE AND PRICE CONTROLS

The Market Mechanism

During normal times countries in the Western world rely to varying degrees on the market mechanism to make many of the decisions which usually are undertaken directly by governments in more socialistic countries such as Russia and China. In a pure market economy the price system determines which goods and services are going to be produced, by what methods and for whom. Such allocations are made by changes in relative prices and incomes in response to the forces of supply and demand. No modern country relies exclusively on the market to determine the welfare of its citizens and all countries intervene to modify the verdict of the marketplace with respect to certain kinds of goods and services, certain groups of people, and certain geographic regions.

Experience with Controls

While all economies have elements of both market and state control, the market is still an important if indeed not the dominant force in the West. During such emergencies as an all-out war, the state is usually compelled to intervene in the market and allocate resources directly to the war effort rather than rely on the price system to determine what percentage of production will be available for civilian as opposed to military use. To ensure that the remaining production is distributed equitably and that it does not end up only in the hands of those who can afford to pay extremely high prices, goods are usually rationed by coupons as well as by prices. Experience in Canada and the United States during the Second World War clearly demonstrated that the administration of such programmes is extremely complex. In addition to controlling the sale and prices of consumer goods, the authorities must plan total production and allocate resources so things are in the right place at the right time. Public acceptance of such programmes is a matter of law buttressed by government propaganda and a spirit of wartime patriotism.

22   Milton Friedman, "Using Escalators to Help Fight Inflation," *Fortune* 90, no. 1 (July 1974): 94-97 and 174-76.

Since the war, many European countries, the United States, and Canada have attempted to cope with periodic inflation by means of wage and price controls without resorting to the extensive planning done in wartime. Britain has imposed such policies no less than five times within the past thirty or so years. It is generally accepted that such measures at best only suppress or hide inflation and are usually followed by a period of market vengeance during which inflation again accelerates.[23]

Erosion of Controls

When wage and price controls exist over a long period of time, their effects tend to become eroded by other types of change. To evade the effect of price controls, management for example can reduce the quality of products. It is relatively simple to make such things as chocolate bars more expensive at a specific price by reducing the proportion of sugar or nuts they contain, and it is practically impossible for authorities to check on the detailed specifications of literally millions of items sold in a complex economy.

On the cost side, management and labour can collude to bring about what is called "wage drift." When wages are not controlled, firms wishing to attract new labour or retain their existing work forces compete by raising wage scales. Under controls, there is a tendency for such firms to "reclassify" or promote workers into higher categories and to relax the rules on overtime pay. Once some firms adopt these practices others must follow in self-defence, and the longer the controls are in place the more widespread these practices become.

Relative Wages and Prices

While unions are constantly trying to get wage increases at least sufficient to compensate for inflation, they are equally concerned about their relative position in the country's income spectrum. Firemen compare their incomes with those of policemen or firemen in other cities, while university professors talk about their position vis-à-vis high school teachers or other professionals. With or without inflation there is a continual jockeying for position as one group follows another to the bargaining table.

Shifts in relative positions occur more rapidly in situations where the settlements of each group include large dollar compensation for inflation. Whenever controls are imposed, some groups will be approaching the end of their contracts while others will have recently concluded agreements which have compensated them for inflation and changed their position relative to those about to enter negotiations. From the moment the controls are implemented a large percentage of the work force views them as being unfair, and the longer they continue the greater the resentment they engender.

23   Michael Parking, "Where is Britain's Inflation Going," *Lloyd's Bank Review*, no. 117 (July 1975), pp. 1-13; and Darryl R. Francis, *Proposed Solutions to Inflation: Effective and Ineffective 53*, no. 7 (St. Louis: Federal Reserve Bank of St. Louis, July 1971): 25-30.

In 1972 the British launched a programme of wage and price controls, and both the government's posture and labour's reaction were predictable. In that year Britain had one of the largest budget deficits in history, and the country's money supply had been allowed to grow by nearly 25 per cent. As conventional economic theory would suggest, the result was rapid inflation. The government insisted that the inflation was due solely to union power, and imposed wage and price controls. Labour retaliated with a series of strikes in key industries, which forced the adoption of a three-day week. The net result was a general election which brought a change in government and a collapse of wage and price controls.[24]

It is usual to implement price and wage controls by imposing a freeze on prices and wages. Price freezes imply fixed relative prices in much the same way that frozen wages imply fixed relative wages. When relative prices are prevented from changing, shortages become commonplace. Even during the brief period of price controls in the United States shortages of chickens developed as farmers refused to produce them because of the unfavourable relationship which existed between the price of chickens and chicken feed. At the same time, shortages of beef developed in that country as farmers exported their production to Canada where the price of beef was higher. The only way to prevent such shortages under fixed prices is to impose detailed production and export controls, and most countries are not prepared to set up the machinery necessary to establish and police such regulations.

Controls in Canada

From the end of World War II until October 1975, compulsory wage and price controls had not been used in Canada. In 1969 this country established the Prices and Incomes Commission which failed to gain labour support for its plan of voluntary restraint.[25] Management offered to support the plan on the proviso that labour would go along. But labour leaders, who are elected to get "more" for their members, found it difficult to endorse a programme that was intended to put a lid on the gains that any one union could obtain. In addition, labour believed that since it takes collusion between management and labour to frustrate wage controls and since no such collusion is required to cheat on prices, it is easier to control wages than prices, making any system of controls biased against labour. Labour also argued that a complete system should also limit profits, interest, and dividends, so that payments to capital as well as to labour would be under control.

In the political campaign that preceded the general election of July 1974, the Progressive Conservative Party advocated compulsory wage and price controls. The Liberals campaigned against controls on the grounds that Canada's inflation was largely the result of increasing world price levels. Since exports and imports amount to roughly 25 per cent of the G.N.P., it

---

24　Lipsey, Sparks and Steiner, *Economics,* 2nd ed. (New York: Harper and Row, 1976), pp. 801-02.
25　Ibid., p. 800.

would be impossible for authorities to totally insulate Canada from external inflationary pressures, particularly those emanating from the United States. In addition, it was pointed out, the federal government has a fundamental constitutional problem associated with such measures, since prices and wages clearly fall under provincial jurisdiction, except perhaps in a situation of national emergency. The Liberals won an overwhelming victory in that election, which suggests in part that the people did not then believe compulsory controls were necessary.

In October 1975, just sixteen months after he had been elected on a platform that opposed compulsory wage and price controls, Prime Minister Trudeau announced that he intended to impose such a programme on Canadians.[26] He argued that since price increases in other countries had started to slow down, inflation in Canada could be contained with the help of controls. He said that any future inflation would be largely the result of excessive wage demands on the part of large unions. Labour's reaction to the programme has been hostile; however, there have not yet been wide-scale strikes to express opposition to the programme.

The controls are intended to break the inflationary psychology in Canada so that long-term labour contracts will not incorporate large increases in wages intended to compensate for inflation that does not occur. If such excessive compensation were won by labour because inflation was expected to be higher than it in fact turns out to be, international cost pressures would merely be replaced by domestic pressures from wage costs. Under such circumstances, proper monetary and fiscal policy would be able to reduce inflation, but only by causing considerable unemployment. That is, the country would have to face the same unacceptable trade-off that had existed when the inflationary pressures were international.

The Canadian controls programme is rather unique, and avoids some of the problems typical of the experience in other countries. First, since the programme was not implemented with a freeze on wage and price hikes, it is more flexible than its counterparts in other countries and ought to lead to a minimum misallocation of resources. Second, the programme takes a long-term view and intends to bring wage increases down gradually over a period of three years. Most other countries tried short-term freezes and labour and management had considerable incentive to wait them out. The result was that such programmes tended to merely temporarily suppress or postpone the inflation.

Labour's main resentment of the controls lies in the fact that they are much more explicit with respect to wage increases than they are about prices and profits. Wage increases are limited to specific and declining percentages over the three-year programme, but while price increases must be justified by increased costs there is no real legal limit on the amount by which prices can rise. The controls on profits are somewhat vague and subject to interpretation. Labour therefore believes that its purchasing power will decline as wage controls bite into their raises and prices continue to increase.

---

26 *Globe and Mail* (Toronto), October 14, 1975.

It is clear that the government intends to rely on conventional monetary and fiscal policy to contain price increases, and is using the controls programme to relieve some of the upward pressure on costs. If the programme works, unemployment created by the tight monetary and fiscal arrangements could be considerably less than it would be in the absence of controls. Strategically the government would have been better off to admit that it was primarily large increases in the money supply that had been causing the inflation, but that these increases were permitted in order to avoid unemployment that would have resulted from a more restricted monetary policy. It could then have pointed out to labour that the controls were primarily designed to prevent massive unemployment in the face of pending restrictions in the growth of the money supply. Such admission would have forced the government to accept at least some of the responsibility for inflation, and might have had undesired political consequences, but they might have made the controls more acceptable to organized labour, the group that can make or break the programme.

It is too early to judge whether or not the federal government's controls programme has had a significant effect on inflation. The programme was imposed at a time when market forces were poised to reduce the rate of inflation and economists were predicting that such a deceleration was imminent.[27] As has been indicated earlier in this study, the rate of inflation in Canada has declined since the controls were imposed, but much of the improvement has been in items such as food which were not subject to controls.

Currently there is speculation that the government will end the programme before it has lived out its scheduled three-year existence. There are two basic questions surrounding the removal of controls: first, how should their withdrawal be accomplished; and second, will they be replaced by a more permanent monitoring agency?

There is fear that bungling in the dismantling of the controls programme could set off another inflationary spiral. Several different scenarios are possible and each has drawbacks. A sudden and complete cessation of the programme would leave some unions with recently-signed contracts with a sense of grievance as contracts currently under negotiation escape the constraints of the programme. To announce a specific future date for early withdrawal would tend to paralyze the collective bargaining process as unions would drag out negotiations beyond the date of decontrol. A system of phased withdrawal by contract date or by industry is also a possibility. Withdrawal by contract date would appear to be equitable in that most contracts would have been subject to controls for two contract years, but such a system would take no account of the strategic position of various industries whose contracts are regarded as "key settlements" in other negotiations or whose product prices are an important cost element to other industries.

Some would prefer a systematic withdrawal phased according to the particular market conditions of industries. Those operating in depressed

27   See, for example, the economic forecasts published in the *Canadian Business Review* 2, no. 4 (Autumn 1975).

markets, such as electronics and textiles, could be exempt first and others would follow as conditions seemed appropriate. Such a system could lead to a serious misallocation of resources because industries which ought to be expanding in response to demand conditions would not be getting proper signals from the price system.

The issue of a permanent monitoring agency to replace the Anti-Inflation Board is more fundamental. Such a body would presumably oversee wage settlements in the public and private sector and insist on public accountability in cases where either prices or wages appeared to increase unduly. The notion of the need for such an ongoing authority is based on a belief that the market mechanism is no longer capable of allocating resources and determining income distribution. It is an endorsement of the ideas of John Kenneth Galbraith, who for years has claimed that governments ought to take a more active role in the economic decision-making process.[28]

Disciples of Galbraith envisage a corporate state in which groups comprised of government officials, business executives, and union leaders would set fairly specific rules which would minimize the role of competition and collective bargaining in the allocation and distributional process. Many economists fear that such a system will lead to slower economic growth and higher unemployment, making it more rather than less difficult to provide a reasonable and equitable standard of living for Canadians. They prefer to allow the market mechanism to make decisions which would promote growth and employment. Most economists would agree that markets do not make due allowance for equity, and believe that a certain amount of redistribution via transfer payments and the tax system is necessary and warranted after the markets have completed their function. They essentially believe though that the gains in output generated by a market as opposed to a planned or programmed approach to production will be more than sufficient to provide compensation to those who are disadvantaged by the impersonal free-enterprise system.

Galbraith and laissez-faire economists are poles apart. It is likely that after the debate has gone on for yet a while Canada will arrive at a compromise system which will be different from the extreme views of either camp, but which will appeal to Canadians.

Impact on the Poor

Experience in other countries has shown that some prices are much more easily controlled than others, and that particular difficulties arise in areas subject to international competition such as raw materials and agricultural products. It is difficult to say whether controls are slanted in favour of the rich or the poor, but at least one study of the United States during the 1971-1972 controls period disclosed that the basket of goods purchased by the typical poor family increased by a higher percentage than did the purchases of the rich. Much of this difference can be accounted for by the higher percentages of income spent by the poor on food and housing,

---

28 Galbraith has written extensively on these issues. One of many references is John Kenneth Galbraith, *Economics and the Public Purpose* (Boston: Houghton Mifflin Company, 1973).

which increased relatively rapidly in price during the period of controls.[29] But one cannot be sure what would have happened to the relative prices of these items in the absence of controls, nor of the employment opportunities which would have been lost to the poor had the government tried more rigorous use of monetary and fiscal policy as an alternative to controls. The study also does not examine the relative changes in income of the rich and poor during that period. Nevertheless, the fact remains that controls do not have the same impact on all income groups.

It is too early to determine the likely impact of Canadian controls on the poor as far as their effect on prices is concerned. They will probably benefit the lower-income group more because they could soften the impact of tight money on labour markets. That is, jobs could be more readily available than they would have been had tight money been implemented without controls.

CONCLUSION

Recent Canadian experience suggests that the domestic relationship between unemployment and inflation has been altered by increased inflation in the rest of the world. Under such conditions it is likely that attempts to reduce the internal rate of inflation to earlier levels would result in massive unemployment. It has also been suggested that such unemployment would be an even greater burden on the poor than the inflation it would replace. Tight labour markets and a system such as indexing to compensate the poor for inflation would seem to be a much more humane policy choice than one which opted to stop inflation by creating more unemployment. Wage and price controls have not been particularly successful elsewhere, and will encounter difficulties in an open economy such as Canada's. Such controls could, however, assist the poor if they have the effect of changing Canadian expectations in a manner warranted by international economic conditions.

29   Mirer, "Distributive Impact on Purchasing Power."

Income Security

DAVID ROSS

The present represents an appropriate time to examine our system of
income security chiefly because the federal government and the ten provincial governments in April of 1973 launched what was billed as an extensive and comprehensive two-year review of social security in Canada (actually it ran for three years). While the review did not live up to expectations, it
represented an important event for those concerned with social security
policy.

The review process was set in motion by the federal government with the
release of its *Working Paper on Social Security in Canada* (commonly
referred to as the Orange Paper).[1] Governments, voluntary social agencies,
church, business, labour, citizens' groups, and academics all responded to
the Orange Paper which increased the interest and extended the debate
significantly.

The current examination of income security and poverty can probably be
traced back to the interest and shock generated in 1968 by the material
contained in the *Fifth Annual Review* of the Economic Council of Canada,[2]
which revealed that 27 per cent of the Canadian population lived in poverty,
very stringently defined, but which perhaps more importantly revealed that
of all the designated poor families in Canada, 68 per cent were headed by

---

1 Health and Welfare Canada, *Working Paper on Social Security in Canada* (Ottawa: Health
 and Welfare Canada, 1973).
2 Economic Council of Canada, *Fifth Annual Review* (Ottawa: Information Canada, 1968),
 ch. 6. The Council also pursued it, but less ambitiously, in their *Sixth Annual Review* (1969),
 ch. 7.

workers; that is, the majority of the poor were working Canadians and not part of the welfare caseload.

During this same period a prestigious, competent and ambitious Commission was established in the province of Quebec by the provincial government to investigate the field of health and social welfare in the broadest terms possible. This Commission came to be known as the Castonguay-Nepveu Commission and since its inception has published dozens of final reports and substudies that have not only raised important questions related to social security, but have provided a wealth of factual information and imaginative but detailed solutions, many of which have been, or are being implemented, in Quebec.[3] Unfortunately, the work of this Commission has not received the widespread public attention outside of Quebec that it justly deserves.

In 1971 an influential volume, *Poverty in Canada,* was published by a Special Senate Committee (known as the Croll Committee) which re-emphasized, expanded upon, and updated many of the points contained in the earlier Economic Council Review, but which was much more extensive in its coverage and criticism.[4] For example, it publicized the fact that the poor may be paying as much as 60 per cent of their income in taxes of one form or another. But the Committee also concluded that the solution to poverty lay in a federally-financed guaranteed annual income.

The Senate Report is important, not only because it sustained the interest generated by the Economic Council's work but because, perhaps for the first time, it introduced to a wide audience the idea of a guaranteed annual income and it spelled out how it might be implemented. Prior to that time, most discussion of the guaranteed annual income was confined to textbooks and it was seldom seriously associated with public policy.

Adding to the interest generated by the Senate Report was the almost simultaneous publication of the *Real Poverty Report,*[5] a volume put together by a group of disenchanted so-called rebels who quit the Senate investigation and believed that the Senate Report would not indict the real culprits responsible for poverty and its perpetuation. *The Real Poverty Report* arrived at many of the same policy conclusions that the Senate Report did, but its tone was angry and it attempted to lay bare the fundamental causes of poverty.

The most recent comprehensive national report on poverty is that of the Canadian Council on Social Development which in 1973 published the findings of its Task Force on Social Security, which deliberated for two years.[6] It contained criticisms of a wide variety of income and service programmes, and while endorsing the guaranteed annual income it came out strongly in favour of a permanent work opportunities programme which represented an important new approach that earlier reports had not taken.

3 Of particular relevance to this study is the following Commission document: *Income Security,* report of the Commission of Inquiry on Health and Social Welfare (Quebec, 1971), Vol. V, Book 2.
4 Senate of Canada, *Poverty in Canada,* report of the Special Senate Committee on Poverty (Ottawa: Information Canada, 1971).
5 Ian Adams, et al., *The Real Poverty Report* (Edmonton: Hurtig Limited, 1972).
6 Canadian Council on Social Development, *Social Security for Canada, 1973* (Ottawa: Information Canada, 1973).

All of the aforementioned activity in the past nine years is now culminating in serious debate concerning the objectives and methods of providing income security, and the following discussion provides an outline for those wishing to follow the debate.

INCOME SECURITY: AS IT WAS AND IS

For purposes of analyzing past and present income security policy it is helpful to divide the low income population into two broad groups: the welfare poor and the working poor. According to Statistics Canada in 1961, the proportions were 32 per cent welfare poor, and 68 per cent working poor; in 1967, the proportions were 36 per cent and 64 per cent; and in 1971 they were 46 per cent and 54 per cent respectively. In 1974 they were 54.7 per cent and 45.3 per cent respectively.[7]

Welfare Poor

The welfare poor are generally those who for some "identifiable" reason are not able or expected to support themselves through employment earnings, and Table 1 provides a breakdown of the welfare poor by "identifiable" reason.

Social welfare is constitutionally a provincial responsibility, but the help that the professional gave the child with the trauma of moving funded under the Canada Assistance Plan (C.A.P.), which enjoins the provinces and the federal government in a 50/50 cost-sharing of social assistance programmes. In a few provinces there still remain some categorical schemes (e.g., for the blind), but these are gradually being phased out in favour of C.A.P. financing.

Prior to 1966 and the passage of the Canada Assistance Plan, social assistance was granted on a categorical basis. If an applicant were blind, widowed, deserted, aged, a veteran, disabled, a long-term unemployed, etc., then he could be placed in a category that "deserved" assistance —however minimal it might be. Generally, if an applicant were employed (regardless of how low his income might be), he would not be placed in a "deserving" category. Most of these categorical schemes were administered by the provincial and municipal governments, but on a cost-sharing basis with the federal government. Family allowances, Old Age Security (O.A.S.), Unemployment Insurance (U.I.), Canada Pension Plan/Quebec Pension Plan (C.P.P./Q.P.P.) are based on public funding from the federal government only, although some provinces have supplemented the federal family allowances.

The C.A.P. was designed to replace the cost-sharing categorical programmes with one general cost-sharing scheme. The qualification for social assistance under C.A.P. was simply "being in need" of social assistance; no longer were there to be any categorical programmes. In fact, C.A.P. went even further to include people not at present in need but who would be if aid were not given. This aid, usually in the form of some service (e.g., medical, day-care, visiting homemaker), was thus designed to be

---

7 Statistics Canada, *Income Distributions by Size in Canada,* 1961, 1967, 1971 and 1974 volumes (Ottawa: Statistics Canada).

TABLE 1

DISTRIBUTION OF SOCIAL ASSISTANCE CASELOAD, BY REASON FOR ASSISTANCE, BY
REGION AND FOR CANADA, 1970*

Reasons for Assistance	Total Respondents and Percentage Distribution					
	Total	Atlantic	Quebec	Ontario	Prairies	British Columbia
Base (Number of respondents)	2,104	417	465	408	402	412
	%	%	%	%	%	%
Permanent disability or illness	41	44	52	36	26	33
Absence of husband	26	28	18	33	36	29
Unemployed	13	14	9	15	13	22
Old age	9	4	13	4	11	7
Temporary disability or illness	8	8	6	11	10	8
Employed but insufficient income	3	3	3	1	6	3

* Based on 1970 Survey of Welfare Assistance Recipients in Five Regions.

Note: Percentage figures do not necessarily add to 100 due to rounding.

Source: Health and Welfare Canada, *Working Paper on Social Security in Canada (1973)*, p. 51.

preventive—that is, to prevent people from falling in need ("onto welfare")
in the first place.

Because the qualification "being in need" could also include the working
poor, it was hoped that full-time earners in this category would also be
allowed to apply for social assistance. Unfortunately, this was not to be. As
is sometimes the case with social policy, enabling legislation is not always
translated into practice by backing it with the necessary funds. The deliberate exclusion of the working poor from C.A.P. is attested to by the survey of
social assistance recipients reported in Table 1 which reveals that only 3
per cent of the total were employed but had insufficient earnings; the
remainder were long-term unemployed, or "unemployable" for specific
identifiable reasons.

To sum up, the system of social assistance to the present day has been
based on the philosophy that if you work you look after yourself, and only if
you are unable to work, for some identifiable and legitimate reason, are you
then deserving of assistance. It has seemingly seldom occurred to legis-
lators that it is possible to be fully employed but still in serious need.

As partial qualification to the above, it is true that in the past, and in
almost all provinces, it has been possible to be on welfare and yet work. But
the amount of exempted work-related earnings has generally been so small
(in the neighbourhood of $25.00-$50.00 monthly) as to make it not worth-

while. The general approach has been to allow individual earnings of a small monthly amount, but above this to match every dollar earned by a dollar reduction in social assistance—in effect, a 100 per cent welfare reduction (tax) rate that amounts to confiscation of earnings.

There have been variations on this general approach. Nova Scotia has had a 50 per cent welfare reduction rate for each dollar earned, and Alberta and Quebec experimented with "phasing in" periods, where the welfare reduction rate begins at a low level, but increases monthly until earnings reach a level where the recipient is no longer entitled to, nor requires, social assistance.

While some of these schemes have undoubtedly been useful, and have granted increased security to welfare recipients striving to regain their skills, independence, and confidence, they all have one feature in common—that the applicant must be on welfare first before he/she can qualify for the limited income supplementation available.

Working Poor

Prior to 1973, no province systematically or clearly granted direct income supplementation to low-income workers not on social assistance. Perhaps this situation is now changing. In 1973, British Columbia began funding a programme to bring the net earnings of low-income earners up to at least the levels of income received by those on social assistance and by 1975 several Ontario municipalities were granting a similar type of assistance.

By late 1974 the province of Saskatchewan began systematically to supplement the earnings of low-income workers. Under that plan, the Family Income Benefits plan, a family head whose income was less than $4,500 plus federal family allowance ($20 per child) would receive full benefits: these were $40 per month for each of the first three children and $30 per month for the fourth and subsequent children under the age of eighteen years. Families whose incomes exceed the basic exemption ($4,500 plus federal family allowances) calculated their Family Income Benefits by reducing the maximum benefits available by one dollar for every two dollars of income they had in excess of the exemption level. Hence, for example, a family with six children would qualify for a portion of Family Income Benefits up to an income cut-off of $10,980, and a family with two children would qualify up to an income level of $6,900.

Also in December of 1974, the province of Manitoba began making payments under an experiment to evaluate the behaviour of low-income families after they have been in receipt of income supplements. The Manitoba experiment was designed in such a manner as to place the experimental families on one of three guaranteed income levels. For example, for a family of four, the levels were $3,800, $4,600 and $5,400 annually. All income received in addition to these basic minimum guarantees would be taxed at three experimental rates, 35 per cent, 50 per cent and 70 per cent. Hence, a family of four with a guarantee of $5,400 annually and a tax rate of 50 per cent would receive some income supplementation until additional income exceeded $10,800. A family's additional income and, consequently, its guaranteed supplement was to be based on the past twelve-month moving average of family income.

Finally, the federal government in its Orange Paper strongly suggested the need for a general income supplementation scheme to provide assistance to the working poor, and in many respects Saskatchewan's plan could be considered the first response to this federal suggestion although the federal government would have preferred one co-ordinated national scheme rather than ten unco-ordinated provincial ones. However, as it has turned out, it now seems that very little will emerge for the working poor by way of income assistance from the federal-provincial review.

It is obvious that the past system of social security has been designed primarily with the needs of the welfare poor in mind, and it has given little direct income support to low-income earners while they are employed. The only direct income programmes available to the working poor have been universal programmes such as family allowances for those workers with dependent children and Old Age Security (O.A.S.) for those workers over the age of sixty-five (or spouses over the age of sixty). Insurance programmes such as Unemployment Insurance, Canada Pension Plan/Quebec Pension Plan and Workmen's Compensation provide assistance to workers during contingencies and old age, but generally not while they are gainfully employed (C.P.P./Q.P.P. pays a pension to workers when they reach the age of sixty-five and Workmen's Compensation pays partial disability pensions to workers).

Because the subject of the working poor is perhaps the largest, most pressing, most complex, and most neglected area in the field of income security policy, it may be appropriate to dwell on past measures, most of them indirect, that have attempted to provide income security for the working poor.

The causes of poverty incomes are three: low wages, intermittent employment, and family size. The following look at past approaches is grouped around these three causes of low income.

(1) To combat low income caused by low wages a series of measures have been tried. First, since 1966 there has been an increasingly centralized and expanded manpower training, rehabilitation and relocation programme at the federal level. Undoubtedly this has helped some increase their wages, but the Economic Council of Canada's *Eighth Annual Review* revealed that retraining only increased earnings by approximately 5 per cent and that relocating only increased earnings by $500 annually.[8] Consequently only those workers bordering on the poverty line could barely escape poverty through either of these manpower measures.

Second, provincial and federal minimum wages are only now becoming sufficient to help individuals and, in a few provinces, family heads with one or two dependents only to escape poverty (see Table 2), but minimum wages are generally not sufficient for maintaining a family at an adequate income level.

Third, discrimination has been a cause of low wages and to combat this there has been an increase in federal and provincial "equal pay for equal work" legislation which to some extent has reduced discriminatory practices by sex as a cause of low wages. For those who may be discriminated

8 Economic Council of Canada, *Eighth Annual Review* (Ottawa: Information Canada, 1971), chs. 6-7.

against because of age the federal government indirectly offsets this through the universal old age assistance programme introduced in 1952, and an income supplementation scheme for the aged, introduced in 1967, which guarantees a basic income to all individuals over the age of sixty-five, plus recent changes that give assistance to spouses over the age of sixty.

TABLE 2

PREVAILING MINIMUM WAGE RATES AND THEIR ANNUAL INCOME EQUIVALENTS, APRIL 1977

Jurisdiction	Hourly Minimum April 1977	Annual Income Equivalent*	C.C.S.D. Poverty Line** for a Couple	E.C.C.-Statistics Canada Poverty Line for a Couple***
Federal	$2.90	$6,032	$6,100	$4,900
Alberta	3.00	6,240	6,100	4,900
British Columbia	3.00	6,240	6,100	4,900
Manitoba	2.95	6,136	6,100	4,900
New Brunswick	2.80	5,824	6,100	4,900
Newfoundland	2.50	5,200	6,100	4,900
Nova Scotia	2.75	5,720	6,100	4,900
Ontario	2.65	5,512	6,100	4,900
Prince Edward Island****	2.70	5,616	6,100	4,900
Quebec	3.00	6,240	6,100	4,900
Saskatchewan	3.00	6,240	6,100	4,900

*   Calculated on a forty-hour-week basis.
**   Estimated for mid-1976. Economic Council of Canada-Statistics Canada poverty lines are based on what is considered necessary for a family's minimum subsistence. Canadian Council on Social Development poverty lines are calculated as 50 per cent of the average Canadian family income and adjusted for family size.
*** Averaged from the Revised Low Income Cut-Offs for two persons in Statistics Canada, *Income Distribution by Size in Canada Preliminary Series* (1975), p. 7.
**** Effective July 1, 1977.

Source: Canada, Department of Labour, *Minimum Wage Rates in Canada* (Ottawa: Department of Labour).

Fourth, an expanded programme of regional economic expansion was centralized within one federal government department in 1969, with the hope that this would lead to both increased incomes in depressed regions and increased employment possibilities. It is too early to judge the results definitively, but while there is reason to believe that the incentives have induced some firms to relocate in selected regions, the impact of the programme has been small and even then it may have been at the expense of employment opportunities in the regions the firms have left.

Fifth, the past forty years have witnessed the passage of permissive legislation for forming labour unions with the intended purpose of increasing worker bargaining power and, hence, wages. There is little doubt that unions have raised wages, but yet there are still areas in the laws governing labour relations that need further changing to facilitate the organizing of low-income workers.

Finally, for those who have been partially disabled on the job and who are able to secure special employment after their recovery and rehabilitation, every province has en employer-funded Workmen's Compensation scheme that permits the payment of partial disability pensions to help offset the low wages earned by the partially disabled.

(2) To combat low income caused by intermittent employment, three general approaches have been followed. The federal government, in a 1945 White Paper, took responsibility for assuring full employment through broad fiscal and monetary controls.[9] With the exception of the years 1958-62, the federal government more or less fulfilled this promise until the year 1968 when unemployment began to rise. It has not since fallen to a level acceptable to either economists or politicians.

In addition to its attempts to produce full employment, the federal government in 1940 assumed the responsibility for a contributory unemployment insurance programme to provide workers with a basic income during periods of unemployment. Amendments to the Unemployment Insurance Act in 1971 increased assistance substantially and also extended coverage for unemployment due to sickness or maternity leave.

Finally, the creation of direct employment programmes such as L.I.P. and O.F.Y., which have been funded by the federal government, are probably due to the high and persistent levels of unemployment since 1968. In addition, most provinces also have direct employment schemes.

(3) To combat poverty incomes caused by family size, family allowance programmes plus child-related tax exemptions have provided some financial assistance to all families, low-income or otherwise. In 1945 federal family allowances were established on a universal basis, and in 1974 the allowances were tripled and made taxable, hence giving proportionately greater aid to low-income families. Aid to families is also extended through the Income Tax Act since dependents can be claimed as deductions and there is now also an exemption to allow for partial costs of day-care.

TABLE 3

THE 1971 WORK EXPERIENCE OF ALL LOW-INCOME CANADIANS

Percentage of All Low Income	Percentage of Working Poor	Weeks Worked
46.1	—	None
3.3	6.1	1- 9 weeks
4.0	7.4	10-19 weeks
6.3	11.7	20-29 weeks
4.4	8.2	30-39 weeks
4.4	8.2	40-49 weeks
31.5	58.4	50-52 weeks

Source: Statistics Canada, *Income Distribution by Size in Canada, 1971*, p. 76.
     (Column 2 was adapted from the source.)

9   Government of Canada, Department of Reconstruction, *Employment and Income* (Ottawa: King's Printer, 1945).

All of the above measures give some assistance to low-income individuals and families, but still, in 1971, 54 per cent of those living below the poverty line were attached to the labour force, and 58 per cent of these worked full-time, as Table 3 indicates. It would appear that there is a strong case for an expanded programme for raising the wages of low-income units. Perhaps a comprehensive and direct programme of income supplementation is the answer.

THE WELFARE POOR VS. THE WORKING POOR

In closing the discussion on aid to both the welfare and working poor, it is necessary to look at one prevailing issue and dispel some of the false notions surrounding it. When discussing the "problems" of the working and welfare poor, quite often the major issue identified is that there is increasingly little financial incentive to continue working because of a generous social security system that "rewards" people for not working.

Unfortunately, while this may be true in a few instances, and more so as family size increases, the wrong conclusion is often reached that social assistance benefit levels are too high. In fact, as Table 4 quite clearly indicates, there are few instances where social assistance plus family allowances, unemployment insurance plus family allowances, or even minimum wages plus family allowances come even close to the conservatively-estimated poverty lines on the Economic Council of Canada.[10]

Two conclusions are evident. First, there is little evidence to indicate that there is a generous system of social assistance. If it does appear generous to the working poor, then it says more about the low wages received from work than it does about the alleged high rates of public assistance.

The second conclusion to be drawn from Table 4 is that while income from minimum wages may be superior to social assistance for small families, it falls behind significantly as size of family increases.

Based on the data in Table 4, it is evident that all forms of assistance to the poor need to be increased to bring families up to even the most stringent poverty line. However, there is also an additional need above this to raise or supplement the income of the working poor so that no worker and his family make less than what they would be entitled to through various forms of public assistance.

INCOME SECURITY: SOME NEEDED AND SUGGESTED REVISIONS

Space limitations only permit a discussion here of direct income and employment programmes but this should not be interpreted to mean that social service programmes are not of equal importance in the overall strategy for providing social security. As I have argued elsewhere, many services must be upgraded and expanded to supplement and complement direct income and employment programmes—services such as day-care, visiting home-

10 The absolute levels in Table 4 apply to 1973, but the relative levels reviewed still apply today with little modification.

TABLE 4

BENEFITS, ON AN ANNUAL BASIS, UNDER SELECTED SOCIAL PROGRAMMES, SELECTED PROVINCES, MARCH 1973

Programme	Couple						Couple with three children aged 6, 10, 15					
	P.E.I.	N.B.	Que.	Ont.	Sask.	B.C.	P.E.I.	N.B.	Que.	Ont.	Sask.	B.C.
1. Employed at the minimum wage with family allowances	2,600	3,120	3,432	3,744	3,640	4,160	2,864	3,384	3,696	4,008	3,904	4,424
2. On social assistance with family allowances[a]	2,613	2,124	2,316	2,448[b]	2,592	3,000[c]	3,905	3,872	3,480	4,620	4,752	5,064[c]
3. On a L.I.P. project, with family allowances[d]	4,680	4,784	4,940	5,044	4,888	5,044	4,944	5,048	5,204	5,308	5,152	5,308
4. Average U.I. benefits, with family allowances[e]	2,704	2,964	3,328	3,484	3,328	3,640	2,968	3,228	3,592	3,748	3,592	3,904
Poverty Line												
Canadian Council on Social Development	4,300	4,300	4,300	4,300	4,300	4,300	6,888	6,888	6,888	6,888	6,888	6,888
Economic Council of Canada-Statistics Canada	3,600	3,600	3,600	3,600	3,600	3,600	5,760	5,760	5,760	5,760	5,760	5,760

a   Basic rates are approximations and these include estimates for fuel and rent. Benefits for couples with children are estimated using average allowances per child.
b   Rate is $2,820 for a couple who are not employable.
c   These rates to be effective June 1, 1973.
d   Based on average wages per week in the province. There are variations within a province, depending on local wage norms and the nature of the job.
e   Based on average weekly benefit payments under U.I. for all beneficiaries in the province for December 1972.

Source: Health and Welfare Canada, *Working Paper on Social Security in Canada (1973)*, p. 13.

maker, housing, legal aid, job placement and retraining, health care and personal social services.[11]

With respect to direct income and employment programmes the best that can be hoped for in the immediate future is an improved and revised edition of the present basic system, but along lines that will provide unblocked routes to a desirable society in the future. Basic reform of the present system is politically impossible at this stage because of an unreadiness to face three fundamental problems: the public's perception of the cause of poverty, the present income distribution mechanism in society, and a changed and expanded definition of remunerative work. Discussion on these three problems is withheld until the final section.

Revision and reform of the present social security system can only proceed appreciably if the objectives of the system are expanded beyond the present singular one of "bringing people up" to a defined subsistence poverty line. I would recommend, as a start, the four objectives set out by the C.C.S.D. Task Force: significantly reducing income inequalities; equalizing opportunities and increasing access to those opportunities that allow individuals, families, and groups to enhance the quality of their lives; expanding work options; and increasing the participation of people in the making of decisions that control their lives.[12]

Social assistance programmes should become more dependent on employment guarantees, where employment is guaranteed by a fund to provide self-initiated work opportunities.[13] Employment guarantees of this type, as opposed to pure income guarantees, are more likely to include people in society rather than exclude them. Moreover, work opportunity programmes such as L.I.P., O.P.Y., and L.E.A.P. have, and continue to, demonstrated that while there may be much measured unemployment in Canada and, hence, few employment opportunities, there is still a vast range and depth of unsatisfied social needs and, hence, work to be done. Consequently, we should be utilizing manpower more effectively through these types of employment programmes rather than enticing it to lay idle through the more traditional type of cash transfer programmes.

Moreover, the size of a work opportunities programme should not be completely defined by the necessity of it retaining a neutral relationship with respect to either the private market or the traditional public sector labour forces. If the programme attracts some workers from the private sector, or if it attracts additional workers into the labour force—such as homemakers and the elderly—then this should not be regarded, as the Orange Paper did, as a problem but perhaps as a value. Surely what is happening is an expansion of the work options for a group of people who are unhappy and/or exploited in their present positions. Obviously, in the initial stages some restrictions will have to be placed on the programme, but in the longer run there must be more aggressiveness in suggesting that

11 David Ross. "A Critical Look at Present and Future Social Security Policy in Canada," *The Social Worker* 41, no. 3 (Winter 1973):2 60-75.
12 Canadian Council on Social Development, *Social Security, 1973*, p. 5.
13 Canadian Council on Social Development, *The Future Course of Work Opportunities* (Ottawa: Canadian Council on Social Development, 1973), and National Council of Welfare, *Beyond Services and Beyond Jobs* (Ottawa: National Council of Welfare, 1974).

social policy should not forever be the residual of economic policy, and hence subordinate to it.

However, recognizing that not all people can or want to take advantage of work opportunities, it will also be necessary to have an income guarantee programme related to family size. Both the Orange Paper and the C.C.S.D. Task Force Report proposed a two-stage guarantee system along the lines initially suggested by the Castonguay-Nepveu report. A higher guaranteed level is suggested for those who are unable to work, or who are performing important unremunerated work elsewhere (e.g., homemakers). A lower guaranteed level is suggested for those who already have employment, but where earned income is inadequate either because of the low-paying nature of the job or because of family size. An adequate income level in this lower guaranteed income programme can be maintained without seriously impairing work incentives via either a negative income tax or tax credit scheme and the mechanics of these various schemes are spelled out elsewhere.[14]

The assignment of people to either income programme can be done in one of three ways: let the individuals themselves choose, let the authorities choose on a discretionary basis, or let an income test separate the applicants. The first method, which was proposed by the Castonguay-Nepveu Report, and which is often criticized as too lenient and costly, would probably be feasible in the presence of a work opportunities programme, an income supplement programme, and where there is increasing emphasis on job enrichment in the private sector. Under these circumstances it is hard to imagine many able-bodied wanting to "loaf" on the higher income guarantee.

The C.C.S.D. Task Force Report leaned towards the income test approach, while the Orange Paper endorsed the use of discretion with its emphasis on a categorical approach. In light of this it is difficult to accept the claim of the Orange Paper that the higher level is in fact a guaranteed income when there is such a large element of discretion involved in the eligibility procedure. In this respect it appears little different from the present method of granting financial assistance through the provincial and municipal social assistance programmes.

One of the primary objectives of the C.C.S.D. Task Force's work opportunities and income support programmes is to reduce income inequalities. With this in mind, the so-called "income-poverty" lines are related to average Canadian family income, and not to some absolute, subsistence poverty level. The Task Force thus established the income line for a family of four at $6,020, which was 50 per cent of the estimated average 1973 family income level of $12,040. It may be remembered that the Real Poverty Report had earlier suggested this approach.

If the social security system has an adequate and comprehensive basic income support plan, then it can be forcefully argued that the social insur-

14 Nicole Martin, "Objectives and Repercussions of the Guaranteed Annual Income," in *Guaranteed Annual Income: An Integrated Approach* (Ottawa: Canadian Council on Social Development, 1973), pp. 149 and 293; and Health and Welfare Canada, "Alternative Approaches to Income Supplementation," in *Income Supplements for the Working Poor* (Ottawa: Canadian Council on Social Development, 1974), pp. 65-107.

ances (Canada and Quebec Pension Plan, Workmen's Compensation, Unemployment Insurance) should become more insurance (risk) and less social-assistance oriented. Under this approach, premiums should be related to risk as much as is actuarially possible and benefits should be more closely related to earnings. In this manner, the social insurances could provide for full and effective protection to all income classes in society. If the social insurances are restructured along these lines, then a leading question immediately arises: Why can't private insurance programmes do the job?

If our experience with private pensions is illustrative, then a major shortcoming with private schemes is that portability is severely curtailed, if not completely eliminated. If one of our social objectives is to increase work options, then the present restrictive and demobilizing effects of private pension schemes can be used as an example of the negative and restrictive aspects of fragmented private programmes that are too often used to tie people to their jobs.

Finally, in any discussion of income maintenance, the question of a separate family allowance programme arises. While the Senate Report recommends abolition of family allowances, the Orange Paper, the C.C.S.D. Task Force Report, and the Castonguay-Nepveu Report all favour maintaining a separate and universal family allowance programme but with benefits taxable. The main rationale for retention appears to be that even though there would be a comprehensive basic income support programme adjusted for family size, the basic income programme must be restricted to families with low incomes even though there is a sizeable middle-income segment that is also in need of family-related payments. The argument is made that to include the middle-income segment in the basic income support plan requires tax exemption levels to be universally revised, which results in a significant and unintended loss of revenue that becomes difficult and unpopular to regain through higher tax rates.

Other arguments in favour of a universal and separate family allowance programme involve either the notion that for purposes of equity all families, regardless of earned income, should receive state payments to adjust for family size and the attendant child-rearing costs, or the notion that the parent attending the child is entitled to an independent income for performing a parental function.

INCOME SECURITY: SOME NEEDED BASIC REFORMS

It would be inappropriate and misleading to terminate a study on income security in Canada at this point. An impression may be left that with a few revisions of the present system all will be well. Unfortunately, this is unlikely to be the case.

It has been strongly argued by Titmuss, Miller, and others that many of today's social problems and injustices stem from inequalities in the distribution of income and employment opportunities.[15] As Table 5 shows,

---

15 Richard Titmuss, "The Social Division of Welfare," in *Essays on the Welfare State* (New Haven: Yale University Press, 1959), pp. 34-55, and S. M. Miller and Pamela Roby, *The Future of Inequality* (New York: Basic Books, 1970).

there has been very little change in the distribution of income in the past twenty years, although certainly there is a wider distribution of basic services because of subsidization of health, education, housing, legal aid, day-care, etc.

TABLE 5

DISTRIBUTION OF FAMILY INCOME IN CANADA BY QUINTILES

Year	Percentage Distribution of Income				
	Bottom Fifth	Second Fifth	Third Fifth	Fourth Fifth	Top Fifth
1951	6.1	12.9	17.4	22.4	41.1
1957	6.3	13.1	18.1	23.4	39.1
1961	6.6	13.5	18.3	23.4	38.4
1967	6.4	13.1	18.0	23.6	38.9
1969	6.2	12.6	17.9	23.5	39.7
1971	5.6	12.6	18.0	23.7	40.0
1973	6.1	12.9	18.1	23.9	38.9

Source: Statistics Canada, *Income Distributions by Size in Canada,* selected years (Ottawa: Statistics Canada).

Because we have failed to reduce income inequality through (alleged) redistribution programmes such as unemployment insurance, universal old age security, the guaranteed income supplement, family allowances, Canada Pension Plan, Workmen's Compensation, and social assistance, we may also have done very little to reduce the basic source of social problems. Also, notwithstanding the fact that very little change in income distribution has occurred in the past twenty years, a backlash against redistribution seems to be developing, as was demonstrated by the Economic Council's 1973 attack on welfare transfers and its apparent ready and favourable reception by the media and the public.[16] Current government efforts to restrain expenditures are also not reassuring and certainly help to explain why the results of the federal-provincial review are so disappointing.

This apparent backlash against further redistribution attempts demonstrates that we may very well need to adopt new approaches if society has reached its limit in terms of "handouts." We may be forced to make fundamental changes in our approach. The time may be at hand to look at the *causes* of continual maldistribution of income in Canada and attack these directly and thus remove the need for redistributive programmes. A big advantage for a strategy effecting a proper distribution vis-à-vis one effecting redistribution is that it can be a one-shot strategy (once it is done, it is done), whereas redistribution is a perpetual never-ending strategy. However, this is not to imply that effecting a proper distribution will occur

16　Economic Council of Canada, *Tenth Annual Review* (Ottawa: Information Canada, 1973), ch. 6, and editorials and comments in most leading newspapers during November 1973.

through a revolution and be accomplished within a short period of time. It will indeed take time to effect and it will take place through piece-meal policy-making, but the piece-meal policies will ultimately result in a proper distribution of income, whereas present policies will simply lead to a continuous programme of redistribution.

To begin to bring about a more equal distribution of income and employment opportunities, it will be necessary to confront three basic issues: the public's perception of the cause of poverty, the maldistribution of income, and the way we presently define remunerative work.

The Public's Perception of the Cause of Poverty

What this country needs is the recognition of "no fault poverty" instead of the present belief that poverty is primarily one's own fault. Because it is widely believed that it is the individual who designs his own circumstances, we have not examined the institutions in society that play a much larger role in determining an individual's destiny. Hence, for example, we have trained generations of social workers to "adjust" and "rehabilitate" the individual when, in fact, social workers should be asking themselves whether they should not be rehabilitating some of society's institutions. Today, fortunately, more and more social workers are recognizing this and are becoming "change agents" as well as, or instead of, counsellors.

A basic argument for the establishment of "no fault" poverty is provided by aggregate data on the poor which reveal that 50 per cent of the poor population in Canada are "working poor" and that these people work whenever they can, and 60 per cent of them work full-time, year round, but still earn poverty incomes. Can we, therefore, say that poverty is their own fault? And can we still maintain the myth that hard work alone brings success? Statistics also reveal that of the other 50 per cent of the poor population, those who are unable to work, 49 per cent are disabled or ill, 26 per cent are deserted women with families, 9 per cent are debilitated by old age, so that 84 per cent of the "unemployable poor" are in poverty for reasons almost totally beyond their control. Can we attribute personal fault?

It is important to debunk the myth of "own fault" poverty because it colours our entire approach to social security. It is certainly the basis for the appalling subsistence standards we expect the poor to live under and it is the basis for making social security demeaning and difficult to obtain. It follows that if indeed poverty is one's own fault, then there certainly is no need or obligation placed on society to help the poor to achieve a life of dignity and self-respect.

Much of the blame for the public's perception of poverty can rightfully be placed on economists. The traditional economic explanation of the job and income distribution process is based on some important critical assumptions that simply do not hold true. These assumptions involve free and competitive markets (in both factor and goods markets), perfect knowledge of all market conditions with a resultant lack of uncertainty, and equal opportunity for all members of society, including equal and easy access to all labour and capital markets. The primary result of these assumptions is to postulate a rather homogeneous labour force and an environment where any member of society can control his or her economic fortunes. In this economist's dream world, and to exaggerate only slightly, everybody is truly a potential Horatio Alger in which it is to be believed that a successful banker has arrived at his position in life because he started out to become a banker, has become a banker, and has faced no obstacles on the way, and where a night-watchman started out in life wanting to become a watchman and also encountered no obstacles. Moreover, if the watchman no longer likes the job and discovers in mid-life that a mistake was made in career selection, then the watchman can become a successful banker, or can open up a business, or whatever. In this unreal world created by economists, workers can shift fluidly from one job market to another when their own situation becomes low-paying, unpleasant or boring as the result of changes in job and market conditions or personal attitudes.

Based in part on this kind of economic interpretation, where individuals are assumed to have virtual total control over the planning of their economic fortunes, an individual is entitled to get back out from the economic system what he puts in, and hence everyone is responsible for looking after one's own welfare. In this ultimate laissez-faire world, the processes of production and distribution are tightly associated and are merely two sides of the same coin.

What traditional economic theory and the general public attitude neglects to recognize is the tremendous role played by circumstances beyond an individual's conscious control, and also the sizeable impact exerted on markets by corporate structures, which is an institution traditional economic theory has long ignored because of its preoccupation with Adam Smith's "invisible hand" and free atomistic markets.[17] Because of the work of economists within the profession, like Galbraith, as well as an increasing number of others, we now appreciate more the role in the distribution process played by luck, birthright, corporate and public interventions, intelligence, and health.[18]

The traditional and widely accepted economic interpretation, however, would have us believe that hard work alone is the prerequisite for success, although, as was indicated earlier, as many as 50 or 60 per cent of our poverty population are the "working poor"—people who work very hard, and have worked very hard all their lives (and at jobs most people in the top

17 For examples of traditional economic thinking, consult two of the most widely adopted introductory economics texts used in Canada: Paul Samuelson and Anthony Scott, *Economics,* 3rd Canadian ed. (Toronto: McGraw-Hill Company, 1971), chs. 3, 4, 22 and 26; and Gordon F. Boreham and Richard Leftwich, *Economic Thinking in a Canadian Context* (Toronto: Holt, Rinehart and Winston, 1971), chs. 2, 4, 9, and 15.

18 J. K. Galbraith has probably led the modern revolution in economic thinking. His work began with the *Affluent Society* (1958), was followed by *The Industrial State* (1967), and has now been capped by his *Economics and the Public Purpose* (1973). Lester Thurow has helped expose the role played by the concentration of wealth in America, *Poverty and Discrimination* (Washington: The Brookings Institute, 1969). Three books that contain the work of "radical" economists are: David Gordon, *Problems in Political Economy* (Lexington, Mass.: D. C. Heath and Company, 1971); David Mermelstein, *Economics: Mainstream Readings and Radical Critiques* (New York: Random House, 1970); and Robert Heilbroner and Arthur Ford, *Is Economics Relevant?* (California: Goodyear Publishing Company, 1971).

four income quintiles would not take) and yet they do not make adequate incomes.

For many, it is perhaps comfortable to assume that some people are born with a strong desire to inhabit the bottom income quintile, and who have consciously decided to make a career out of being poor. However, what a new interpretation of the distribution process should teach us is that a person ends up being where he is in life primarily through a complicated set of circumstances playing on him. Certainly hard work is often necessary, but it is neither essential nor sufficient for purposes of being economically successful.

Maldistribution of Income

Once one has accepted "own fault" poverty, then it is also natural to accept and vigorously defend the present distribution of income in Canada that perpetually allocates 40 per cent of total income to the top quintile, and 5 per cent to the bottom quintile.

The rationale for the present distribution process is based on the value of productivity, or on what one allegedly contributes to the economic system. Admittedly, this may have been possible to measure, or at least to visualize, when the overwhelming majority of the work force was producing tangible goods, but today it is not only difficult to visualize, but increasingly impossible to quantify when two-thirds of the work force is engaged in the production of non-tangible services (e.g., how do you unambiguously measure a unit of education, of legal aid, of health care?). But the distributional implication of the value of productivity doctrine is that one is unquestionably entitled to that amount of the community's output which one has directly created. Arguing from this sanctified value or productivity doctrine, therefore, one can quite easily defend the proposition that one simply "gets out of the system what one puts in."

However, as social scientists and others look closer at the economic system with all its imperfections and shortcomings and examine the role that non-economic power relationships play, it is likely more accurate to sum up the distributional process with the statement that one "gets out of the system what one takes out," and what one takes out depends more on power (of which some may be legitimate economic power) than on contribution to the community's wealth disguised as "value of productivity."

A new theory of income distribution should begin by stressing that the total wealth of goods and services produced in the community is what it is, in both size and composition, because of the joint contributions of all of its citizens as they perform in all of their roles and carry out all of their activities, market and otherwise. This means, among other things, getting away from the option of defining our community's wealth of goods and services in the narrow and traditional gross national product sense where "wealth" or useful "things" are only legitimized and valued as they are exchanged and priced in markets. In our highly sophisticated, urbanized, interdependent and publicly-supported economy, it becomes less and less defensible to isolate an individual's contribution to the community's wealth and determine a distributional share according to alleged contribution. Perhaps this was more the case in a frontier society where markets scarcely existed and self-sufficient individuals and families did basically carve out their own existence in isolation from other members of society. In frontier society, individuals did produce the bulk of their own goods and services and they may have had an economic and moral right to consume all of their output themselves.

In today's economy, however, we should recognize the extreme inter-dependence required not only in the production process, but in the whole process of living together in viable communities, and we should also recognize the limited control an individual has over his productive contributions. Consequently, we should strive for a more equal distribution of the community's total goods and services. Economic life should not be one big gamble with winner take all, and we should not adhere rigidly to the sacred law of supply and demand which permits individuals to take from the community's total of goods and services whatever they legally can. The law of supply and demand is simply a sophisticated cover-up for society's endorsement of "survival of the strongest." And as long as the "strongest" maintain control over society there is little chance for an acknowledgement of a different distribution process.

When the distribution process is seen in this light it should become hard to get worked up, as others have, about news stories concerning mothers on welfare (who presumably do good jobs of raising their children) who are occasionally found cheating the welfare system of a few dollars in order that their children can eat. If raising children is a worthwhile and necessary contribution to society, should these parents not be entitled to an adequate portion of the community's wealth? Rather, what society should get incensed about, to take only one example, is the professional who legally and proudly takes out $100,000 of goods and services from the community's total (and thus leaves reduced shares for others) on the basis that because of his training and life-long hard work he actually contributes $100,000 of the community's wealth in the first place. Fortunately, we are now beginning to recognize that an individual's income of $100,000 does not automatically or likely reflect his real contribution to the community's wealth and, consequently, is not a justification for his taking that amount out, as Friedman and Kuznets have shown.[19]

Unfortunately, many people fail to appreciate that the professional enjoyed many years on "elegant social welfare," first as a public school student and later at a publicly-supported university. Moreover, society constructs numerous artificial situations and regulations on his behalf that permit the making and retaining of large incomes. First, class size at university is undoubtedly restricted to "safeguard" professional quality. Second, the professional association has undoubtedly been given the dubious right to control the examination and licensing of practitioners, and in many circumstances society has even removed the possibility of there being competition among the admitted members of a profession by allowing them to establish formal fee schedules or to adhere to informally-agreed-upon

19   Milton Friedman and Simon Kuznets in a classic study demonstrated quite clearly how, and by how much, various professional groups were able to obtain incomes in excess of what a competitive market would permit. See their *Income from Independent Professional Practice* (New York: National Bureau of Research, 1945).

schedules. Moreover, as Gillespie and Maslove have shown, the present system of taxation does not work particular hardships on high-income earners, even though they benefit heavily from the rules laid down in society.[20]

Conversely, if one were to look at the other end of the income scale it would be possible to discover other sets of unfavourable artificial situations and regulations, public and private, that keep low wage earners in that position, and restrictions that keep others out of the labour market altogether.

As a result, therefore, of public regulations, subsidies, luck, and other institutional factors, it becomes difficult to believe and defend the notion that a person's salary is an accurate reflection of his contribution to society and, therefore, a basis for determining how much he should take from it.

This new interpretation of the distribution process leads to the conclusion that there is strong justification for a programme to permanently correct the maldistribution of income and employment opportunities, and which is not based on a feeling of charity but rather one of entitlement. There is nothing "natural" or sacrosanct about the present income distribution mechanism. In the past it may have served the goal of economic efficiency very well and at a time when the efficient development and use of all of the economy's factors and resources were necessary because there truly existed an economy of scarcity. But in the North American post-scarcity society, it is no longer necessary to perpetuate the economic efficiency goal which requires that "you get out what you put in," and the more so when artificial interventions no longer permit the practice of this classical distribution ideal anyway. Surely the time has come for a more planned and public decision-making approach to both employment and income distribution, with the prime objective being social development and not pure economic efficiency.

Redefining and Redesigning Remunerative Work

It will not be an easy process to bring about an economic system that provides a proper distribution of income. Obviously, two broad strategies have to be followed. First, those powers, practices, and institutions that permit people to earn high incomes have to be changed. Second, low-income earners have to be assured of higher earnings through employment.

To effect a fair distribution of income it will be necessary to create work and employment and to assign incomes to these employments so that people can have a proper income in the first place. It seems that any method of redistributing income that does not involve employment or contributing to society in some way will be construed simply as a transfer or a redistribution of incomes from those who work to those who do not work. So it is necessary to develop new forms of work and hope that over time these

20 Irwin Gillespie, "The Incidence of Taxes and Public Expenditures in the Canadian Economy," esp. Table 2.3, Study no. 2 for the Royal Commission on Taxation (Carter Commission, 1966), and Allan Maslove, *The Pattern of Taxation in Canada,* a study prepared for the Economic Council of Canada (Ottawa: Information Canada, 1972).

forms will become recognized as legitimate forms of work and that the incomes attached to them will become legitimate forms of income and will not be regarded as social assistance or cash transfers.

It will perhaps take some time for programmes such as L.I.P., O.F.Y. and other publicly-created work opportunities to be fully recognized as legitimate work, but we must soon begin defining work through a political process which will also not likely involve equal participation by all citizens but which will certainly be more democratic than the marketplace mechanism where the decisions are made through a dollar "voting" process that is heavily skewed in favour of the wealthy.

A growing body of literature reveals that much of the current thinking about our present forms of work involves a questioning of whether only the market should legitimize work activities and, hence, largely determine who receives direct income payments and, more importantly, who does not.[21] Today people are rejecting this role played by the impersonal market and replacing it with the belief that whatever society collectively wishes to call work, and hence reward, it can do so.

For example, why should land speculators and dope-peddlers receive direct payments from the market, but not mothers, university students and those who perform needed services in the community? Unfortunately, work activity is still predominantly legitimized by direct monetary reward and is perhaps one reason why homemaking and raising children leave the performers of these activities with a feeling of doing non-legitimate or non-useful work in society. Perhaps if mothers and homemakers were rewarded directly, there would be less desire to seek "work" (which often in itself proves meaningless to the individual) in a "legitimate" job outside the home and in the marketplace. It has often struck me as odd that our values in society either compel a parent to accept or lead a parent to feel that sewing canvas covers for snowmobiles in a factory is more virtuous and useful than tending a child at home and administering and responding to that child's unique intellectual and emotional needs. It certainly appears to answer the question as to whether people or goods are more highly prized by our society.

There is a growing awareness that the market alone should not determine what is legitimate work. There is a concern that because of a bad distribution of income, there is an overemphasis on the production of material goods at the expense, and in some cases exclusion, of needed personal services. A new definition of work would permit a community's output of goods and services to have more personal services than are now provided through the private market mechanism and probably fewer goods.

---

21   David Ross, "Work: For Love or Money," *Canadian Welfare* 49, no. 6 (November-December 1973): 6-10; David Woodsworth, *Social Policies for Tomorrow* (Ottawa: Canadian Council on Social Development, 1971); William Dyson, *Social Policy in Canada: A Quest for Humanization* (Ottawa: The Vanier Institute of the Family, 1973); Gail Stewart and Kathy Starrs, "Reworking the World," a proposal submitted to the Challenge for Change programme of the National Film Board, 1973; Albert Rose, "The Work Ethic and Welfare Reform," *The Social Worker* 41, no. 1 (Spring 1973): 37-46; National Council of Welfare, *Statement on Income Security* (Ottawa, April 1971); and Canadian Council on Social Development, *New Concepts of Work* (Ottawa: Canadian Council on Social Development, 1974).

In closing, it should be stressed that new forms of work will also have to recognize the increasing demands being placed on remunerative work, not only as a device for obtaining income, but also as a meaningful activity to the individual performing it.

CONCLUSION

Canada has a fairly complex, disparate, comprehensive and inadequate system of income security that is in need, and in the process, of minor revision. Unfortunately there has been little questioning of the basic causes of the problems that give rise to the need for a public system of income security. But yet, if we are ever to escape the continuous "transfer-handout," "haves-have nots" world that plagues those who are trapped by circumstance, then we must begin to look at basic causes, and ultimately to basic reforms, not only in the income security system but in the way we live our lives.

Health and Inequality: Unresolved Policy Issues

ROBIN F. BADGLEY
and
CATHERINE A. CHARLES

The quest to make access to good health care more equitable was the basis for the gradual development of national health insurance in Canada. Before then, a mosaic of private and public measures served unevenly the Canadian people. How much illness and physical disability a man experienced were deeply influenced by his social circumstances. While much has been done by government to make access more equitable to health care, sharp disparities still exist which profoundly affect the life chances of many Canadians.

This situation was recognized by Allan J. MacEachern when he introduced the 1966 Medical Care Act in the House of Commons. He then asserted the Act would "insure access to medical care to all of our people, regardless of means, of pre-existing conditions, of age or other circumstances which may have barred such access in the past." Fully adopted across Canada by 1971, in addition to its four major provisions, the Act further stipulated: "The plan must make available on uniform terms and conditions to all insured residents . . . all medically necessary services rendered by medical practitioners . . . on a basis of 'reasonable access to insured services by insured persons.'"[1]

---

1 Canada, *Medical Care Act,* 14-15 Eliz. 2, ch. 64, assented to December 21, 1966.

Based upon the experience of pre-existing government measures and also derived from the structure of private health insurance, the Act was redistributive in its intent to alter access to health care. Now fully implemented, the operations and impact of this extensive and expensive measure are seen here from the perspective of four issues:

(1) What aims were intended to be met? Are they being achieved?
(2) What impact has the legislation had in reducing the unmet health needs of Canadians?
(3) Has access by Canadians to health services changed? What measures are used to determine the dimensions of equity in access to health care?
(4) How have the payment arrangements of the Act affected the allocation of incomes among health workers?

The impact of any new legislative measure can be expected to take some time before its full consequences may be known. Likewise, the terms of any particular public reform may have unanticipated and unequal consequences. The rich social diversity of Canadian society precludes the occurrence of uniform aspirations or social opportunities. Coupled with these facts is the nature of disease itself, which may involve circumstances resulting from congenital or environmental conditions. None would contest the moral justification to provide specialized medical attention to patients suffering from unusual conditions, an acknowledged necessity which in terms of available health resources may constitute a form of positive discrimination in the allocation of scarce resources. For these several reasons there is no more likely to be a homogenization of health services than of Canadian society itself.

The critical issue is not if differences along social lines exist in the use of health services. They do. The relevant questions involving services organized and paid for by government are: under what circumstances and with what consequences are they provided. The terms and the implementation of health legislation are sensitive indices of a country's intent to improve the well-being of its people. These programmes also measure how social power is distributed within a society. By reviewing the history and current status of one measure, national health insurance, a fuller understanding can be gained about how Canadian society works, and in this instance, what has been done and what remains to be done in achieving a reasonable degree of equity in the provision of good health care.

THE DEVELOPMENT OF NATIONAL HEALTH INSURANCE

While national health insurance as it is known today has been in operation for less than a decade in Canada, its legislative and policy roots go back to colonial times. In addition to the hospitals set up to care for the indigent sick by religious nursing orders, the Legislative Assemblies of Lower and Upper Canada acknowledged in the 1840s the principle of the responsibility of the state in the care of the sick. Initially modest, this support included: grants for the construction of general hospitals; direct support for voluntary and religious charities; and contributions to the training of medical students. The colonial assemblies also made provisions for quarantine and the custody of the insane.

The massive emigration of destitute persons from Ireland in the late 1840s resulted in substantial emergency support for the indigent sick and hospitals. In 1848, for instance, 42,540 patients were treated in emigrant hospitals which were supported directly from the British Colonial Office and the provincial assemblies. This crash programme reinforced the emerging principle of public support for hospitals, one which was acted upon differently in various parts of the country.

The support of general hospitals in Ontario, for instance, grew substantially during the 1870s. In calling for more public funds in 1872 the Ontario Inspector of Asylums and Prisons asserted:

> Government aid may properly be given for two reasons; first, for the relief of suffering and cure of disease, and secondly, for the practical training of medical students . . . .
>
> The fact that 2914 patients were received and treated during 1871 by these 10 Institutions, shows pretty conclusively that the first reason . . . is well sustained. Government should make wise provision either in granting aid to hospitals already established . . . or in the founding of new Institutions.[2]

The revenues of ten general hospitals in Ontario in 1871 came from: 64.2 per cent, provincial legislature; 12.9 per cent, municipal taxes; 10.3 per cent, paying patients; and the remainder from endowments and public subscriptions. Elsewhere in Canada a variety of public programmes evolved for the support of hospitals. These measures included grants for construction, legislation setting up municipal doctors' schemes on the prairies and the establishing of public health departments. While some Friendly Societies were started, their membership was limited to specific trades. Many soon dropped out of sight. None of these programmes was intended to provide access to health care as a right for all persons regardless of their circumstances.

The first major proposal for a national health insurance plan was made in the 1919 political platform of the federal Liberal Party. In *Industry and Humanity* W. L. M. King had developed a framework for a broad programme of social services, much of which was to be developed after his death. These early proposals were intended as electoral bait. Occasionally dusted off for public discussion, they were shelved for three decades in turn by the jousting for power of the minority government of the 1920s, the impact of the Great Depression, the brittle constitutional debates over the federal-provincial jurisdiction on taxation, and then by World War II. When an ambitious post-war national health insurance plan floundered on the shoals of reaching acceptable revisions in tax-sharing arrangements with the provinces, Ottawa went ahead by itself with an incremental grants-in-aid health programme in 1948. National hospital insurance was started a decade later.

Both programmes were popular. In each case they provided sizeable new revenues for the poorer provinces. The federal government at this time had little enthusiasm to introduce a programme of national health insurance. Its

---

2 Ontario, Legislative Assembly, *Sessional Papers 1872-73, Fifth Annual Report of the Inspector of Asylums and Prisons for the Province of Ontario, 1871-72* (Toronto: Hunter, Rose & Co., 1873), pp. 66-67.

volte-face on the issue was stimulated by Saskatchewan's successful 1962 programme and an effort to break a skein of minority governments. The 1966 Medical Care Act, implemented in July 1968, was hailed as Lester Pearson's belated "centennial birthday present." By 1971 all provinces and territories had accepted the terms of this cost-sharing programme. Subsequently its terms were revised (Bill C-37, 1977), but its basic principles about universal coverage and reasonable access remained intact.

In introducing the medical insurance legislation in the House of Commons on July 12, 1966, Allan J. MacEachern said that the Act would "insure access to medical care to all of our people, regardless of means, of pre-existing conditions, of age or other circumstances which may have barred such access in the past."[3] Eight years later another federal health minister asserted that these aims had been achieved for, "though short of perfection," the Canadian health system "is the equal of any in the world."[4]

This conclusion was endorsed by the federal deputy health minister in 1975 who asserted: "The greatest benefit has been the provision of financial accessibility to health care .... The only deterrents to seeking care are the time and trouble involved."[5] These observations by Lalonde and LeClair are not valid. They represent hopes for the future, not facts of today.

HEALTH NEEDS

The intent of the three national health acts introduced since 1948 was: to increase the supply of health personnel; to equip adequately and to build modern health facilities; to remove "hindrance of any kind" in making health services available; and to achieve "the highest possible health standards for all our people."[6] Implicit in these programmes was the recognition that many Canadians could not readily afford the price tag of obtaining optimal health care and a large reservoir of unmet health needs existed.

The idea of health needs which is used here refers to an individual's state of health or illness which either is recognized by a person or diagnosed by a physician. Used in this sense a health need is a static concept subject to qualitative definition. In contrast, the notion of demand refers to the extent to which an individual, regardless of how healthy or ill he may be, actually uses available health resources.

Demand is counted by the number of patients who visit doctors' offices, who use hospitals, or who are the direct consumers of health care. Because information for accounting purposes is required by statute or administrative procedure, the concept of need is ignored in official reports in favour of the economic concepts of supply and demand. For these reasons most of the health information which we have today in Canada concerns the demand for health services.

---

3 Allan J. MacEachern, in Canada, *House of Commons Debates,* final session, 27th Parliament (July 12, 1966): 7549.
4 Marc Lalonde, *A New Perspective on the Health of Canadians: A Working Document* (Ottawa: Information Canada, April 1974), p. 5.
5 Maurice LeClair, "The Canadian Health Care System," in *National Health Insurance: Can We Learn from Canada?,* ed. S. Andreopoulous (New York: John Wiley and Sons, 1975), p. 42.
6 *Royal Commission on Health Services,* vol. 1 (Ottawa: Queen's Printer, 1964), pp. 3-12.

Such information which is available indicates that there have been and still are extensive unmet health needs afflicting the Canadian people. During World War II the rejection rate was 32.5 per cent for medical reasons among armed services' recruits. The evidence of the Canadian Sickness Survey of 1950-51 confirmed the extent of widespread illness with 7.1 per cent of the population having a permanent physical disability.[7] An estimated 3.1 per cent of Canadians were then so severely or entirely disabled that they could not work or perform usual activities.

In 1962-63 it was estimated that 100 million man-days of labour were lost through illness with attendant economic costs of $1,630 million or 3.8 per cent of the gross national product. The "silent" unemployed, those individuals who were handicapped, numbered about three-fifths of the unemployed persons in the country.[8] Another estimate in 1965 concluded that about one out of five persons in the population had some form of major disability, "of whom half had mental or emotional problems."[9]

The results of the International Collaborative Study on Medical Care Utilization which obtained information about 15,608 individuals in Saskatchewan, Alberta and British Columbia in 1968 confirmed previous trends. The level of physical impairment in the four regions was between 8 to 11 per cent with 13 to 18 per cent of the respondents reporting chronic health problems, and one out of ten persons had been confined to bed for at least one or more days during the two weeks prior to the sruvey.[10] From these several sources it is apparent that as a baseline estimate at least some 770,000 Canadians in the mid-1970s suffered from a major physical handicap or a severe chronic disability.

This burden of illness is not evenly distributed among the Canadian population. It handicaps the poor and certain minority groups more severely than the average or well-to-do income groups. The Canadian Sickness Survey found that the lower income group had significantly more physical disability than the higher income groups, a point partially confirmed by the results of the International Comparability Study and the Ontario Medical Association's 1973 Pickering Report. Specific and more limited surveys in small Newfoundland fishing villages, in Sterling County, Nova Scotia and in Wheatville, Saskatchewan buttress this conclusion.

The introduction of national health insurance in Canada was based on the premise that all individuals, regardless of their health status, should have equal access to health services. The programme did not initially take into account the fact that to improve the health of socially and medically disadvantaged groups, special programmes and health promotion efforts are required to alter this situation. At no time has any level of government tackled directly the question of the scope of the health needs of the population in the context of the adequacy of health services to meet these needs. Although it has been well known in Canada since the Montreal health

7 Dominion Bureau of Statistics, *Illness and Health Care in Canada. Canadian Sickness Survey 1950-51* (Ottawa: Queen's Printer, 1960), pp. 25-27.
8 *Royal Commission on Health Services*, pp. 510-14.
9 Statistics Canada, *Perspective Canada: A Compendium of Social Statistics* (Ottawa: Information Canada, 1974), p. 29.
10 David L. Rabin, ed., "International Comparisons of Health Care," *Milbank Memorial Fund Quarterly* 50, no. 3 (July 1972): pt. 2.

survey of the 1930s (Marsh-MacLeod) that the poor and the unemployed experience more ill health than affluent individuals, no study on this issue has yet been commissioned by government in Canada regardless of its political philosophy. Most of the concern has been with the resources, the operation and the costs of the health system, not with persons whom it is intended to serve. This "medicine first, the public second" attitude was voiced by Lord Brain in his 1966 Commission on Health done for Newfoundland. In *A Last Word,* in volume three he concluded:

> Modern medicine is extremely expensive and is likely to remain so ... medicine will have to have a higher priority in national finances than that now given .... Within the medical budget priority should be given to central facilities for diagnosis and treatment, then to research, and finally to raising the general level of medical care for all people.[11]

The inadequacy of information on the health status of Canadians cited in the 1964 Royal Commission on Health Services merits reiterating. "Little or no effort has been made so far in Canada to establish an integrated system of data collection to supplement the well established mortality statistics. Frequent references are made to the inadequacy of data concerning Canada's health status and health needs." The report concluded "these data need to be improved to adapt them to today's health problems."[12] New information on this still unresolved question will begin to appear as reports of the 1978 Canadian national health survey are issued.

ACCESSIBILITY TO INSURED SERVICES

The 1966 Medical Care Act stipulated that there be "reasonable access to insured services by insured persons." Achieving a measure of equality for a population in obtaining "reasonable access" to health services depends on two necessary conditions. If services are available, there is the implication that, regardless of social and economic circumstances, within reasonable limits they will be uniformly used. The second prerequisite relates to the actual geographical distribution of the resources which may be sought out, in this instance, insured services. Neither of these assumptions upon which a level of "reasonable access" to insured health services is contingent has yet been realized in Canada.

Since its introduction in 1968, national health insurance has had certain direct consequences in re-ordering the shape of the Canadian health system. The scope of private enterprise in health affairs has been somewhat curtailed, a government-run health bureaucracy has emerged to administer and control insured services, and the traditional autonomy of the established health professions is being gradually converted into a public service profession. The benefits for the public have been real, but more difficult to gauge. The shift from a mix of health insurance plans to a largely state health insurance scheme has contributed to an overall increase in the use of medical services across Canada. For the one out of five Canadians who live in poverty, the often punitive economic effects and the stigma of being

---

11   *Royal Commission on Health*, 3 vols. (St. John's: Government of Newfoundland and Labrador, 1966).
12   *Royal Commission on Health Services*, p. 141.

charity cases have been partly excised. From available polls it appears that the public is satisfied with national health insurance. But like Pip in *Great Expectations* who rose from a blacksmith's apprentice to being a gentleman, their concern has now shifted to stress the qualitative aspects of medical treatment and its availability.

Since 1968 government has been largely preoccupied with structural changes within the federal and provincial ministries of health, the periodic re-negotiation of federal-provincial cost-sharing arrangements, and above all in the search for ways to control rising health costs. With few exceptions (e.g., the Manitoba White Paper on Health Policy, Ontario's underserviced doctors' programmes), the question of accessibility to health services has not been directly dealt with by provincial government programmes or reported upon in official documents. It is widely assumed (viz., Lalonde and LeClair statements) that all is well. But as *Perspective Canada 1974* observed, "an additional concern is the adequacy of health services . . . in this area, apart from hospital costs and capabilities, practically no statistics are available."[13]

What has apparently changed little since national medicare is how health services are selectively used by individuals of different social backgrounds. Other deeply-rooted values about how men live and in particular their ideas about health have remained firmly entrenched. A man's education, his ethnic origins, the nature of his family responsibilities and the level of his income still collectively mould his outlook on life. These factors influence his recognition of illness, when he seeks care, from whom such treatment is sought and how he follows a particular medical regimen. In the context of what is known about human behaviour, it is hardly surprising that a single state measure like national health insurance has had only a limited impact in altering these deeply-rooted social values.

The Canadian Sickness Survey of 1950-51 found that low-income males between twenty-five to forty-four years, while comprising 14 per cent of men in this age group, experienced 30 per cent of the disability days of men in all income levels. Likewise, low-income men between forty-five to forty-six years made up 16 per cent of all males and they accounted for 35 per cent of all disability days. While no comparable national survey has subsequently been completed, some two decades later similar trends occurred in Saskatchewan which started its medicare plan in 1962.[14] During the first years of this programme 10 per cent of the highest income group made little use of insured health services for which there were no direct financial barriers. In contrast, almost half (47 per cent) of the lowest wage earners did not use these services. While this disparity had been reduced six years later, the proportion of non-users by income was 10 per cent and 30 per cent respectively.

The use of elective services in Saskatchewan varied by income over this period with the higher income group making a more extensive use of these

---

13 Statistics Canada, *Perspective Canada*, pp. 29-30.
14 R. G. Beck, "Economic Class and Access to Physician Services under Public Medical Care Insurance," *International Journal of Health Services* 3 (1973): 341-55; R. G. Beck, "The Effects of Co-payment on the Poor," *Journal of Human Resources* 9 (1974): 129-42; R. G. Beck and J. M. Horne, "Economic Class and Risk Avoidance: Experience under Public Medical Care Insurance," *Journal of Risk and Insurance* 43 (1976): 73-86.

benefits than persons with lower incomes. With the exception of the use of hospital services, how medical services were used varied directly with income. Between 1963-1971 the average dollar value of health services for each person in Saskatchewan rose from $67.04 to $109.25. For the lowest income group this increase was $36.10 and for the highest, $61.24. During this period the differential by income level (lowest to highest) more than doubled (from $30.96 to $66.10). In short, all had gained but high-income earners had gained the most in terms of using services.

For a three-year period in Saskatchewan (April 1968-August 1971) a co-payment policy was adopted (regardless of the billing method), involving user charges of: $1.50 per office visit and $2.00 per home, emergency or hospital out-patient visits. The intent of this policy of deterrent charges was to limit the abuse of services and to serve as a means of containing health expenditures. Between 1963-1967, the average cost of insured services per beneficiary rose from $22.05 to $26.77, or by about 5 per cent per year. With the introduction of user charges in 1968, there was an expenditure reduction in insured health services followed between 1969-1971 by increases of 12.5, 11.4 and 12.2 per cent respectively. Simultaneously, the medical fee schedule was increased in 1968 by 20 per cent. While the co-payment programme was in effect the general reduction in the use of services attributed to user charges was between 6 to 7 per cent. This reduction was of the order of 18 per cent among the lowest income groups, a change which involved family physician but not specialist services.[15]

Other post-medicare surveys corroborate the relation between income level and how health services are used. In a small praire town given the pseudonym of Wheatville, while the total volume of illness reported had declined slightly, five years after an initial survey the disparity in use of medical services by income levels had widened.[16] The 1968-69 International Collaborative Study on Medical Care Utilization of 15,608 individuals living in three Western provinces found a disparity in income in the self-reporting of health experience with what was recorded in official health agency charts. Lower income groups, in contrast to other workers, substantially overreported their use of doctors or the volume of their visits to hospital.[17] While since the start of medicare, official reports in Quebec indicate an overall rise in the use of health services, there are contradictory findings from two surveys about the impact of the programme. Lower income groups in Montreal had apparently increased their visits to physicians in contrast to higher income groups. However, no marked before-after changes in how services were used took place in the Eastern Townships, a region stretching from Montreal to the American border. These results suggest either a genuine variation between these areas or, more likely, they may be accounted for by the different study methods, time frames and analytic procedures which were used.[18]

15   Ibid.
16   R. F. Badgley, R. W. Hetherington, V. L. Matthews and M. Schulte, "The Impact of Medicare in Wheatville, Saskatchewan," *Canadian Journal of Public Health* 58 (1967): 109-16.
17   Rabin, ed., "International Comparisons," and Gordon H. Josie, ed., "World Health Organization International Collaborative Study on Medical Care Utilization," in *Report on Basic Canadian Data* (Saskatoon: University of Saskatchewan, 1973).
18   P. E. Enterline et al., "The Distribution of Medical Services Before and After 'Free' Medical Care: The Quebec Experience," *New England Journal of Medicine* 289 (1973): 1174-78, and

The findings of the 1977 Report of the Committee on the Operation of the Abortion Law indicate significant differences between what is known publicly and what may happen in practice in using medical services. Included among its extensive surveys was a study of 4,754 abortion patients in eight provinces. One out of five of these women paid extra medical fee charges which averaged $73.71, a practice which affected more women who were young, less well educated and foreign-born.[19]

From these several reports, while national health insurance has removed major financial barriers little else has changed in how patients go about getting health care or how it is provided to them. As measured by income a person's social class still affects the type and the amount of health services which are obtained. Instead of being reduced in these respects, the gap has widened. Not enough time has elapsed since state medicine was enacted in Canada to conclude that the social importance of these personal attributes may not disappear in time. But from the experience of other nations with state medicine, this redistributive outcome is unlikely to occur soon or by itself. If equal access to health care, regardless of an individual's background, is to be attained, special programmes will have to be developed, in particular, to change the embedded cultural values associated with poverty.

DISTRIBUTION OF SERVICES

What is meant by social equality in health services has been narrowly, if ever clearly, set out in Canadian legislation. The terms of the 1966 Medical Care Act, for instance, required that the insurance plan provide comprehensive medical services, allow for universal coverage of the population, have portable benefits for individuals moving between provinces, and be administered by a public authority. In an injunction upon which the federal cost-sharing contribution was contingent, the Act further stipulated that insured services were to be provided on a basis "that does not impede or preclude, either directly or indirectly, whether by charges made to individuals or otherwise, reasonable access to insured services by insured individuals."

Certain unspecified assumptions, three vaguely-defined terms and a narrow Thomist interpretation of sections of the Act by its administrators have curtailed its broad intent from being fully realized. The Act stipulated that its terms of reference be reviewed within five years. If the conditions enacted then by the House of Commons were not then being met, Ottawa could withhold its portion of funds from the provinces of this cost-sharing agreement. While new financial arrangements were reached in 1977, the legislation required the provinces to continue to respect the basic national standards which had been initially set. At no time has there been a detailed public review of the extent to which these terms are in fact being met.

L. Munan, J. Vobecky and A. Kelly, "Population Health Care Practices: Epidemiologic Study of the Immediate Effects of Universal Health Insurance," *International Journal of Health Services* 4 (1974): 285-95.

19 . "Cost of Health Services," in *Report of the Committee on the Operation of the Abortion Law* (Ottawa: Government of Canada, 1977), ch. 15.

The legislation did not define what was intended by "reasonable," "access," or the "otherwise" conditions. Economic advisors to certain provincial premiers when the Act was being negotiated have subsequently recounted with glee how they "beat the feds" by changing the bill's initial wording from "available" to "access." "Available" insured services, so it has been contended, would have required a provincial government to provide insured personnel and health facilities on a geographical basis proportional to where people lived. In contrast, the substitution to "accessible" services (sic) meant that insured services could be used under the Act's terms wherever they happened to be located. By winning this exercise of lexical gamesmanship, it was felt that rights of patients embodied in the concept of insurance had been preserved and possible encroachment by the state on the autonomy of the health professions thwarted for the time being.

The special meanings attributed to these two words does not accord with common usage nor are they so specified in the Medical Care Act. Both words are used interchangeably to mean that an article or service is either "within one's reach" or "able to be reached." Further, if "reasonable" means tolerable or fair, then the Act requires that insured services be provided where they can be reached when needed by individuals. It is clearly not the stated intent of the Act that health personnel providing insured services unilaterally decide where they choose to work nor that such facilities be allocated by health administrators, unless these resources generally and reasonably accord with the needs and distribution of the population.

The idea of "reasonable" access raises the question of which, among many standards, is to be adopted. This word's definition put into operational terms can include an optimal state, an established majority pattern, or a statistical average. The last measure, one which is commonly used in health statistics is the basis here for reviewing the distribution of health personnel and facilities.

There is an inverse relation in the social equation of income and health resources by residence in Canada. The number of the rural poor, already sizeable, is typically underestimated in many official reports. *Perspective Canada 1974* reported that while 23.9 per cent of the population in 1971 lived in rural areas, 54.8 per cent of the nation's low-income families lived in these areas. But Treaty Indians, because they are official wards of Ottawa, for instance, are excluded from the calculation of the national wage index, unlisted in the health statistics of several provinces, and along with other residents living in isolated areas, usually not considered in many research ventures (viz., the Pickering Report or the International Comparability Study on Medical Care Utilization). In contrast (and not unexpectedly), health resources, like other specialized professional and technical services, cluster in large towns and cities. While these services are available, and indeed under special circumstances used by rural residents, rural people rely on adjacent health services for a majority of their medical attention. It is for these reasons that where a man lives in Canada still determines to a large extent his accessibility to health care, and on occasion from whom and what type of medical care he receives.

Since the introduction of national medicare, the economically affluent provinces have continued to add substantially to their already extensive health manpower resources. While the disparity in the supply of physicians, for instance, between Ontario, Alberta and British Columbia and several "have-not" provinces had narrowed, none of the latter by 1974 had attained physician-to-population ratios achieved by the former over a decade earlier. The Ontario physician-population ratios in 1961 and 1974 were 1:776 and 1:568; for British Columbia, 1:758 and 1:562. In contrast, the ratios for Newfoundland were 1:1,991 and 1:836; and for New Brunswick, 1:1,314 and 1:923. Comparable disparities between the cities and rural areas exist in the distribution of physicians within most provinces.

Some well-informed observers have contended that medicare has reduced sharp regional morbidity differences, and health care is now being provided more than in the past on a basis of health needs of patients than depending upon the availability of professional workers. This point is as yet unproven. In some cases, such as the Saskatoon Community Clinic tradition, regional and class differences may disappear once a patient actually receives care.[20] But overall the issue is still unresolved: sharp differences persist at the point of entry to getting care, and once in the health system in the type of care which is received.

Extensive information about one elective surgical operation, hysterectomies, indicates considerable latitude in how the Medical Care Act's stipulated conditions are interpreted.[21] The age-adjusted rate for this operation per 100,000 women rose annually by 12.8 per cent from 1967-1971. Where women lived was related to how often this operation was performed. Alberta, New Brunswick and Saskatchewan consistently exceeded the national average while this operation was less often done in Manitoba and Newfoundland.

In Alberta, the province with the consistently highest rate, there were sharp variations between selected rural and urban hospitals, and in Edmonton and Calgary, based on their ownership between major city hospitals. In Edmonton, the likelihood of the operation being done was 1.8 times as great in one hospital as contrasted with a second hospital. In Calgary, one hospital's hysterectomy rate was 6.8 times that of another major hospital. The Saskatchewan rates per 100,000 women were 851 for Regina, 488 for Saskatoon, and 273 for Estevan. When these rates were adjusted to exclude "unjustified" operations, i.e., medically not-indicated surgery, the rates respectively were 747, 454 and 227. The rate for Regina exceeded that for Saskatoon by 65 per cent, and for Estevan's rate by 229 per cent. The pressure brought by the Saskatchewan Medical Care Insurance Commission subsequently led to more extensive reviews of hospital surgical practice leading to some sharp reductions.

In commenting tersely on a similar distribution of hysterectomy operations, the *Manitoba White Paper on Health Policy* concluded that these

20   Samuel Wolfe and Robin F. Badgley, *The Family Doctor* (Toronto: Macmillan Co., 1973).
21   Statistics and Research Division, Alberta Hospital Services Commission, "A Comparison of the Frequency of Hysterectomies in Alberta and Other Provinces 1967-73," 1974. (Mimeographed.) "Report of the Hysterectomy Committee," *College of Physicians and Surgeons of Saskatchewan, Newsletter*, October 11, 1974.

"striking differences . . . imply either a phenomenal incidence of ailments not on the face of things *regionally* determined, or something peculiar about regional medical views on the fraction of wombs . . . that need to be excised."[22] How the Act's stipulation that "all medically necessary services" be provided is interpreted, it would appear, varies considerably.

In Manitoba, Metro Winnipeg residents in 1970, in contrast to those of rural Parkland, received twice as many general history and physical examinations; had 2.5 more specialist consultations; had 42 per cent fewer hospital admissions; generated 40 per cent more medical care costs; had 42 per cent fewer appendectomies, but 52 per cent more hysterectomies performed; received 3.5 times more services from neurosurgeons; and overall had 25 per cent more major surgical operations.

Over 500 of the province's medical specialists were based in Winnipeg, less than forty in six other regions of the province. In contrast to Winnipeg and Parkland, "the 7.2 per cent of the population in Northern Manitoba receive but 0.9 per cent of Manitoba's psychiatric care, only 2.9 per cent of its total care by surgeons, and a mere 1.7 per cent of its care by anaesthetists." The substitution of specialist medical care, with general medical practice means that "treatment at the level of the 'state of the art' suffers."[23]

The higher rates of total days of care and hospital admissions for Parkland is an established trend for rural areas in Canada. Because rural residents may be scattered in a vast area, rural doctors tend to admit patients to hospital more frequently to facilitate their care. With the exception of these trends, the other sharp discrepancies in medical care between the two Manitoba regions may mean that:

(1) the actual medical needs of Winnipeg residents required more surgery and specialist consultations;

(2) urban residents were receiving a substantially higher quality of medical attention than rural residents;

(3) extensive unnecessary medical attention was being provided to the Metro Winnipeg population;

(4) a combination of the above three points.

National health insurance has not brought about a redistribution in the provision of health care on a basis which is reasonably equitable for all Canadians. This is the dominant fact that stands out after a decade's experience with this social security measure. The present inequitable situation is unlikely to be altered much by the limited options which are being tried. These include a regrouping of health and social services, the modest moves towards regionalization and the extension of community health services. Because the Canadian health system is bound by constitutional terms of authority, operates under a mix of private and public controls and retains many open-ended features, no major changes in its structure can be anticipated. What this means is that until a "reasonable" level of equity is reached, the health and the life chances of some Canadians will be profoundly affected.

22   Manitoba, *White Paper on Health Policy* (Winnipeg: Department of Health and Social Development, 1972), p. 27.
23   Ibid., p. 26.

THE DIVISION OF LABOUR IN HEALTH SERVICES

Health costs in the 1970s became a major item in federal and provincial budgets. The costs of health care in 1976 averaged well over $500 per person and accounted for 7.3 per cent of the gross national product. With the nation's annual health bill exceeding $12 billion, more stringent controls began to be introduced by government.[24] In an open economic system the income levels of workers are held to be a function of the competitive marketplace. This situation has never been fully realized in the Canadian health system where the payment of health workers has been partly determined by non-competitive social forces. The professions paid by fees have held a guild-like monopoly which has been sanctioned by provincial licensing codes. In the past salaried hospital workers had low, non-competitive incomes which were held in restraint under the ethic that their services were provided either as a charity or a public service.

High levels of inflation coupled with the almost total payment of health services by government have redefined within a decade how health workers have seen important aspects of their work. The previously independent professions in the negotiation of their fee schedules have assumed some of the attributes of trade unions. As lower-echelon health workers have extensively joined unions and started to seek wage parity with comparable non-service occupations, strikes have become more common. With the exception of the threatened physicians' boycott in the 1930s in British Columbia and the twenty-three-day Saskatchewan doctors' strike in 1962, this labour tactic was neither used nor considered in the past by other health workers. In contrast, and shortly after the start of national health insurance, there have been some fifty to sixty strikes or threatened strikes since 1970 by all categories of health workers.

In handling these disputes government is the employer, the arbitrator and the judge. Its record here is not exemplary. The law has not been equally enforced either across Canada or as it applies to different health occupations. No doctors, for instance, who have collectively "withdrawn their services," i.e., gone on strike, have been publicly sanctioned. In contrast, the leaders of certain other health unions have been fined and, on occasion, have been sent to prison. The process of arbitration favours management, namely, government which appoints its referees, establishes the rules of arbitration. This situation has only slowly started to change.

The recent trend across Canada in arbitration is shifting from ad hoc settlements to a principle of equal proportional wage settlements among health job categories. While put forward as an equitable measure, as in the case of Ontario's interns, nurses or non-professional hospital workers, the consequences of this policy led to inequitable results in terms of disposable income and actual capital gains.

An annual 5 per cent wage increase over ten years, for instance, for a base salary of $5,000 increases a worker's annual gross income to $8,145. A similar rate of pay increase for a starting salary of $25,000 results after a decade in an income of $40,725. While the ten-year increment is 62.9 per

24 Department of National Health and Welfare, *Health Insurance and Resources Directorate* (Ottawa, 1977).

cent for both jobs, the *gross annual income gap* between the two positions widens from $20,000 to $32,580. In terms of *absolute gross income,* the holder of a $25,000 job over a decade gains $264,156 more than the worker who is paid $5,000. The current federal-provincial progressive income tax scale, when applied for a family of four members, reduces the income disparity in the first year to $12,690. But by the tenth year this gap widens to $17,952.

The across-the-board proportional wage settlements now being adopted for public service occupations maintain and extend a rigid income structure with direct social class implications. Between 1960 and 1970 the average net income of doctors increased more rapidly than the income of other self-employed professionals, but this rate subsequently levelled during the 1970s.[25] Physicians, however, with average annual incomes of $44,585 in 1974 still remained the highest-paid major professional group in the country with an average annual increase of 7.5 per cent between 1967 and 1974.

Traditionally at the income apex among health workers, the financial pre-eminence of medicine grew substantially under national health insurance. In 1966 the gap between the physicians' average income and the general duty staff nurses' average salary was $20,325; this amount increased to $32,009 by 1974. For a comparable period the differences in average annual incomes between physicians and other health workers were:

	1966	1974
nurse's aide	22,209	36,653
female laboratory technician	21,873	34,757
hospital chambermaid	22,365	36,797

The hospital administrator was the only major health occupation which kept pace with, and in fact gained on, medicine during this period.

Current income policies of government have not dealt with the basic issue of "how much is enough?" for various health workers. Wage settlements have not been considered in the context of actual job functions nor in terms of their income redistribution consequences for workers at the top and the bottom of the health job hierarchy. During this period no uniform wage guidelines have been developed by provincial health ministries. Their strategy still remains one of ad hoc bargaining tactics. In this situation each health occupation seeks its strongest bargaining position. This has been the case for medicine, for instance, which contended that it lost ground in comparison with lawyers, dentists, accountants and lower-income health workers.

The wage settlements reached in the 1970s were a function and a measure of the social power of various health occupations. During this short period the highly visible wage settlements gained by hospital workers were real in terms of the wages paid to all civilian employees, but led to only ephemeral changes within the health system. The direct result of national

25 Canadian Medical Association, *Quickbase* (Ottawa: Department of Statistics, Systems and Economic Research, 1977), and Health Economics and Statistics Division, *Salaries and Wages in Canadian Hospitals: 1962 to 1975* (Ottawa: Department of National Health and Welfare, 1977).

health insurance was that this system grew more rigid and unequal in terms of direct income and associated benefits, between groups of workers. The positions of the doctor and the hospital administrator, already on the top in terms of income and status, were entrenched relative to lower-echelon health jobs.

As controls tighten on health expenditures, more rather than less labour unrest will likely challenge the income allocation structure among health workers. If these controls are imposed "across the board" or indexed for all occupational groups to changes in a provincial gross product, existing income disparities will remain, the gap in real income will widen, and the comparative yardstick of earnings paid to private enterprise will continue to spur a sense of invidious discontent among health workers.

EQUITY AND HEALTH POLICY

The attempt to obtain a clear-cut statement of social policy in health affairs is an elusive and complex exercise. The concept of social policy in common usage refers to a course of action followed by government. But in practice this word has many meanings. It may refer to an accomplished fact, an intention to act or express an ethical judgment. In Canadian health affairs it is not always clear who is responsible for statements about health policy. Important structural changes, for instance, in services can and are made by senior civil servants without any public announcement or legislative review. Public addresses made by health ministers either may be statements of policy or trial balloons to test public opinion. For their part royal commissions may be used as substitutes for action, their recommendations may be selectively drawn upon, or ignored. Legislation which represents a formal commitment by government to pursue a particular course of action relies for its success upon the allocation of necessary enabling resources. If sharp criticism is met, and this is not uncommon, or the will of government shifts, new measures may be withdrawn or retain only a wallpaper validity. For these reasons it is not surprising, as a senior health administrator has observed, that to understand the nature of health policy in Canada, the imagination of an Aesop or a Lewis Carroll may be required.

In considering the country's health policies, we look to simple and elementary considerations. Rather than considering what has been said by health authorities at public meetings, to the press or in the legislatures, we are concerned with the social consequences of those health measures, however initiated, which have moulded the nation's health system and have affected each Canadian's health status. Stripped of its institutional and fiscal complexity, the persuasive rhetoric of vested interests, or often a reliance on self-serving outcome measures, the provision of health services revolves around certain basic issues.

We do not now know enough about the unmet health needs of Canadians. What is known indicates that national health insurance, a necessary first step in removing an economic barrier, will have to be positively extended if special health needs of particular groups are to be substantially reduced. There is also strong evidence that health services, as was the case before this legislation was passed, continue to be used and distributed selectively depending upon where a man lives, his social circumstances, and the supply of health resources. Health legislation has broadened, not narrowed, the income disparity between different levels of health workers. This change, coupled with inflation, has fostered a trend toward unionization and resulted in a growing number of strikes by health workers.

These health policy issues either have seldom been raised in Canada or, when asked, have rarely been directly answered by responsible health authorities. The all-too-few attempts by independent observers to analyze the country's health system have often been ignored, or, if read, rejected as charged advocacy. Government for its part has been rarely forthright in its public review of health services. The small library of reports commissioned by Ottawa or the provinces is usually little more than an apologetic for the status quo. Because government has determined which questions are to be asked, or, more important, ignored, the conclusions of health commissions have rarely gone beyond recommendations which tinker with the organization of health services, the structure of health ministries, or means to control health costs.

More can be learned about current health policies by considering the range of basic social issues that have not been dealt with than becoming mired in the details of recommended but unimplemented programmes. Up to the present in Canada the esthetic of style in health policy has been an emphasis on planning for planning, not in dealing with the setting of programme objectives, ensuring they are reached, or assessing their impact on the health of the population. At no time has there been a major review by government of the organization, the costs and the staffing of hospitals, the linch-pins of the nation's health system. While studies elsewhere (e.g., U.K. Registrar General, U.S. National Health Survey, etc.) clearly document that the poor, certain minority groups, and individuals living in isolated areas experience more ill health and receive less medical attention than do the majority of a population, virtually no publicly-collected baseline information about the health experience of these groups is now available in Canada.

Emmett Hall, the chairman of the 1964 Royal Commission of Health Services, regarded medical care legislation "as but a segment of the whole health services' complex." Much more was required if good health care was to be provided. He concluded: "We will rightly stand condemned by history if we fail to do what our people need and what our resources and our know-how make readily possible."[26] Health care is not provided equitably to all Canadians. Little public effort has been directed toward this objective. The result has been that it is the poor and the disadvantaged who still experience unequal chances within a public programme intended to benefit all Canadians. As long as this situation exists it is a cruel mockery of the unfulfilled pledge by government "to ensure access to medical care to all of our people regardless of means, of pre-existing conditions, of age or other circumstances."[27]

26   Emmett M. Hall, "Implications of a Health Charter for Canadians," in *Health Services in Canada* (Ottawa: Mutual Press, 1966), p. 20.
27   Allan J. MacEachern, in Canada, *House of Commons Debates,* final session, 27th Parliament (July 12, 1966): 7549.

5

Housing Policy

DAN BURNS

INTRODUCTION

Housing is one of the major public issues of our time. During the past five years there has been a steady stream of commentary from journalists, academics, government officials and task forces, and from the public at large. There have been extensive changes in the level and the nature of government's role in this field.

We will begin this chapter with an outline of the evolution of housing policy in Canada at the federal government level and discuss briefly the place of the provincial and municipal governments. With respect to provincial and local government activity, the bulk of the discussion will be about Ontario, the area with which we are most familiar.

We shall see that housing policy in Canada has moved from being an economic policy—that is, a policy related to the housing market, to one which combines this focus with others. It is these other foci which make housing policy such an important part of social policy today. Perhaps the most important of these is the growing role that housing programmes now play in government approaches to income distribution. Although by most measures of quality, Canadians are the best housed nation in the world, these high standards and a sustained period of inflation have created severe problems of high housing costs for many Canadians.

After this historical review we will turn to a discussion which will set housing policy in the context of some of the major forces operating within the housing industry and on housing generally. This broader scene forms the backdrop to an identification of some of the most important areas of debate in Canadian housing policy today.

The final portion of the chapter deals with the future. What general direction is being taken in housing and what directions might be taken?

By and large, we have taken the attitude that this chapter should introduce the reader to the field. As a result, the author's view is presented only occasionally. Undoubtedly the overall treatment given also indicates a great deal about my own views.

Housing policy is a large and complex area. This chapter can only touch on some of the major debates and problems. For those interested in following up on some of the questions raised here, a brief reading listing has been included.

OUTLINE HISTORY OF HOUSING POLICY

This brief history will review the efforts of federal, provincial, and municipal governments since the closing years of World War II. Since so much of housing activity in Canada has taken place within the context of the National Housing Act, we will begin with a discussion of the federal role in housing.

THE FEDERAL GOVERNMENT

David Donnison in his excellent book *The Government of Housing* has proposed a useful framework for tracing the evolution of national housing policies which we will make use of in this chapter. He terms the first stage of his three-stage categorization an assisted free market approach. At this stage, the emphasis is on strengthening mortgage and other financial markets in order to ensure a healthy flow of funds to residential construction. In addition, a strong emphasis is placed on increasing the productivity of the residential construction industry. In short, the economic goals of increased efficiency and overall growth are pursued. Until recently, these objectives dominated Canadian housing policy.

The Canadian government got involved in housing in a substantial way in the last years of World War II. This involvement was part of a whole series of social and economic programmes brought in by the Liberal government of that day in the train of a number of reports on the problems that would face post-war Canada (including in particular the Marsh Report on Social Security in 1943 and the Curtis Report on post-war reconstruction in 1944) and in the face of greatly increased popularity of the Cooperative Commonwealth Federation (C.C.F.) in the later years of the war. The federal government was shifting to a basically Keynesian approach to managing the economy. In 1944, a National Housing Act (N.H.A.) was passed and in 1945 a new crown corporation, the Central Mortgage and Housing Corporation (C.M.H.C.), was created to implement the N.H.A. C.M.H.C. also took over all the earlier housing programmes, the most important of which were the wartime and veteran's housing programmes.

The two major thrusts written into the 1944 N.H.A. were the joint loan and direct assistance to municipalities for social housing. Since there was almost no social housing built in those years, the joint loan was C.M.H.C.'s primary tool until 1954. C.M.H.C. would participate to the extent of 25 per cent of the total for first mortgage loans, the rest to be provided by approved lenders. This effort was intended to stimulate construction and to build confidence in the residential mortgage market. In 1954, the direct participation approach was replaced by mortgage insurance.

The use of mortgage insurance after the 1954 overhaul of the N.H.A. lowered the risks involved to lenders. The operative interest rate was set by the Governor General in Council (in effect, the Cabinet) and has been extensively used by the federal government as a tool to accomplish its general management of the economy. Fairly small changes in the residential mortgage interest rate can create fairly large changes in the rate of construction. Smith, working with the statistics for 1957-65, estimated that a 1 per cent change in the interest rate would create a 9 per cent change in housing starts.

Also in 1954, changes were made to the Bank Act which allowed the chartered banks to re-enter the residential mortage field and thus increase the overall supply of residential mortgage funds. All in all, including insurance companies, savings and loan associations and so on, there are about 120 approved lenders (eligible for N.H.A. mortage insurance) in Canada.

Although these provisions have been aimed at promoting the construction of single-family dwellings, there has always been a floor on eligible incomes (relative to the dwelling's price) and, to cut out high income borrowers, there have also been ceilings on the amount of mortgage obtainable. These levels have been revised upwards several times over the past twenty years.

All in all, it is fair to say that the major thrust of government policy right up until 1964 was to lower mortgage costs, create a strong mortgage market, help foster a productive building industry and, by these means, to promote home ownership. In Donnison's terms, this is an assisted free market approach.

There was some social housing built by government in the 1949-64 period as well. From 1944 to 1949, this housing was built through a federal-municipal partnership arrangement. In 1949, this was replaced by a more constitutionally appropriate approach: the federal-provincial partnership. The year 1949 also marked the end of the wartime and veteran's housing programmes which had provided about 50,000 units up to that point. Virtually no housing was built by federal-municipal partnerships in the 1944-49 period.

The federal-provincial partnership approach lasted until 1964. Although the partnership might provide 100 per cent of a project's capital cost (75 per cent federal and 25 per cent provincial), municipalities, at least in Ontario, were required to ask for projects. In addition, they had to cover a proportion of any operating losses and provide services to the site. The payments made by the partnership in lieu of property taxes did not cover the necessary municipal expenditures.

As a result of these factors and of widespread local antipathy to public housing in general, very few requests were forthcoming. The recessions of

1958-59 and 1962-63 and a cumbersome development procedure did not help either. All in all, only about 15,000 public rental units were built in the whole country during this fifteen-year period.

However, the partnerships did manage to assemble several large tracts of land. In Ontario, the Malvern area in northeastern Metropolitan Toronto is probably the most famous.

In 1960, the N.H.A. was amended to permit loans for student housing and to municipalities for the construction of sewage treatment plants and trunk sewer lines.

In 1964, the N.H.A. received a major overhaul. New provisions were introduced allowing 90 per cent loans for public sector rental housing projects and for land assembly projects by the provinces, their agencies, or municipalities where these had been enabled by provincial statute. A formal urban renewal programme was introduced. Municipal corporations and non-profit corporations were made eligible for loans under the limited dividend section of the Act. This section had been available to entrepreneurs since 1946. The limited dividend approach essentially exchanges a preferred interest rate (below market) for a limited rate of return, initial rents at below current market levels and a fifteen-year agreement which relates rent increases to increases in operating costs.

The result of this was that the cumbersome federal-provincial partnership was superseded in many of the provinces over the next few years and in Ontario immediately. The partnership provisions remained in the Act for those provinces unable to undertake housing programmes on their own.

Although a large number of municipalities were interested in urban renewal, especially for their business districts, the middle 1960s still saw very little social housing being built outside Ontario and not much even there.

However, during the late 1960s, the assisted free market approach was increasingly seen as inadequate. A sustained period of inflation cut into the economic position of the poor and in few markets were price increases as strong as they were in housing, particularly in the home ownership market. As a result we have had a period of fairly fundamental realignment of the federal housing effort. It now, basically, conforms to Donnison's second type of government housing policy. He termed this a social housing approach.

With this approach, primary reliance is still placed on free market activity. However, a whole series of direct intercession programmes are also used to provide housing for those whose needs cannot be met by the private market.

Tentative steps in this direction were made by the 1964 amendment to the N.H.A. and the subsequent reaction of a number of provincial housing corporations, particularly the Ontario Housing Corporation. The process of change picked up momentum after the election of the first Trudeau government in 1968. The minister then responsible for housing, Paul Hellyer, announced the formation of a Task Force on Housing and Urban Development which, breaking precedent, he led himself. After a whirlwind tour of the country, this Task Force reported in January 1969.

Among its recommendations were the promotion of non-profit housing, substantial public development, income supplements, much less reliance on current public housing programmes, regional planning, an urban ministry, an end to "old style" tear-it-all-down urban renewal, and a new towns programme. Some of these recommendations, such as the proposing of an urban ministry, were implemented soon after. Others are part of the N.H.A. amendments passed by Parliament in the summer of 1973. In 1969, however, Hellyer resigned from the Cabinet in protest over the lack of action on his Task Force's recommendations.

During the life of the Task Force, funding for further public housing and urban renewal projects was frozen. Although the freeze for public housing was lifted, no new urban renewal schemes have been funded since 1968.

Paul Hellyer's successor as the minister responsible for housing, Robert Andras, announced in 1969 a major redirection of the federal housing effort aimed at providing housing for low-income Canadians. Andras and C.M.H.C. set up a series of Task Forces to review existing policy on urban assistance (urban renewal, sewage treatment), the mortgage market, native housing, and low-income housing. The year 1970 also saw a special $200 million Innovations Fund spent in a search for innovative methods of housing low-income families.

During 1971, a Ministry of State for Urban Affairs was created and, in conjunction with this, a broad-ranging series of monographs on urban Canada, organized by N. H. Lithwick, were published.

During 1971 and 1972 C.M.H.C. and the new Urban Affairs Ministry tried to absorb the reports of its task forces, assess its position and look for new directions. All during this period, large parts of the work done for these task forces, especially for the Task Force on Low Income Housing, were leaked. Much of this was very critical of federal housing efforts.

First was a report authored primarily by Melvin Charney entitled *The Adequacy and Production of Low Income Housing,* generally referred to as the Charney Report. It strongly attacked C.M.H.C.'s preoccupation with housing starts, pointing out that most low-income Canadians live in older housing. It argued for a major government commitment to rehabilitation. Also attacked was the Innovations Fund which had resulted in very few new tenure or quality ideas and whose cost savings came primarily from building smaller units or special savings on land costs.

After the leak of a draft of the overall Low Income Housing Task Force's final report, the task force chairman, Michael Dennis, and one of its other principal authors, Susan Fish, published their report privately as *Programs in Search of a Policy: Low Income Housing in Canada.*

In June 1972, the government brought extensive amendments to the N.H.A. before Parliament. These amendments, bringing changes and additions to seven major programme areas, were:
   (1) A Neighbourhood Improvement Programme (N.I.P.) aimed at upgrading existing residential areas as a replacement for urban renewal.
   (2) A Residential Rehabilitation Assistance Programme (R.R.A.P.)—a grant and loan programme aimed directly at housing rehabilitation.
   (3) An Assisted House Ownership Plan (A.H.O.P.) which offered a limited interest rate subsidy.
   (4) For non-profit housing corporations, 100 per cent loans at preferred rates of interests and other assistance.

(5) For co-operative housing associations, much wider access to government funds on a similar basis to non-profits.
(6) An increased Land Assembly Programme.
(7) More funds for the Housing Research and Community Planning provisions of the N.H.A.

Although this bill was not passed before the October 1972 general election, it sparked a great deal of criticism and many further proposals. In January 1973, there was a federal-provincial housing conference. As a result of these criticisms and meetings, a revised bill to amend the N.H.A. was brought before Parliament on January 30, 1973.

In addition to improvements in the earlier proposed changes, three new elements were added:

(1) A New Communities Programme—special monies were set aside for this purpose outside the regular land assembly provisions.
(2) Extension of access to all programmes was opened to Indians living on reservations.
(3) A Purchaser Protection Plan—the mortgage insurance programme was extended to provide for the completion of faulty new houses financed under the N.H.A.

These amendments were the culmination of an overhaul process which the N.H.A. has received in order to suit it for a national housing policy of the social housing programmes. Although, as we have seen, there have been social housing programmes in the N.H.A. from the very beginning, they were largely unused until the mid-1960s. In the late 1960s, the major shift in federal housing efforts towards social housing made the overhaul necessary.

However, the use of this type of approach has also brought forth new issues. One of the most important is the question of the role of housing as an income-support programme. Housing policy has become an important part of the overall debate concerning the appropriate mix of income transfer and social service programmes and the appropriate design of overall support efforts.

It has also created new strains and conflicts within C.M.H.C. itself. C.M.H.C. has had to incorporate social housing programmes and its accompanying philosophy into what was basically a financial institution with an approach based on support of a free market approach and the conservatism of a financial institution. To resolve this, many people have suggested that C.M.H.C. should be divided into a Canadian Central Mortgage Corporation and a Ministry of Housing; it does not seem likely that this will happen in the near future.

The change to social housing approach also strengthens demands that the nation go further in its housing efforts. Donnison has termed the third stage of policy evolution the use of a comprehensive housing policy. With such a policy, the national government ceases to play simply a residual role. It sets overall targets for housing and subtargets for areas such as land development or the availability of mortgage funds, and does its best to ensure that these targets are met. For example, both the Dennis Report and the Canadian Council on Social Development have urged the government to move in this direction.

However, since both the federal and provincial governments are committed to leaving housing production and distribution primarily to private enterprise and unplanned market activity, it is unlikely that we will see the emergence of a comprehensive housing approach from either level of government. The primary activity is most likely to be the reform of a social housing approach to place it on a more adequate footing.

Some of these areas of reform, and where we might go from here, form the subject matter of the second half of this chapter. For the moment, it is sufficient to point out that the type of evolution and debate we have outlined with respect to housing policy are paralleled in many other areas of social policy as well as in the development of the Canadian variation of the welfare state taken as a whole.

Before we get to that discussion, we will very briefly look to the roles of provincial and local governments, drawing heavily on the experience of Ontario.

PROVINCIAL AND MUNICIPAL ACTIVITY

Until very recently, the provinces and municipalities of Canada have not played a large role in general economic policies, confining themselves to the capital investment and social programmes assigned to them by the British North America Act. What little activity there was in the field of housing was primarily within the federal-municipal and federal-provincial provisions of the 1946-64 versions of the N.H.A.

On the other hand, many provinces, in particular Ontario and Quebec, have felt that ultimately the provincial and municipal governments should implement the social housing programmes in Canada. The 1964 amendments to the N.H.A. reflected this sort of perspective and the provincial housing corporations, particularly the Ontario Housing Corporation (O.H.C.), have provided most of the social housing in Canada to date. The issue of ultimate division between provincial efforts and municipal ones is still very much an open question throughout Canada. In Quebec, a strong reliance has been placed on municipal governments since the middle 1960s. Recently Ontario has begun to move in this direction as well.

O.H.C.'s public housing projects for families have raised strong opposition in many parts of Ontario—so much so in Metropolitan Toronto that it is very unlikely that more than a handful of units will be approved. In this context, and also in the context of strong municipal agitation in the province for more responsibility generally and in the housing area in particular, the province has authorized local governments to enter the field of providing housing once again.

It should be added that in its ten years of existence, O.H.C. has in fact developed a broad set of housing programmes. It has a home ownership programme, House Ownership Made Easy (H.O.M.E.), which is based on subdivisions developed by O.H.C. There are also large programmes for student housing and senior citizens' housing. Its mortgage-lending operations. which have been primarily used to provide mortgages for houses on H.O.M.E. lots and to help finance the development of condominiums, are now important enough to be placed in the hands of a separate institution, the Ontario Mortgage Corporation.

Ontario's municipalities have a wide range of roles as well, quite apart from the recently conferred right to create non-profit housing corporations. They have always been primarily responsible for housing quality in Ontario. They adopt codes for building and have the option of developing maintenance and occupancy by-laws to set standards for existing housing. They will be the implementers of the new N.I.P. programme, as well as the province's grant/loan housing rehabilitation programme, the Ontario Home Renewal Programme (O.H.R.P.). They exercise immense control over the amount of residential building land available through their general Official Plan, zoning by-law, and subdivision control powers, and through such direct activities as the construction of main sewage, water, and transportation facilities. The approach they take to this is strongly conditioned by the realities of municipal tax bases. Confined primarily to the property tax and provincial transfers as revenue sources, most local governments in Ontario are extremely loath to promote the building of more modest houses on smaller lots—houses they view as being unable to provide the tax revenue required to finance the necessary extra services. Some have even imposed a special cash impost tax of up to $1,500 on each new lot developed. Overcoming the limitations of the local tax base is one of the major urban problems in Canada today and is a very real constraint on our housing policy.

The province of Ontario has a Housing Action Programme (H.A.P.) at the moment which has taken limited account of this, offering grants to municipalities allowing more inexpensive houses. More generally, the Ontario government is currently committed to passing on any further unconditional transfers that they may get from the federal government to local governments. Local governments, on the other hand, are arguing that they should have access to a much broader tax base quite apart from further transfer payments.[1]

Although most of the Canadian experience has been with either direct provincial or municipal building, there has been some third-sector activity and some provinces have strongly supported this kind of approach. The first two sectors are private sector housing and public sector housing. The third sector is generally defined as including all non-governmental, non-profit or co-operative housing. An emphasis on a voluntary philosophy is generally strong throughout the third sector. Nova Scotia has supported building co-operatives for a long time and the government of British Columbia had a strong support programme to complement the more favourable provisions of the 1973 N.H.A.

In many ways, the provinces and the municipalities are at the centre of debate in Canada today. For most social housing programmes, the federal government is now simply the banker for other levels of government and the third sector. In the next section, which will delve into the debates of today in more detail, we shall again have cause to comment on the question of

1   See, for example, Office of the Metropolitan Chairman, Municipality of Metropolitan Toronto, *Municipal Tax Reform* (February 1974).

jurisdiction and varying philosophies among different levels of government.

WHERE ARE WE NOW?

Throughout the previous history, we have focussed our attention on the evolution of the roles of governments. For the rest of this chapter we will pay more attention to the broader context in which housing policy is operating. In this section, we will briefly identify some of the major environmental forces, the thrust of government policy as it relates to them, and then try to identify the focus of debate in each area. The particular environmental forces chosen for discussion are not the only ones that could have, nor are they totally separate—all are interrelated. However, this is not the place to try and present a general theory of social and economic development or even a thorough treatment of urban development. We are settling for the more modest task of having a look at some of the major questions that bear on housing policy.

The most important force is that of urbanization. Not only are our urban areas undergoing massive growth, but this growth is concentrated in a very few of our largest urban complexes. The large internal migration to these areas is complemented by the almost complete concentration of recent immigrants in the same areas.

For a long time, the thrust of government policy was to assist this urbanization process as much as possible. Mortgage insurance and later federal programmes to aid in major servicing projects helped underwrite the massive suburban developments of the 1950s and 1960s. During the same period, big firms grew and were encouraged by government to grow in the development and construction industries.

Physical planning and physical planning controls, at both the provincial and municipal levels of government, also developed during this period. Official plans, zoning by-laws, subdivision control, and standards for the construction of new buildings are now found almost everywhere. These give governments the power to make some impact on the shape, form, and quality of urban growth. The effects of government power have been many and varied. Some major effects are less poor housing built; municipalities enabled to impose minimum lot sizes and thus put a bottom price on the new house market; and the rate of physical growth has been limited in many places, helping to raise land prices. These, combined with long processing time, reinforced the trend toward large, well-financed development corporations with one foot in construction, the other in large-scale land purchase and development linked to major financial institutions. On the other hand, new housing is no longer built far in advance of regular municipal services, is usually accessible to schools, and is no longer right on top of industry, particularly noxious industry.

We will return to the question of large development corporations, but for the moment let us look at some of the issues that have risen from massive, concentrated urbanization. The focus of debate has moved, both nationally and provincially, from how to make urban development more efficient to the question of spreading urban growth throughout the country. The federal government has created a Department of Regional Economic Expansion, C.M.H.C. has created a fund to buy the land for new towns, and Ontario has acquired several new town and satellite town sites.

Many local governments have come to oppose all but the slowest of growth rates and this lends further urgency to the situation. It has also generated tension between them and those provinces with the highest rate of urban growth. Ontario, for example, is finding it difficult to persuade local governments to utilize its Housing Action Programme, which is aimed at speeding up servicing and planning approvals to put more residential land on the market.

The crux of the problem is that housing is a major element in any active government effort to influence the pattern of regional development. We will return to this question later.

Before turning to the next issue, a brief mention should be made about the other side of the urbanization coin: the remote areas with declining populations. Governments have been extremely reluctant to invest money in non-urban, non-industrialized areas though they contain much of our worst housing. Only recently have special rural and northern programmes been developed to complement the meagre use of existing government programmes.

The past ten years have seen a rapid increase in the proportion of rental housing in our urban areas. There has also been a large change in its composition. We now have a number of rental property companies with large holdings. The form of this housing has also changed, now consisting primarily of high and medium density housing.

The increase in land prices and mortgage interest rates have continued to make rental housing a more efficient user of both land and capital, an attractive alternative. However, this relationship has brought some major changes in government policies in its wake.

Most provinces have now revised their landlord-tenant laws to curtail the rights of landlords and extend those of tenants, who now are not only more numerous but also far less likely to have any kind of personal relationship with their landlord.

Over almost all of the period since the last war, rents have increased at a slower pace than either income or the consumer price index. However, the gradual introduction of minimum building standards, the elimination of some of the worst of our urban slums, and the abandonment of some of our worst rural slums has eliminated a great deal of our low-rent housing. To reach the people now unable to reasonably afford "standard" housing, we have introduced a wide range of residential rental programmes discussed earlier in this chapter.

On the other hand, in the last couple of years the strong inflation in the rest of the economy is being reflected in increases in rent levels as well. Rent control has once again emerged as a major public issue. This issue has added another dimension to what I believe to be the central point of debate about the rental sector in Canada today. This is: to what extent are we going to take rental housing out of the private enterprise sector? And, as a corollary to this, once we have embarked on this enterprise, at what point can we stop? It seems to me that this is one of the really crucial issues in modern Canadian housing policy.

The debate between those who favour a social housing approach and those who favour a comprehensive approach is primarily fought in terms of the rental sector (and land development, which we shall discuss later). The question of housing as a key element in state income and wealth distribution policy is being debated primarily in relationship to rental housing. Issues of alienation, relative power, and community are also strongly represented in the discussion of the future of this sector. We shall return to some of these questions in the next section of this paper.

Before we do, though, I would like to turn briefly to the development and construction industries in Canada. Even more than in rental housing, land development has come to be dominated by a few broadly-based companies. Although, as we have indicated above, this situation has generally been encouraged by governments on efficiency grounds, the current result is that instead of using a few carrot-on-a-stick techniques to encourage change in residential markets, governments are now often involved in direct bargaining/negotiation. Ontario's Housing Action Programme, for example, is taking an approach which will involve actual contracts with the large landowners. The government of British Columbia has gone one step further—to buying a controlling interest in one of the province's largest development companies.

The construction industry in Canada, on the other hand, is still largely made up of small and medium sized firms. Because of the cyclical character of construction and the fragmented nature of the companies and unions involved, this sector is characterized by a higher than average rate of unemployment and bankruptcy. This does not mean that this sector is terribly inefficient. In fact, the industry is one of the most effective in the world, when it is building.[2]

These, then, are some of the major environmental factors with which government housing policy must work—massive urbanization, large changes in the nature of the development and rental property industries, and the emergence of a large number of other government activities such as planning and standard-making that strongly affect housing conditions in Canada. Before we turn to the future, though, a brief discussion of one other major environmental factor is in order, and that is social values.

One aspect of this is that the overwhelming majority of Canadian citizens would prefer to be homeowners. There are many facets of this: security of tenure, which brings a measure of control over our environment; equity build-up which brings economic status; easier access to credit; and many others. Government policy has tried to reflect these values. Although a number of the rights which have been associated with private property in Canada have been curtailed, there is still a fairly strong similarity between the views of government, private enterprise and homeowners.

2   For a further discussion of housing policy as it has been directly influenced by developers and the construction industry, see James Lorimer, *The City Book* (Toronto: J. F. Lorimer & Co., 1976).

When it comes to rental housing, though, a whole series of conflicts emerge. Tenants have only a measure of security of tenure and no share in the equity build-up or capital gains associated with their housing. To assure these for tenants would mean abandoning rental housing as private property and making ownership co-operative, non-profit, or government housing—each of which offers the tenant far more of what most people value in housing than renting does today.

Although private rental housing is a very small part of the housing stock in many European nations (less than 20 per cent in Britain, for example), it comprises a very large part of ours (40 per cent in 1971). Abandoning it would mean a total change in our development, construction and property industries. Most Canadians would not favour such large-scale nationalization. So the crucial question is this: Can we get what people want out of our housing production and distribution system without effectively nationalizing it? We will look at some of the answers being proposed.

WHERE DO WE GO FROM HERE?

We have chosen to divide this section along the lines developed by John Jordan in his excellent essay, "Housing in the Future of Ontario Society," which was part of *A Study of Housing Policies in Ontario: General Report* published by the Ontario Welfare Council.[3] The first will be entitled "Towards Comprehensiveness," and the second, "Beyond Comprehensiveness."

1. Towards Comprehensiveness

The issues in this section include both those which might be termed internal to housing policy and those which try to relate housing to other areas of public policy, both social and economic.

Within housing policy, the primary effort seems to be in getting the financing, production, and planning aspects of housing production to work together well enough so that we can avoid unintended roadblocks and achieve as high an annual output of housing as we possibly can. To be successful, this effort must mean taking several steps in the direction of a comprehensive housing policy. Things like ensuring the flow of mortgage funds become combined with specific targets for residential land development and a set of targets for housing production, perhaps even with sub-goals for distribution—so much for social housing, so much for sale at various prices, and so on. Government planning activities at all levels are subjected to intense pressure to ensure that their day-to-day activities support the achievement of such targets as much as possible. This kind of approach was the major proposal of the Advisory Task Force on Housing Policy in Ontario (The Comay Task Force) and is now the focus of the efforts of Ontario's new Ministry of Housing.[4]

3 Ontario Welfare Council, *A Study of Housing Policies in Ontario: General Report* (Toronto, October 1973).
4 Ontario, Advisory Task Force on Housing Policy, *Report* (Toronto: Queen's Printer, August 1973).

Before one gets very far into trying to direct housing production, one runs into the effects of the business cycle and the efforts of governments, particularly the federal government, to make general economic policy in relation to this. If general government policy is trying to slow down or "cool off" the economy through the use of such tools as restricting the money supply (which results in higher interest rates) or cutting government expenditures, then the housing sector will get hit quickly and hard. Housing starts are very sensitive to increases in interest rates.

As in many other things, the poor make a disproportionately large contribution to cooling out the economy. Not only do they bear the brunt of unemployment but as vacancy rates drop, they end up with rent increases, in the worst housing, or doing the bulk of the doubling-up. Since in part at least, the adoption of social housing policies and aspects of comprehensive policies by governments in Canada have been aimed at achieving distribution goals for housing, this type of situation brings housing policy into direct conflict with general economic policy.

Several approaches have been suggested to overcome this. Some have argued that housing ought to be removed from the mainstream of the economy. Such measures as separating the residential mortgage markets from other capital markets and a stronger public role in the financing and production of housing have been proposed.

Others, arguing that not only should government not move from managing the economy to administering it, but also that residential construction is a crucial part of general economic policy, have suggested other policies. Primarily the argument holds that in time of economic expansion, governments should ensure the building of enough housing of all types and that a substantial excess capacity or vacancy rate exists throughout our housing stock. This would create an adequate supply of housing when construction falls off. Unemployment insurance and other income policies can be used to relieve the other burdens recessions place on the poor.

Neither of these has really been tried, but the attempt to achieve some kind of balance between housing policy goals and management of the economy does lead us to two other areas which must be included before these approaches could really work. One of these is endemic to discussions of policy in Canada—the problems of divided jurisdiction. At the moment, the federal government is responsible for general economic policy and is the primary banker for public sector and third sector housing activities. The provincial governments are the primary producers of social housing and control most public sector land development. Both levels have substantial programmes in the field of assisted home ownership. Local governments control physical planning and the provision of the hard services that are necessary before any housing can be built at all.

In this context, how can we create a comprehensive approach that extends to areas outside the jurisdiction of any one level of government at all? Although the federal government does, from time to time, express its general goals with statements like, "We hope for 225,000 starts this year," it rarely goes beyond this. Its funding of provincial, local and non-profit activity is not any more specific, although it is consistent with whatever general goals are announced and the general commitment to spend most federal funds on social housing. Provincial governments, in their turn, have established some form of relationship with their municipalities. Who establishes the volume of social housing built? Who builds it? How will physical planning be related to housing production? These and many other questions have not been clearly answered in this system.

When any government tries to become more comprehensive, as the government in Ontario is trying to become now, it must attempt to convince the other levels of government to move along with it. In Ontario, this has meant a consistent effort to convince the federal government to guarantee several years' basic funding for provincial programmes (a guarantee not provided so far). It has also brought an effort to get local governments to produce housing policies which the province insists must be consistent, in a general way, with its own goals. These policies must not only suggest targets of various kinds, but must also indicate that local physical planning activities will proceed with the housing policy and targets clearly in mind.

If we are to have more comprehensive housing policies in Canada, I believe they must come from the provincial governments. To accomplish this, the federal government must be willing to make longer term commitments with its housing funds and provinces must find some way of getting the co-operation of their local governments. This is not only because of the current provincial responsibilities for social housing, but also because of their roles in physical and regional development planning and programmes, social services, income security, and such physical services as sewage treatment and the provision of water. At this level lie the largest number of related public activities required to make housing policies more broadly based.

The other area that we are brought to rapidly when thinking about housing questions is the relationship of these to income policies. Housing lies at the nexus of income and wealth distribution policies. Since the fairly firm adoption of a social housing approach in Canada during the last ten years, and especially during the last five, the income transfer portions of housing programmes have become very important. Thus, not only are these subjects of discussion in the current federal-provincial review of income security policies in Canada, but we also have had numerous suggestions that an income, or demand for housing, approach should form the basis of our distribution of housing policy. That is, if we created a housing allowance or similar scheme, might we not be able to stop the practice of providing assisted housing on quite different bases from those at different levels of income? This was a major recommendation of the Federal Low Income Housing Task Force, for example.[5] This approach would offer help where people are now at, not wherever subsidized housing happens to be located—if there is no waiting list, that is. It also overcomes one of the major problems of our current assisted housing, a problem held in common with many other social welfare programmes, that of creaming or high-grading. High-grading means that in order to minimize either administrative problems or operating losses, or both, the managers of assisted housing might

5   Michael Dennis and Susan Fish, Programs in Search of a Policy (Toronto: Hakkert, 1972).

not accept those with a record of evictions, credit problems, or perhaps not even a substantial proportion of very low income families.

On the other hand, a demand for housing allowance presents some obvious problems. It spends a lot of money that does not create any more new housing, at least in the short run. Much of the money may just pass through and into the hands of landlords or those selling their homes after the allowance is introduced, and, like any major change in income policy, it has to be considered in relation to the current state of the minimum wage, labour market, and so on. At any rate, it is clear that the income or demand component of housing policy is crucial to any fully comprehensive approach. At this point, it should also be mentioned that, especially in the absence of a substantial vacancy rate, some form of rent regulation or control may be required to prevent these new income transfers from simply ending up as windfall gains in the hands of the landlords. Governments that do not like the idea of controls or regulation are loath to introduce this kind of support in an inflationary era when they are beset with demands for rent control or regulation.

This also brings us back to the question of the future of the rental sector. It is clear that a rapid expansion of public sector (provincial and municipal), non-profit, limited-dividend, and co-operative housing coupled with rent regulation amounts to a partial nationalization of the rental sector. From that time on, any expansion of the private rental sector will be very largely dependent on a variety of public decisions.

It seems to me that if we are going to extend a large measure of security of tenure and economic security as well, though it may not involve an equity position, to our tenant population, then we are going to have to effectively nationalize, or perhaps socialize is a more accurate term, a large part of our rental housing. By this I do not mean that provincial governments will or should go out and expropriate all of their landlords. Rather, most additions to the rental stock would be created either by governments or preferably by small, relatively independent non-profit and co-operative corporations, whose approach would hopefully include a large measure of participation on the part of their tenants or members, at least in the case of co-operatives. In addition, some part of the existing rental stock should be bought by these same groups.

Only in this kind of framework can housing demand and supply policy work effectively together in the contribution both to alleviating poverty and a broader access to the security offered by a broader distribution of wealth, whether that wealth is directly personal or available through security of tenure and relatively stable rents.

I should say, though, that we are a fair way from this position in most parts of Canada. British Columbia is a partial exception, having both limited increases in rents to 8 per cent per annum and spectacularly increased the production of non-private sector housing. Most governments will try and walk the tightrope that increases social housing and does not alienate tenants too much but still keeps the private sector building rental housing. It will not be an easy tightrope to walk, either politically or administratively. Even more so at a time when private rental housing does not offer much of a return and non-residential construction does. In some areas, non-private producers may well find themselves the only builders of new rental housing whether they really want it that way or not.

Before we turn to other issues, some mention should be made of other areas of public policy that must become linked to housing policy as governments try to direct more events and try to do this in as comprehensive a manner as possible. The most important one, in my mind, is one that we have discussed above—housing and regional development. As more provincial governments attempt to influence or perhaps even direct the distribution of employment and thus urban growth, the more we will see new towns and major government residential land developments. Other areas which are being discussed now in relation to housing, and will likely be even more in the future, include housing and social services, especially in relation to housing for special groups such as the aged and the handicapped, environmental protection, the management of housing, the quality of housing design and the tax policies of various levels of government. These are, of course, only the major areas. Brief essays such as this one can really only scratch the surface of a policy area as complex as housing.

2. Beyond Comprehensiveness

Although a more broadly based policy is an obvious necessity, there is more optimism about the real potential of a comprehensive or systematic approach in this field than can be really justified.

One of the major reasons for this is contained in the extremely useful distinction made by Michael Chevalier between the calculable and the incalculable. It is obvious that the basic concerns of housing policy are with aspects of our society that are calculable, that is, capable of being precisely described, primarily through the use of statistics. Things such as starts, household incomes, facilities, and average dwelling size become our goals and the measures of our success or failure. However, it is more likely that aspects of social life such as lifestyle, security, control of one's immediate environment, and neighbourhood are far more important aspects of housing in people's lives than these statistics.

Another reason can be outlined by the use of a brief analogy from the field of physical planning. In that field it is very difficult if not impossible to achieve the goals laid down in official plans for periods such as twenty-five years in the future—particularly when all the actual programmes that are intended to build toward that state are developed on an annual basis and are very sensitive to short-run changes in conditions in the community in question. What has come out of this situation is an attempt to build fairly open-ended plans which try to look only at the mid-term future, say, three to six years, in the hope that these plans will be neither as utopian as Official Plans nor as pragmatic and adaptable as most line programmes.

By and large, discussions of housing policy are in the same boat—either utopian and state speculation or what the hell do we do this year! Thus, discussions of comprehensiveness have tended to focus on what the ideal state of affairs might be if all policies worked together rather than on how do we get the crucial two or three together for the next few years.

Norbert Prefontaine, a senior officer of the federal Department of National Health and Welfare, reflecting on his experience with attempts to systemize social policy made this comment:

> I think I see sufficient evidence to say that our common approach to, and understanding of, social policy is inherently wrong-headed . . . our intentions to the contrary, it is literally ill-directed. It follows from this that if our present inadequate understanding is further systemized, our efforts to develop an adequate social policy will have the net effect of systematically damaging what in the past we have damaged only randomly.[6]

Nothing could summarize more clearly the limits of the potential for comprehensive housing policy.

Where does this leave us? It seems to me that it leaves us with a clear commitment to approach housing in a way that leaves a great deal of choice to its final users. Within general guidelines that guarantee some measure of tenure and economic security in the public and public-related housing sectors and insure a positive income redistributive effect, housing should reflect local and individual priorities, lifestyles, and not simply the numerical corollaries of grand central goals.

John Jordan, in the essay mentioned above, goes beyond this, arguing that housing policy should be situated ". . . directly in the context of the major strains and tensions of a post-industrial society. It is to suggest that we start to conceive of our housing policy as one of the means by which we seek to provide a realistic reintegration of social structure and culture." In his essay, he has contrasted the continuing strength of the values of a quieter era in a time dominated by largeness, in institutions and cities, and rapid change in technology and many other things. Housing policy, he argues, can play a major role in bridging this dichotomy of values and the real state of affairs. In conclusion he states:

> In terms of moving from our present policy, it is very useful to begin by grappling with its limitations growing out of its restricted notion of housing as a calculable system, and beginning the exploration of the incalculable dimensions of housing in Ontario. Finally, it may be worth pointing out that a shift in the housing policy toward the type we are speaking of is not one that demands an increase in the role of government. The sovereign consumer has considerable opportunity to balance the calculable and the incalculable elements in his housing decisions. Today, however, the sovereign consumer has been reduced to economic man. But tomorrow the question will be, as Norton Long has put it, whether we will be developing our policy on the notion of man as consumer or rather on the notion of man as citizen.[7]

I can think of no better note on which to end our brief voyage on the stormy waters of housing policy.

CONCLUSION

As in all essays of this kind, we have just been able to scratch the surface of some of the major issues in Canadian housing policy today. Housing is

---

6 Quoted by John Jordan, from Ontario Welfare Council, *A Study of Housing Policies in Ontario*, ch. 3, "Housing in the Future of Ontario Society."

7 Ibid.

intimately related to most other areas not only of social policy but of economic policy as well.

BIBLIOGRAPHY

This list contains only a few of the available books and reports on housing policy in Canada and elsewhere. However, many of those included do have extensive bibliographies of their own and these should be consulted by those who wish to read extensively in this field.

Aaron, Henry J. *Shelter and Subsidies: Who Benefits from Federal Housing Policies?* Washington, D.C.: The Brookings Institute, 1972.

Armitage, Andrew, and Audain, Michael. *Housing Requirements: A Review of Recent Canadian Research.* Ottawa: The Canadian Council on Social Development, May 1972.

Bryant, R. W. A. *Land: Private Property and Public Control.* Montreal: Harvest House, 1972.

Canadian Council on Social Development. *Beyond Shelter: A Study of N.H.A. Financed Housing for the Elderly.* Ottawa: Canadian Council on Social Development, July 1973.

_____. *Is There a Case for Rent Control?* Ottawa: Canadian Council on Social Development, January 1973.

Canadian Council on Urban and Regional Research. *The Management of Land for Urban Development.* A collection of Conference Papers. Ottawa, April 1974.

Central Mortgage and Housing Corporation. *Canadian Housing Statistics.* Ottawa (an annual publication).

City of Toronto. *Living Room: An Approach to Home Banking and Land Banking for the City of Toronto.* Toronto, December 1973.

Economic Council of Canada, *Towards More Stable Growth in Construction.* Ottawa, 1974.

Fraser, Graham. *Fighting Back: Urban Renewal in Trefann Court.* Toronto: Hakkert, 1972.

Hamilton, S. W. *Public Land Banking—Real or Illusionary Benefits?* Vancouver, B.C.: Urban Development Institute of Ontario, January 1974.

Jordon, John. "Canadian Policy Towards Co-operation Housing: A Study of Values in Conflict." Unpublished M.E.S. thesis, York University, Toronto, 1973.

_____. *Co-operation Housing: Program Review and Proposal.* Ottawa: Central Mortgage and Housing Corporation, 1971.

Nevitt, A. A. *Housing, Taxation, and Subsidies.* London, England: Thomas Nelson and Sons, 1966.

Ontario. Ministry of Community and Social Services. "Housing and Social Policy in Ontario." March 1973.

Ontario. Department of Municipal Affairs. *The Maintenance of Property—A Program for Ontario.* July 1970.

_____. *Brunetville—A Neighbourhood Reborn.* March 1972.

Ontario, Ministry of Housing. *Housing Ontario/74: An Initial Statement of Policies, Programs and Partnerships.* Toronto, May 1974.

Ontario Association of Housing Authorities. *Good Housing for Canadians.* Toronto, 1964.

Ontario Economic Council. *Subject to Approval, A Review of Municipal Planning in Ontario.* Toronto, 1973.

Ontario Habitat Foundation. *Voluntary Activity in Housing: A Policy and Program for the Third Sector.* Prepared for the Advisory Task Force on Housing, Province of Ontario. Toronto, May 1972.

Ontario Welfare Council. *Housing in Ontario: A Sourcebook.* Toronto, October 1973.
_____ . *The Municipal Role in Housing.* Toronto, October 1974.
Peter Barnard Associates. *Managing Public Housing in the Province of Ontario.* Submitted to Ontario Housing Corporation. Toronto, December 1971.
Reid, M. *Housing and Income.* Chicago: University of Chicago Press, 1962.
Richardson, Boyce. *The Future of Canadian Cities.* Toronto: New Press, 1972.
Rose, Albert. *Regent Park—A Study in Slum Clearance.* Toronto: University of Toronto Press, 1958.
Sayegh, Kamal S. *Canadian Housing: A Reader.* Waterloo, Ont.: University of Waterloo, 1972.
Social Planning Council of Metropolitan Toronto. *The Rent Race: A Study of Housing Quality, Shelter Costs, and Family Budgets for Social Assistance Recipients in Metropolitan Toronto.* Toronto, March 1974.
Wheeler, Michael. *The Right to Housing.* Montreal: Harvest House, 1969.

Immigration and Social Policy

GRACE M. ANDERSON

INTRODUCTION

Few countries have experienced as much public concern with the questions raised by continuous immigration as has Canada. Successive waves of immigrants have altered the ethnic composition of the population from being a nation composed mostly of persons of French and British backgrounds to a nation made up of a mosaic of different ethnic heritages. The first immigrants to come in large numbers after Confederation, in addition to the British, were immigrants from Northern and Eastern Europe. Then, in the mid-twentieth century large numbers from Southern Europe arrived. In the 1970s the centre cores of the largest metropolitan cities—Toronto, Montreal and Vancouver—have seen the influx of many non-white immigrants—Caribbean and American Blacks and Asians from India, Pakistan and Hong Kong.

These changes reflect changing world conditions as well as the changing needs of a country which is rapidly becoming a highly industrialized, urbanized nation. In the nineteenth century many western and some northern areas were opened up to agriculture and to mining. But the twentieth century is noted for the growth of the cities, growth which is assisted in large measure by the continued influx of immigrants as well as rural migrants displaced through the increasing mechanization of farming.

In the last century immigrants were left largely to fend for themselves. Now many programmes are available to assist them, although these are frequently available only on a piecemeal basis.

HISTORICAL OVERVIEW OF IMMIGRATION

The history of immigration since Confederation has been dominated by the emphasis placed by Canadian governments upon the special status conferred upon the two "founding races,"[1] English and French.

The 1870-71 census, the first census after Confederation, revealed that the two largest groups in Canada at that time were the French with a total of 1,082,940 and the British—the English, Scots, Welsh, and Irish—with a combined total of 2,110,502. If taken separately, none of the latter outnumbered the French. There were 706,349 Englishmen, 549,946 Scots, 7,773 Welshmen, and 846,414 Irishmen. Other groups were much smaller, the only sizeable one being the Germans with 202,991. There were 29,662 Dutch, 21,496 Negroes, then listed as "Africans," and small groups of Swiss, Italians, Spanish, Portuguese, and other nationalities. The Ukrainians were not mentioned. The Chinese community, probably already numbering several thousand and concentrated in British Columbia, was not present in this census, as the province did not enter Confederation until 1871.[2]

The dominant and rival ethnic groups, English and French, attempted to maintain the balance of power between them, and, wherever possible, to improve upon the existing situation. Anglophones often supported immigration of persons from Northern Europe and more especially from Great Britain whereas the Francophones, while traditionally maintaining an anti-immigration stance, attempted to sustain high birth rates until comparatively recent times.[3]

The first Canadian Immigration Act came into force in 1869. It limited the number of passengers a ship could carry. Other than that restriction, however, the main requirement for immigrants for the next fifty years was little more than the ability to walk off the ship.

Travelling conditions were hazardous. In 1847, for example, of 109,690 immigrants who sailed from Europe more than 16 per cent died en route. Those who survived were left to fend for themselves after arrival. Many engaged in farming, an occupation in which some had no previous experience.[4]

The period between 1845 and 1924 is often referred to as the time of the "open door" policy. It was an era of almost free migration without controls. Although entry itself was easy, once again there were frequently great hardships to be endured in the early years of becoming established.[5] Asians and Blacks, however, were not included in this policy of easy entry. Jews

1 Although referred to as "races" in the literature, these are really ethnic entities. English and French are both of the same race, Caucasian. Census figures have to do with ethnic origin, reckoned through the male line.

2 Freda Hawkins, *Canada and Immigration: Public Policy and Public Concern* (Montreal: McGill-Queen's University Press, 1972), p. 34.

3 See Council on French Life in America, "The Fertility Crisis in Quebec," in *Critical Issues in Canadian Society*, ed. Craig L. Boydell et al. (Toronto and Montreal: Holt, Rinehart and Winston, 1971).

4 Canada, Department of Manpower and Immigration, "Immigration to Canada," Fact Sheet, Info/9 (Ottawa: Department of Manpower and Immigration, Immigration Information Service, 1969), p. 1. (Mimeographed.)

5 The latter part of this period is vividly documented for men who worked on the outer fringes of society in Edmund Bradwin, *The Bunkhouse Man: Life and Labour in the Northern Work Camps* (Toronto: University of Toronto Press, 1972).

also found entry to be problematic. Dawson[6] describes in detail the early settling of Western Canada by a variety of ethnic groups, the Doukhobors, Mennonites, Mormons, German Catholics and French Canadians who either homesteaded or else purchased cheap land.

The Canadian Family Tree[7] sketches very briefly the backgrounds of Ukrainians, Norwegians, Icelanders, Finnish and many other groups which settled in Canada in the nineteenth and early twentieth centuries, as well as giving an overview of Canadian ethnic histories in general.

Throughout the latter quarter of the nineteenth century gains from immigration were minimal. In spite of the steady arrival of immigrant ships, there was an ebbing away of gains of new arrivals through a trek southward to warmer climates in the United States. "By 1871 only 8 per cent of the population was of ethnic origin other than British, French, or native Indian and Eskimo. By 1881 the percentage had risen to nearly 9 and by 1910 to nearly 10."[8] Jenness reports that during the twentieth century Canada has been a net receiving country (p. 6).

"A crucial episode in the history of Canada was played out during the fourteen years of Wilfrid Laurier's administration, 1896-1911."[9] In those years official immigration policy changed from being *laissez faire* to actively seeking immigrants thought to be in the most highly desirable categories. Clifford Sifton, the dynamic newly-appointed minister of the interior under Laurier, in 1896 proposed that immigration priority "should be granted to agriculturalists who would populate and farm Western Canada" (Troper, pp. 6-7). White farmers from the American Midwest were actively sought out and encouraged to migrate to Canada. In order to advertise this programme thirty men were designated as Canadian government agents in the years 1896 to 1911 and they were settled in offices in the United States, mostly in farming centres of the Midwest, to entice farmers northward and to provide favourable publicity for Canada (Troper, p. 30).

The Canadian Immigration Act of 1906 and the subsequent act of 1910 provided the impetus to reject entry by "undesirable elements" on the grounds of medical problems, pauperism, and "moral turpitude." The government not only was granted powers to deny entry for individuals and to deport those already in the country, but it could also prohibit entry of *groups* of immigrants. "The act of 1910 more specifically enumerated and defined prohibited classes and added race as a classification factor for immigration into Canada" (Troper, p. 23).

While the policy was initially pro-agriculturalist, it became racist when Oliver followed Sifton as minister responsible for immigration:

---

6 C. A. Dawson, *Group Settlement: Ethnic Communities in Western Canada* (Toronto: Macmillan, 1936).

7 *Canadian Family Tree: Centennial Edition 1867-1967* (Ottawa: Queen's Printer, 1967).

8 *Report of the Royal Commission on Bilingualism and Biculturalism,* Book IV, *The Cultural Contribution of Other Ethnic Groups* (Ottawa: Queen's Printer, 1970), p. 18. See also the table, "Ethnic Variations in the Canadian Population," p. 19, and R. A. Jenness, "Canadian Migration and Immigration Patterns and Government Policy," *International Migration Review* 8 (Spring 1974): 5.

9 Harold Martin Troper, *Only Farmers Need Apply* (Toronto: Griffin Press, 1972), p. 1.

TABLE 1

IMMIGRATION TO CANADA BY CALENDAR YEAR, 1852-1972

Year	Immigration	Year	Immigration	Year	Immigration	Year	Immigration
1852	29,307	1882	112,458	1912	375,756	1942	7,576
1853	29,464	1883	133,624	1913	400,870	1943	8,504
1854	37,263	1884	103,824	1914	150,484	1944	12,801
1855	25,296	1885	79,169	1915	36,665	1945	22,722
1856	22,544	1886	69,152	1916	55,914	1946	71,719
1857	33,854	1887	84,526	1917	72,910	1947	64,127
1858	12,339	1888	88,766	1918	41,845	1948	125,414
1859	6,300	1889	91,600	1919	107,698	1949	95,217
1860	6,276	1890	75,067	1920	138,824	1950	73,912
1861	13,589	1891	82,165	1921	91,728	1951	194,391
1862	18,294	1892	30,996	1922	64,224	1952	164,498
1863	21,000	1893	29,633	1923	133,729	1953	168,868
1864	24,779	1894	20,829	1924	124,164	1954	154,227
1865	18,958	1895	18,790	1925	84,907	1955	109,946
1866	11,427	1896	16,835	1926	135,982	1956	164,857
1867	10,666	1897	21,716	1927	158,886	1957	282,164
1868	12,765	1898	31,900	1928	166,783	1958	124,851
1869	18,630	1899	44,543	1929	164,993	1959	106,928
1870	24,706	1900	41,681	1930	104,806	1960	104,111
1871	27,773	1901	55,747	1931	27,530	1961	71,689
1872	36,578	1902	89,102	1932	20,591	1962	74,586
1873	50,050	1903	138,660	1933	14,382	1963	93,151
1874	39,373	1904	131,252	1934	12,476	1964	112,606
1875	27,382	1905	141,465	1935	11,277	1965	146,758
1876	25,633	1906	211,653	1936	11,643	1966	194,743
1877	27,082	1907	272,409	1937	15,101	1967	222,876
1878	29,807	1908	143,326	1938	17,244	1968	183,974
1879	40,492	1909	173,694	1939	16,994	1969	161,531
1880	38,505	1910	286,839	1940	11,324	1970	147,713
1881	47,991	1911	331,288	1941	9,329	1971	121,900
						1972	122,006

Source: Canada, Department of Manpower and Immigration, 1972, *Immigration Statistics* (Ottawa: Information Canada for Department of Manpower and Immigration, 1974), p. 4.

The virtual sealing of the Canadian border to black Americans by 1911 was not the product of direct parliamentary action. Rather, it was an outgrowth of citizen agitation with which the Immigration Branch sympathized . . . the process of exclusions shifted over a ten-year period from haphazard stop-gap discouragement of black settlement to a well-polished mechanism completely geared toward preventing Negroes from crossing the border into Canada.[10]

Departmental Secretary L. M. Fortier claimed to have "observed that after some years of experience in Canada [Negroes] do not readily take to our climate on account of the rather severe winter" (Troper, p. 127).

The total immigration into Canada from the United States between 1896 and March 1912 was 785,137 (Troper, p. 148). The large majority of these immigrants were white farmers. It may well be asked what lasting effect this was to have upon Canada during the remainder of the twentieth century. One American magazine observed in 1903: "It is not only the Northwest of Canada which is being invaded by American settlers and American capital, but the entire Dominion is becoming Americanized, though the inflow is naturally more marked in particular localities."[11]

Blacks were not the only persons who experienced discrimination. In 1908 Mackenzie King, then deputy minister, officially accepted the principle of Asiatic exclusion, and by 1912 there was an almost total exclusion of Asians from Canadian entry for purposes of immigration. As illustrative of the lengths to which the Canadian government was prepared to go, a passenger ship carrying potential East Indian Hindu immigrants was chased from Vancouver harbour by a Canadian naval vessel on July 23, 1914.[12]

The years 1910 to 1913 were peak years for immigration as settlers poured into the country by boat and many headed westward. Others settled in the cities in Eastern Canada. The best land in the United States had already been pre-empted. Canada still had land available for settlement, its cities were comparatively small but growing rapidly, skilled workers were in high demand, because Canada had few facilities for training the technicians it required within its embryonic industrial system or educational establishments. Immigrants came in massive waves during these years. During the war years (1914-1918) immigration was curtailed from Europe and reduced to a trickle from other parts of the world.

Throughout the 1920s immigration again flowed into the country, but never in the numbers seen in the pre-war period. The effect of the stock market crash in 1929 was not felt until over a year later, when its seriousness was realized and its devastating effects were experienced throughout North America. Once again immigration was reduced to a trickle throughout the thirties. Small numbers of refugees from Nazi anti-Semitism policies came to Canada in this period.

10   Ibid., p. 121.
11   Ibid., p. 156.
12   Canadian Broadcasting Corporation, "Come to Us," television immigration documentary, November 24, 1974, Larry Zolf. See also Ted Ferguson, *A White Man's Country: An Exercise in Canadian Prejudice* (Toronto: Doubleday, 1975). A theoretical discussion of prejudice and discrimination in Canada is to be found in Jean Leonard Elliott, *Immigrant Groups* (Scarborough, Ont.: Prentice-Hall, 1971), pp. 9ff.

During World War II (1939-1945) immigration was again reduced to a trickle from continental America and was cut off almost entirely from Europe. Immediately after cessation of wartime activities in 1945, the Canadian government began to consider a policy of encouraging immigration. But shipping was at a premium and the servicemen, and in some cases their overseas., brides, were given priority. Scarcely was this process completed when the question of admittance of "displaced persons" or refugees from camps in Europe needed urgent consideration. There was also the question of the settlement of the members of the armed forces of Poland who did not wish to be repatriated. Finally, there were pressing problems of labour shortages in Canada, on the farms, in domestic service and in the textile industry.

An Order-in-Council (P.C. 3112) in July 1946 was passed "which provided for the admission from the United Kingdom and Italy of ex-servicemen from the Polish armed services."[13] Nearly 5,000 men entered Canada under this scheme. Many of them were initially directed to agriculture, mining, and to other labour-short areas.

The solution of the European refugee situation was found through making the necessary arrangements with the International Refugee Organization, "as a result of which some 166,000 displaced persons entered Canada between 1947 and 1952."[14]

Workers for the farms were sought in these immediate post-war years. Shortages of food in Europe and elsewhere gave an added impetus to the search for workers. Advertising in England was exuberant and optimistic of the prospects for new immigrants, and more especially was this true of Ontario House in London. But England, a highly industrialized country, was not the best location to search for immigrants for rural Canada, and the Canadian government eventually made arrangements with the government of the Netherlands to provide farm workers commencing in 1948. By 1952 discussions were undertaken with the Portuguese government to import farm workers and railway section hands from the Azores.

The ban on entry of former enemy aliens was lifted in 1948 so that workers were accepted from Italy, and a few years later from Germany.

In the immediate post-war period native-born youth from the farms and returning servicemen frequently sought more remunerative employment in the cities. The immigrants initially went to the farms but the majority eventually found their way to the cities also, so that the problem persisted and new rural workers were constantly being sought. Moreover, Canada's problems were being intensified in the cities by the "brain drain" of skilled and professional people to the United States during the post-war years.[15] These workers were initially replaced by attracting qualified immigrants from Northern Europe. Eventually, when these sources of supply dried up pro-

13   Anthony H. Richmond, *Post-War Immigrants in Canada* (Toronto: University of Toronto Press, 1967), p. 7.
14   Ibid., p. 9.
15   See Louis Parai, *Immigration and Emigration of Professional and Skilled Manpower During the Post-War Period*, Special Study No. 1, Economic Council of Canada (Ottawa: Queen's Printer, 1965); and Louis Parai, a paper presented to the Research Committee of the International Sociological Association, Waterloo, November 1973.

fessionals and skilled workers were taken from Southern Europe and from countries of the "Third World," with frequent protests from the latter nations that they could ill afford to give their most qualified persons to Canada.

A new Immigration Act came into force in 1953 which limited or prohibited entry of immigrants for reasons such as "ethnic group . . . peculiar customs, unsuitability, having regard to the climatic . . . conditions . . . probable inability to become readily assimilated . . ."[16] and so on. These regulations attached to the Act were amended in 1956 to give preference to persons of British birth whether from the United Kingdom or from the "white" Commonwealth countries. French citizens were also included, although few actually immigrated. Additionally, United States citizens were counted in the most favoured category. "The second order of preference was given to immigrants from western European countries if they had certain approved economic qualifications" (Richmond, 1967, p. 13). Persons from other countries could not enter unless sponsored by a close relative. Hawkins has written vividly on the consequences of sponsorship, chain migration, and the potentiality for explosive growth. "By the mid-fifties it was calculated that one Italian immigrant meant forty-nine Italian relatives, and the potential for family sponsorship was even higher" (p. 51). Sponsorship was to become a very contentious issue in the years ahead. Moreover, this aspect of the act was to change the very nature of the restricted immigration policy. W. L. Mackenzie King had stated that the Canadian people on the whole "do not wish as a result of mass immigration to make a fundamental alteration in the character of our population."[17]

When the labour market was tight in Canada during the fifties the authorities were inclined to interpret the new regulations somewhat leniently. This prompted one Member of Parliament to remark, "If you put pants on a penguin, it could be admitted to this country."[18]

In the sixties the sponsorship movement accelerated and inhabitants in large metropolitan areas such as Toronto, Montreal and Vancouver noticed large ethnic settlements in the heart of their cities. The ethnic groups were frequently from Southern Europe, Italy, Portugal and Greece. In addition, Montreal was acquiring an Arab urban intelligentsia from the Middle East.

In the years between 1953 and 1966 several crises in Europe sparked waves of immigration to Canada and elsewhere. From the crisis of November 1956 and until December 1958 a total of 37,566 Hungarian refugees were admitted on compassionate grounds.[19]

In 1957 the Suez crisis prompted many Britishers to consider emigration. Shortly thereafter, 108,989 British immigrants arrived in Canada.[20]

During the sixties, many would-be immigrants from the less favoured nations arrived in Canada as visitors and remained to work. Eventually this

16 Richmond, *Post-War Immigrants in Canada*, pp. 11-12.
17 Quoted in D. C. Corbett, *Canada's Immigration Policy: A Critique* (Toronto: University of Toronto Press, 1957), p. 36.
18 Quoted in G. A. Rawlyk, "Canada's Immigration Policy, 1945-1962," *Dalhousie Review* 42, no. 3 (1962): 287.
19 See Hawkins, *Canada and Immigration*, pp. 114-17, and John Kosa, *Land of Choice: The Hungarians in Canada* (Toronto: University of Toronto, 1957).
20 Hawkins, *Canada and Immigration*, p. 114.

situation drew the attention of the governments, both provincial and federal, following questions in the House of Commons. Joseph Sedgwick, Q.C., was retained as counsel to inquire into allegations of aliens who were reported to be detained unlawfully.[21] He recommended both prosecution and deportation, and suggested that merely detaining and deporting was insufficient. He pointed out that remaining in Canada is a privilege, not a right, and that the methods of dealing with it should be resolved in favour of Canada (II, p. 17). However, the issue was a very sensitive one among the Canadian electorate and Members of Parliament were being pressured to take an individual case to the floor of the House, often with the backing of the ethnic group in question.

In the meantime, illegal immigration was rampant and newspapers such as *The Toronto Star* featured many articles on the process. Towards the end of the decade pressure was mounting in some quarters for governmental action to be taken.[22]

In 1966, after several years of study and consideration, the Canadian government released a White Paper on Immigration delineating factors which should be taken into account in the formulation of a new policy and proposals for the direction it should take.[23]

On August 16, 1967, new immigration regulations were introduced which amended the Immigration Act (R.S.C., 1952, c. 325). "Educational preference has now replaced racial discrimination as the major criterion of Selection."[24] The system of selection was published and was based upon universalistic criteria. It has become popularly known as "The Points System."[25] In addition to being universally applicable and without discrimination in terms of race, colour, religion or national origins, two other notable features of the new immigration policy were:

> It is expansionist; it proposes the basis for a steadily active immigration policy adapted to Canada's manpower needs for economic growth.... It confirms, and in some respects extends to sponsored relatives as immigrants most of the privileges which are now enjoyed by Canadian citizens and by other people who are already permanent residents. Future immigrants will have fewer sponsorship privileges until they have lived in Canada for five years and become citizens.[26]

> Under the "points system" which came into being on August 16, 1967, the applicants are assessed on a number of criteria on the basis of a maximum of 100 points. Independent candidates (i.e., those without relatives sponsoring or nominating them) should attain at least 50 points to be admissible. The number of points allowed for independent applicants in each of the following categories is as follows:

21　Joseph Sedgwick, "The Sedgwick Report, Part I" (Ottawa, April 1965), and "The Sedgwick Report, Part II" (Ottawa, January 27, 1966). (Mimeographed.)

22　For indications of the extent of the problem see Grace M. Anderson, *Networks of Contact: The Portuguese and Toronto* (Waterloo: Wilfrid Laurier University Press, 1974).

23　Canada, Department of Manpower and Immigration, *Canadian Immigration Policy* (The White Paper on Immigration) (Ottawa: Department of Manpower and Immigration, 1966).

24　Hawkins, *Canada and Immigration*, p. 11.

25　*Office Consolidation of the Immigration Act* (Ottawa: Queen's Printer, 1968).

26　Canada, Department of Manpower and Immigration, "Immigration to Canada," p. 7.

Education and training	Maximum 20 points
Personal assessment	15
Occupational demand	15
Occupational skill	10
Age	10
Arranged employment	10
Knowledge of English and French	10
Relative in Canada	5
Employment opportunities in area of destination	5

For nominated immigrants the number of points required is calculated according to the closeness of the kin relationship. The minimum for admission of the applicant varies from 20 to 45 points.[27]

With the sweeping away of the "favoured nations" basis for acceptance of immigrants new waves of entrants appeared in Canada. The greatest advantage in the new regulations appeared to be for the non-white nations. Well-educated Indians and Pakistanis, as well as Blacks from the Caribbean entered Canada and were able to sponsor others. Simultaneously large numbers of immigrants from the United States also entered Canada. Many of these wished to escape the racial violence and tension of cities to the south of the border. Some came to avoid the draft into the armed forces, and as a negative response to the American involvement in the Vietnam War.

Cities such as Toronto were aware, as the sixties drew to a close, that the origins of immigrants arriving in their city was radically changing. In the early sixties the increase in Southern Europeans had been noted. In the late sixties, the shift to a larger proportion of West Indian immigrants was evident.

> Between 1946 and 1970, the largest number of Canadian immigrants came from Britain, Italy, the United States and Germany in that order. . . . Over the past three years, the number of immigrants from Europe has been decreasing, while immigrants from the United States and the West Indies have dramatically increased. These trends are accentuated in the first half of 1971. According to 1970 estimates, British and Italian are still the two largest ethnic groups. . . . Negro has risen to third place from seventh in 1966; Portuguese still occupies fourth place in rank; East Indian . . . moved into fifth place.[28]

This movement was felt particularly in Toronto since that city became the major recipient of immigrants during this period.

Although the basic premise that some nations were to be more favoured than others was officially removed, the situation was not one of total equality. The location and the size of the visa offices in part determined how many applicants could be processed. Some offices always operated with insufficient staff to handle the applicants promptly and some had a backlog of one or two years.[29]

27 Anderson, *Networks of Contact*, pp. 43-44.
28 Ontario, Department of the Provincial Secretary and Citizenship, *Current Immigration Trends: Research Report* (Toronto: Department of the Provincial Secretary and Citizenship, Research Branch, 1971), pp. 2, 15.
29 See Hawkins, *Canada and Immigration*, chs. 9 and 10.

In 1967 visitors were given the opportunity to apply for landed immigrant status while already in Canada. This step had been recommended in the first Sedgwick report as one way of combatting some of the problems associated with the presence of relatively large numbers of "visitors" illegally working in Canada. However, while many took advantage of this aspect of the new regulations, others entered Canada with the intention of working before they received the necessary permission to do so. The problem expanded in scope enormously with this unanticipated turn of events. In addition, an Immigration Appeal Board was also set up that year and began to hear appeals late in 1967 (Hawkins, 1972, p. 166). "Visitors" who had thus been rejected could extend their stay in Canada for many years. By July 1970 it was obvious that the situation was out of hand as the Board was flooded by appeals and a considerable backlog of appeal applicants had been accumulated. Mr. Joseph Sedgwick, Q.C. was again called in to study the situation. His report was available in October of that year.[30]

A period of amnesty was announced for "visitors" to declare themselves and to make application for remaining in Canada as landed immigrants. Appeals in the mass media, in English, French, and in many other languages were made over a period of many months. It was also announced that the opportunity for persons to apply within Canada would be withdrawn very shortly and therefore all resident "visitors" were urged to make application immediately. About 50,000 persons came forward at this time and on November 1, 1973, the period of amnesty was ended and all future applicants were received only in the countries of origin. However, the problem of working "visitors" remains. It has been suggested that only one-third or one-quarter of the total number actually came forward at that time.

As the policies of the post-war period are examined, it is apparent that the acts and regulations have been guidelines which were applied more or less stringently from time to time according to the labour requirements of the country. (It is well known that immigration volume follows the economy with a time lag of about one year.)[31] This process of labour control has been referred to as the "tap-on, tap-off" policy, as overseas offices are requested to restrain immigration in a time of recession or to encourage it in a period of prosperity. However, in part, the process is automatic since word filters back to the sending countries during periods of high unemployment, and immigration slows down.

With the influx of many immigrants of non-English and non-French background, the Canadian government's official policy of "Bilingualism and Biculturalism" was questioned by spokesmen for the other immigrant groups. Yuzyk spoke of the Third Force and tried to organize it through conferences; but he had limited success because of the disparity of those he wished to include.[32] Frequently it was the second and third generation

30   Joseph Sedgwick, *Report on Applicants in Canada* (Ottawa: Queen's Printer, 1970).
31   Ontario, Department of the Provincial Secretary and Citizenship, *Current Immigration Trends*, pp. 4-6.
32   See Elizabeth Wangenheim, "The Ukranians: A Case Study of the 'Third Force'," in *Canadian Society: Sociological Perspectives*, ed. Bernard R. Blishen et al., 3rd ed. (Toronto: Macmillan, 1968), pp. 648-66.

FIGURE 1

POST-WAR IMMIGRANTS TO CANADA AND EMPLOYMENT RATES, 1946-1970

In thousands

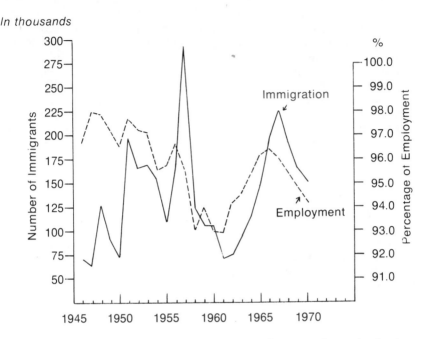

Source: Ontario, Department of the Provincial Secretary and Citizenship, *Current Immigration Trends: Research Report* (Toronto: Department of the Provincial Secretary and Citizenship, Research Branch, 1971).

immigrants who were most vocal on this issue, and often Ukrainians were in the forefront:

> Senator Paul Yuzyk, Manitoba-born of Ukrainian origin, in his maiden speech in the Canadian Senate on May 3, 1964, discussed the emergence of a "Third Force" made up of all those Canadians who are of non-English and non-French origin. Senator Yuzyk cited 1961 census figures to show that this Third Force now constitutes 26 per cent of the population of Canada, but its proportion in the three Prairie provinces ranges from 48 per cent to 53 per cent. Senator Yuzyk suggested that the ethnic groups which constitute this Third Force have, because of their minority status, much in common and that as a united group they can hold the balance of power between the English and the French.[33]

This speech doubtless came as a response to the formation on July 19, 1963 of the *Royal Commission on Bilingualism and Biculturalism* "to recommend what steps should be taken to develop the Canadian Confederation on the basis of an equal partnership between the two founding races, taking into account the contribution made by the other ethnic groups to the

33 Ibid., p. 648.

cultural enrichment of Canada and the measures that should be taken to safeguard that contribution. . . ."[34]

The Government's response to *Book IV* of the *Report of the Royal Commission on Bilingualism and Biculturalism* was announced by the Prime Minister, Pierre Elliott Trudeau, on October 8, 1971, in the form of a new policy of multiculturalism within a bilingual framework. A series of programmes was subsequently announced to implement this new official policy.[35] Members of all ethnic groups were encouraged to retain aspects of their cultures. The two *official* languages remain, but unofficially Canada is becoming much more multilingual as waves of new immigrants arrive with their varied languages and backgrounds. In the early and mid-seventies in areas of heavy ethnic concentration, languages other than those traditionally taught have begun to make their appearance in high school curricula of the largest urban centres.

THE ISSUES

The question of open or, alternatively, selective immigration raises at least three major issues: should we have open immigration or should we be selective, and if we select, on what basis should this be done? How many immigrants should Canada admit? When?

In the historical overview it is apparent that a completely open policy for white immigrants, and a very highly restrictive one for non-whites, was operated until 1924. The settling of large tracts of land in Western Canada was of major concern. The immigrants who were most attracted at this time to this process were from Northern Europe.

By 1924, a radical change in policy took place when a system of priorities was set up according to national background of the prospective immigrants. Britain and France, together with the United States and the "white" Commonwealth countries were declared to be the most favoured nations from which immigrants would be accepted. But within these countries very little selectivity was exercised provided that the persons were willing to work. While this policy appeared on the surface to be a change of direction, in reality it continued to produce the same type of immigration which had taken place during the previous century. New pressures came into being and this act prompted new barriers to be raised against them.

The act which came into force in 1953 was designed to accelerate immigration which would be geared to "absorptive capacity." This phrase was employed to get around an awkward situation in which it was thought desirable to exclude persons from countries whose nationals were thought to be assimilated less easily, and yet to avoid the *appearance* of racial or ethnic prejudice. It was selective in terms of estimated assimilative ability, and this was usually gauged by race, ethnicity and religious background.

Gradually the regulations were relaxed and interpretation of the act became much more liberal in the late fifties and early and mid-sixties so that

---

34 *Report of the Royal Commission on Bilingualism*, pp. 235-36, also gives further details of this mandate.
35 An outline is given in Hawkins, *Canada and Immigration*, pp. 368-89.

large numbers of immigrants from Southern Europe were able to enter Canada at that time.

In centennial year, 1967, a partial change in emphasis in policy took place. While the original act was retained, the regulations governing it changed very drastically. The criteria for selection switched from stressing race, ethnicity and religion to stressing occupational skills and education. A universalistic system was introduced. This opened Canada to many highly educated persons of the formerly little-favoured nations and races. Non-white racial groups entered in relatively large numbers, especially in certain occupations in which there were critical manpower shortages. The largest metropolitan cities experienced an influx of Blacks from the United States and the Caribbean, Indians and Pakistanis, and Chinese from Hong Kong. Many of these recent entrants are highly educated.

How many immigrants Canada should admit is still debatable. In the nineteenth century the railways were actively promoting immigration. Initially they needed labour to build the railbeds and lay the tracks. When sufficient immigrants and native-born workers were not forthcoming they opted for the importation of Chinese coolies for completion of these tasks. After the railway lines were completed across the continent the companies sought to actively promote immigration as a means of filling up the wide expanses of prairie with a farming population in order to make their companies viable, both as passenger and as freight carriers. (It is, of course, well known that the completion of the Canadian Pacific Railway to the Pacific coast was part of the bargain under which British Columbia entered Confederation. The railway was one of the means by which Canada was being united as a nation.)

The owners and managers of private industries in the cities and small towns also frequently viewed an open immigration policy as desirable, for they looked to it to provide the necessary labour, both skilled and unskilled for their plants and workshops at competitive prices.

Labour unions have traditionally been opposed to policies which favoured large-scale immigration. They have regarded it as the cause of the maintenance of lower wages affecting their membership, and especially the native-born. In the twentieth century, unions with large proportions of foreign-born workers have sometimes modified their position in this regard.

However, the dichotomy has continued into the twentieth century. The traditional patterns of viewing the labour market are frequently upheld. Employers and managers often support an "open door" policy which, in the nineteenth century was dubbed a "take millions" policy, whereas native-born workers have continued to favour a much more restrictive policy. Foreign-born workers, on the other hand, often express support of continued large-scale immigration, especially where it favours their own ethnic group.

While Quebec remained traditionally hostile to large-scale immigration, Prime Minister Diefenbaker in 1957 advocated a policy of "populate or perish,"[36] but nevertheless during his years as Prime Minister, immigration

36 Ibid., p. 127.

was restricted as indicated by the statistics. Other areas of the country varied according to region and to ethnic background, as a study by Jones and Lambert demonstrates.[37] As Hawkins clearly points out in her book (1972), the major determinant of immigration policy has been current labour requirements. This has become very explicit in recent years when the separate functions of Manpower and Immigration have been linked in one department. However, the labour policy is often formulated in terms of immediate market needs, whereas immigration policy needs to be formulated on a steady, long-term basis. This "tap-on, tap-off" process can be expected to induce antagonism in the contributing countries.

Our policies have frequently been modified for humanitarian reasons. The sponsorship programme in recent years has been an example of this policy. Native-born Canadians are usually sympathetic to individual cases, yet there had been much criticism, both in public and in private, of the admittance of large numbers of unskilled labourers, especially in times of high unemployment. One recent study has indicated that these minimally-educated immigrant workers do find jobs and that the "points system" may not be a very adequate measure of future effectiveness of unskilled labour.[38]

The admittance of refugees has been a continuing process in Canadian history. Ukrainians, Jews, Poles, Latvians, Lithuanians, Czechoslovakians, Hungarians, Tibetans and Asian Ugandans and many others have all been admitted to Canada, with little selectivity exercised in some cases. Often the question is raised, "How many refugees can Canada absorb without severe detriment to the quality of life of its own people?"

In a freely elected democracy such as Canada, decisions are often based upon political expediency. The politicians are subjected to all sorts of pressures from groups and individuals within their own ridings. The political process operates in the short run under these conditions. But immigration policy needs to be made with long-run objectives in mind. One way out of this dilemma, taken from time to time by the Canadian government, has been the appointment of relatively autonomous Commissions and Boards of Enquiry. These can offer advice which is designed to obviate some of the long-run problems. But whether this advice will be heeded may depend upon public opinion and pressures brought to bear upon the politicians by special interest groups.

Political expediency may also be dictated by foreign policy considerations. For example, requests for increased immigration from the Soviet Union will only be made when it is thought that this will not upset the sometimes-precarious negotiations in other areas.

The question of when to admit larger volumes of immigrants has in recent years been tied to the labour market, as discussed earlier. In the nineteenth and early twentieth centuries this was thought to be a self-regulatory proc-

37 Frank E. Jones and Wallace E. Lambert, "Attitudes Toward Immigrants in a Canadian Community," in *Canadian Society: Sociological Perspectives*, ed. B. Blishen et al., rev. ed. (Toronto: Macmillan, 1964), pp. 95-104.
38 Anderson, "Canadian Immigration Policy and Non-Policy," in *Networks of Contact*, pp. 43-67.

ess for the most part. Now the Canadian government attempts to plan the process. Nevertheless, sponsorship, if allowed to grow unfettered, can make a shambles of any planning. Thoughtful people are asking the question, "How much sponsored immigration can we afford to allow?"

The entrance of persons who have entered Canada illegally also brings other questions to the surface: "Are we willing to allow citizenship to a large number of persons who have already indicated their contempt for the law?" "Will this eventually bring the laws of the country into disrepute?" and "How much law-breaking can a nation afford and still remain under the rule of law?"

"Is it a right or a privilege to enter Canada?" Since 1924, at least, politicians have usually emphasized that it is a privilege which can be denied. It is only in recent years that the right of appeal has been granted. The mass media has sometimes raised the issue of how long this process should be allowed to drag on, while those denied entry continue to remain in this country until they have exhausted all recourse to the full legal process in a series of appeals. "Should the reasons for denial be made public?" Formerly, immigration officials were given considerable leeway in exercising their judgment as to the suitability of the applicant. There is relatively little room for the exercise of discretion in the new "points system." One important question which is allowed little consideration is, "Will the applicant become a law-abiding, responsible citizen eventually?" Obviously the question of the interest of the individual may be in conflict with the interests of the state in some cases.

Hawkins (p. 279) has rightly pointed out that there was an unintended bias in the legal system of appeals "in favour of those countries where the exercise of political pressure and the use of influence were common practice." Is it desirable that this bias should continue?

In a consideration of the issues Canadians recall that they are a "nation of immigrants." Often, throughout our history, immigrants have been called in to provide the skills that we lacked and at a time when we were unable to provide them for ourselves. Immigrants have continued to also fill the positions in the labour market that native-born Canadians declined to occupy. They have often worked at the most hazardous and least-remunerated jobs, sometimes in isolated locations or under unfavourable working conditions. Each ethnic group says proudly, "We helped to build Canada," and many have made a sizeable and sometimes unique contribution. Small wonder, then, that immigration and ethnic groups continue to be a major topic for research and specialization in Canada to an extent seldom exceeded in other parts of the world.[39]

PROGRAMMES OF IMMIGRANT AID

Recent programmes and services for immigrants have been described by Hawkins (1972, p. 279) as

> piecemeal and inadequate and that, in general, the immigrant has had better service before arriving in Canada than after. Many officers expressed the view

---

39 S. D. Clark, "Sociology in Canada: An Historical Over-view," unpublished paper presented to the International Sociological Association meetings, Toronto, 1974.

that there had been a continuing failure at both federal and provincial levels to provide proper services for immigrants in Canada.

In some cities the municipality also attempted to provide some services, largely through (often partial) financial assistance to voluntary agencies. The official provision for the needs of immigrants on arrival in this country has been largely a post-World War II development. The Department of Manpower and Immigration sees one of its prime responsibilities as the assisting of members of the work force to obtain suitable employment.[40] This includes courses to retrain immigrant workers and directing them into courses to gain a facility in one of the official languages, where necessary. In the early fifties, language courses for "New Canadians" were frequently handled on an unpaid voluntary basis, often through interested organizations such as churches. Later, these courses were transferred, for the most part, to Adult Education Centres. Frequently these were run in conjunction with Community Colleges. Workers were offered a subsistence allowance both for themselves and for their dependents while they studied.

Other aspects of immigrant need frequently fell initially within the area of services provided by the Department of Citizenship (which in 1966 became the Citizenship Branch of the Secretary of State's Office). It

> would be more concerned with the social, political, and cultural integration of immigrants. The Citizenship Branch would continue to work with the provinces and voluntary organizations in the provision of classes for immigrants in language training and citizenship. There would in fact be two language-training programs, one oriented to employability and the other to the integration process generally.[41]

Hawkins suggests, however, that the agreement separating the functions of immigrant servicing into the Immigration Branch of the Department of Manpower and Immigration and the Citizenship Branch of the Secretary of State's Office has created a "federal twilight zone" of responsibility (p. 156). To this is added in the provinces of Ontario and Quebec a Department of Immigration and Citizenship to stimulate both immigration and services for immigrants and to provide research facilities. There are also services provided by some municipalities and voluntary organizations on both the national and local level. It is readily appreciated that the bewildered immigrant is confronted with a battery of services operating in a more or less unco-ordinated manner. Some cities attempt to bring services together under an umbrella organization such as a City Social Planning Service. In other areas immigrant services are facilitated by an International Institute. For immigrants belonging to well-organized ethnic groups, an ethnic association may assist them by operating either as an independent group or through an ethnic church group. C.O.S.T.I. is well known in Southern Ontario as a group which assists Italian immigrants and in some areas services Portuguese immigrants also. Religious organizations have frequently provided services, especially for their own members. These include The Jewish Immigrant Aid Services of Canada, Service d'Accueil

40　For details of the objectives of the Department, see Hawkins, *Canada and Immigration*, p. 392.
41　Ibid., p. 155.

aux Voyageurs et aux Immigrants (S.A.V.I.) in Montreal, Catholic Immigrant Aid Society, The Baptist Federation of Canada, and the Salvation Army. There are many others.

Often the voluntary organizations look after the immediate needs of the new arrivals. The larger ones, which operate with trained social workers fluent in several languages, attempt to meet most of the needs which confront immigrants in a strange land.

Often local ethnic associations will attempt to fill gaps of which they are particularly aware through special services. This is frequently done with the assistance of government grants. Sometimes this includes the publishing of lists of services in the mother-tongue of the immigrants. Usually, however, these services are specific to a particular ethnic group. Because the funding of these programmes is uncertain, their services tend to be sporadic. Nevertheless, they often fill a crucial role during times of heavy immigration and sometimes before a second generation has grown to maturity in Canada to provide bilingual personnel.

Voluntary associations often provide services for mothers of young children. They offer translation services and general information on government services available to the immigrant for the asking. Often they operate in an area of the city which is known to be an immigrant reception district. These neighbourhood, and sometimes store-front offices, appear to the immigrants to be more accessible than those services available in large government buildings, especially to immigrants coming from a peasant background or from totalitarian countries, where all forms of contact with the government might be regarded with distrust.

But still gaps remain in the services, or, more frequently, in bringing those in need in touch with the services provided. Often these gaps have been initially filled by ethnic travel agents, owners of restaurants and by proprietors of food stores in ethnic neighbourhoods. Often these services are freely provided. In some cases, though, considerable fees have been charged for services such as translation or assistance with income tax forms which are available free or at a nominal charge elsewhere. Sponsored, almost-illiterate, immigrants are, of course, the most vulnerable.

In some areas certain retired people with linguistic skills are well known in a particular ethnic community for rendering service to needy immigrants, either with no charge or for a minimal fee. Informally, librarians may be approached through the children, or school teachers, for help in finding an agency for coping with a specific problem.

The topic of immigrant programmes is vast. The answers are usually very specific to a particular location in Canada, to a particular ethnic and religious group. To find one's way through the maze of helping organizations and services, both formal and informal, requires the resources of a very intelligent person with fluency in English or French. The amazing thing is not how little help the immigrants receive but rather how much they locate in spite of all the inadequacies of the system. The referral systems of the voluntary organizations and government agencies help to form a network of services, which although often lacking in particular programmes, nevertheless co-opt the assistance of individuals to fill the needs where possible. The real problem lies in getting immigrants in touch with some portion of this network of assistance.

THE CURRENT SITUATION

At the present time there is a ferment of activity going on in Ottawa in regard to immigration, but much of this is taking place beyond public view.

A Task Force of the Citizenship Branch, Secretary of State's Office, has examined the federal responsibilities for immigrant services. In an early report it found "that there was a serious state of under-development in the area of services and programs for immigrants, migrants and refugees in Canada."[42]

> As well as the Canadian Immigration and Population Study, an Interdepartmental Committee is examining the proposals of a recent Task Force on Services and Programs for Immigrants, Migrants and Refugees and is expected to make recommendations to Cabinet in the near future.[43]

The Department of Manpower and Immigration in Ottawa has been conducting a longitudinal study on "The Economic and Social Adaptation of Immigrants" over a period of several years. This study is particularly interesting because it follows the same group of immigrants over a three-year period. Comparisons are made with a control group of Canadian residents who also received questionnaires. The findings are based on responses from 2,037 persons and deal with topics such as employment experience and income, residential mobility, cultural identity and motivation. Hidden within the wealth of statistics are hints of the lifestyle of immigrants during the initial period of adjustment, e.g., "Immigrant workers were twice as mobile as the average Canadian resident."[44]

The Green Paper on Immigration finally made its appearance in February 1975. But public interest in the topic of immigration had been greatly underestimated, for only 5,000 copies were published and many highly-interested persons waited several months before copies became generally available. The Green Paper itself consists of four volumes dealing with different aspects of immigration. Volume 1 discusses immigration policy perspectives. In volume 2 the evolution of policy since Confederation is reviewed. Volume 3 gives statistical data, much of which had not been readily available previously. The fourth volume reports on the longitudinal study mentioned above.[45]

42 Ibid., p. 152.
43 Ibid., p. 141.
44 Canada, Department of Manpower and Immigration, *Three Years in Canada: First Report of the Longitudinal Survey on the Economic and Social Adaptation of Immigrants* (popularly referred to as vol. 4 of the Green Paper) (Ottawa, 1974), p. 75.
45 Canada, Department of Manpower and Immigration, *Immigration Policy Perspectives: A Report of the Canadian Immigration and Population Study* vol. 1 of the Green Paper (Ottawa: Department of Manpower and Immigration, 1974); *The Immigration Program: A Report of the Canadian Immigration and Population Study*, vol. 2 of the Green Paper (Ottawa: Department of Manpower and Immigration, 1974); *Immigration and Population Statistics: Canadian Immigration and Population Study*, vol. 3 of the Green Paper (Ottawa: Department of Manpower and Immigration, 1975); and *Three Years in Canada: First Report of the Longitudinal Survey on the Economic and Social Adaptation of Immigrants* (Ottawa: Department of Manpower and Immigration, 1974).

The policy alternatives are presented on the general supposition that immigrants are to fill Canadian manpower needs—the entire policy is tailored to suit Canada's economic needs. But in what ways would this have been different if the policy had had a predominantly humanitarian orientation? The stated aim of the policy is to shape change "to yield the largest measure of self-fulfilment for present and future generations of Canadians" (vol. 1, p. 1). We find it hard to like self-centred people; are self-centred nations any more attractive?

In spite of the general tenor of the policy statement, the first chapter of volume 1 concludes, "the character of our society demands a policy approach that is non-discriminatory and humane; one that emphasizes the dignity of the individual immigrant, and the value of his or her potential contribution to the Canadian community" (vol. 1, p. 17).

The Green Paper was designed to stimulate discussion among the general population and to present a set of alternatives. Basically the Green Paper asks, how much growth do Canadians want, and what are the social costs of immigration, as well as the advantages? Some of the most intriguing facets of this discussion are the gaps in policy directions which were not discussed and which pose a series of intriguing questions. How, for instance, do we prevent immigrants from congregating in the largest metropolitan centres? Can we persuade them to settle in less-populated parts of the country? How would this be enforced without resorting to dictatorial methods?[46]

Several interesting, although rather technical, documents supplement the Green Paper. They examine in detail such topics as the impact of immigration on language imbalance between English- and French-speaking groups.[47] It is well known that the majority of immigrants prefer to assimilate to English-speaking Canada. One study compares the Canadian population policy, which is intimately tied to immigration policies, with those of the United States, Australia and Israel. Space precludes further discussion of these enlightening papers.[48]

Shortly after the Green Paper documents were published a commission was set up to tour the country and to receive briefs.[49] Many disparate

46 See Grace M. Anderson, "Gaps in Green Paper Raise Intriguing Questions," *Kitchener-Waterloo Record*, June 28, 1975, and other Southern Ontario Newspapers for further discussion of this topic, and "Special Issue: The Green Paper," *Canadian Ethnic Studies* 7, no. 1 (1975).

47 Jacques Henripin, *Immigration and Language Imbalance: Canadian Immigration and Population Study* (Ottawa: Department of Manpower and Immigration, 1974).

48 Raymond Breton, Jill Armstrong, and Les Kennedy, *The Social Impact of Changes in Population Size and Composition* (Ottawa: Manpower and Immigration, 1974); Larry Epstein, *Immigration and Inflation* (Ottawa: Department of Manpower and Immigration, 1974); Freda Hawkins, *Immigration Policy and Management in Selected Countries: A Study of Immigration Policy and Management and their Implications for Population Growth in the United States, Australia and Israel* (Ottawa: Department of Manpower and Immigration, 1974); Warren E. Kalbach, *The Effect of Immigration on Population* (Ottawa: Manpower and Immigration, 1974); Anthony H. Richmond, *Aspects of the Absorption and Adaptation of Immigrants* (Ottawa: Manpower and Immigration, 1974); Nancy Tienhaara, *Canadian Views on Immigration and Population: An Analysis of Post-War Gallup Polls* (Ottawa: Manpower and Immigration, 1974).

49 Special Joint Committee on Immigration Policy of the Parliament of Canada, 1975.

opinions and briefs were collected ranging from groups such as the Canadian Civil Liberties Association to others like the Young Women's Christian Association. Ethnic groups were usually not reticent to make their voices heard also.

During the summer of 1975 the Canadian Council on Social Development commissioned Professor William Nichols to undertake a research project on informed reaction to the Green Paper. The discussion in his subsequent report revolves around the kind of country Canadians want in the future —but since there is no consensus he concludes that "the changes have been overlaid on top of older policies."[50] Nichols presents three basic paradigms of the goals of Canadians, namely, personal self-interest, national economic interest, and human interest. He suggests that these three are conflicting goals, so that persons tend to react ambiguously. Problems he discussed with groups and individuals across the country concern the size of population thought desirable in the future for Canada, the distribution of population and cultural composition and character. The report emphasized that the government services tended to focus on needs of the breadwinner and to ignore other equally urgent needs of the immigrant family members.

Many other conferences and discussion groups, both large and small, academic or laymen, formal and informal, met across Canada during the period immediately following the publication of the government Green Paper documents. However, many specialists voiced the opinion that discussion is inappropriate in this highly complex and technical field. Others emphasized that certain topics cannot be discussed openly without sparking a public furor. Sensitive issues include the carrying of diseases to this country from other areas of the world, and the appearance of activities which are thought to be associated with the illegal entry of would-be immigrants.

Much discussion was generated around the topic of whether the proposal-alternatives put forward in the Green Paper are tinged with racism. The regulations of 1967 attempted to create, through the points system, a non-discriminatory admission policy. However, certain crucial incidents in Canada's past have made a lasting impression on many ethnic groups: the Komagata Maru incident in 1914 where East Indians were turned away, the scapegoating of Jewish persons in World War II in Montreal, the internment of West Coast Japanese Canadians during the early part of that same war—these incidents recall prejudice and discrimination which many Canadians would prefer to forget. But the question remains as to how many non-white immigrants Canadians are prepared to receive. One television commentator described Canadians as "a nation of Archie Bunkers." If the government pushes too hard for increased non-white immigration it may experience a severe backlash. Often Canadians find that their ideology, based upon the Judeo-Christian tradition, favours non-discrimination but that their experience in the economic marketplace favours restrictive policies. How will the Canadian people resolve this dilemma? Presumably the government can only "make haste slowly." It can

50   William M. Nichols, *What Kind of Canada Do We Want? A Special Project on Population and Immigration Policies* (Ottawa: The Canadian Council on Social Development, 1975), p. 20.

legislate against discrimination but legislation cannot eliminate prejudice which can be applied in very subtle ways. Unless the government can find ways of preventing the conglomeration of large non-white ghettos in the major metropolitan centres without abrogating human rights, they are liable to run into roadblocks in the attempted passage of further non-discriminatory legislation. After all, politicians are only in office in the short run (which, of course, they try to prolong as much as possible). Eventually political expediency usually wins out over considerations of fair play and humanitarian interests.

On November 24, 1976 the long-awaited new immigration act was given first reading in the House of Commons, Ottawa.[51] Basically the proposed act outlines the setting of an annual global ceiling on the numbers of immigrants from all countries who are allowed to enter the country. It also proposes that a visa obtained in the country of origin be required of both immigrants and visitors for entry into Canada. The purposes of the new act are listed at length and include proposed legislation "to support the attainment of such demographic goals as may be established by the government of Canada from time to time in respect of the size, rate of growth, structure and geographic distribution of the Canadian population" (p. 5).

The act also stipulates that the standards of admission are to be "that they do not discriminate on grounds of race, national or ethnic origin, colour, religion or sex" (p. 5). Canada affirms her continued interest in upholding her humanitarian traditions with respect to convention refugees. Also, immigration policy continues to be regarded as a tool to "foster the development of a strong and viable economy and the prosperity of all regions in Canada" (p. 5).

This proposal implies that immigrants would initially be directed to parts of the country needing their labour and services, and presumably away from the largest metropolitan areas.

The trend of government thinking was apparent when the Immigration Department was subordinated to the Department of Manpower where economists dominate the research division. Citizenship is separated from Immigration and is a subdivision of the Office of the Secretary of State, as also is the Directorate of Multiculturalism.

The ethnic press has already reacted strongly against the new law stating in some cases that photographs and fingerprints will be demanded (although the format of the visa has not been given in the act).[52] It is also proposed that the number of appeals permissible be lowered.

While representatives of ethnic associations and media are attacking the bill for being too constrictive, other Canadians have reacted against the bill as not being sufficiently rigorous in blocking immigrant entry during times of economic difficulty. They question whether Canada needs more immigrants in view of ecological issues such as pollution, overcrowding and congestion, lack of housing and shortages of energy.[53]

51 Canada, Parliament, *An Act Respecting Immigration to Canada, First Reading*, Bill C-24, The House of Commons of Canada, The Minister of Manpower and Immigration, November 24, 1976.
52 See "Immigrantes Amenazados," *El Popular*, December 13, 1976.
53 Anthony H. Richmond, "Environmental Conservation and Immigration: A New Racist Ideol-

IMMIGRATION AND SOCIAL POLICY

It is apparent that the subject of immigration has been approached piecemeal, and that there is no overall social policy. For one thing, the newly-arrived immigrants find that the implementation of government policy takes place at the federal, provincial and municipal levels. There are usually social service programmes to take care of the various and sundry needs of the immigrants but it would take a highly-literate and articulate person, fluent in one of the official languages, to be able to find his way through the maze of red tape in order to take advantage of these available services. Some ethnic groups have attempted to solve this problem by having specialized local agencies to handle immigrant problems in the language of the recently arrived. Frequently these programmes are handled by volunteers or are underwritten by short-term grants and are therefore leading a tenuous existence. Voluntary organizations have the advantage that they try to avoid the formal settings and rigid office hours of many government agencies. Usually immigrants who are lone representatives of an ethnic group in an area find themselves in very great need of assistance and they are the ones who have the most difficulty finding persons who can help them. By the time large numbers of an ethnic group settle in an area, programmes are set up to help them. But by then, the period of greatest need has passed. A strange irony!

A recent example of piecemeal social policy is the case of the high incidence of industrial accidents among Italian workers and the "hot-line" set-up in Toronto to attempt to control dangerous working conditions. Many are working for small construction contractors where safety regulations may be disregarded. While this telephone programme is a very commendable action at the local level, it is just one example of a single, small piecemeal solution to a massive country-wide social problem among many groups of immigrant workers.

CONCLUSIONS

Because such a large proportion of the population of Canada's major metropolitan centres is made up of immigrants, it is clear that piecemeal or inadequate social policies will have major repercussions when needs are not met and problems abound. While trying to integrate social policies to make them equally applicable to all sectors of the population, we run the risk of neglecting urgent social needs of a disadvantaged and frequently inarticulate segment of our Canadian society.

The production of a series of ethnic histories of immigration to Canada has already commenced. More than twenty have been projected, several have already been published. Considerable amounts of original research material have been incorporated into some of these volumes.[54]

ogy?" York University, Toronto. (Mimeographed.) Summary version of a paper presented at the Bicentennial Conference on "The New Immigration: Implications for the United States and the International Community," Smithsonian Institution on Immigration and Ethnic Studies, Washington, D.C., November 15-17, 1976.

54 Henry Redecki with B. Heydenkorn, *A Member of a Distinguished Family: The Polish Group in Canada* (Toronto: McClelland and Stewart, 1976); Grace M. Anderson and David Higgs, *A Future to Inherit: Portuguese Communities in Canada* (Toronto: McClelland and Stewart,

In conclusion, Canada is still in the midst of hammering out an immigration policy on the anvil of public opinion. The issues are complex, informed laymen are few, and the public speaks with many voices. It is apparent, however, that we are about to embark on a set of policies which stem from new compromises of many widely-differing viewpoints.

BIBLIOGRAPHY

Anderson, Grace M. "Gaps in Green Paper Raise Intriguing Questions." *Kitchener-Waterloo Record*, June 28, 1975.

_____. *Networks of Contact: The Portuguese and Toronto.* Waterloo: Wilfrid Laurier University Press, 1974.

_____, and Higgs, David. *A Future to Inherit: Portuguese Communities in Canada.* Toronto: McClelland and Stewart, 1976.

Bradwin, Edmund. *The Bunkhouse Man: Life and Labour in the Northern Work Camps.* Toronto: University of Toronto Press, 1972.

Breton, Raymond; Armstrong, Jill; and Kennedy, Les. *The Social Impact of Changes in Population Size and Composition.* Ottawa: Manpower and Immigration, 1974.

Canada. Department of Manpower and Immigration. *Canadian Immigration Policy* (The White Paper on Immigration). Ottawa: Department of Manpower and Immigration, 1966.

_____. *Immigration Policy Perspectives: A Report of the Canadian Immigration and Population Study.* Vol. 1 of the Green Paper. Ottawa: Department of Manpower and Immigration, 1974. *The Immigration Program: A Report of the Canadian Immigration and Population Study.* Vol. 2 of the Green Paper. Ottawa: Department of Manpower and Immigration, 1974. *Immigration and Population Statistics: Canadian Immigration and Population Study.* Vol. 3 of the Green Paper. Ottawa: Department of Manpower and Immigration, 1975. *Three Years in Canada: First Report of the Longitudinal Survey on the Economic and Social Adaptation of Immigrants.* Popularly referred to as vol. 4 of the Green Paper. Ottawa: Department of Manpower and Immigration, 1974.

_____. "Immigration to Canada." Fact Sheet, Info/9. Ottawa: Department of Manpower and Immigration, Immigration Information Service, 1969. Mimeographed.

_____. *1972, Immigration Statistics.* Ottawa: Information Canada for Department of Manpower and Immigration, 1974.

Canada. Parliament. *An Act Respecting Immigration to Canada, First Reading.* Bill C-24. The House of Commons of Canada, The Minister of Manpower and Immigration, November 24, 1976.

Canadian Broadcasting Corporation. "Come to Us." Television immigration documentary. November 24, 1974. Larry Zolf.

Canadian Family Tree: Centennial Edition 1867-1967. Ottawa: Queen's Printer, 1967.

Clarke, S. D. "Sociology in Canada: An Historical Over-view." Unpublished paper presented to the International Sociological Association meetings, Toronto, 1974.

Corbett, D. C. *Canada's Immigration Policy: A Critique.* Toronto: University of Toronto Press, 1957.

Council on French Life in America. "The Fertility Crisis in Quebec." In *Critical Issues in Canadian Society*, pp. 6-11. Edited by Craig L. Boydell et al. Toronto and Montreal: Holt, Rinehart and Winston, 1971.

1976); Stanford Reid, ed., *The Scottish Tradition in Canada* (Toronto: McClelland and Stewart, 1976). Other ethnic histories will follow as they are completed. Each of these histories gives accounts of the early struggles of immigrant pioneers from their own perspectives.

Dawson, C. A. *Group Settlement: Ethnic Communities in Western Canada.* Toronto: Macmillan, 1936.

Elliott, Jean Leonard. *Immigrant Groups.* Scarborough, Ont.: Prentice-Hall, 1971.

Epstein, Larry. *Immigration and Inflation.* Ottawa: Department of Manpower and Immigration, 1974.

Ferguson, Ted. *A White Man's Country: An Exercise in Canadian Prejudice.* Toronto: Doubleday, 1975.

Hawkins, Freda. *Canada and Immigration: Public Policy and Public Concern.* Montreal: McGill-Queen's University Press, 1972.

_____. *Immigration Policy and Management in Selected Countries: A Study of Immigration Policy and Management and their Implications for Population Growth in the United States, Australia and Israel.* Ottawa: Department of Manpower and Immigration, 1974.

Henripin, Jacques. *Immigration and Language Imbalance: Canadian Immigration and Population Study.* Ottawa: Department of Manpower and Immigration, 1974.

"Immigrantes Amenazados." *El Popular,* December 13, 1976.

Jenness, R. A. "Canadian Migration and Immigration Patterns and Government Policy." *International Migration Review* 8, no. 1 (1974): 5-22.

Jones, Frank E., and Lambert, Wallace E. "Attitudes Toward Immigrants in a Canadian Community." In *Canadian Society: Sociological Perspectives*, pp. 95-104. Edited by B. Blishen et al. Rev. ed. Toronto: Macmillan, 1964.

Kalbach, Warren E. *The Effect of Immigration on Population.* Ottawa: Manpower and Immigration, 1974.

Kosa, John. *Land of Choice: The Hungarians in Canada.* Toronto: University of Toronto, 1957.

Nichols, William M. *What Kind of Canada Do We Want? A Special Project on Population and Immigration Policies.* Ottawa: The Canadian Council on Social Development, 1975, p. 20.

Office Consolidation of the Immigration Act. Ottawa: Queen's Printer, 1968.

Ontario. Department of the Provincial Secretary and Citizenship. *Current Immigration Trends: Research Report.* Toronto: Department of the Provincial Secretary and Citizenship, Research Branch, 1971.

Parai, Louis. *Immigration and Emigration of Professional and Skilled Manpower During the Post-War Period.* Special Study No. 1, Economic Council of Canada. Ottawa: Queen's Printer, June 1965.

_____. A paper presented to the Research Committee of the International Sociological Association, Waterloo, November 1973.

Redecki, Henry, with Heydenkorn, B. *A Member of a Distinguished Family: The Polish Group in Canada.* Toronto: McClelland and Stewart, 1976.

Reid, Stanford, ed. *The Scottish Tradition in Canada.* Toronto: McClelland and Stewart, 1976.

Report of the Royal Commission on Bilingualism. Book IV, *The Cultural Contribution of Other Ethnic Groups.* Ottawa: Queen's Printer, 1970.

Richmond, Anthony H. *Post-War Immigrants in Canada.* Toronto: University of Toronto Press, 1967.

Sedgwick, Joseph. "The Sedgwick Report, Part I." Ottawa, April 1965. (Mimeographed.)

_____. "The Sedgwick Report, Part II." Ottawa, January 27, 1966. (Mimeographed.)

_____. *Report on Applicants in Canada.* Ottawa: Queen's Printer, 1970.

Special Joint Committee on Immigration Policy of the Parliament of Canada. 1975.

"Study Will Pave Way to New Immigration Act." *The Toronto Star*, August 21, 1974.

Tienhaara, Nancy. *Canadian Views on Immigration and Population: An Analysis of Post-War Gallup Polls.* Ottawa: Manpower and Immigration, 1974.

Troper, Harold Martin. *Only Farmers Need Apply.* Toronto: Griffin Press, 1972.
Wangenheim, Elizabeth. "The Ukrainians: A Case Study of the 'Third Force'." In *Canadian Society: Sociological Perspectives*, pp. 648-65. Edited by Bernard R. Blishen et al. 3rd ed. Toronto: Macmillan, 1968.
_____ . *Aspects of the Absorption and Adaptation of Immigrants.* Ottawa: Manpower and Immigration, 1974.
_____ . "Environmental Conservation and Immigration: A New Racist Ideology?" York University, Toronto. (Mimeographed.) Summary version of paper presented at the Bicentennial Conference on "The New Immigration: Implications for the United States and the International Community," Smithsonian Institution on Immigration and Ethnic Studies, Washington, D.C., November 15-17, 1976.

Social Policy Concerning Women*

MARGRIT EICHLER

Until quite recently, Canada, along with many other countries, explicitly endorsed a principle of sex inequality. The Common Law of England stated that "A woman is not a person in matters of rights and privileges, but she is a person in matters of pains and penalties"—which is as apt and concise a description of the situation of Canadian women as one might ever hope to compose.

In 1948, the U.N. General Assembly adopted unanimously the Universal Declaration of Human Rights which states that "All human beings are born free and equal in dignity and rights." In 1967, when the Royal Commission on the Status of Women in Canada was established, the Universal Declaration of Human Rights was interpreted by the Royal Commission to imply that Canada, as a memberstate of the United Nations, "is, therefore, committed to a principle that permits no distinction in rights and freedoms between women and men. The principle emphasizes the common status of women and men rather than a separate status for each sex. The stage has been set for a new society equally enjoyed and maintained by both sexes."[1]

The principle of sex equality has finally been accepted in broad terms. Its incorporation into specific laws is still lacking in some areas, such as the criminal law and the current family law. Its implementation and realization in all areas is an entirely separate question. A case in point is the situation of

* I wish to thank Mary Eberts for her extensive help with the references, and Carolyn Presser for her help in locating many of the needed legal documents for this paper.
1 Canada, Royal Commission on the Status of Women, *Report* (Ottawa: Information Canada, 1970), p. xi.

women on the labour market. All of Canada now recognizes the principle of equal pay for equal work, but this has, so far, not led to a significant change in the discrepancies between the salaries of male and female employees. Nevertheless, legal expression of the principle of sex equality is a necessary, if not sufficient, condition for sex equality in Canadian society, and as such of high importance.

The establishment of the Royal Commission on the Status of Women helped redefine the scope of women's problems. The *Report* of the Commission carefully and in detail documented many of the ways in which Canadian women are disadvantaged. It covered a wide range of problems—from the position of women in the economy over education and the position of women in the family to problems of taxation, immigration, political participation and criminal justice. Coming, as it did, at a time when the social climate was receptive to a discussion of problems concerning women, due to the Women's Liberation Movement, the *Report* triggered a number of important changes and served as a focus for action for further changes. In many ways, 1970 can therefore be regarded as a watershed for women's rights—as will be seen, many of the laws were rewritten or amended in or after that year—but the water still has a long way to run to reach the sea of sex equality.

The progress, as well as the lack of progress, that has been made can be gleaned from the annual reports of the Advisory Council on the Status of Women. The 1975-76 report summarizes what happened to the recommendations of the Royal Commission until 1976. In May 1976, of the 122 recommendations of the Royal Commission that fell within federal jurisdiction, 50 had been implemented, 53 had been partially implemented, and 19 had not been implemented.[2]

In the following, I shall try to trace briefly the increasing acceptance of the principle of sex equality through its gradual acceptance in three especially important areas: *suffrage*, the *labour market*, and *family law*. I shall then attempt to point out in what ways social reality deviates from the principle of sex equality in each of these areas. Lastly, I shall attempt some general assessment to what degree—and in what areas (if in any)— sex equality has been achieved and what remains to be done if full sex equality is ever to become a social reality in Canada.

THE POLITICAL PARTICIPATION OF WOMEN

In the nineteenth and early twentieth centuries, the Election Act of the Dominion of Canada decreed that "No woman, idiot, lunatic or criminal shall vote." Nevertheless, in the early nineteenth century, some places in Quebec gave women a limited right to vote. In 1849, however, a statute was passed which forbade women to vote in any election, including local and provincial elections.[3] The right to vote was won by women during and after the First World War. Manitoba, Saskatchewan, and Alberta were the first

2 Canada, Advisory Council on the Status of Women, *Annual Report 1975-1976* (Ottawa, 1976).
3 *Decisions of the Judicial Committee of the Privy Council Relating to the British North America Act, 1867 and the Canadian Institution 1867-1954*, vol. 2, pp. 637-38.

provinces to enfranchise women in 1916, prior to federal enfranchisement. British Columbia and Ontario followed suit in 1917, Nova Scotia in 1918, New Brunswick in 1919, Prince Edward Island in 1922, Newfoundland in 1925, and Quebec only enfranchised women in 1940.[4]

The federal vote was won more swiftly than the provincial vote in some of the provinces. The War-time Elections Act of 1917 specified that

> Every female person shall be capable of voting and qualified to vote at a Dominion election in any province or in the Yukon Territory, who . . . is the wife, widow, mother, sister or daughter of any person, male or female, living or dead, who is serving or has served without Canada in any of the naval forces, of Canada or of Great Britain in the present war . . . .[5]

A year later, the Act to confer Electoral Franchise upon Women specified that

> Every female person shall be entitled to vote at a Dominion election who,—
> (a) is a British subject;
> (b) is of the full age of twenty-one years and upwards;
> (c) possesses the qualifications which would entitle a male person to vote at a Dominion election in the province in which said female person seeks to vote . . . .[6]

Women thereby had won, in 1918, the right to vote in all federal elections—however, this did not yet mean that women could serve in all political offices. The right to sit in the House of Commons was granted temporarily in 1919, and made permanent in 1920. In the federal election of 1921, a woman was elected to the Dominion Parliament. It was Agnes McPhail who was the successful candidate of the United Farmers of Ontario. However, "It is a matter of some interest to note that as late as 1928 the Chief Justice of Canada reasoned that while a woman might be elected as a member of the House of Commons, it was questionable whether a woman might be appointed a member of the Privy Council."[7] It was not until 1957 that the first woman was appointed to the federal Cabinet.

In the 1920s, women had won the right to vote in all federal elections, in most provincial elections, and to be elected to the House of Commons—but they did not yet have the right to be appointed to the Senate. This right was won through the indefatigable work of many women's groups, unceasing petitions and the decision of the Judicial Committee of the Privy Council of Britain to overturn a decision of the Canadian Supreme Court. It was a drawn-out battle which extended over ten years, and is one of a number of cases in which the Supreme Court of Canada proved itself to be less than progressive as far as the status of women is concerned.

In 1916, the year in which Albertan women were enfranchised, two Edmonton women who had come to observe the trial of a group of prostitutes were asked by the Crown Council to leave the court, "on the ground that the evidence in such cases was unsuitable to be heard by a mixed

---

4 Maxine Nunes and Deanna White, *The Lace Ghetto* (Toronto: New Press, 1972), p. 32.
5 Canada, Statutes of Canada 1917, sec. 33A (1) added to *The Dominion Elections Act* by *The War-time Elections Act*, 7-8 Geo. 5, ch. 39, sec. 1(c).
6 Canada, Statutes of Canada 1918, 8-9 Geo. 5, ch. 20, sec. 1(1).
7 *Women's Bureau '73* (Ottawa: Information Canada, 1974), p. 29.

audience"[8]—apparently the prostitutes themselves did not count when establishing the existence of a "mixed audience." The two women were angered and sought the advice of Emily Murphy, a prominent journalist. Murphy suggested that the women accept their ejection but press for the establishment of a women's court to try cases involving women. Murphy was enlisted to head the campaign for such a demand, and the result was that in the same year the Attorney-General of Alberta established a women's court and asked Murphy to become its first magistrate. Murphy was sworn in in June 1916—the first woman in the entire British Empire to occupy the post of police magistrate.[9]

During Murphy's first day in court, the counsel for one defendant objected to the magistrate's jurisdiction on the grounds that a woman is not eligible to hold public office. This point was raised repeatedly, and finally taken to the Supreme Court of Alberta over the appointment of a second female magistrate, Alice Jamieson, who had been appointed a magistrate in Calgary in December 1916. A conviction of hers was appealed on the grounds "That the said Mrs. Alice J. Jamieson is not a police magistrate and has no capacity for holding the appointment of police magistrate and is incompetent and incapable of holding the said appointment."[10] The appeal was denied by the Supreme Court of Alberta which ruled, in 1917,

> I therefore think that applying the general principle upon which the common law rests, namely that of reason and good sense as applied to some conditions, this Court ought to declare that in this province and at this time in our presently existing conditions there is at common law no legal disqualification for holding public office in the government from any distinction of sex. And in doing this I am strongly of the opinion that we are returning to the more liberal and enlightened view of the middle ages in England and passing over the narrower and more hardened view, which possibly by the middle of the nineteenth century, had gained ascendency in England.[11]

This decision is significant because it justifies the eligibility of women for public office *in principle*. Some years later, the Supreme Court of Canada was to decree otherwise.

The question of the eligibility of women for public offices arose again when in 1919 the Federated Women's Institutes of Canada unanimously approved a resolution to the Canadian government requesting that a woman be appointed to the Senate. The request was not acceded to, and for about ten years regular petitions for a female senator were filed by various women's groups. One of the problems with such an appointment was the ambiguity in the British North America Act (B.N.A. Act) concerning the eligibility of women to serve in the Senate. The B.N.A. Act states that "The Governor General shall from Time to Time, in the Queen's Name, by Instrument under the Great Seal of Canada, summon qualified Persons to the

---

8   Eleanor Harman, "Five Persons from Alberta," in *The Clear Spirit: Twenty Canadian Women and Their Times*, ed. Mary Quayle Innis (Toronto: Published for the Canadian Federation of University Women by University of Toronto Press, 1966), p. 162.
9   Ibid.
10   R. v. Cyr [1917-18], 12 Alta. L.R. 320, at p. 326 (Alta. Sup. Ct., App. Div.).
11   Ibid., at p. 336.

Senate; and, subject to the Provisions of this Act, every Person so summoned shall become and be a Member of the Senate and a Senator."[12]

The question, then, was whether women were persons as conceived under the Act.

When many years of petitioning proved unsuccessful in getting a woman appointed Senator, Murphy decided to test the constitutionality of female personhood by petitioning for an Order-in-Council which would direct the Supreme Court of Canada to rule on the question. She was successful in having the petition accepted, and needed four other "interested persons" to plead the case. She invited Nellie McClung, Louise McKinney, the Honourable Irene Parlby, and Henrietta Muir Edwards to join her in pleading the case.

The case reached the Supreme Court of Canada in March of 1928. In the "Persons" reference Chief Justice Anglin ruled that women were *not* qualified persons in the sense of the B.N.A. Act and therefore were not eligible for appointment to the Senate.[13]

The five women (who were no persons) immediately requested and received an Order-in-Council giving them leave to appeal to His Majesty's Privy Council. The case was argued in London in 1929. In October of that year the Judicial Committee of the British Privy Council reversed the decision of the Canadian Supreme Court. The judgment concluded that ". . . their Lordships have come to the conclusion that the word 'persons' in s. 24 includes members of both the male and female sex, and that, therefore, the question propounded by the Governor General should be answered in the affirmative, and that women are eligible to be summoned to and become members of the Senate of Canada, and they will humbly advise His Majesty accordingly."[14] The first woman senator was finally appointed by Mackenzie King in 1931. It was Clarine Wilson. By 1929 women in Canada had finally won the right not only to vote at the federal level, but also to sit in both chambers of the Canadian government.

However, the representation of both sexes is a separate question. The concern with women's issues in Parliament is low, to say the least. The federal Advisory Council of the Status of Women has, ever since its establishment, been concerned about the slowness with which bills referring to the status of women move through Parliament. Katie Cooke, first Chairperson of the Council, once asked: "Did you know that a private members' Bill to make the Beaver an official Canadian symbol was introduced on 14 January 1975 and has already had second reading? WHY? Because thousands of letters have been received supporting its cause." The Bulletin of the Advisory Council then goes on to ask: "Could it be that the beavers of this country bear more import to our parliamentarians than the women? And the beavers don't even vote!"[15]

Women are, at the present time, still pitifully underrepresented in all major political bodies. Between 1917 and June 1970, there have been 134

---

12 Sec. 24 of *The British North America Act, 1867*, 30 & 31 Vic., ch. 31 (U.K.).
13 Harman, *The Lace Ghetto*, p. 174.
14 Edwards et al. v. Attorney-General of Canada et al. [1930], A.C. 124, at p. 143.
15 Canada, Advisory Council on the Status of Women/Conseil consultatif de la situation de la femme, *Bulletin* (Ottawa, March 1975), p. 2.

federal and provincial elections, and 6,845 people have been elected. Of these, 67 were women—that is just under 1 per cent of the total.[16] In the spring of 1977, there were eight female M.P.s out of a total of 281 M.P.s. In order to at least partially understand the lack of female political representation and the lack of concern with issues relating to the status of women in Canada, we need to look at least at two other areas which are of particular import to women: the labour market and the family.

WOMEN ON THE LABOUR MARKET AND THE LAWS PERTAINING THERETO

The participation of women in the labour market has increased drastically since the beginning of this century and seems to be still on the rise. In 1911, 13 per cent of the labour force was female. In 1974, 34.4 per cent of the labour force was female. The participation rate of women in the labour force was 39.7 per cent in 1974. Of the regularly employed women, more than half are presently married. This presents a major change with respect to the access of women to paid work—in fact, the right to paid labour is hardly disputed any longer, although it is not expressly specified as a right in the Canadian Bill of Rights or elsewhere. Nevertheless, speaking in very general terms, sex discrimination in employment is, by now, illegal in Canada.

The prohibition of discrimination on the basis of sex is typically contained in provincial human rights legislation and, occasionally, in Labour Standards Codes. Legal protection of the rights of employed women comprises, at a minimum, three aspects: the right to engage in a certain type of employment irrespective of sex if and when such employment is available, the right of equal pay for equal work, and lastly, safeguards for women in the case of pregnancy. We shall deal with each of these aspects in turn.

Basic to any principle of sex equality, and probably the one issue that generates most support in the general public is the principle of equal pay for equal work.

By now, the legitimacy of the principle is quite widely accepted. The first equal pay legislation in Canada was Ontario's, passed in 1951.[17] Since then, the other provinces have passed similar legislation, with the Yukon being the last province to enact equal pay legislation in 1973.[18]

16   Canada, Royal Commission on the Status of Women, *Report*, p. 339.
17   See *The Female Employers Fair Remuneration Act, 1951*, S.O. 1951, ch. 26.
18   After Ontario, the other provinces followed suit in this order:
Saskatchewan: *The Equal Pay Act*, S.S. 1952, ch. 104;
Canada: *Fair Employment Practices Act*, Stats. Can. 1952-53, ch. 19;
B.C.:   *Equal Pay Act*, S.B.C. 1953 (2nd sess.), ch. 6;
Man.:   *The Equal Pay Act*, S.M. 1956, ch. 18;
N.S.:   *Equal Pay Act*, S.N.S. 1956, ch. 5;
Alta.:   *An act to amend the Alberta Labour Act*, S.A. 1957, ch. 38, sec. 41;
P.E.I.:   *The Equal Pay Act*, S.P.E.I. 1959, ch. 11;
N.B.:   *Female Employees Fair Remuneration Act*, S.N.B. 1960-61, ch. 7;
N.W.T.:   *Fair Practices Ordinance*, O.N.W.T. 1966 (2nd sess.), ch. 5;
Nfld.:   *Newfoundland Human Rights Code*, S. Nfld. 1969, No. 75, sec. 10;
Yukon: equal pay added to *The Labour Standards Ordinance* by O.Y.T. 1973 (1st sess.), ch. 13, sec. 2.
These are references to acts as they were originally passed. By now, many of them have been amended. For a detailed discussion of current equal pay legislation, see Gail C. A. Cook and

Nevertheless, the following types of discrimination are still perfectly legal in Canada:

> Employers under federal jurisdiction—such as banks, airlines, insurance companies and telephone companies—can refuse to hire or promote people on the basis of age, sex or marital status. . . . Employers under federal jurisdiction can, and do, provide women employees with smaller pension plans and insurance benefits than those provided for male employees.[19]

Overall, as far as the legal aspects of the right to equal pay for equal work irrespective of sex is concerned, the groundwork has been done. However, equal pay for equal work legislation, though constituting needed, necessary and laudworthy pieces of legislation, do not solve the problem of equal remuneration for women if it just so happens that most of the women in the labour force are concentrated in those occupations which happen to have very low pay rates—as, indeed, is the case in all parts of Canada. For, as the New Brunswick Female Employees Fair Remuneration Act stipulates, a difference in the rate of pay between a female and a male employee based on any factor other than sex (such as a slightly different type of work) does not constitute a failure to comply with the principle of equal pay for equal work. The notion of "equal pay for work of equal value" is somewhat more progressive, but is, as yet, only being discussed.[20]

The problem of sex-typing of occupations has, of course, been recognized. At the legal level it has been addressed through forbidding employers to discriminate in hiring and conditions of employment on the basis of sex. This prohibition is usually incorporated in provincial Human Rights legislation. Most provinces have, by now, enacted legislation that is supposed to ensure equal employment opportunities.[21] It is instructive to consider the time gap which occurred in most provinces between introducing equal opportunity legislation for minority groups and extending the protection to women. In the case of Alberta, it took five years; in the case of British Columbia, thirteen years; Manitoba, seventeen years; New Brunswick, fifteen years; Newfoundland had no gap at all; Nova Scotia had a gap of sixteen years; Northwest Territories, twelve years; Saskatchewan, sixteen years; and the Yukon, eleven years.[22]

Most of the legislation that affects the working conditions of employees is provincial legislation. At the federal level, there are so far two acts which address the problem of sex discrimination in employment: the Unemployment Insurance Act of 1971 which stipulates that there be no sex discrimination in the referral of workers referred by the National Employment Service, and the Fair Wages and Hours of Work Act which decrees that all government construction contracts must include a provision which prohibits the contractor from discriminating on the grounds of sex.

Mary Eberts, "Policies Affecting Work," in *Opportunity for Choice*, ed. Gail C. A. Cook (Ottawa: Statistics Canada in association with the C. D. Howe Research Institute, 1976), pp. 174-77.

19 Canada, Advisory Council on the Status of Women, *Fact Sheet on Human Rights* (Ottawa, October 1976).
20 See, for example, Ontario Ministry of Labour, *Equal Pay for Work of Equal Value, A Discussion Paper* ([Toronto,] 1976).
21 See Cook and Eberts, "Policies Affecting Work," pp. 177-83.
22 See Table A.5.1 in Cook, ed., *Opportunity for Choice*, pp. 187-88.

At the legal level, the preconditions for equal pay for equal work and non-discrimination in employment seem to be present. However, so far no improvement in the discrepancies between female and male earnings is discernible. On the contrary, after a detailed study of male-female wage differentials between 1946 to 1971, Gunderson concluded, "The male-female wage differential appears to be growing over time. Full employment policies cannot be relied upon to narrow the differential. And most important from a policy point of view, equal pay legislation does not appear to be capable of narrowing the differential."[23] Nor is there any indication that the representation of women in higher paying occupations has in any way increased so far. Laudable as the existing legislation is, it is unlikely to effect radical changes in the placement of women and men in different occupations. The problem is, at least partially, one of policing discrimination.

Let us consider a hypothetical, but not at all unlikely, case. A woman with a B.A. in English and a man with a B.A. in Psychology both apply to the Personnel Department of a university for a job. The woman is referred to the library which is predominantly female staffed, with low rates of pay, and the man is referred to the administrative service of the university, which, in its upper echelons is predominantly or exclusively male-staffed with very high rates of pay. They both accept their job offers, with the man earning initially 100 per cent more than the woman. In a few years, his salary may exceed hers by 200 per cent, since pay increases for both employees are on a percentage basis. How can one ever prove that discrimination has occurred? And yet, the overall pattern has once again been repeated in two particular cases.

The last type of legislation that needs to be considered in the context of labour laws concerning women is maternity legislation and protective legislation in general. While Canada compares well with other countries with respect to its equal pay legislation (which, however, is ineffectual, as we have seen), it compares quite poorly with respect to maternity legislation. Basically, most but not all employed Canadian women have the right to a total of approximately seventeen weeks of unpaid leave of absence before and after delivery. After a two-week waiting period, women are eligible for Unemployment Insurance. In addition, women cannot be fired for reasons of pregnancy only.[24]

Although these changes constitute a slight improvement over previous regulations, the present laws still put the woman under fairly severe economic pressure at a time when her expenses jump drastically due to the birth of a new child. Some of the European countries have much further

23   Morley Gunderson, "Time Pattern of Male-Female Wage Differentials: Ontario 1946-71," *Industrial Relations* 31, no. 1 (1976): 57-71. See also Lynne McDonald, "Wages of Work: A Widening Gap Between Women and Men," *The Canadian Forum* 55, no. 650 (May 1975):5.
24   Maternity leave is available under legislation in only seven of the thirteen Canadian jurisdictions—federally and in the following provinces: British Columbia (since 1921), New Brunswick (1964), and Ontario, Manitoba, Nova Scotia, Saskatchewan. With regard to the other jurisdictions, it is up to the employer or the terms of the collective agreement as to whether a woman gets leave. The provisions of the *Unemployment Insurance Act* (Stats. Can. 1970-71-72, ch. 48, particularly secs. 30 and 46) are available to women across Canada.

advanced legislation concerning maternity leaves. Here, Canada definitely lags behind other highly-industrialized countries.

While maternity laws definitely are needed and should be greatly improved to avoid penalizing the woman for bearing children, the value of other protective legislation is much more doubtful. While in principle it seems desirable to improve the working conditions of women, it should be just as desirable to improve the working conditions of all employees, female or male. The main problem with protective legislation is that, as a rule, the onus is on the employer to provide the extra service. For example, there are several Acts which require employers to provide a female employee with transportation to her home if she finishes work between some time after midnight and the morning hours (Saskatchewan Labour Standards Act of 1967; Manitoba Employment Standards Act of 1970, Ontario Employment Standards Act of 1970, Quebec Industrial and Commercial Establishments Act of 1964). Since the employer consequently has to pay an additional cost for a female employee that he does not have to pay for a male employee, this may act as a disincentive to employ women in such occupations or may lead him to avoid putting women on the often-better-paid night shifts. There are few situations imaginable in which men would not profit from having any protection that is given to women extended to them (with the exception of maternity-related laws, although paternity leave should also be legally recognized). Equality would be better served by extending protective labour laws to men, which would make women and men more equally desirable employees.

Overall, we can state that great strides have been made in terms of equal pay legislation, and equality of employment legislation. Why then is it that so little change for the better, if any, is discernible with respect to the status of female workers?

The main answer is that occupations in Canada are still sex segregated and that women still hold the low-paying, low-prestige occupations. There is a tradition of channelling women into low-paying occupations, such as clerical and secretarial jobs, and there is some evidence that occupations decrease in their comparative rate of pay as they become more female.[25] Secondly, many women still have interrupted career patterns—they work until the birth of their first child, drop out of the labour force until the last child is in school, and then return into the labour force. At that stage, they are not in a good competitive situation. Most of their skills will be obsolete by then, and they are older—a double stroke against them. Then there are the employers' expectations that young women will follow just this pattern—irrespective of whether the women themselves plan to do so or not—and it may thus become a self-fulfilling prophecy. Lastly, the policing and enforcement of non-discrimination is extraordinarily difficult. Hiring into and promotion to supervisory and managerial positions is always based on a variety of factors, one of them being the personality of the candidate. In principle, this must be considered a legitimate concern, since by definition supervisory and managerial personnel must be capable of

25 Margrit Eichler, "The Double Standard as an Indicator of Sex-Status Differentials," paper delivered at the American Sociological Association Meetings in Montreal, 1974.

dealing with subordinates (and superordinates, for that matter). However, since the image that most employers have of women does not, as a rule, include their potential for authority positions, it is highly likely that qualifed women will be excluded from authority positions because of their sex rather than because of lack of ability.

In the United States, this problem has been addressed through equal rights legislation which uses negative sanctions against employers who do not meet certain standards of percentages of female employees in various types of positions. If one shares the conviction that the present legislation (or more like it) will not suffice to radically alter the problem of sex segregation in occupations, and if one wishes to avoid the route of negative sanctions, then the other alternative that offers itself is to use positive incentives for employers who do wish to employ women in currently sex-segregated occupations. One might, for instance, give special tax advantages to businesses based on the number of women who are employed in positions of authority. Once the balance has been righted and women have had a chance to establish themselves in these positions, the positive incentives could be discontinued. If Archibald's study can be at all generalized, simply experiencing work with women in positions of authority should be an effective means of reducing the currently-existing sex stereotypes.[26]

So far, we have looked at political and economic rights and restrictions of women. By far the greatest restrictions, however, are experienced by women through their family roles. An examination of the legal as well as the social constraints of women in their family roles will lead us to the heart of the problems that are obstructing the route to sex equality.

WOMEN IN THE FAMILY

At the present time, the legal obligations of husbands and wives are still quite dissimilar. Basically, the husband is held responsible for the economic well-being of his family, including that of his wife, and the wife is held responsible for the management of household affairs and child-care.[27] In cases of divorce, for example, children are usually awarded to the mother rather than the father. Indeed, a father usually must prove that his former wife is an "unfit mother" in order to win custody of his children. In return, the wife loses the economic contributions she has made to the family during the duration of the marriage. Her work as housewife and mother is not financially rewarded, although, if children are involved, it is only through her raising them that the husband was capable of accumulating any assets (if there be any).

A recent case put this problem into sharp focus. In Murdoch v. Murdoch,

> The appellant wife and respondent husband were married in 1943 and, until 1947, worked on various ranches, hiring themselves out as a couple. Under this arrangement the husband broke horses and looked after cattle while his

26   Kathleen Archibald, *Sex and the Public Service* (Ottawa: Queen's Printer, 1970), p. 47.
27   Work patterns have been documented in Martin Meissner et al., "No Exit for Wives: Sexual Division of Labour and the Cumulation of Household Demands," *Canadian Review of Sociology and Anthropology* 12, no. 4, Part 1 (1975): 424-40; and Susan Clark and Andrew S. Harvey, "The Sexual Division of Labour: The Use of Time," *Atlantis* 2, no. 1 (Fall 1976): 46-47.

wife did the cooking for the work crews. In 1947, the husband and the wife's father purchased some property and operated it as a dude ranch until it was sold in 1951, at which time the husband realized $3,500 as his share of the proceeds. In 1952, the husband purchased another property which was sold in 1958, when the property in issue, . . . was purchased. In all of the purchases the property was held in the name of the husband and in none of the purchases did the wife make any direct financial contribution. However, during the period 1947 to the date of separation in 1968, the husband was, for five months of each year, away on stock association business and during these periods the wife contributed physical labour to the various ranching operations on the properties successively occupied by the spouses. Her contributions involved doing chores and included haying, raking, swathing, mowing, driving trucks and tractors, dehorning, vaccinating and branding cattle.[28]

She therefore claimed an undivided one-half interest in the property. In October 1973, the Supreme Court of Canada ruled that

> Since the wife had made no direct financial contribution to the acquisition of the property claimed by her, there was no basis for finding a resulting trust in her favour. Moreover, the fact that the wife had performed various services in connection with the husband's ranching activities did not give her any beneficial interest in the property claimed.[29]

Nobody disputed in this case that the wife worked as hard as the husband. The dissenting Judge Laskin maintained that in addition to a small direct financial contribution, the wife contributed indirectly through her labour. Yet, the presently-existing laws did not give her any interest in the jointly-accumulated assets. The inequality in evaluating the contributions of the spouses is obvious.

In similar cases that have come to trial since the Murdoch case, some women did win a half-interest or less, while others were denied any part of matrimonial property. Basically, the Murdoch case seems to have changed the legal structure such that both a financial contribution on the part of the wife and proof of a common intention between the parties to own the disputed property jointly seem necessary before a woman has a chance to be awarded an interest in a property which is held in her husband's name—no matter how great her non-monetary contributions may have been.[30]

Presently, the family law is under revision, both at the federal as well as at the provincial level. This discussion will therefore address itself to what would be needed (rather than what currently exists) to insure equality of the sexes, since the Law Reform Commission in its Working Paper 8 on Family Property explicitly states this as its aim:

> We associate ourselves with the concept of equality before the law for married persons of both sexes and believe that it is the coherence and justice inherent in the concept of legal equality that gives the true substance to the argument

---

28 Murdoch v. Murdoch [1973], 41 D.L.R. (3d) 367 (S.C.C.). This statement is taken from the headnote of the case, at p. 367.
29 Ibid.
30 Stella Bailey, "Matrimonial Property: What Has Happened Since Murdoch?" *Branching Out* (September/October 1976), pp. 35-40.

that there is a need for significant change in the law governing family property relations.[31]

In their working paper, the Law Reform commission discusses three different types of property regimes: (1) Separation of Property coupled with Discretion in the Court, (2) Community of Property, and (3) Deferred Sharing. The basic thrust of all three regimes is to recognize marriage as a legal, social, and *economic* partnership in which both spouses, irrespective of whether one of them functions as a housewife part of the time or all the time, share equally in those assets that were accumulated during the duration of the marriage.

While such a conception is a giant step forward, especially on the backdrop of such blatant sex inequality as was manifested in the Murdoch case, there are also some problems in such a conception. While obviously the economic value of housework must be legally recognized in some way, a law that would give half-interest in any accumulated assets to *any* spouse would legally equalize the contributions of wives when clearly there are important differences in the amount of contribution that is being made. There is clearly a difference in value if a wife does the household work for one adult man and herself only or if, to take the other extreme, she cares for several children, works part-time or full-time, and in addition does most of the housework. Clearly the contribution of the second wife is greater than that of the first, and its economic value may be greater than the economic value of the contribution of the second husband—in which case the wife should receive more than half the assets that were accumulated during marriage, while the first wife may have earned less than half. It seems that such a differentiation between the value of different contributions should be taken into account when new laws are being formulated. Failing that, the contribution of wives will still be reckoned on the basis of the husband's achievements rather than on her own—in other words, the ex-wife of a rich husband will receive substantially more assets than the ex-wife of a poor husband, irrespective of the relative contribution of any one of the spouses.

EVALUATION OF SOCIAL POLICIES CONCERNING WOMEN AND OUTLOOK INTO THE FUTURE

Three areas of social policy which greatly affect the status of women have been briefly surveyed: political rights of women, the position of women on the labour market, and family law. One fact that stands out is that the main gains that have so far been made are legal gains, while at the same time the Supreme Court of Canada has in several crucial decisions shown itself to be somewhat less than helpful as far as female equality is concerned. Of these decisions, two have been briefly discussed: the denial of personhood of women and the Murdoch v. Murdoch decision. Another case which falls into the same category is the Lavell case.

The Lavell case is of particular importance since it was the first attempt before the Supreme Court of Canada to use the Canadian Bill of Rights of

31　Canada, Law Reform Commission, *Family Property*, Working Paper 8 (Ottawa: Information Canada, March 1975), p. 3.

1960 to secure equality for Canadian women. Lavell, an Indian woman, married a non-Indian man as a result of which her name was deleted from the Indian Register. In contrast, an Indian man who marries a non-Indian woman retains his Indian status. She appealed her loss of Indian status, charging sex discrimination. The Canadian Bill of Rights decrees that "It is hereby recognized and declared that in Canada there have existed and shall continue to exist without discrimination by reason of race, national origin, colour, religion or sex, the following human rights and fundamental freedoms . . . ."[32] Mrs. Lavell was not granted Indian status, on the grounds that the Bill of Rights does not make existing legislation inoperative, and that equality before the law means simply equality of treatment in the enforcement and application of the laws of Canada before the enforcement authorities and the ordinary courts of the land.[33] A Western feminist group thereupon very appropriately mailed out a black-bordered engraved card which read:

> IN MEMORIAM. The Canadian Bill of Rights, born in April 10, 1960, passed away August 27, 1973.
> Its short, valuable life was dedicated to the freedom of MAN; its sudden, untimely death occurred when woman expected to be included.
> "Here lies one who meant well, tried a little, and failed much."
> Remembered with sorrow and regret by the women of Canada.[34]

In spite of the failure of the Bill of Rights to serve as an instrument of change towards sex equality, in the political and economic area great strides towards achieving legal sex equality have been taken, and in the family area sex equality has been declared a goal and steps to achieve it are currently being considered.

Why, then, is it that in spite of such legal changes the improvement in the social, economic and political position of women is very small? Why is it that not more women are in important political offices, that the gap in earnings between female and male employees does not seem to shrink, that there are so few women in supervisory and managerial positions? Why do the laws concerning equal pay and equal employment conditions have no visible effects?

The answer must be sought in the interaction of the three areas—family, labour market, and politics, rather than in any one of them. Women are still the ones in Canada who do the housework and the child-rearing. While both activities have economic effects, they are of a fundamentally different nature. Housework is a private service. Child-care is a public service. If a wife and mother is incapable of fulfilling her household and child-rearing tasks, and if the father is likewise incapable, the state will take over the child-rearing functions, but not the housework functions. Women are therefore in great numbers fulfilling public and private functions for which they are not being paid. For the private functions, they should be paid privately. That is, indeed, what the proposed new family property law is

32 *Canadian Bill of Rights*, R.S.C. 1970, Appendix III, p. 457.
33 Attorney-General of Canada v. Lavell; Isaac et al. v. Bedard [1973], 38 D.L.R. (3d) 481 (S.C.C.), at p. 500.
34 Personal possession.

striving for: financial reward for housekeeping tasks. But most women, for parts of their life, are also fulfilling a public function: care of children. And for that they should be paid by the state.

It is the ironic conclusion that we may have to draw from the failure of the present laws to usher in sex equality that this may perhaps be achieved only in an indirect manner. One of the reasons that economic non-discrimination laws will not work is that there are sufficient numbers of women willing to take jobs which pay little because their only other option is even less attractive, namely, to remain housewives without any pay after their children are grown. Little money is, after all, better than no money, or so most people think. And two of the contributing reasons that not more women are in politics are clearly (1) that many women find themselves without the time, due to child-care and household obligations, and (2) that social expectations are still such that women are prepared for motherhood and housewifery rather than public lives.

If mothers were paid, this would have a more drastic effect on creating equality in the labour market than any of the means that have so far been employed. If one could earn an attractive salary for child-care, a number of women might choose to engage in this type of work for a limited number of years rather than work for lesser pay outside the home. This would necessitate a drastic re-evaluation of the need for, the recompense for, and the general working conditions of, many of the female jobs. It would likewise, for the first time, give women an option to work outside the home or to work in the home. Presently, many mothers must seek paid work due to the financial problems of the family, and others cannot accept paid work due to the unavailability of alternative child-care arrangements or the lack of money to pay for those services which do exist. With pay, mothers could choose to hire someone else to perform the child-care services part of the time or they could choose to stay at home for a number of years. Employers would have to compete by offering attractive pay and employment conditions. As long as the public service functions of child-care will not be recognized and financially rewarded, all attempts to achieve sex equality will remain incomplete and, at best, only partially effective.

The Elderly and Social Policy

SHANKAR A. YELAJA

There are three basic themes running through any consideration of aging and social policy: economic insecurity after retirement is a forced condition of poverty for the aged; the psychological impact of being old in Canada is severe because older people do not have any significant societal functions and roles to fulfill; societal values and attitudes are the chief causes of benign neglect in developing a progressive social policy for old people. This paper will review social policy and services for the aged in Canada. It is argued that for the development of a comprehensive social policy for the aged, we must come to grips with the economic insecurity, psychological alienation and societal neglect experienced by the aged.

The ratio of people over sixty-five years of age in relation to the total population is increasing by approximately 1 per cent every ten years in Canada. In 1921, the older people (i.e., those above sixty-five years of age) made up 4.8 per cent of the total population numbering 8,775,600. But as the decades passed, the percentage of older people in the population grew at a rate faster than the total population. In 1935 Statistics Canada reported that there were 1,834,200 elderly people (8.3 per cent). Projections indicate there will be about 2.6 million elderly Canadians by 1985, or 10 per cent of the nation's population. Perhaps the single most significant change in the character of Canada's population by 1985 will be this dramatic change in its age structure. Clearly, Canada's population will undergo a significant aging process in the remaining quarter of this century.[1]

1 *Population Projections for Canada and the Provinces, 1972-2001* (Ottawa: Statistics Canada, 1974).

The increasing life span results in people living longer after retirement. In 1931, the life expectancy at birth in Canada was 60.0 years for males and 62.1 years for females. By 1966, this expectancy had increased to approximately 68.8 for males and 75.2 for females. The discovery of wonder drugs and the conquering of diseases that previously took a heavy toll on human lives are the main factors contributing to increased life expectancy.

With the current decline in the birth rate, and the accelerating trend towards earlier and mandatory retirement ages there will be a higher proportion of older people in the nation's population. As the retirement age decreases and life expectancy increases, we can expect that an increasing number of persons will thus be defined as "older people."

It is significant to remember that old age and retirement are co-related in an industrial society such as Canada. Old age and retirement from the work force are synonymous in our society. As soon as a person retires from working life, the status of old age or of "senior citizen" is confirmed. It does not matter how he feels about his self-worth and his contributions to society; the fact that he is retired from the mainstream of work places him in a role and status of being old. The work ethic is still a very strong force in shaping the values of our society; indeed, it can be seen as one of the cornerstones of our society. With the industrial age came the adage, "The devil makes work for idle hands," expressing the work ethic that a man who does not work has no worth. Work was seen as a means of realizing the individual's fulfillment. There is no doubt that the affluence of Western society is in large measure due to adherence to the work ethic, as supported by Max Weber's thesis, The Protestant Ethic and the Spirit of Capitalism.[2] Unfortunately, however, the philosophy of the work ethic has a detrimental effect on older people. In a society where work and earned income are primary factors in determining status, older people are forced into social isolation from the mainstream of society.

Retirement from the active work force has, first of all, grave and serious economic consequences. Retired older people face a dual economic crisis: their total income is so drastically reduced that it barely makes ends meet; and benefits under our various governmental income security programmes force these older citizens into a state of continual dependency, a dependency which turns out to be both economic and psychological. There is a basic positive correlation between having the money to live adequately and comfortably and having a happy retirement. Only 40 per cent of Canadians have adequate incomes in their retirement years, while 60 per cent either fall below the "poverty line" or are on the fringe of it and struggle along at subsistence levels. Of the 1,866,905 men and women receiving old age pensions in 1973, 467,053 were getting the maximum supplement. The maximum supplement, added to the basic monthly allotment of $112.95 to everyone, means a single person with no income will be paid a pension of $192.18 a month ($2,306.16 a year), while a married couple receives $183.31 each (for a combined total of $4,395,84 a year) on the maximum supplement. The Canadian Council on Social Development, in September 1973,

2   Max Weber, The Protestant Ethic and the Spirit of Capitalism, trans. Talcott Parsons, with a foreword by R. T. Tawney (London: G. Allen & Unwin, Ltd., 1930).

placed the poverty line at $2,580 annually for a single person, and $4,300 for a married couple.

In 1976 the Council updated its figures and placed the poverty line at $3,660 for a single person, and $6,100 for a married couple. However, in estimating poverty line there is a slight difference of interpretation between the Council and other national organizations, including the Senate Committee on Poverty, Economic Council of Canada, and Statistics Canada. Table 1 is illustrative of differences in estimating the poverty line. It is abundantly clear that the perceptions of poverty and consequently decent standards of living (in monetary terms) are by no means uniform. Nevertheless, for a majority of older people in Canada there appears to be no escape from the devastating effects of inadequate income and poverty.

The Special Senate Committee's study on poverty in Canada defined old age as one of the significant factors contributing to poverty. Table 2 is illustrative of the incidence of poverty among people sixty-five years of age and over in relation to their age groups.[3]

It was estimated that about two-thirds of the people over sixty-five were below the 1967 poverty-income level. One of the main reasons for the high incidence of poverty among older people is related to the fact that during most of their working lives, so many of them were not able to pay into a pension plan. Housewives, male workers who were not members of unions, store workers, casual workers, and farm workers were not covered by pension contributions. These are the people for whom the threat of income insecurity on retirement poses grave and serious consequences.

The problem of income insecurity following retirement is made more serious by inflation. The rising consumer price index affects everyone, but it affects most heavily the older people with fixed and inadequate incomes. In a recent survey done by the United Church of Canada[4] to enquire about older people's concerns, it was found that the high cost of living and lack of money to meet the daily necessities of life were among the chief factors that occupied the minds of older people. Important as is the psychological well-being, acceptance and emotional security of older people, financial security is of crucial significance.[5]

In the Toronto survey by the United Church cited earlier, senior citizens were asked, "What is the one most important problem that senior citizens face in their life?" Psychological problems, notably loneliness and the need for companionship, were considered the most important by nearly half (48%) of the respondents. Of these, 34 per cent stated loneliness, 9 per cent boredom or loss of interest in life, and the remaining 5 per cent stated their feeling of being unwanted by society.

So traumatic has been the psychological crisis of being old that recent statistics show a high rate of suicide among senior citizens. Most of the suicides occur immediately or soon after retirement. The suicide rate has

3 Report of the Special Senate Committee on Poverty, *Poverty in Canada* (Ottawa: Queen's Printer, 1971).
4 United Church of Canada, "Senior Citizen's Media Research Project," unpublished final report, May 1974.
5 M. Giletson, "The Emotional Problems of Elderly People," *Geriatrics* 3 (1948): 135-50.

TABLE 1

POVERTY LINE UPDATED, 1976

Family Size	Senate Committee Poverty Line 1974	Senate Committee Poverty Line 1975	Senate Committee Poverty Line 1976	Economic Council 1976	Canadian Council on Social Development 1976	Statistics Canada (Revised) (Pop. 500,000 or More) 1976	Statistics Canada (Updated) 1976
1	$ 3,100	$ 3,490	$ 3,981	$2,759	$ 3,660	$ 3,787	$2,759
2	5,130	5,810	6,635	4,598	6,100	5,488	4,598
3	6,145	6,970	7,962	5,516	7,320	7,003	5,516
4	7,200	8,140	9,289	6,369	8,540	8,329	6,369
5	8,200	9,300	10,616	7,356	9,760	9,310	7,356
6	9,970	10,470	11,943	7,356	10,980	10,222	7,356
7	10,970	11,630	13,270	7,356	10,980	11,208	7,356
8			14,597	7,356	10,980	11,208	7,356
9			15,924	7,356	10,980	11,208	7,356
10			17,251	7,356	10,980	11,208	7,356

Notes: Whereas the Senate report set the poverty line at 50 per cent of the average Canadian family income adjusted to family size, making provision for inflation and gross national product, Statistics Canada has determined it by adjusting the low income lines developed in 1961 for increasing prices as reflected in the Consumer Price Index.

Revised estimates on the poverty line are based on changing consumption patterns which now indicate that families who spend 62 per cent or more of their income on food, clothing and shelter (as opposed to the 70 per cent criterion used in the updated lines) are in straitened circumstances. These limits are also differentiated by size of area of residence. For example, using the revised limits, the poverty line for a family of four in 1974 ranged from $5,527 in a rural area to $7,601 in cities of half a million or more people.

Source: Report of the Special Senate Committee on Poverty, *Poverty in Canada* (Ottawa: Queen's Printer, 1971).

TABLE 2

DISTRIBUTION OF LOW INCOME AND ALL UNATTACHED MALES AND FEMALES BY SELECTED CHARACTERISTICS, 1967 (AGE GROUP)

Age Group	Males with Low Income (000s)	All Males (000s)	Incidence of Low Income (%)	Females with Low Income (000s)	All Females	Incidence of Low Income (%)
14-24 years	42	155	26.9	85	177	48.1
25-34 years	13	128	10.3	11	72	16.0
35-44 years	14	91	14.8	8	47	17.9
45-54 years	19	94	20.2	25	78	31.6
55-64 years	34	97	35.3	59	136	43.6
65-69 years	25	53	47.0	51	83	61.6
70 years and over	74	113	65.9	124	177	70.1

Source: Report of the Special Senate Committee on Poverty, *Poverty in Canada* (Ottawa: Queen's Printer, 1971), p. 22.

jumped from seven per 100,000 population in 1961 to twelve per 100,000 in 1971. There is evidence to support the statement that the suicide rate among the age groups of sixty-five to sixty-nine years in males and fifty-five to fifty-nine age group in females is proportionately higher than the other age groups.[6] How a person adjusts to old age is a reflection of how he has dealt with previous life crises, but the crisis of old age can defeat people despite their successful dealing with past life crises. It is linked to the whole idea of loss. The loss of vigour, attractiveness, social achievement, memory and physical well-being deeply threaten a person's feelings of security and can lead to what is known as "reactive depression." In such a psychological state, an older person is reacting to entering a phase of his life over which he or she has absolutely no control.[7] The depression may linger on and lead some older people to end it all rather than suffer through it. A psychiatrist has equated the reactive depression of older people with that of an extended grief reaction. A person can mourn the loss of his own ability to function as a valuable member of society.

Retirement is undoubtedly the most common precipitating factor of crisis in senior citizens. It means loss of image, valued work, self-esteem and income. The crisis can affect full participation in social and economic roles. In one of the theories of social gerontology called the "Process of Disengagement" developed by Cumming and Henry, it is argued that older people become incapable of and uninterested in fuller participation in a variety of their roles.[8] Briefly, the theory posits a trajectory of human activity that starts with socialization and primary induction into the society, moves to full engagement by assumption of responsibility in secondary and tertiary networks of social relations and finally moves toward a progressive and irrevocable disengagement from social involvement as a preparation for withdrawal and cessation of all activity (death). However, the theory of disengagement is refuted by the study of aging in three industrial societies by Shans, Townsend, et al.[9] Their study suggests that there is incomplete evidence for total disengagement and practically none for the theory that old people themselves take the initiative in "disengaging." Although extensive social interaction may decrease, there is no evidence of the decline of intensive, local, social interaction. Indeed, as a compensatory response to the enforced loss of economic and civil responsibility, a more intensive type of interaction becomes meaningful. The theory proposes that full participation in social and economic roles and activities is dependent upon perceived opportunities and acceptance of senior citizens for what they are.

In Canadian society, values and attitudes toward aging and older people are in large measure responsible for our present social policy and services. Two dominant values still persist and have profound implications for the aged: the worship of youth and the denial of aging. In our society, youth is respected and is seen as the prime force in life. The public media, advertising campaigns to sell goods and services, the employment market, and

6 *The Financial Post*, November 2, 1974, p. 31.
7 H. Feifel, "Older Persons Look at Death," *Geriatrics* 11 (1956): 127-30.
8 E. Cummings and W. E. Henry, *Growing Old* (New York: Basic Books, 1961).
9 Ethel Shans and Peter Townsend et al., *Old People in Three Industrial Societies* (New York: Atherton Press, 1968).

fashions are all geared to the needs of the young. The advertisement for Clairol hair colouring sums it all up, "You're not getting older; you're getting better!" In our excessive emphasis upon youth and its place in society, we have developed a negative attitude toward aging and older people. We do not think there is much good about being old in Canada. We use denial of aging as our defense mechanism. Quite simply, we do not like old people because they remind us of our own mortality. The fear of death is so strong that we push human mortality and all that is associated with it into a far corner of our minds. We do not want to be reminded of death and yet, like birth, it is a reality of life.

In agricultural societies of the world, the aged are looked upon in a positive way. These societies also accept death as a natural part of life. Preparation for the acceptance of death is built into cultural traditions. Older people are easily assimilated and integrated into the society.[10] For example, in India there is a strong stigma attached to the removal of older people into institutions. It is expected that elderly parents will be cared for by the eldest son when it is feasible and practical. Older people have a function to perform; their authority is held in high regard and their wisdom is sought after and respected. In Kenya, despite sweeping technological changes and the attendant consequences for family life, recognition is given to the preservation of its cultural traditions. One of the significant traditions is the role performed by the elderly in the tribal decision-making process. The "Harambee movement," which has attempted to integrate Kenya's cultural traditions with modern technological changes, has made a conscious and concerted effort at ensuring the fullest use of tribal structure and maintaining the role performed by Kenya's senior citizens. On my visits to Ethiopian institutions caring for elderly who were displaced due to the famine conditions in Northern provinces, it was a thrilling experience to find that the Ethiopian social workers were proposing to develop a programme that would provide care on a family basis—each family being provided with a small house to accommodate its grandchildren, relatives and members of the extended family, with farming as the main occupation for the elderly. It was recognized that divorcing older people from their family and land (farming) would prove to be a traumatic shock and a devastating experience. These glimpses of the continuing usefulness of the aged in agrarian countries starkly highlight the customary treatment of the elderly in the Canadian industrial society! Modern Canadian housing is not built to accommodate the extended family or aged parents. Our political, educational and family structures focus on youth as valuable and discourage the continued participation of the elderly in social institutions.

Having described the current status of the elderly in Canada, let us now look at the development of the pieces of social legislation which attempt to alleviate the psychological, economic and social problems of the aged. Since exact dollar figures and the formula for computing benefits fluctuate in response to economic factors, we shall consider these items in the perspective of their ultimate effectiveness and purpose rather than their specific and current monetary value.

10 Matilda Riley, et al., *Aging and Society* (New York: Russell Sage Foundation, 1969).

CANADA PENSION PLAN

Although the Canada Pension Plan came into being in 1966, the beginnings of pension legislation can be traced to the development of industrial pension plans that allowed employees to have contributions deducted from their income and held by their employers toward a pension fund. By 1960, the total number of private plans in operation was approximately 12,000. In 1960, the total number of employees participating in Canadian pension plans was estimated at 1,800,000 out of a labour force of about 4,400,000 (excluding 1,165,000 self-employed, family workers and agricultural workers).

In 1959 there was a study of over eight thousand plans administered through trusts, insurance companies and Canadian government annuities. The study revealed that the total annual contributions amounted to $567 million and the total assets of the plans amounted to $4,825 million. This tremendous interest in planning for old age is all the more impressive when it is considered that before 1963, apart from government and municipal schemes, there was only "persuasive" legislation in the granting of tax benefits for those pension plans which complied with certain requirements.

The Pension Benefits Act was passed in 1963 in Ontario. This was the first legislation making pension plans compulsory and the unique feature of this act was that pensions were transferable when an employee changed jobs. With the advent of the Canada Pension Plan in 1966, the compulsory feature was dropped. The Pension Benefits Act 1965 retained the portability, solvency and funding features and was designed to promote uniform pension legislation throughout the provinces. Quebec has similar legislation.

Shortly after the federal government announced details of the Canada Pension Plan, a comparable plan was announced by the province of Quebec. Both of these plans were enacted in 1965 and became operative on January 1, 1966.[11]

Although Quebec operates a distinctly different plan from that of the Canada Pension Plan, the acts are closely co-ordinated and operate virtually as a single programme. Together they cover almost all members of the labour force in Canada. Benefit credits accrued under the plans are portable throughout Canada. A contributor who may have worked for more than one employer during his lifetime will accumulate pension credits regardless of where he may have worked. Every contributor must have a social insurance number so that his pensionable earnings may be accurately recorded for benefit purposes.

In order to participate in the plan, an individual must be between the ages of eighteen and seventy and earn more than $900 annually as an employee, or at least $900 if he is self-employed. In 1977 contributions are made on earnings between $900 and $9,300 a year by both employees and self-employed persons. No contributions are made by persons while they are receiving disability pensions. Although contributions are made on annual earnings, benefits are calculated on total earnings.

11   *Canadian Employment Benefits and Pension Guide Reports* (Don Mills: CCH Canadian Ltd., Publishers of Topical Law Reports, 1972), pp. 15-16.

Canada Pension Plan benefits are classified under three main headings: Retirement Pensions, Survivors' Benefits, and Disability Benefits.

From 1970 to 1974 inclusive, retirement pensions became payable to contributors who were sixty-five years of age or over provided that if they are under seventy they are retired from regular employment. Amendments effective in January 1975 eliminated this requirement and retirement pensions are now payable at age sixty-five, retired or not.

Survivors' Benefits became payable in February 1968. They are paid to, or on behalf of, the survivors of a deceased contributor who has made contributions for the present maximum qualifying period of three years for those whose benefits commence before 1975.

Disability Pensions[12] became payable in 1970. A contributor is considered to be disabled if he has a physical or mental disability that is so severe and likely to continue so long that he is incapable of pursuing a gainful occupation. Disability pensions are available only if contributions have been made to the plan for the present minimum qualifying period of five years.

OLD AGE SECURITY

The Old Age Security Act came into operation in 1952. Under this act the federal government pays a monthly pension to all persons aged sixty-five or over who meet the necessary residence qualifications. Until 1966, the pension was payable only to those over age seventy, but an annual one-year reduction to age sixty-five was completed in 1970. Parliament has recently approved provisions whereby Old Age Security Pension benefits are adjusted four times instead of only once each year to keep pace with the cost of living.

The Old Age Security pension (demogrant) is not subject to a "means or needs" test and is payable at a flat rate to all persons who qualify as to age and residence, regardless of income or wealth. Under the Income Tax Act, the Old Age Security pension is subject to federal income tax and is added to other income, if any, for the calculation of tax.

GUARANTEED INCOME SUPPLEMENT

A Guaranteed Income Supplement is a monetary payment added to the Old Age Security pension of a pensioner who has no income or only a limited amount of income.

The Guaranteed Income Supplement was established by amendments to the Old Age Security Act. The supplement, which first became payable on January 1, 1967, was initially set at $30 but has been increased periodically. Current single maximum rate is $100.62.

The 1972 amendment provided that effective April 1, 1973 the amount of the Guaranteed Income Supplement would be escalated annually to reflect the full amount of any increase in the consumer price index, reductions in the index causing no reduction in the supplement.

12 *Bureau of Statistics and Canadian Employment Benefits and Pension Guide Reports* (Ottawa: Queen's Printer, 1972).

A Guaranteed Income Supplement may be paid to a recipient for six months after he leaves Canada. This differs from the Old Age Security pension in that a pensioner may be paid until death if he meets certain residence requirements. A pensioner must have been in Canada for twenty years after age eighteen in order to export the pension.

Every applicant for a supplement must, in his application, make a statement of his income for the year before. Additional statements may also be filed when the applicant in the current fiscal year, or prior thereto, retires or loses his private pension income. An applicant is required to prove his marital status and in most cases where the applicant is married the application will only be dealt with after the applicant's spouse has filed a statement of income for the base calendar year or has submitted an application for a supplement for the current fiscal year. Changes in marital status may result in changes in the supplement. Benefits received under the Canada or Quebec Pension Plans are excluded from income when determining the supplement.

Under the Guaranteed Income System spouses are also covered. Spouses' allowances are monthly benefits under the Old Age Security Act to pensioners' spouses between the ages of sixty and sixty-five who meet the residence and income requirements. Spouses' allowances first became payable in October 1975. They were designed to fill a gap often created by illness of one or both partners in a marriage resulting in two people trying to get by on the income of only one. However, this bill and the provisions are not without controversy because when the pensioner dies the spouse's allowance ceases, leaving the survivor with a considerable loss of income (the Old Age Pension is, of course, also lost with death).

Other federal legislation which provides financial assistance to the aged includes the Old Age Assistance Act, the Disabled Persons Act, the Blind Persons Act, and the Pension Fund Societies Act. These acts make payments to elderly Canadians who meet highly specific requirements and are available to a relatively small number of the population.

GUARANTEED ANNUAL INCOME SYSTEM

Many people who are presently retired worked in an era before pensions were common. Income protection in the form of comprehensive pension plans and adequate health insurance did not exist. Consequently, these pensioners live on fixed incomes following their retirement. Recognizing this problem, Ontario established the Guaranteed Annual Income System (GAINS) in July 1974 to provide a basic income for qualifying residents sixty-five years of age or older. In order to qualify for GAINS benefits the person must meet the eligibility criteria including age, residency and income. GAINS payments to the elderly are administered by the Guaranteed Income and Tax Credit Branch of the Ontario Ministry of Revenue, which decides periodically the minimum amount of money required by an individual to live above the poverty line. This amount is called a Guaranteed Annual Income level, and at this time of writing the annual guarantee is $3,352 for a single person and $6,704 for a married couple. If the total income falls below this level the Ontario government will make payments to bring it to the GAINS level.

SOCIAL SERVICES

Social services which provide direct service to the elderly may be divided into those delivering health care and those which regulate housing.

Health care services under the federal-provincial relationship fall within the administrative jurisdiction of the provincial government. We will focus here on the health services for the aged in Ontario and comparable schemes in other provinces.

The Ontario Health Insurance Plan, operating under the legislative provisions of the Health Insurance Act, 1972, is a comprehensive government-sponsored plan of health services for Ontario residents. It provides a wide range of benefits for medical and hospital services. Residents of Ontario —regardless of age, state of health or financial means—are entitled to participate in the plan. Prepayment is a requirement of any premium-based insurance programme. The Ontario Health Insurance Plan, therefore, is no exception. Premiums are set by regulations. Monthly premium rates in 1976 were $16 for a single person and $32 for a family (with two or more eligible persons). However, effective January 1, 1972 premiums were abolished for residents of Ontario sixty-five years of age or over who have lived in Ontario at least one year immediately prior to making application. In the case of married couples, if one spouse is under the age of sixty-five but the other is over, the insurance can be transferred to the name of the older spouse in order to qualify for premium-free insurance.

OHIP provides a wide scope of benefits for medical and hospital services including physicians' services and hospital services as prescribed under the plan. Extended Health Care (nursing homes and homes for the aged) and home care are also provided for patients eligible and requiring these services.

We must, however, note services not covered by OHIP. These are:
- any hospital charges for private or semiprivate accommodation;
- hospital visits solely for the administration of drugs;
- charges for dental care (except those services provided for an in-patient and performed in an approved hospital, and by a dental surgeon who is a member of the hospital staff);
- eyeglasses, artificial limbs, crutches, special braces and other such appliances;
- private-duty nursing fees;
- drugs taken home from the hospital;
- transportation charges other than approved ambulance service
- health certification services for employment, life insurance or recreational activities;
- cosmetic surgery;
- acupuncture;
- any services other than those provided by approved hospitals or practitioners as specified in the plan.

The exclusion of these services affects the comprehensive and total coverage of health care for all age groups, but, more importantly, for older persons it means additional expenditures on the already limited financial resources available.

Local health units employ one or more public health nurses who are of special service to old people. Upon request, a nurse will visit and assess the needs of the older person and the family. She does not usually give direct nursing care but acts as a referral to medical and welfare services in the community.

For nursing service on a visiting basis, the Victorian Order of Nurses may be called. Charges are based on actual cost, adjusted according to ability to pay. The services of a visiting homemaker are also available in many centres. Under the Homemakers and Nurses Services Act, the province subsidizes the municipality in providing both of these services to those who are not able to pay.

Organized Home Care Plans have been developed in some areas providing the services of doctors, visiting nurses, homemakers and others, such as physiotherapists, to enable patients to leave hospital earlier than they otherwise could, or to avoid entering hospital. In the case of early discharge from hospital, services' are covered by the Ontario Health Insurance Plan.

The provincial government of Alberta has developed a $3 million programme to provide extended health care to Alberta's 127,000 aged. The programme covers the cost of eyglasses, hearing aids, dentures, dental work, and medical equipment such as braces, crutches and wheelchairs. The service is available to persons over sixty-five years of age. The professional groups involved bill the government directly for services and senior citizens need only to present their Alberta Hospital Care Insurance card. This programme is the first of its kind in Canada. As has been seen from the discussion of Ontario Health Services, there is very little health legislation specifically for the aged. Perhaps Alberta's large step forward will persuade other provinces to follow suit.

The Ontario Drug Benefit Plan was instituted on September 1, 1974 by the Ministry of Health in order to assist special segments of the population with the high cost of health care by providing certain approved drugs free of charge to the province's elderly, blind, and disabled on low incomes.

Since the elderly constitute a "population at risk" in respect to several chronic diseases, they may spend up to twice as much as the average citizen on drug costs. These costs have created an overwhelming financial burden for many senior citizens living on fixed incomes. As of August 1, 1975, a revised Ontario Drug Benefit Plan was introduced. This plan covered all persons aged sixty-five years and over (who have resided in Ontario for twelve months and who are citizens or landed immigrants). Those eligible are able to receive prescription medicines covered by the Drug Benefit Plan. In order to receive the benefits, all medicines must be prescribed by a physician, dentist or other qualified health practitioner, and the prescription must be filled in Ontario. Furthermore, only the drugs listed in the Ontario Drug Benefit Formulary are supplied free of charge.

In this extension of government-sponsored health coverage to drug benefits, the Ontario government followed precedents set by three other

Canadian provinces—British Columbia, Manitoba, and Quebec—in acknowledging the principle that inability to pay should not deprive anyone of essential health care needs.

On general principle, the programme is laudable. In its particular application, its adequacy and economic feasibility might be questioned. For instance, the exclusion of compound drugs from the Formulary necessitates that the physician prescribe two single drugs in place of one if the medicine is to qualify for free coverage. The elderly patient thereby ends up with the confusion and inconvenience of taking two pills instead of one and the taxpayer, via the government, ends up paying the pharmacist two dispensing fees. Such inefficiencies could be eliminated by minor revisions to the plan, just as other restrictions that threatened overutilization have been.

Several Ontario cities have low-cost housing projects for older persons. When the Ontario Housing Corporation was formed in 1964, it inherited thirty-six senior citizen housing units developed under the previous federal-provincial partnership. At the end of five years, the corporation had 2,700 units under management and another 7,500 under construction. For the most part, these dwellings consist of one-bedroom units complete with stove and refrigerator. In some of the larger complexes, provisions are made for a central dining room where the residents may buy their meals at a reasonable cost.

The formal request for senior citizen housing usually comes from the municipality. In some cases churches, service clubs or similar organizations suggest the project to municipal offices. It is up to the municipal council to ask the Ontario Housing Corporation for a survey of need and effective demand. Need refers to whether or not a housing shortage exists, and effective demand signifies the number of people who would actually move into available units. If the recommendations put forward by O.H.C. on completion of the survey are accepted by the municipality, then the corporation can go ahead with the building project in consultation with the municipality. The federal government lends O.H.C. 90 per cent of the capital sum and the province lends the balance. Both are repaid with interest.

To be eligible for admission to a unit, an individual should be over sixty years of age and a resident of the community where the unit is located. There can be exceptions to the rules to meet individual needs. Actual admission to senior citizens' housing is based on priorities determined by a point rating system which takes into consideration such things as the applicant's living conditions at the time, his income, and the portion of his income spent on rent. Rents are based on the tenant's income. Charges for utilities are included in the overall rent.

Residential care includes homes for the aged, rest homes and nursing home care. Elderly persons, no longer able to manage at home, may find accommodation in one of the sixty-two homes operated by charitable or religious institutions or in a municipally-operated home for the aged. The former are administered by their own board of directors with the province subsidizing building costs and operating costs not met by income from residents. All give some nursing care but some offer special (senile) or bed care. Municipalities also provide homes for the aged. They are intended for any residents over sixty unable to care for themselves. Persons with means or pensions pay all or part of the cost of care. Municipalities may also provide "special home care" whereby persons eligible for homes for the aged are placed as boarders in private homes.

Rest homes are primarily for persons needing nursing but not hospital care or treatment. They give long-term nursing care.

Privately-operated nursing homes, ranging from converted houses with a few residents to large commercial operations, accommodate many old people who need nursing care but are not eligible for admission to hospitals. Care for persons without means may be financed by the municipality, reimbursed up to 80 per cent by the province.

OTHER SERVICES

The community service which seems to be in vogue at this point in time is the senior citizen drop-in centre. It is usually a place where people who are living independently may come for the day to participate in various activities. Very few communities in Canada seem to have established drop-in centres for senior citizens. There is a gradual recognition that community-based social and recreational services are needed to cope with various psychosocial problems of the elderly in our society.

The only type of counselling that seems to be directly relevant to the needs of the aged is pre-retirement counselling. This is a relatively new innovation and has been received with enthusiasm. Courses on pre-retirement planning are being conducted by universities, industries, and business organizations. Leaders of pre-retirement groups are being trained with the idea that "living can ge ageless." They become knowledgeable on such topics as physical health, work after retirement, individual concerns with retirement and consumer information. Also included in the curriculum are legal issues which may come up, housing considerations and discussions around understanding retirement. An understanding of retirement would include attitudes toward retirement, the implications of increased free time and the need for preparation. The Ontario Ministry of Community & Social Services has put out what we consider an excellent resource kit on pre-retirement information which covers all of the above-mentioned topics.[13] The advent of this type of counselling is a very necessary service if we are to live in a society where compulsory retirement exists.

CRITIQUE OF PRESENT SOCIAL POLICY

In reviewing the income maintenance programme and social services for the aged, the major criticism is that in Canada there is no comprehensive national social policy concerning aging and the aged. [14] Income maintenance programmes are patchwork endeavours designed to meet the most serious contingencies and needs. The existing programmes fail to provide a guaranteed adequate standard of living for the aged. In the organization

13 Pre-Retirement Resource Kit from the Pre-Retirement Library, Ministry of Community and Social Services, Ontario, Youths Recreation Branch, Summer 1972.
14 Daniel Jay Baum, The Final Plateau: The Betrayal of Our Older Citizens (Toronto: Burns and MacEachern, 1974).

and delivery of social services for the aged, there is little or no recognition of sociopsychological effects of aging and their profound consequences for the older persons in our society. In short, present social policy fails to come to grips with the complex problems of the aged and of aging in Canada. The recently-adopted policy statement by the Canadian Council on Social Development on retirement in Canada is based on broad-range studies of retirement age and income. Their examination of the status of our older citizens living on retirement incomes finds much inequality and stop-gap legislation in dealing with this problem.

Income maintenance programmes for the aged are most inadequate in terms of their cash benefits and supplements. A person who has made regularly the maximum contributions to the existing programmes during his earning years and who qualifies for the maximum benefits must expect a retirement income that is on the poverty line. That is to say, that approximately 60 per cent of the people over sixty-five must live at a bare subsistence level even though most of the programmes are now keyed to the cost of living index.

In this frame of reference, the attempt to plug the holes and continue the patchwork approach is shocking. The present income maintenance programmes simply fail to guarantee a standard of living that is a right of every citizen including the aged.

Health care for the aged is inadequate. The level of income and the quality of health care are positively correlated. Because of the inadequacy of income maintenance programmes, most older citizens are also deprived of quality health care. Aging often makes necessary an increased amount of spending for health care. Lack of adequate income affects proper nutrition and the availability of drugs. It also affects the quality of the accommodation that older people can afford in the housing market. There have been some attempts to integrate comprehensive health care and services for the aged with income maintenance programmes such as the step taken by the Alberta government. There is a need for a national policy in this regard.

If the present trend toward emphasizing institutional care for the aged continues, Canada will have attained the dubious distinction among the countries of the world of having the highest proportion of older citizens in institutions.[15] These institutions may range from nursing homes for the chronically ill to "retirement villages" for the relatively healthy. Lack of adequate incomes is one of the primary reasons leading to higher institutionalization of older people. Community services for this group are just beginning and we are slowly recognizing the fact that the aged can be taken care of in their own homes and that, in fact, this is the desirable type of care for nearly 80 per cent of older citizens.

The psychological consequences of alienation, disengagement, despair and a feeling of worthlessness among our senior citizens will continue as long as there is a separation between "we" and "they." Retirement at age sixty-five accounts for this separation. Our policy of compulsory retirement forces retired individuals to accept the proposition that they are worthless from a market economy point of view. Lack of post-retirement work oppor-

15 Nathan Markus, "Home Care for the Aged," *Canadian Welfare* 50, no. 1 (1974): 17-19.

tunities accentuates the psychological effect. Our present tax structure and benefit programmes penalize the senior citizen who wishes to work after the mandatory retirement age. For people who have been steeped in the work ethic since childhood, it is a source of stress and demoralization to find themselves being "paid" to do nothing in retirement. Our current social policy does nothing to help this growing segment of our society feel useful or needed. Indeed, we would seem to be wasting a valuable national resource by turning our backs on the elderly and not mobilizing their wisdom and experience toward the goals of our society.

A COMPREHENSIVE SOCIAL POLICY

We have criticized the existing social policy but now it is necessary to suggest alternatives. In the development of a comprehensive social policy, it is assumed that *living can be an ageless phenomenon*. Too many of our social programmes are based on age groups that force an artificial separation between life stages. The economic, psychological and social needs of the aged are not radically different from those of any other group in society. As such, in the development of a comprehensive social policy, we need to bear in mind that the elderly are and will continue to be an integral part of the society.

The substance of our proposal is centred around the Guaranteed Annual Income for the aged, and indeed for every person in our society. G.A.I. should be viewed as a right for all people leaving the work force. It should be seen as a right and not as a privilege or a reward for contributions to society, but rather as an integral part of the concept of human rights. The fact that G.A.I. would be available to everyone whose earnings and income fall below a certain level of acceptable standard of living would help eliminate the stigmatization and separation of older people from the rest of society. The complex provisions of many programmes should now be consolidated into one comprehensive guaranteed annual income programme which would also provide adequate health care, housing, and improvement of the psychological self-image of the aged.

Public support for a guaranteed annual income is growing. According to the latest survey conducted by a Montreal firm for the Canadian Council on Social Development, 88 per cent of Canadians now support some form of G.A.I. Only 67 per cent favoured the idea when a national survey was conducted in 1971. The Special Senate Committee on Poverty chaired by Senator David Croll has strongly recommended that the government of Canada implement a G.A.I. programme using the Negative Income Tax method on a uniform national basis. The committee's report further recommended that the proposed G.A.I. programme be financed and administered by the government of Canada, and that the plans be designed to cover *all Canadians* who need it.[16]

There is also a need to revise our policy of compulsory retirement at a certain age. Instead of compulsory retirement, we need a graduated and flexible retirement policy that will prepare for disengagement, eliminate the

16　Report of the Special Senate Committee on Poverty, *Poverty in Canada*, p. xv.

abruptness of retirement, and offer greater freedom of choice to workers for retirement between sixty and seventy years with room for exceptions at either end. Toffler, in his book *Future Shock*,[17] suggests that society must be ready to look at retirement more as an individual phenomenon and not on the basis of a mandatory retirement age for all, regardless of individual needs. There is a further need to provide meaningful work opportunities for people during the post-retirement period. Meaningful work opportunities help reduce and can even eliminate the psychological trauma accompanying retirement. Work enhances feelings of self-worth and of being contributing members of society. The New Horizons programme of the federal government is noble in its intent to accomplish this task, but needs to be greatly expanded before it can make an impact on older people.

Community services for senior citizens must be developed across Canada and should be integrated with total service programmes for other age groups. The emphasis of community services should be to provide for all of the needs of the elderly within the community. This would include housing, health care, recreation and leisure opportunities as well as psychological and counselling resources. Ideally, community services should be neighbourhood-based and should provide opportunities for interaction with family and friends of older people.

Educational opportunities for new learning and new careers for older people must be found and developed. The Ontario Commission on Post-Secondary Education[18] has strongly endorsed the proposition that education must be universal. It asks for diversification at all levels. It argues that because ours is a pluralistic society, it follows that if educational services are to be universally available they must also be diverse. The Commission recommends a policy that will allow for free flow of *students at all ages* and at all times during their lives in and out of the school system. Some universities, such as Trent and Victoria, are experimenting with courses of study for older persons. Certainly, the continuing education programmes developing across Canada can do much to enrich the lives of our senior citizens.

Another important educational approach is the preparation of the population for retirement. In 1974 Wilfrid Laurier University and the Faculty of Social Work offered courses on pre-retirement counselling which were highly popular. Much more needs to be done and can be done to utilize existing educational institutions in preparing Canadians for retirement and in exploring avenues to new careers for older people.

CONCLUSION

The older people in Canada experience three major problems: economic insecurity, social neglect and psychological alienation. *Economic insecurity* is due to the lack of adequate income after retirement. The various governmental social security programmes for the aged fail to guarantee a "standard of living" that can be considered above the "poverty line."

17   Alvin Toffler, *Future Shock* (New York: Random House, 1972).
18   Report of the Commission on Post-Secondary Education in Ontario, *The Learning Society* (Toronto: Ministry of Government Services, 1972).

Because older people have *no significant social role* to perform they feel isolated and alienated from the mainstream of society. Societal neglect of senior citizens is a major factor in the lack of progressive social policy. In the development of such a policy, we must come to grips with the consequences of these problems. Re-examination of compulsory retirement provision of a guaranteed annual income, pre-retirement and post-retirement counselling and post-retirement career opportunities for older people are some of the elements that should make up the design of social policy for the aged in Canada.

The challenge of constructing a viable social policy for the aged of Canada is an awesome one. I have tried to outline some of the economic, social and psychological problems faced by our senior citizens today. I have dwelt, however dryly, on the provisions of our "finger in the dyke" approach to these problems. And I have suggested some solutions which might prove to be more comprehensive and constructive. But in concluding this essay, there is one last important point to be made. The onus of the problem does not rest upon our social policy alone—it rests with each of us as individuals and collectively as a society! Our societal neglect of the aged, however we may try to rationalize it, is a denial of our own mortality. To form a just and humane policy that accommodates the needs of the aging members of our society necessitates the realization that aging is a natural function. Today we have the opportunity to guide the policy that governs us—tomorrow!

BIBLIOGRAPHY

"Age Stigma: Rhetoric and Reality." Editorial, *Social Policy* 7, no. 3 (November-December 1976): 2.

Audain, M. J., et al. *Beyond Shelter. A Study of National Housing Act Financial Housing for the Elderly.* Ottawa: Canadian Council on Social Development, 1973.

Auerbach, L., and A. Gerber. *Implications of the Changing Age Structure of the Canadian Population.* Perceptions 2. Study of Population and Technology. Ottawa: Science Council of Canada, July 1976.

Baum, Daniel J. *The Final Plateau: The Betrayal of Our Older Citizens.* Toronto: Burns and MacEachern, 1974.

Bellak, Leopold. *The Best Years of Your Life.* Toronto: McClelland and Stewart, 1975.

Brown, J. *How Much Choice? Retirement Policies in Canada.* Ottawa: Canadian Council on Social Development, 1975.

Bryden, Kenneth. *Old Age Pensions and Policy Making in Canada.* Montreal: McGill-Queen's University Press, 1974.

Canada. Department of Health and Welfare. *Hospitals and the Elderly—Present and Future Trends.* Ottawa: Health and Welfare Canada, Long Range Health Planning Branch, 1975.

Canada. Senate. *Final Report of the Special Committee of the Senate on Aging.* Ottawa: Queen's Printer, 1966.

Canadian Conference on Aging. *Conference Proceedings.* Toronto, January 1966, and Ottawa, November 1966.

Canadian Council on Social Development. *Statement on Retirement Policies.* Ottawa, March 1976.

Canadian Welfare Council. *The Aging in Canada.* Ottawa: Canadian Welfare Council, 1966.

Coward, Lawrence E. *Some History on Pensions in Canada.* Don Mills: CCH Canadian Ltd., 1964.

Curtin, Sharon R. *Nobody Ever Died of Old Age.* Toronto: Little, Brown and Company, 1972.

Davies, R. E. G. *A Critical Review of the Senate Report on Aging.* Ottawa: Canadian Welfare Council, 1968.

Etzioni, Amitai. "Old People and Public Policy." *Social Policy* 7, no. 3 (November-December 1976): 21-29.

Hart, G. *Non Profit Housing for the Aged and Other Special Groups.* A Policy for Central Mortgage and Housing Corporation. Ottawa, August 1976.

Health Services for the Elderly. *The Final Report of a Working Group of the Federal Provincial Advisory Committee on Community Health.* Ottawa: Community Health Directorate, Health and Welfare Canada, August 1976.

Hepworth, Philip H. *Personal Social Services in Canada: Access and Delivery.* Ottawa: The Canadian Council on Social Development, 1975.

Hunnisett, Henry S. *How to Survive Retirement in Canada.* Vancouver: International Self-Counsel Press, 1976.

Louis Harris and Associates. *The Myth and Reality of Aging in America.* Washington: National Council on the Aging, 1975.

Markus, Nathan. "Home Care for the Aged." *On Growing Old* 12 (February 1974).

Ontario Conference on Aging. *Aging is Everyone's Concern: The Proceedings of the First Ontario Conference on Aging.* University of Toronto, May 31-June 1, 1957.

The Ontario Health Insurance Plan: General Guide. Pamphlet issued by the Ontario Ministry of Health, 1976.

Schwenger, C. W. "Integrated Application of Community Resources to the Aged." *Canadian Journal of Public Health* 58, no. 12 (December 1967): 535-40.

_____ . "Health Care for Aging Canadians." *Canadian Welfare* 52, no. 6 (January-February 1977): 9-12.

Toward a National Policy on Aging. Vol. 1. Proceedings of the 1971 White House Conference on Aging, November 28-December 1, 1971, Washington, D.C.

Yudelman, John. *The National Context.* A report on government programmes concerning the elderly. Toronto: Pensioners Concerned (Canada) Inc., 1974.

Native Peoples and Social Policy

E. PALMER PATTERSON II

No one who reads the newspapers or watches television can miss the fact that native peoples are in the news. They have emerged as an important element in the total national scene in a way which has not been matched in more than a hundred years. The decline of the native as an important subject in history books is a story that has been told elsewhere (Walker, Patterson). The post-World War II world has seen the emergence into self-consciousness and political independence of many indigenous peoples who had been overcome by the European expansion of the last several centuries.

The promotion of the multicultural society and the cultural mosaic in Canada has contributed to the re-emergence of the native people as an important segment of Canadian society. Canadian Indians are, therefore, receiving greater consideration. Undoubtedly the arrival of Europeans has caused native Canadians gradually to adopt large elements of educational, organizational, and communications techniques introduced by the new-comers. At a time when the immigrant European and other ethnic groups have been asserting the values of their cultural traditions, the native peoples have been rediscovering and redefining their own outlook on their traditions.

In an atmosphere which will allow the survival of diverse cultural traditions the native peoples are seeking to achieve their cultural survival. New leaders, new organizations, new techniques of communicating their points of view and some new friends are contributing to a new interest in an awareness of the Indian and Inuit in Canada today. Several recent books by

Indians have reached wide audiences. Harold Cardinal's *The Unjust Society*, Waubageshig's *The Only Good Indian*, Edward Ahenakew's *Voices of the Plains Cree*, and George Manuel's *The Fourth World* are among the most important of these for presenting to both the student and the general reader a picture of how Indians view the Indian's experiences in Canada in the last several centuries.

CANADIAN INDIAN HISTORY

The history of the native peoples in Canada has been one in which they have moved from political, social, religious, economic and artistic independence to a status of subjection and control. Generally speaking, the advance of foreign domination has proceeded from east to west and from south to north.

Small groups of people who identified with each other and with adjacent small groups have gradually come, as a result of the impact of the new-comers, to identify themselves as "tribes" and as Indians. The loss of autonomy in all the categories of culture indicated above has been accompanied by the development of new units of identification. While each group of people has had its own unique experience, they have also shared in many experiences which are the products of Indian-white contact. The pace of change and adaptation which characterized the aboriginal culture was accelerated. The pressures for change came from the contact situation and from the ramifications of changes proceeding from contact.

Technological and material elements were the first parts of aboriginal culture to be altered. This gradual alteration led in many cases to dependence on European goods and technology. These changes, though voluntary at the start, became irreversible. Shifts in political and social status occurred, epidemic diseases affected social life, shifts in residence occurred, and change in natural resources led to more extensive and intensive cultural change generally. The dynamics of change were taken out of the hands of the native people. They were obliged to react to the actions of the invaders.

The purpose of the earliest Europeans was to acquire fish. Perhaps by the late sixteenth century, but certainly by the early seventeenth century, it was furs that became the main economic motivation for European activity in Canada. A complementary relationship developed between natives and newcomers. The Indian way of life, as hunters, fishermen, and gatherers, fitted into the economic interests of the European very well. They were partners. The native had much to offer—not only pelts, but food, geographic knowledge, techniques of transportation, diplomatic relations, established trade routes, medicinal knowledge, and the offer of friendship to a handful of foreigners.

Rivalry between the Europeans in north-eastern North America led to the natives becoming involved as allies in the European wars. The competition for furs led to more deadly wars between the eastern Algonkian-speakers and the Iroquoian-speakers of Eastern Canada and the adjacent United States, from at least the early seventeenth century down to the early nineteenth century. Native involvement with Europeans changed the partnership relationship to one of superior/inferior. The autonomy of the native peoples was replaced by subjection and control. Voluntary acceptance of European cultural items was replaced by forced change as the basis of Indian-white linkage was altered.

Even where the fur trade continued to be the major basis of the European economic interest, native people changed from partners to employees. When pelts were no longer available in significant numbers, natives sought employment as guides, canoemen, porters, suppliers of meat and labourers around the trading post. Native patterns of residence and group composition changed also. The social unit changed from the small band to assemblies of two hundred or more people who settled around the trading post/mission station/administrative and police office.

In the third quarter of the eighteenth century there were probably less than 100,000 people of European extraction resident in Canada. This population did not require much land. The end of the eighteenth century and early nineteenth century witnessed the beginning of a significant change in population. The American Revolution and developments in the British Isles led to an influx of settlers from those areas. The small French-speaking population was rapidly augmented by a large English-speaking population. These people were agriculturalists. They wanted land for farming, and the colonies' administrators, wishing to attract settlers, took steps to provide land. Some of the new immigrants were Iroquois allies of the British, who came along with other Loyalists.

In order to provide land, treaties of land surrender were signed with the Indians of Upper Canada. In Quebec and the Maritimes no such treaties of surrender had been made by the French in their occupation. Neither did the British government do so, when they took over from the French. Generally speaking, the French did not recognize an aboriginal right in the land, and the British received the territory from the French as though the matter was settled. From the late eighteenth century through the nineteenth century into the twentieth century, in Ontario, Manitoba, Saskatchewan, and Alberta, as settlement was anticipated or began to occur, treaties of land surrender were signed with the Indians. These are the "Indian Treaties." There were other treaties of friendship, alliance, and trade. But more often than not, when treaties, treaty rights, and other such phrases are used, land surrender treaties are meant.

CANADA'S SOCIAL POLICY TOWARD INDIANS

A new notion of the Indian began to emerge which can be correlated with the new economic emphasis of the incoming whites. At the same time, a conscious social policy came into being. Indians were to be converted into farmers. Aboriginally most of the Indians of what is today Canada had been hunters, gatherers, and fishing folk. Only the lower Great Lakes area and parts of the St. Lawrence River Valley had contained agriculturalists, and these people had been largely removed from the scene by the mid-seventeenth century. If the hunters became settled farmers, large tracts of land would become available to the new burgeoning European population. In addition, the Indians placed on the reserves could undergo a process of culture change at the hands of Indian administrators, Christian clergy, and teachers. This policy of involuntary culture change leading toward the eventual cultural, if not biological, assimilation of the Indian became the policy. It was to be applied from the early nineteenth century until the second half of the twentieth century.

As European settlement spread, the Indians ceased to be numerically important; as agriculture spread, the Indian became peripheral to economic life. As geographical knowledge increased and technology developed new systems of transportation and new applications of energy for transport, Indians declined in importance as aids to travel. Their technology became associated with sport and recreation instead of business and commerce. Their importance as allies diminished when one large neighbour emerged, after the War of 1812, with whom peaceful relations were sought.

Official correspondence dealing with Indians began to decline. The Indian figured less and less as an important subject of government concern. The policy toward Indians underwent what some observers have regarded as its most important alteration in the early nineteenth century. Duncan Campbell Scott, a senior Indian administrator and early writer on the history of Indian administration, described this change. His words contain a reference to the problem of periodization in the reconstruction of Indian history:

> The time divisions which are convenient for the larger purposes and scope of this history [of Canada] have no significance for Indian Affairs. The administrative changes which occurred in 1763 [the Treaty of Paris] and 1841 [the Union of Upper and Lower Canada] did not effect the Indians in their government, and the date of Confederation serves but to mark the responsibility for Indians then cast upon the Dominion. The year 1830 may be fixed as the limit of the first regime in Indian affairs. Before that date a purely military administration prevailed, the duty of the government being restricted to maintaining the loyalty of the Indian nations to the Crown, with almost the sole object of preventing their hostility and of conserving their assistance as allies. About 1830 the government, with the disappearance of the anxieties of the first period, began to perceive the large humane duties which had arisen with the gradual settlement and pacification of the country. The civilization of the Indian became the ideal; the menace of the tomahawk and the firebrand having disappeared, the apparent duty was to raise him from the debased condition into which he had fallen due to the loose and pampering policy of former days. Protection from vices which were not his own, and instruction in peaceful occupations, foreign to his natural bent, were to be substituted for necessary generosity. When the Dominion in 1867 gathered up and assumed the responsibility of the colonial governments to the Indians of the provinces this policy was not changed, but a great expansion in its current occurred, and the development of the new western territories largely increased the burden.[1]

The gifts and presents of former days of hunting and military alliance —cloth, guns, ammunition, foods, trinkets—were replaced by articles suited to the practice of agriculture—plows, domestic farm animals, seed, axes, and saws, but the implementation of the new policy was much less

---

1 Duncan C. Scott, "Indian Affairs, 1763-1841," in *Canada and Its Provinces*, ed. Adam Shortt and Arthur B. Doughty, vol. 4 (Toronto: University of Toronto Press, 1913), pp. 695-96.

systematic than a superficial reading of the intentions might indicate. The various human agents of culture change—administrators, clergy, teachers, police—were working with, and themselves constituted, conditions which made the realization of their task of assimilation extremely unlikely to succeed. The slogans "advancement and protection" and "civilization and Christianity" and "the Bible and the plough" were the ideals that were voiced. But the means by which these goals were to be accomplished proved ineffective. Staffs changed frequently, were not well-trained for their work, and had little or no understanding of the culture of the people they wanted to change. The isolation of reserves and non-reserve Indian peoples meant that intensive contact was lacking. Indian indifference and/or resistance to and resentment of the changes being pressed on them lessened the impact. The Indians, where they wanted change, wanted selectivity in change. They wished to retain control over their culture change. They did not accept the assumption of the Euro-Canadians that Western civilization was superior to the culture they already had.

The methods used to effect change, and the attitudes and behaviour of the Euro-Canadians, including settlers and miners as well as administrators, clergy, teachers, and policy, aroused frustration, resentment, insecurity, and defensiveness in the Indian. Where resistance to change could not be made overtly it was made covertly. Efforts to suppress use of the native languages meant that students, forbidden to speak their own languages in school, used them out of earshot of teachers. Customs forbidden by administrators and/or clergy were practised away from their eyes and in altered forms.

The white population grew and Indians became peripheral to the life of nineteenth-century Canada. Without the vote and without economic or organizational power, they were ignored. If thought about at all, they were viewed as undergoing assimilation. In the late nineteenth and early twentieth centuries it was thought that the natives would take a long time to become "civilized" but that they would do so eventually. Some commentators on the process pointed out that it had taken the Germanic forebears of the English several centuries to evolve into the English people. The Indians were compared with various North European groups who had come under the influence of the Roman Empire and Western Christianity.

As individuals were seen to assimilate, it was thought that whole communities would do the same. Some observers saw cultural assimilation as the only alternative to biological extinction. While some thought that the Indians were a "vanishing race," others noticed that among the Indians of the Maritimes, Southern Quebec, and Ontario, there had begun to be a very slight rise in population by the mid-nineteenth century. The census reports showed a rise in Indian populations in Canada generally. The decline had been checked, due in part, it has been suggested, to some European admixture.

Further, the Indian Act of 1876 meant the creation of the status "Indian." It also left a population of people who were Indian or Indian/white (as were the status Indians), but who were not Indians under the Indian Act. These people are known as Métis, and increasingly in the late twentieth century are also called non-status Indians. Though outside the jurisdiction of the federal government's Indian administration, the non-status Indian experienced the discrimination and prejudice practised on the status Indians. In many cases they could not find a sense of community with Euro-Canadians or status Indians, but only among their own people. In these circumstances they have in many cases developed a strong sense of their own identity.

In the last decades they have increasingly organized themselves, locally, provincially, and nationally, to call attention to their condition. Although not included as Indians under the Indian Act, some have asserted that they are natives under the British North America Act and as such have a claim on the federal government for special assistance beyond that which comes through the local and provincial governments. An indication of their identification of themselves as native peoples can be seen in the titles of their organizations, for example, Union of Non-Status Indians (Nova Scotia), British Columbia Association of Non-Status Indians, and Native Council of Canada, the national organization.

Allen Harper notes both the policy of assimilation and the low view widely held of Indian culture:

> Indeed, the policy of "transforming the Indian into a white man," has had few critical dissenters in Canada. This objective has been coupled always with little appreciation of Indian culture. In all the literature there is hardly a kind word for a single aboriginal virtue which might conceivably command respect on the part of the whites and deliberate preservation on the part of government administrators.[2]

It might be more accurate to say that even when virtues were noted they were thought to be inferior to the larger or better virtues which would come when the old culture was demolished and the Euro-Canadian culture had replaced it. John McLean's *The Indians of Canada: Their Manners and Customs* (1889, 1970) is an example of what would probably be regarded as some of the most enlightened opinion of the nineteenth century. He remarks, "The change that must inevitably come to all inferior races has at last fallen upon them."[3]

Certain general characteristics of this policy may be noted. Firstly, Crown sovereignty was asserted over the land and native interest in the land was alienated by treaties of land acquisition where rights of conquest were not presumed. In British Columbia the land policy shifted from land treaties, comparable to those in the prairie provinces, to a policy of denying native rights in the land altogether. Secondly, the basic economic activities of the native peoples were made to conform to the economic interests of the white occupiers. Though the particular economic emphasis shifted from furs to farming as the Euro-Canadian society developed, in both cases the initiative for pressures to change were produced, whether intentionally or unintentionally, by the interests of the dominant segment of the emerging society.

2　Allen G. Harper, "Canada's Indian Administration: Basic Concepts and Objectives," *America Indigena* v, no. 2 (April 1945): 128.
3　John McLean, *The Indians of Canada: Their Manners and Customs* (1889; Toronto: Coles Publishing Company, 1970), p. 321.

Accompanying the loss of land and the domination of the economy was the pressure to conform to the cultural values and forms introduced by the newcomers. This included, as has been seen, pressures on the Indians to take up European religion, language, education, dress, customs, and law. The paternalistic methods and the ethnocentric attitudes which lay behind these direct and indirect, planned and unplanned measures for culture change have increasingly been commented upon by Indians in the 1970s. Some writers have concentrated on what they see as a malicious intent on the part of the Euro-Canadians in their dealings with the native people. Cross-cultural conflict, ethnocentrism, paternalism, and exploitation characterize the history of Indian-white relations, the policy of Indian administration, and its day-to-day application.

After the War of 1812 the native peoples were increasingly seen as expendable. They would either assimilate or die out. Their administration was created to aid their assimilation, but white society was not going to be seriously affected. Wherever the land and resources the Indians held were wanted by whites, these could be had through the machinery of a government controlled by the white settler population.

It was assumed that the European culture with which Indians were presented was so manifestly superior that all but the most conservative and unrepentantly traditionalist (the words used were "pagan," "heathen," "savage"—all pejorative) would see and take the option to become "civilized," "Westernized," and "Christianized." It was, however, frequently admitted that the persons and mechanisms which were being used to implement the policy of assimilation were not always the best. Programmes were neither thought out, nor administered efficiently; goods did not arrive or came spoiled and unusable. Indians who were discriminated against and abused exhibited resentment, bitterness, withdrawal, and unwillingness to assimilate. Where recognized, these were seen as flaws in the system, bugs to be worked out by new personnel and new techniques for applying the policy.

This approach can be seen in the European missionaries and clergy who evangelized, shepherded, taught, and practised medicine among Indians. They were among the earliest to comment on the declining buffalo herds and to call for shifts to agriculture to avoid future famine when herds disappeared. Wishing to introduce European Christianity and European culture, they were partners with the government in acculturation. At the same time, they sometimes acted as intermediaries between government, white society, and the Indians.

While firmly committed to drastic changes in the life of the Indian, they also frequently noticed specific abuses and called attention to ways in which the ideals of the programme for culture change were being undermined by the methods used. Nevertheless, they were themselves guilty of some of the most dramatically destructive forms of behaviour in dealing with the native peoples and their culture. The European system of child discipline and the residential schools which applied that system have frequently been commented upon for the harmfulness and bitterness of their effects upon Indians.

Among the clergy, there were some who thought of incorporating greater or lesser amounts and kinds of native cultural tradition into the Christianity they presented. Only in the third quarter of the twentieth century have notions of "native Christianity" become an alternative where Indians are concerned, although for centuries it was the common pattern for Christianity to become indigenous as it spread, and even in the heyday of nineteenth-century European imperialism this had a few advocates. Henry Venn of the Church Missionary Society of England is an example. However, it was not often seen as a procedure suited to New World Indians, certain pioneering efforts by the Jesuits notwithstanding.

Diamond Jenness, one of the most outstanding figures in the study of Canadian Indians, summarized the conditions in the 1920s. His description relates policy and practice to each other and both of these to the atmosphere of the Euro-Canadian society of which they were the expression and reflection. What Jenness found was prejudice against Indians across the country, though with less in Quebec than in most other provinces. Generally, the "average Canadian" looked down on Indians as inferior and undesirable, to be shunned as companions, or fellow labourers. Native people suffered from the neglect of their "guardians." They were unable to alter their conditions because of their isolation, small numbers, lack of the vote, poverty, and lack of skills in making their case. They reacted with an attitude of apathy and discontent. For their administrators they were an infinite meal ticket. The education offered to the Indians was frequently of poor quality and few of them went beyond the primary grades. Their health was also neglected, and disease and malnutrition were endemic among many.[4]

We have been surveying approximately three centuries of first British and then Canadian policy toward Indians, from the late seventeenth century to the second half of the twentieth century, to review what happened to the native peoples of Canada, what occurred to create new categories and groupings, what policy and practice contributed to create out of many diverse peoples "the Canadian Indian." While each people had its unique events, certain experiences have recurred widely, affecting many groups, though not necessarily all peoples.

THE DEVELOPMENT OF CANADIAN INDIAN ADMINISTRATION

In 1755 an important step was taken in the development of Indian administration and policy. In order to hold Indians more effectively to a British alliance, and to unify and centralize their administration, two superintendencies of Indian affairs were created. The northern superintendent dealt primarily with the Iroquois and matters relating to their affairs. His southern counterpart dealt with the Cherokees, Choctaws, Creeks, Chickasaws, and their affairs. These officers were appointed by London following reports of William Johnson and Edward Atkins. These men became the first two appointees, though Johnson, who took the northern superintendency, is by far the better known of the two. An important aspect of their duties was the

---

4   Diamond Jenness, "Canada's Indians Yesterday; What of Today?" *Canadian Journal of Economics and Political Science* 20, no. 1 (February 1954): 95-100.

regulation of trade and commerce and securing of and retaining adherence to treaties of alliance. Efforts were made to control land purchases as well. The Proclamation of 1763 has become one of, if not the most famous, documents of the early Indian-white relations. It was set in the context of heightened antagonism by many western tribes against European encroachment, cutbacks in gifts of friendship, and the disappointment felt by many Indians at the removal of the French from competition in North America. The Proclamation regulated the sale of Indian land, prohibited westward expansion of the white settlers, and attempted to create a huge Indian reserve. The policy of friendship, alliance, and giving of presents is that already referred to in the remarks of Duncan Campbell Scott.

The point has been made that the basic Indian policy in Canada for the last 140 or so years began to take shape in the 1820s and 1830s. This policy of assimilation can be seen to be developing in various official reports, legislation, and official statements. As has already been indicated, the implementation of the policy did not necessarily conform perfectly to the policy as stated or as anticipated. Various factors which intervened between the thought and the action have been noted. It is useful for a better understanding of the policy to take a closer look at some of the highlights of its career. It would be inaccurate to assert that it has undergone no change since its formulation in the early nineteenth century, but the basic policy has remained. Many of the basic attitudes of the Euro-Canadians, the basic analysis of what the Indian is and should be, have not changed much. Many of the stereotypes which pertain today have been the product of the kinds of interaction that have occurred between Indians and non-Indians. This is particularly likely to be the case when the Indian ceased to be an important economic, military, and numerical segment of the total population.

A review of the broad outlines and historical circumstances after the War of 1812 has already been given. After the war, economies were called for. Appropriations of money for Indians were among the categories to be pared. Presents were not only expensive but clashed with the newly-emerging policy of forced culture change. Missionaries and other Indian "experts" argued that equipment for hunting and migratory existence restricted the ability of the whites to work effectively on the Indians to change them. Further, the annual distributions of presents created opportunities for behaviour, such as carousing, gambling, and drinking, which were contrary to the larger changes deemed necessary. In this way various interests of the whites coincided in Indian administration.

The earliest report suggesting a change in policy from one designed "to conciliate the Indians, to insure their services, and to supply their wants as warriors in the field: and afterwards, in terms of peace, to assure their allegiance towards the British Crown, and their good will and peaceful behaviour towards the white settlers,"[5] is associated with the name of Major General Darling, Deputy Superintendent General of Indian Affairs. General Darling urged the necessity to "civilize and educate" the Indians and to substitute for the annuities and gifts livestock and farm implements. This

5 "The Report on the Affairs of the Indians of Canada," *Journal of the Legislative Assembly of Canada, 1844-45*, Appendix E.E.E., Section 1, p. 6.

suggestion seems to have been anticipated in a more general way in 1822 and 1827 by the Earl of Bathurst and Viscount Goderich, the Colonial Secretaries in the respective years.

In 1828 Sir George Murray approved General Darling's suggestions, and himself requested of Sir John Kempt, Lieutenant-Governor of Lower Canada, to report on measures that would be "necessary for the moral and religious instruction of the Indians, and how far the labours of the Missionaries in this respect have been beneficial, or may require assistance; and whether the measures which have hitherto been adopted for the protection of the Indians, in the lands and property to which they are fairly entitled, have been effective."[6]

Kempt made several proposals: first, Indians should be collected together and settled in villages, and a portion of their land set aside for cultivation; second, provision should be made for evangelizing them as well as for providing them with a European type of education and training in agricultural pursuits; third, they should be provided with aid to build houses, get food, seed, implements—at least a portion of the expenses to come from money which would otherwise be spent on their annual presents; and fourth, missionaries should be provided in particular locations, with English Methodist missionaries replacing the American Methodists who were so active.

It is not necessary to pursue the development of the policy in detail to be able to observe in its early formulation the principles of "protection and advancement," "Christianity and civilization," and "the Bible and the plough," which have already been mentioned. Parallel developments were taking place in the administration of Indians in Nova Scotia and New Brunswick at about the same time. There, the influx of settlers and the policy of forced change produced situations similar to those in Upper and Lower Canada.

From time to time through the mid-nineteenth century, investigations were made by government into the progress being made in the programme of culture change. The first major report in Canada was made in 1844. It was reported that the Indians of Canada East had long been evangelized by Jesuits but were otherwise little or not thought about by government. They remained as they had been in 1763, "unenlightened" and "docile" followers of their religious pastors. The Indians of Canada West, on the other hand, were reportedly coming to a much larger extent under more recent efforts at culture change. Their pastors were often Methodists, and the Indians had been "raised" above those of Canada East. However, the nearby presence of white communities frequently had a degrading and debauching effect on the Indians, who were robbed and cheated when dealing with the whites.

One interruption in the emergence of the assimilation policy needs to be noted. In the late 1830s Sir Francis Bond Head tried to reverse the policy and remove Indians of northern Upper Canada to Manitoulin Island. There the Indians would not be touched by whites generally or missionaries in particular. This proposal—Head actually began the process for removal,

6   Ibid., p. 7.

though his actions were largely nullified by later events—was based on Head's view that the Indians of Upper Canada were incapable of significant cultural adaptation beyond that which was described by the words "debauched" and "debased" as a result of contact with whites. He saw the missionaries' efforts as unsuccessful and largely wasted.

How much Head was influenced by the pressures for releasing more Indian land to the white settlers is not clear. The Indian removal of the Five Civilized Tribes (the Trail of Tears) which was taking place in the United States in the 1830s likely had an influence, though it is undocumented. The cross-fertilization of thought between Canada and the United States on Indian policy is a subject which has been touched on from time to time but would bear more investigation.[7]

A major protest was mounted against Head's views on Indian policy and his particular application of these views. This approach did not supplant the embryonic policy of his predecessors. In fairness to Head it should be noted that his proposal for removal was a modification of a previous scheme by Sir John Colbourne to re-settle Indians on Manitoulin Island in order to isolate them from the evil influences of white settlers. The difference Head introduced into the programme as far as overall policy was concerned was the abandonment by him of the idea of culture change.

Culture change and isolation continued as issues of debate in the nineteenth century. In order to secure the desired changes to accomplish assimilation to white society, it was necessary to isolate the Indians from white society, the argument went. Were these not contradictory conditions? Would it really be possible to accomplish assimilation if the Indians were not given the full range of white society to experience? As far as the experience of the Indians was concerned, the argument was largely theoretical because they did in fact generally experience the worst influences of the culture contact situation. Almost the whole range of contact was adverse rather than positive for them. Evangelization and Western education contributed to their battering just as did disease, alcohol, and land loss.

A Royal Commission of 1856 proposed "separation without isolation" as the way to give "protection and advancement." This proposal was based on studies in the neighbouring state of Michigan which showed that controlled separation was more important for protection than was isolation alone. In 1857 an Act of the Government of the Province of Canada re-asserted the goal of assimilation. It laid out procedures for individual Indians to gain citizenship status at the point of their being fully assimilated. This legislation anticipated by three years (1860) the transfer of Indian administration to the Province of Canada. After two years as part of the Crown Lands Department, a separate Indian Affairs Department was created which brought together under its centralized control all of the various functions which had to do with Indians such as sale of land, education, welfare,

7 Several years ago when the writer first read Freeman Blake's *History of the Indians in British North America* (1870), there was stuck in the back of the particular copy he got on Interlibrary Loan a clipping from *The Nation*, Thursday, February 3, 1870. It was a notice of Blake's booklet praising it, and hoping "that even before this country [the United States] undertakes to annex Canada, it will annex its Indian policy."

health, and finance. This centralized Department, what J. E. Hodgetts calls a "clientele" department, would, it was hoped, correct many of the inadequacies and inefficiencies which had been reported by the 1856 Commission.[8]

By the terms of the British North America Act (1867), Section 91(24), control over Indians and lands reserved for Indians was given to the federal government. New legislation incorporated the administrative legislation of the Province of Canada. In 1868 an Act was passed "providing for the organization of the department of the Secretary of State of Canada, and for the better management of Indian and ordnance lands." Provision was made for conforming Indian affairs in Nova Scotia, New Brunswick, and Quebec to the Act. Land, alcohol, election of chiefs, and jurisdiction of chiefs' authority were all dealt with. The loss of Indian status by women who married non-Indians was provided for as well as the surrender of Indian status by enfranchisement.

After the acquisition of Rupert's Land by the new Dominion of Canada, a much larger area and a much larger number of Indians came under Canada's control. The decade of the 1870s was a busy one for administering the new territory and the new peoples. The most important events for the Indians were the creation of the Northwest Mounted Police, the signing of the "number" treaties by which the land of the three western interior provinces—Manitoba, Saskatchewan, and Alberta—were alienated from the natives and made available to whites, and the writing of the Indian Act.

The Indian Act (1876) defined who was legally an Indian. While the definition is patrilineal, it has both a group and an individual aspect. The vast majority of Indians must be members of legally-recognized bands. These bands may have land treaties, may live on reserves and receive annuities, or they may not conform to any of these. Racial or biological criteria are not crucial. A person may be racially Indian and not legally an Indian, or a person may be legally Indian and not racially Indian (as in the case of non-Indian females who marry Indian males and thereby become Indians). Legal status is derived from the husband. In the case of an illegitimate child of an Indian mother, the child is legally an Indian.

The condition of the status Indian, i.e., the Indian who is recognized as such under the Indian Act, is one which has been much discussed and commented upon. Allen Harper, in his essay "Canada's Indian Administration: The Indian Act," observes: "But the restrictions peculiar to their special status do not prevent them from going and coming as they choose, incurring obligations, entering into contracts, sueing and being sued, or being subject generally to the laws of the land in much the same manner as all other persons."[9]

To accelerate the process by which Indians would cease to be Indians and become totally assimilated, legislation was passed to provide for the legal surrender of Indian status and the relinquishing of all land claims and other

---

8   Most of this discussion is based on J. E. Hodgett's *Pioneer Public Service* (Toronto: University of Toronto Press, 1955). See ch. 13, "Indian Affairs: The White Man's Albatross."

9   Allen G. Harper, "Canada's Indian Administration: The Indian Act," *America Indigena* 6, no. 4 (October 1946): 299.

interests. Both as individuals and as groups this enfranchisement was possible. Although it is still possible, few Indians become enfranchised. Perhaps most of those who do so are Indian women who marry non-Indians and automatically lose their Indian status. Although at one enfranchisement included receiving the vote, this is no longer an element of the status change, since Indians (status Indians) have the vote as do non-Indians (Euro-Canadians, non-status Indians, Inuit, and persons of other races who are Canadian citizens). In the mid-1880s, legislation was passed to provide for elected band councils. This was intended as an introductory step, training Indians in the constitutional and political usages of the Euro-Canadian society.

Federally, Indians received the vote in 1960 under the Diefenbaker government. On the provincial level most Indians had already received the vote by 1960. British Columbia was the first to give Indians the vote (1949) and other provinces followed. Nova Scotia was the exception to this situation. In that province the Indian right to provincial vote pre-dates that of all other provinces. The restrictions on Indian voting in the provinces varied, but while Indians generally could not vote, some Indians in specific categories could. The general import of the exceptions seems to have been that certain individual Indians, in particular cases, could be presumed to be more assimilated. Other Indians had made contributions to the general society which warranted the vote being given to them. War veterans fitted into this category.

Perhaps the two most well-known efforts of government to implement the policy of assimilation through suppression of important native customs are the cases of the potlatch and the Sun Dance. Agitation over the Northwest Coast Indians' custom of potlatch arose from administrators and clergy, as well as among some assimilationist-oriented Indians. Pressures on Ottawa to make the custom illegal resulted in an amendment to the Indian Act (1884) which made the celebration of the potlatch or assisting in celebration a misdemeanour and punishable by two to six months' imprisonment. This "Potlatch Law" remained in effect from 1884 to 1951.

The Sun Dance was an equally significant and popular religious ceremonial of the Plains Indians, Blackfoot, Cree, and Assiniboine. It was described in sensational terms, as was the potlatch, and suppressed. An Amendment to the Indian Act in 1895 made engaging or assisting in the Sun Dance an offence punishable by two to six months' imprisonment. This law was removed in the Indian Act of 1952.

In the case of both these activities it was not only a matter of their being contrary to religious and social custom of the Euro-Canadian. In each case it was argued by some of the opponents that the time and money put into the ceremonies could be more usefully spent elsewhere. The ceremonies, therefore, should be suppressed as part of the effort to alter the Indians' economic values and pursuits. Indians continued, whether in secret or openly, to participate in potlatch and Sun Dance. These customs, as with so many others, underwent alteration, but their retention and survival may symbolize the Indian response to their administrators.

Even Indian participation in what were essentially tourist entertainments were frowned upon. Attendance at and participation in rodeos and stampedes produced conflicting views among whites. Administrators and clergy saw these activities as wasteful if not positively harmful to the Indian. They wasted time, money, and risked health. On the other hand, promoters of the festivities regarded Indians as a necessary component in the events to give the maximum tourist attraction.

THE WHITE PAPER AND INDIAN RESPONSE

The most significant event in terms of policy and Indian response was the *Statement of the Government of Canada on Indian Policy, 1969*, the White Paper which evoked a storm of Indian comment and public attention. The policy was based on the premise, "No Canadian should be excluded from participation in community life, and none should expect to withdraw and still enjoy the benefits that flow to those who participate." Indians should have "full and equal participation in the cultural, social, economic and political life of Canada." In order to achieve these results, six major areas of concern had to be dealt with:

1. Legislative and constitutional bases of discrimination must be removed.
2. There must be positive recognition by everyone of the unique contribution of Indian culture to Canadian society.
3. Services must come through the same channels and from the same government agencies for all Canadians.
4. Those who are furthest behind must be helped most.
5. Lawful obligations must be recognized.
6. Control of Indian lands should be transferred to the Indian people.[10]

The federal government proposed: to repeal the Indian Act and give Indians control of title to their lands; to turn over to the provinces the responsibility of Indians who would henceforth be treated as all other citizens of a province are treated; to make substantial funds available for economic development as an interim measure while the changes in responsibilities from federal to provincial authority were taking place; and to begin closing down the Indian Affairs Department, transferring responsibility for federal programmes already underway to other federal departments.

Articulate Indians and leaders of Indian organizations across Canada were stunned by the proposal. For many months prior to the policy statement, they had attended consultation meetings with representatives of Indian Affairs. They interpreted the policy statement as a new effort to press Indians to assimilation after the style of the termination policy of the Eisenhower administration in the United States.

"Paternalism," "arrogance," "infallibility of the Great White Father," "credibility gap," "disruption of relationship with government"—these were the phrases used by Harold Sappier, President of the Union of New Brunswick Indians, to describe the document.[11] The National Indian Brotherhood used more restrained language but it was just as emphatic in its rejection of the main thrust of the policy statement:

10 *Statement of the Government of Canada on Indian Policy, 1969* (Ottawa: Queen's Printer, 1969), p. 6.
11 *Bulletin 201* (Toronto: Anglican Church of Canada, 1970), p. 25.

We know it was not the intent of the new policy but we feel the end result of the proposal will be the destruction of a Nation of People by legislation and *cultural genocide* . . . the minister [of Indian Affairs] proposes to solve the problem by evading the responsibility of the Federal Government under the British North America Act.

We must have control of our lands; our funds and all other responsibilities . . . but we cannot accept the means proposed. [My italics.][12]

The National Indian Brotherhood pointed out that in the consultations they have never advocated provincial takeover of federal responsibilities. The consultations were a show. The federal government was neither hearing nor understanding, or else they chose to ignore the Indians. The Hawthorn-Tremblay survey, commissioned by the Department of Indian Affairs, and representing much time, effort, and money, had recommended that the Indians be accorded a unique status, "citizens plus." This suggestion had been ignored. The signers of the National Indian Brotherhood's statement concluded:

We view this as a policy designed to divest us of our aboriginal, residual and statutory rights. If we accept this policy, and in the process lose our rights and our lands, we become willing partners in cultural genocide. This we cannot do.

We realize all too well, perhaps better than you, that the winds of change are blowing, and that we too must change to keep pace with the times. But a policy must be devised that will enable us to keep pace with you as a people. A people not only with a past but a future. A future as Indian People, and as Canadians.[13]

The government-commissioned survey of the contemporrary situation of the Canadian Indian made public, for those who did not already know and would read it, the fact of the Indians' social, economic, educational, and health disadvantages. It also pointed to a possible delegation of federal responsibility to provincial governments without violating the British North America Act or requiring its revision. This can also be done without contravening the letter or spirit of treaties. In other words, an increased role in Indian affairs by provincial governments is neither unconstitutional nor in violation of treaty obligations undertaken by the federal government.

Some scholars dealing with the constitutional status of the Indian hold that the British North America Act and court decisions together point toward greater federal responsibility for non-status Indians and Inuit. The Supreme Court of Canada has held that Inuit (Eskimo) are also "Indians" under the British North America Act even though they are not Indians under the Indian Act.

It will be seen that the problem is not merely one of contrasting the position of the Indian with that of the non-Indian, for distinctions must be drawn within the class to which the British North America Act refers. *An individual may be an Indian within the meaning of the Constitution, yet be untouched by the codification of special federal law embodied in the Indian Act.* [My italics.][14]

---

12 Ibid., p. 27.
13 Ibid., pp. 28-29.
14 Kenneth Lysyk, "The Unique Constitutional Position of the Canadian Indian," *Canadian Bar Review* 44 (1967): 514. The article is on pp. 513-53.

Since 1969 there has been a proliferation of native organizations. Government offices, federal and provincial, have increased in numbers. These offices have also increased their attention to native peoples. A shift in forces has occurred. Assimilation, ending the Indian Act, doing away with reserves, are still matters of concern to Indians. Each new book or article or interview or speech by an Indian may make comments on one or more of these subjects. But there is now an emphasis on more immediate issues, short-term issues which can be worked out by government and Indians.

Treaty claims and compensation for land, economic and educational assistance, increased autonomy in local government, and control of local schools and curriculum are specific issues to be dealt with. The Land Claims Commission can be an instrument for these purposes. The post-White Paper scene has been one in which the Indians have pursued a variety of lines of approach to secure a greater voice in the determination of Indian policy. They are demanding Indian control of Indian Affairs, of reserves, of band membership, of local education, of economic development, and of a new Indian image to be projected to the non-Indian.

Indian organizations are recognized as the mechanisms through which money and assistance can be channelled, in addition to the established routes through bands and reserves. Increasingly, these organizations have come under attack from both assimilationist-oriented Indians and from others who subscribe to the colonial and neo-colonial model of Frantz Fanon. The Indians have emerged as an influential factor, if not the controlling factor, shaping their future. Although the growth of Indian organizations and articulations of concerns have been developing for many years, no single event has been so important as the White Paper of 1969.

Assimilation, in the circumstances of Indian resurgence, seems unlikely in the foreseeable future. The continuation of communities of Indian peoples making their own synthesis—a development which provides continuity with the past—seems the most likely prospect, given a larger element of self-government, economic self-sufficiency, and local control of education. Separation in the sense of one or more separate and politically independent native states is an unlikely development. Integration of mutually respectful communities co-operating within the context of the "cultural mosaic" is an alternative which is seen by some as a desirable living accommodation. The exact nature of such an arrangement has not been worked out, nor is it likely it could become a static relationship of two or more parties in any case. Presumably whatever characteristics "integration" would have, it would be dynamic and responsive to changing conditions in the larger context of Canada as a whole. George Manuel, in his book *The Fourth World*, indicates some of the conditions of this integration: "Real integration can only be achieved through voluntary partnership . . . the way to end the condition of unilateral dependence and begin the long march to the Fourth World is through home rule."[15]

What is being suggested is not that Indians be another ethnic group in the sense that immigrant peoples to Canada and their descendents constitute

15   George Manuel and Michael Posluns, *The Fourth World* (Don Mills: Collier-Macmillan of Canada, 1974), p. 217.

ethnic groups. For the Indian, Canada is both the motherland and the "New World."

> If the exiled condition in which Eastern Europeans believe themselves can only be ended with a change in the relationship between their Mother Country and the neighbouring Great Powers, our exile can be ended only with a change in our relationship with Canada. We do not expect the same freedom and autonomy in our Mother Country as they demand in theirs, and ours. This is equality.[16]

It may be that the period of the last few years and the next few will prove to be a period of change or at least of fluidity in Indian policy which opens up the possibility for significant changes in Indian policy. Indian resurgence, reawakening, or whatever term may be used, has provided a new, and no doubt Indians intend, powerful ingredient in the mix which will constitute future Indian policy.

TOWARD A NEW SOCIAL POLICY

In the past the tendency on the part of Indian administration has been to see Indians in terms of three stages—"traditional," "transitional," and "assimilated." "Assimilated" was seen as the ultimate goal, the final solution of the "problem" of Indian communities. Change from "traditional" was interpreted as inevitably leading toward "assimilated," though it might be slow and diverse and, in the case of individuals, might never be achieved. Thus, a person might be regarded as "transitional." The Indian resurgence, indeed the growing self-consciousness and "reawakening" of Indians, non-status Indians, Métis, and Inuit, seems to suggest that the formulation, "traditional-transitional-assimilated" is an inadequate model for expressing what the evidence reveals.

The native resurgence, by defining and crystallizing a new identity, may be creating a greater resistance to total assimilation while seeming superficially to be moving in that direction. The paradoxical situation which results might be, in that event, selective borrowing, leading to change with continuity, separate identity through adaptation. There are signs everywhere among native peoples that this is what is happening.

To deal with this situation, government and society must re-adjust their image of the native. Despite the multicultural heritage and the cultural mosaic, native peoples' efforts to retain their identity have not been met with respect and acceptance. Non-natives, government, and society generally, will be obliged to understand that native culture is not only teepees, moccasins, birchbark canoes, and hunting, fishing, and gathering. Undoubtedly, values and customs are related to social and economic life, but native culture in the late twentieth century need not be that of the fifteenth century to have meaning and value for contemporary natives. As Western civilization has changed in the last several centuries, so has native culture. Natives are calling for a larger role in determining the future direction of their cultural change. To do this, they seek such things as local governmental control on reserves; teaching native languages in schools; control of

16   Ibid., p. 220.

band membership; a more solid economic base for reserve and non-reserve peoples, in part based on a viable education and preservation of communities.

Native input into administrative decisions will be maximized if natives are the decision-makers, but without financial and economic viability this will be unlikely to occur. Historically, natives have been drawn into the prevalent economic activities of the newcomers: fur trade, agriculture, commercial fishing, canning, ranching, and now urban industry. Consultation, where it has occurred, has been based on the assumption that native peoples must "fit in" and that, generally speaking, they will want to. When "fitting in" and assimilation have not happened, explanations have been sought in the failure of the administrative methods to work properly. Incompetent staff, too rapid turnover of staff, lack of staff, ill-conceived and badly-executed programmes, and so forth, have been held responsible. Little attention has been paid to the positive preference of natives for control of their own culture and adaptation. "Ethnocentrism" is the term applied to a view which sees the ways of one's own culture as the only ways to operate. Policy based on ethnocentrism leads to a failure to listen to and to believe in the other point of view.

The existence of native people bespeaks the failure of the policy of assimilation to produce a loss of a separate identity. Changes which have occurred have produced varying degrees of continuity with the past. The varied responses and conditions of native peoples today indicates the appropriate direction of future policy. Variety, sensitivity, and attention to local and regional differences are indicated. The corollary of these elements is a maximum native input and native control. The process of native history outlined above was from a situation of autonomy to a loss of autonomy—in economic, technological, political, social, and religious terms—and more recently to movements to regain as much native control of their own affairs and their future direction as is possible.

The direction will not necessarily be a unilinear one. The film "To Walk in Dignity" presents a variety of adaptations already occurring. Uniformity of development presupposed by the historic native policy has in fact produced a variety of responses. Meaningful policy must take these into account. Seen in this light, "Canadian Indian" or "Canadian native" is not a single, uniform category, but is itself a variety, a cultural mosaic, which also possesses unities within its variations. These differences range from those who have a high degree of continuity with traditional culture to people who are highly acculturated to one segment or another of the Euro-Canadian society. These represent a variety of responses which are likely to continue, rather than stages in an inevitable process, leading toward uniformity and/or disappearance.

Coming to grips with these realities by agencies of government administration and by society generally will require greater sensitivity to more subtleties and nuances among native peoples, and the concomitantly greater flexibility, knowledge, and variety in responding to the differences. Application of this generalization could mean that an arrangement developed for one time, place, circumstance, and group must be re-thought and re-worked through continuous consultation to be employed among other groups. Thus, a "land solution" in the James Bay area may not necessarily apply in the Northwest Territories.

Canada's native peoples are not a "problem" which can yield to a "solution." They constitute a distinctive, varied, and on-going part of Canadian culture, population, and life. As such, they will continue to occupy a place in Canada's social policy.

10

Child Welfare in Ontario

JOHN MELICHERCIK

INTRODUCTION

Under the prevailing interpretation of the provisions of the British North America Act child welfare services, like most other social services, are considered a provincial responsibility. While presently the federal government shares in the cost of some child welfare programmes, primarily through the Canada Assistance Plan, the development of specific services has always been left to provincial or local initiatives and auspices and thus no uniform pattern of such services emerged across the country. Each province wove its own particular patchwork of private and public programmes, reflecting the cultural, political, economic, and geographic peculiarities of the region.

As a consequence a study of child welfare policies and programmes in this country requires one to focus on specific conditions and provisions in individual provinces. This paper examines the development of policies and programmes in one Canadian province—Ontario. From an historical perspective, this province was first in Canada to develop public provisions for the welfare of children. In subsequent years, a number of its legislative and organizational efforts, such as the child protective legislation, the system of children's aid societies, and day-care legislation, have been copied by other provinces. While in more recent years other provinces, particularly British Columbia and Quebec, took the initiative in developing some organizational innovations in child welfare, especially in the area of integration of services, Ontario still remains a good example of the process that shaped the child welfare provisions in Canada and of the programmes that this process produced.

CHILD WELFARE AS A SOCIETAL RESPONSIBILITY

The child shall enjoy special protection, and shall be given opportunities and facilities, by law and by other means, to enable him to develop physically, mentally, morally, spiritually and socially in a healthy and normal manner and in conditions of freedom and dignity. In the enactment of laws for this purpose the best interest of the child shall be the paramount consideration.[1]

This statement is taken from the Declaration of the Rights of the Child adopted unanimously by the United Nations General Assembly on November 20, 1959. While it is only a principle or a goal to be striven for, and not a reflection of actual conditions in many parts of the world, it is remarkable that the United Nations could agree on such a document. Among other things, the Declaration clearly states that assuring the well-being of children is a societal responsibility, thus making child welfare an essential area of public social policy of every country. This may seem to many today as a statement of the obvious. However, in most countries, including Canada, the acceptance of this principle is a relatively recent development.

For a long time children were considered basically the property of their parents, or more specifically of the father, to be dealt with as he saw fit. Under the old Persian, Egyptian, Greek, Gaelic, and Roman law the father had absolute power over his children. Infanticide was lawful and the father could sell his sons or daughters into slavery. While, generally, speaking, fathers loved their children and did not desire to kill them or sell them or rule them in an arbitrary or selfish way, they had the right to do so and the state enforced this right instead of interceding on behalf of the child. Under Roman law this absolute power did not end when the child reached his majority but continued throughout the father's life.[2]

The principles and attitudes of Roman law provided the foundation for the legal systems of most European countries and this carried the notion of almost exclusive parental jurisdiction into the twentieth century, not only in the European countries themselves but also in their former overseas colonies to which they exported their legal systems, such as French Canada. The role of the state was for a long time confined to enforcement of parental rights, and whatever organized activities on behalf of children emerged were usually carried out by religious institutions and other benevolent organizations.

While England and her colonies, including English-speaking Canada, have not based their legal systems on the Roman model, the concept of children's rights and of societal responsibility for their well-being was nevertheless slow in development. However, it was in England where the earliest experiments of state intervention on behalf of children took place. It was the impact of the Industrial Revolution, which was first felt in that

1   United Nations, *Declaration of the Rights of the Child* (New York: United Nations Office of Public Information, 1959), p. 1.
2   Grace Abbott, *The Child and the State* (Chicago: University of Chicago Press, 1949), p. 3.

country, that inspired legislative attempts to control the evils of child labour.[3]

However, the road from the earliest expressions of societal responsibility for the well-being of its children to the development of a universal charter of children's rights has been long and often meandering. It took different turns in different jurisdictions and in each jurisdiction different milestones marked its progress.

Some familiarity with this road and with its major milestones is an important prerequisite to any rational consideration of current social policy issues regarding children or child welfare. Since the focus of this paper is on child welfare policy issues in Ontario, it is appropriate, if not essential, that we start with at least a brief review of how child welfare programmes and policies developed in this province.

EARLY BEGINNINGS

Life in the early settlements of what is presently known as Ontario was tough but relatively simple. The chief tasks were those of clearing land and building homes. The principal characteristic of the economic, social and cultural system was self-sufficiency. The family constituted the basic institution of that pioneer society and a strict code of honesty and morality was imposed by the sanctions of the neighbourhood group.[4]

However, there was little formal legislation in the early days. Man was free to do as he pleased with his own property. Children were considered almost a part of man's property and there was only his good will to prevent him from dealing with them as he did with his property. This is not to suggest that parents were particularly abusive of their children, but rather that parents had both the right and the responsibility to provide for their children as they could or as they chose.

However, following the War of 1812 life started changing in Upper Canada. For one thing, the population started growing rapidly and small towns started forming along the shores of Lake Ontario. Many of the new settlers came as single individuals without the support of a strong family group. A mobile labour force started emerging and so did many new problems. Unemployment was one of them, destitution and crime were others. The conditions of many families deteriorated to the point where the political bodies could not ignore what was happening to the children.[5]

The first child welfare legislation was enacted in 1779. It was called An Act to Provide for the Education and Support of Orphaned Children and it provided for the binding of an orphaned child in an apprenticeship until he or she reached the age of twenty-one.[6] This mode of child care was prevalent at that time both in Great Britain and in the United States and it was

---

3 Ibid., p. 79.
4 S. D. Clark, *The Social Development of Canada* (Toronto: University of Toronto Press, 1942), p. 205.
5 Ibid., p. 208.
6 Upper Canada, *An Act to Provide for the Education and Support of Orphaned Children, 1779*, 5 Geo. 2, ch. 85.

transplanted to Canada. In subsequent years this provision was extended to include abandoned children as well as children of parents who were dependent upon public charity.

In the 1870s the emphasis started shifting towards institutional care. In 1874 two pieces of legislation were enacted which illustrate this development. The first one was the Public Aid to Charitable Institutions Act. It provided for partial financing and for some inspection of children's institutions.[7] The second one was called An Act Respecting Industrial Schools. This act represented the first attempt to define a neglected child. It also introduced legal residence as a basis for determining financial responsibility if the parents could not be made responsible for his maintenance.[8]

Several additional pieces of legislation affecting children were enacted during the next decade and each represented some improvement on existing provisions. However, by then public awareness of the plight of many children was growing and so was the concern among humanely-minded citizens. This development was greatly assisted by a Toronto journalist, J. J. Kelso, who spearheaded an energetic effort to develop better provisions for the protection of dependent or neglected children. Among other things, he organized a fresh air fund and in 1891 was instrumental in organizing the Children's Aid Society of Toronto. He became the first president of this organization. The stated objectives of the Children's Aid Society were "to care for and protect neglected children, to secure enactment and enforcement of laws relating to neglected children or juvenile offenders, to provide free summer excursions or other measures of recreation . . . and generally to advocate the claims of neglected children."[9]

However, the most significant milestone was reached in 1893 when the Ontario government enacted the Act for the Prevention of Cruelty to and Better Protection of Children. This legislation provided an encouragement for the formation of Children's Aid Societies (similar to the one established in Toronto) in the cities and towns of Ontario. Officers of these societies were authorized to intervene on behalf of a neglected child as defined in the new legislation. It also introduced foster homes as a form of child care and the cost of such care was to be paid to municipalities. Full guardianship was also given to the new organizations.

This was an important and remarkable piece of legislation. It empowered private organizations to administer a provincial statute and use public funds for that purpose. Under its provisions, some twenty Children's Aid Societies were organized within one year and by 1910 there were seventy-two such societies covering practically all major cities and towns in Ontario. With numerous modifications, this network of child welfare organizations survived to the present day. This legislation clearly established the concept of public responsibility for assuring a minimum standard of well-being of all children in Ontario. And it was only fitting that J. J. Kelso, who was largely responsible for mobilizing public opinion in favour of child protective

7 Ontario, *An Act to Regulate Public Aid to Charitable Institutions, 1874,* 37 Vic., ch. 33.
8 Ontario, *An Act Respecting Industrial Schools, 1874,* 37 Vic., ch. 29.
9 Ian Bain, "The Role of J. J. Kelso in Launching of the Child Welfare Movement in Ontario" (unpublished thesis, University of Toronto, School of Social Work, 1954), p. 12.

measures, was appointed the "Superintendant of Neglected and Dependent Children in Ontario."[10]

TRANSITION INTO THE TWENTIETH CENTURY

It was apparent that some fundamental changes were taking place in Ontario around the turn of the century. The social implications of these changes were not fully realized—as they never are during such periods —but life in Ontario was obviously becoming more complex. The main contributing factor was probably the rapid industrialization and urbanization of the province. This development was introducing new problems for which there were no established provisions. In the area of child welfare, neglect, child labour, delinquency and illegitimacy were the major concerns. With the exception of juvenile delinquency, which fell under both federal and provincial jurisdiction, all the others were considered necessary. There was a prevailing tendency to use suppression as a method of dealing with the growing problem and even charitable efforts were often mixed with correctional measures.

Following the enactment of the child protection legislation, several additional measures were enacted in quick succession. In 1894 the Dominion Parliament enacted an Act Respecting the Arrest, Trial and Imprisonment of Youthful Offenders and one year later a juvenile court was established in Toronto. This was the first operating juvenile court in North America. Further legislation was introduced in 1897 to regulate maternity boarding houses to control the immigration of children into Ontario. A practice was developing of hiring unattended children into the province as cheap labour.

Further legislative provisions occurred in 1908 with the introduction of the Juvenile Delinquents Act of Canada. This was federal legislation which is still in effect in an amended form.

In 1911 the Illegitimate Children's Act was added. It required the father of an illegitimate child to provide maintenance for his child. In the same year the Infants Act was enacted, dealing with the appointment of guardians, disposal of property, custody and religion of children and related matters. Legislation under this name is still in effect in the province.[11]

BETWEEN THE WARS

Some new initiatives in the child welfare field have taken place during the post-war period. World War I speeded up the process of industrialization and with it people's awareness of the vulnerability that human beings are exposed to in a modern society. There was also a growing acceptance of the role of government in developing social legislation to assist people in a variety of situations beyond their control.

One important provision reflecting these new attitudes was the Mothers Allowances Act which was passed in 1920. This legislation represented a

---

10 Ibid., p. 21.
11 For more details of this early legislation, see P. Ramsey, "The Development of Child Welfare Legislation in Ontario" (unpublished thesis, University of Toronto, School of Social Work, 1954).

departure from past measures in that it assisted certain categories of mothers to maintain their children in their home and away from institutions which still tended to be the prevailing mode of providing care for dependent children. To be sure, only "deserving" mothers were eligible for such assistance but its significance lay in the fact that it attempted to keep families together and used provincial funds on behalf of children.[12]

The year 1921 saw two additional provisions added to the provincial child welfare legislation. The first one was the Adoption Act which enabled anyone of full age to adopt another person younger than himself. The other was the Children of Unmarried Parents Act which replaced earlier (1877) legislative provisions for illegitimate children. Both of these acts represented progressive steps in the field of child welfare.[13]

A further substantial updating of the child welfare legislation took place in 1927 when a new Children's Protection Act and a rewritten Adoption and Unmarried Parents Act emerged. However, these enactments were the last significant measures in the child welfare field for almost two decades. The great depression diverted attention to other matters and so did the Second World War. There were two possible exceptions. In 1930 the province established a Department of Public Welfare which included a Child Welfare Branch. This new branch took over the administration of the three above-mentioned pieces of legislation, which until then were administered by the Department of the Provincial Secretary.

The other development worth noting took place during the World War II years. Women were urged during this period to leave their homes and work in war industries or replace men in essential jobs and thus free them for war service. In order to make this possible the federal government offered subsidies for setting up day-care centres for children between the ages of two to fourteen. Ontario was the only province which took advantage of this offer. It added a Day Nurseries Branch to its Department of Public Welfare and by the end of the war it operated some thirty day-care centres across the province.[14]

By comparison with other provinces, Ontario had come a long way in the field of child welfare by the end of the Second World War. However, new needs and new expectations were now being identified and most of the child welfare programmes as we know them today evolved during the post-World War II period.

THE POST-WORLD WAR II PERIOD

The development of child welfare programmes in Ontario during the post-World War II period was shaped by a variety of forces and factors. A few of them stand out.

The first factor was the rapidly-increasing number of children. Like other parts of Canada, Ontario experienced a sharp increase in the birth rate

---

12   Joseph E. Laycock, "New Directions in Social Welfare Policy," in *The Prospect of Change*, ed. A. Rotstein (Toronto: McGraw-Hill, 1965), p. 313.
13   Ramsey, "The Development of Child Welfare Legislation," p. 27.
14   Canadian Council on Social Development, *Day Care* (Ottawa: Publication and Information Branch of the Canadian Council on Social Development, 1972), p. 4.

during the middle and late forties. This rate peaked in 1947 (when it reached 27 births per 1,000 of population) and it remained relatively high for the next decade.[15] A sharp increase in any population group will usually attract to it the attention of policy-makers in a democratic society.

A second significant factor had to do with the rising expectations of all segments of the population during this period. This was part of an international phenomenon but it had a particular relevance for child welfare in Ontario. Most of the parents of the post-war children had experienced the deprivations of the depression in their childhood and they wanted to assure something better for their children.

Another factor which was influential was related to the newly-experienced prosperity both of many individuals and of the government. Personal incomes, as well as governmental revenues, were rising and this made the increasing expectations appear to be feasible and realizable.

One would be inclined to believe that such conditions would generate a rapid development of progressive child welfare policies, programmes and services. Some promising signs emerged. In 1946, the Day Nurseries Act was enacted, which provided for licensing of day-care and nursery school facilities and grants of 50 per cent of the operating costs for day nurseries under municipal by-laws. Ontario was the only province with such legislation. Other progressive policies and programmes also eventually emerged but their development was not rapid, at least not during the 1940s and 1950s. There were some influences at work which had a restraining effect.

To begin with, a strong sentiment prevailed that the well-being of children can and ought to be assured by their parents except in special circumstances of personal misfortune or gross incompetence. Thus the emphasis initially tended to be on provisions geared to deal with conditions such as the orphaned or out-of-wedlock children and neglectful parents. Since this task appeared relatively modest, it was probably not unreasonable that it was largely left to private auspices—religious or secular. This attitude fitted well into the philosophical stance of the Ontario government of this period and was undoubtedly reinforced by it.

It was thus not surprising that the first significant developments in programmes for children in the post-war era took place in the private sector.[16] These developments, however, did not consist so much of establishing new programmes but rather of a substantial expansion and refinement of previously-established programmes. As described before, by now Ontario had legislation dealing with child neglect, out-of-wedlock children and adoptions. This legislation was administered by a network of largely private Children's Aid Societies. In addition, Ontario also had a sizeable number of child-care institutions, which tended to be custodial in nature. However, during the pre-war era the Children's Aid Societies were rather small in size and staffed by volunteers or lay personnel. The institutions, on the other

15 Canada, Dominion Bureau of Statistics, *Vital Statistics* (Ottawa: Queen's Printer, 1964), p. 18.
16 A substantial amount of the information contained in the section on the post-World War II period was acquired by the author in conversations with leading figures in the child welfare field during this period.

hand, tended to be quite large but similarly staffed. In the late forties and fifties these characteristics began to change.

The first change had to do with a growing emphasis on professionalizing the existing services. As more professionally-educated social workers became available, they started finding their ways into positions of leadership in the Children's Aid Societies and into some of the child-care institutions. This, together with new insights into child development, started producing some shifts in the child welfare services. It was increasingly recognized that custodial care, particularly for young children, can be quite detrimental to their healthy development. This realization led to the closing of numerous custodial children's institutions and to gradual transformation of others into treatment-oriented centres.

The swing away from custodial child care, however, had some marked effects on the Children's Aid Societies. It increased their responsibilities and the volume of their work. The volume increased even more with the rising birth rate. It was becoming obvious that voluntary auspices were hard pressed to come up with the necessary funds to finance the rapidly-growing and professionalizing services.

Thus it was hardly surprising that increasingly the Children's Aid Societies began to look to the province and to the local governments for funds. By 1950 the Children's Aid Societies were already reimbursed by the municipal governments for child-care costs, but they had to raise private funds for any additional services. It was increasingly recognized that it was undesirable to wait until a child became neglected and then remove him from his parents. However, there were no provisions for financing services to families and this was gradually recognized as the main weakness of the existing programmes.

Some significant legislative changes occurred in 1954. The three previously-existing pieces of provincial legislation pertaining to child protection, unmarried parents and adoptions were incorporated into a single new Child Welfare Act.[17] This act contained some improved provisions for financing children's services, but there were still hardly any funds available to finance services to families, unless individual Societies were able to obtain some resources from community fund-raising organizations. The financing of child care, while improved, retained one undesirable feature in that it was still necessary to establish the legal residence of the mother and charge the costs to the municipality where she last resided for one full year. This provision was particularly hard on unmarried mothers who frequently moved to a different community to be delivered of their child in order to hide their condition. Their efforts were often negated when the local government of her original municipality had to be notified about the birth of her child.

The new act, however, also introduced two significant changes in the mandate of the Children's Aid Societies. The first one enlarged the definition of child neglect by adding to it the failure to meet the emotional needs of a child. This provision enabled the Children's Aid Societies to intervene in situations where not only the physical but also the emotional well-being of the child was threatened. The second change placed a two-year limit on

17   Ontario, *Statutes of Ontario, 1954*, ch. 8.

the length of temporary care that a Children's Aid Society could provide for a child. At the end of two years the child would either have to return to his parents or be made a permanent ward and thus be eligible for adoption. Its intent was to prevent children from spending long years in foster homes or institutions without any definite long-range planning. Both of these provisions were somewhat controversial, but were generally viewed as progressive by those working in the child welfare field.

While the Children's Aid Societies tended to be viewed as the main instruments through which the well-being of children was protected in Ontario, other services were also developing and it was becoming apparent that more were needed. The child population was rapidly increasing and the pressure on all existing facilities was very heavy. During the 1960s all existing programmes were expanding by leaps and bounds, but it was also becoming apparent that new legislative provisions were needed. Public attitudes also appeared to be shifting and substantive changes in child welfare programmes appeared not only possible but inevitable.

Several quite progressive pieces of legislation pertaining to child welfare emerged around the middle of the sixties. In 1963 the Children's Institutions Act[18] was enacted, providing partial financing to approved institutions. Through successive amendments, this financing increased from the original 50 per cent of the operating costs to 80 per cent by 1967. This facilitated the development of new children's institutions.

In 1965 a completely revised Child Welfare Act[19] was enacted. Probably the two most striking features of this revised legislation were the addition of preventive services to the functions of the Children's Aid Societies and the provision of complete public funding for their operations. Great things were expected from this new act, which was considered by many as a model of progressive child welfare legislation.

Also in 1965 a new Training Schools Act[20] was introduced, updating many of the previous provisions. Some noticeable improvements in the programme of the training schools also began to evolve.

One year later, in 1966, a thoroughly-revised version of the Day Nurseries Act[21] was enacted and this legislation was also widely viewed as the most completed and comprehensive of any province in Canada. It specified clear standards for facilities, programmes, and personnel, and provided for payment of 80 per cent of the operating costs. In 1967 the government issued a White Paper on Services for Children with Mental and Emotional Disorders. This document outlined comprehensive plans for programmes and facilities for troubled children. While legislative action was slow in coming, it eventually did arrive in the form of the Facilities for Children Suffering from Mental and Emotional Disorders Act and the Children's Mental Health Centers Act.[22] This legislation provided for strict licensing and for standards in programmes and personnel. It also assured full public financing for approved facilities.

18 Ibid., *1963*, ch. 14.
19 Ibid., *1965*, ch. 14.
20 Ibid., ch. 132.
21 Ibid., *1966*, ch. 37.
22 Ibid., *1969*, ch. 10.

These examples of legislative activities in the field of child welfare during the sixties are illustrative of the significant shifts in the social conditions which required new provisions in public attitudes which were supportive, if not demanding, of some new provisions, and in the position of the provincial government which introduced these provisions. However, as usual, there was a lag between the plans, or even legislative provisions, and their full implementation. By the end of the decade Ontario had, on paper at least, some of the most progressive provisions for the well-being of children that could be found in any jurisdiction. But there was hardly the feeling that the problems and needs of children were adequately dealt with. Expenditures were mounting, but so were doubts about the programmes, their effectiveness, and their adequacy. Many of the recently-introduced programmes were attacked as outmoded or of dubious value. The expert opinion tended to be divided in its assessment of what was wrong or of what needed to be done. The private sector was diminishing as a significant entity in the provision of the large-scale programmes which seemed to be needed and the government appeared to be worried about the rapidly-rising costs and the criticisms it was receiving about its programmes.

And thus in the early seventies a new attitude started to emerge, both in government and in segments of the general public, which seemed to emphasize re-examination and re-organization of child welfare policies and programmes. The birth rate was by now dropping rather sharply (to about 17 births for 1,000 of population), there were many competing claims for the available resources, and there was doubt about the direction to take. It became the period of studies, reports, conferences, and of debate.

PRESENT PROGRAMMES AND POLICIES

It is probably unavoidable, if not necessary, that after every period of rapid development or expansion, there is a tendency to pause, take stock, and direct a critical look at what has been accomplished. There certainly has been a rapid development of child welfare programmes in Ontario during the post-war years. However, as was indicated earlier, this development usually occurred as a reaction to the pressures of emerging problems rather than as part of a carefully thought-out long-range plan. In such situations new programmes tend to be placed on top of old ones, often without sufficient regard for how they will fit together. There is seldom a clear vision of the overall structure that the individual units are supposed to create. Such development of programmes and policies would correspond to what has been referred to in the literature as the "muddling-through" approach, which tends to be characteristic not only of Ontario but also of Canada as a whole in the area of social policy development. Given these conditions, it is then necessary to take stock of the child welfare programmes that Ontario presently has, examine how they fit together, what apparent gaps or weaknesses exist, and what is the shape of the overall structure.

What then are the present major programmes and policies? Probably the main programme is the Child Welfare Act of 1965. Under its provisions some fifty Children's Aid Societies are presently operating in Ontario, covering all the organized territory of the province. Technically, these Societies can be considered as private organizations since they are governed by boards of directors elected by the membership of each Society. In practice, however, they are under strong influence from the Ministry of Community and Social Services and, to a lesser degree, from the municipal governments of the localities in which they operate. This influence comes largely, and inevitably, from the fact that about 75 per cent of the income of these organizations comes from the Ministry and the remainder from the municipalities, following a rather complex formula. The budget of every Society has to be approved by the Children's Bureau of the Ministry, which also has the right to monitor and supervise its operations. The municipalities have to approve their portion of the budget and they also appoint four members to the board of directors of each Society.

Given such conditions, it could be argued that the Societies, in fact, are already more public than private and periodically proposals are forwarded to bring them even more, if not completely, under public control. In the long run such a development will probably be inevitable.[23]

The Children's Aid Societies are required by the legislation to perform the following functions:

a. investigating allegations or evidence that children may be in need of protection;

b. protecting children where necessary;

c. providing guidance, counselling and other services to families for protecting children or for the prevention of circumstances requiring the protection of children;

d. providing care for children assigned or committed to its care under this or any other act;

e. supervising children assigned to its supervision under this or any other act;

f. placing children for adoption;

g. assisting the parents of children born out of wedlock and the children born out of wedlock;

h. any other duties given to it by this or any other act.[24]

In addition to this general mandate, the legislation also provides the Societies with the necessary authority to carry out those functions. Very specific criteria for the use of this authority are also provided and so are some standards of service. It is a rather comprehensive legislation which compares favourably with similar provisions in other jurisdictions. It gives the Societies an effective instrument to use in situations of child abuse and child neglect. Under the child-care provisions, the Children's Aid Societies were able to develop rather extensive foster home and group home programmes—which serve thousands of children. They also may purchase specialized child care from private facilities when this is required. The provisions concerning unmarried parents and the adoption of children are adequate and quite progressive. Probably the most remarkable aspect of

23 See, for example, Task Force on Community and Social Services, *Report on Selected Issues and Relationships* (Toronto: Queen's Printer, 1974).
24 Ontario, *Statutes of Ontario, 1964*, ch. 14, sec. 6(2).

the legislation is the provision which requires the Societies to provide preventive services. However, this is also where some of the weaknesses of this programme start emerging.

While the legislation appears to be very good, the present implementation does not live up to its potential. This is most obvious in the area of services to children in their own homes and other preventive services. The major problem seems to be restricted funding for this function on the part of the Ministry. While there are almost unlimited funds for services to children removed from their homes, the programmes for children in their own homes do not seem to rate the same priority. This is unfortunate since, without a preventive emphasis, all the other services will never be able to cope with all the emerging needs of the children in the province.

Another problem affecting the implementation of this legislation is related to the capacity of some of the Children's Aid Societies to develop imaginative programmes and to staff them with competent personnel. They obviously will need some help in this area if the full potential of this legislation is to be realized throughout Ontario.

The next major provision for children in Ontario is the Training Schools programme. While quite often the training schools are not listed under the heading of child welfare, their professed function is rehabilitation of some troubled children who, in most respects, are no different from children served by other programmes. Section 2 of the Training Schools Act states that the purpose of these schools is to provide children with "training treatment and with moral, physical, academic and vocational education." While every child has to be committed to it by a court, the reason for such committal can be either a contravention of some statute (section 9) or a finding that the parent or guardian cannot control the child or provide for his social, emotional or educational needs and no other child welfare service is capable or available to remedy the problem. Thus, it would appear that external circumstances would frequently determine whether a troubled child enters the training school system or some other child welfare programme.

There are presently fourteen schools operated under the jurisdiction of the Ministry of Correctional Services. When a child is committed to a school, he becomes its ward until he or she reaches the age of eighteen years, unless the wardship is terminated earlier on the recommendation of an advisory board.

The physical facilities and the programmes of individual training schools seem to vary considerably—some have a strong rehabilitative focus, while others perform essentially a custodial function. These differences in standards are hard to understand since they are all under the administrative control of the Ministry. It seems to illustrate that having a number of facilities under a single administrative structure does not, by itself, assure a uniform quality of service.

There is now also an extensive after-care programme operated by the Ministry and it is apparent that in recent years great progressive strides have been made in the training school programme. However, because the past philosophy of this programme was essentially custodial and punitive, it seems to be a slow process to transform the training schools into effective centres of treatment and rehabilitation for troubled children.

Day nurseries are now widely recognized as an essential part of any effective child welfare system. They can be considered both as a preventive and as a rehabilitative service and should be viewed as a basic public utility as necessary to a modern society as is public education.

Ontario had an early start in the development of day nurseries. Apart from private efforts in this area, Ontario was the only province to take advantage of the war-time provision by the federal government to establish publicly-supported day nurseries.

The present legislative provision is the Day Nurseries Act of 1966. It enables municipalities to establish nurseries under their own auspices or to purchase services for people in need from private licensed day nurseries. The province reimburses the municipal governments 80 per cent of their costs. The licensing regulations are quite comprehensive and progressive, dealing not only with facilities but also with programmes and personnel.

Good legislation, however, does not automatically result in good and adequate programmes. It is a prerequisite but in itself it is not sufficient. The implementation of these provisions has been uneven. In 1971 only sixty-three day-care centres were in operation.[25] It would appear that some municipalities are deterred by the fact that they have to raise 20 per cent of operating and 50 per cent of capital costs. It is also apparent that the priority ranking of day care varies from municipality to municipality and so does the availability of the service.

Another large and expensive segment of the child welfare system in Ontario is represented by an assortment of children's institutions. As was pointed out in the historical overview, this was the earliest approach to assisting children. Their nature has changed over the years and there have been pro- and anti-institutional periods. At this time, institutional programmes are considered indispensable. However, since they are essentially rehabilitative rather than preventive, questions could be raised over the disproportionate amount of funds that is being allocated to this type of programme, as compared with programmes which serve children in their own homes.

The present children's institutions in the province range from specialized treatment centres to small group residences and they are financed or supervised under the provisions of several pieces of legislation administered by at least two ministries.

The Children's Board Houses Act of 1957 deals with the facilities at the residential end of the spectrum. It essentially requires that all premises used to house five or more unrelated children have to be registered. This registration attempted to enforce standards of hygiene and safety as far as the premises are concerned. The legislation does provide some protection against irresponsible operators, but at best assures only some minimum physical standards.

25   Canadian Council on Social Development, *Day Care*, p. 24.

The Charitable Institutions Act of 1962-63 covers residences for unmarried mothers and for young men and women. The regulations set standards for physical accommodation that must be provided and for staffing of the institution. Approved institutions receive grants under this legislation covering 80 per cent of operating costs and some funds for new construction. The act is administered by the Ministry of Community and Social Services.

Other legislation in this category is the Children's Institutions Act of 1963. This act establishes standards for institutions operated for children requiring specialized group care. Approved institutions qualify for grants covering 80 per cent of operating costs and capital grants on a full bed basis. In 1971 some twenty-seven such institutions were approved, providing accommodation for almost 800 children.[26]

Similar provisions exist under the Homes of Retarded Children Act, with the obvious difference that these facilities are operated for retarded children. Both of these acts are administered by the Ministry of Community and Social Services.

The specialized treatment end of the institutional spectrum is covered by the Children's Mental Health Centres Act of 1969. This legislation is administered by the Ministry of Health and it provides for the establishment of government-operated children's mental health centres and for the licensing, inspection and financing of private institutions which meet the requirements of this act. The regulations are very specific, covering facilities, programmes and personnel. Approved institutions receive grants covering all operating costs according to an established formula.

In addition to the institutional sector just described, there are a number of other organizations which contribute some important elements to the child welfare system in Ontario. The best known among them are the hospitals and clinics, some public and some under private auspices. Then there are services operated by various boards of education. Organizations such as Big Brothers, Big Sisters and the "Y" also play significant roles in some communities. Various drop-in centres operated by churches and other groups are also part of the picture, as are homemaking services and family service agencies. The latter ones certainly play an important role in the prevention area since all effective child welfare is essentially family-centred.

The difficulty here, however, is that not all communities have all the services listed. Some have only one or two, smaller ones may have none at all. They are usually an important factor in the child welfare practice of larger cities but are seldom present in small towns.

Then there are the income maintenance programmes which provide a necessary foundation for any child welfare system. In Ontario these programmes are the Family Benefits Act and the General Welfare Assistance Act. It is not intended to discuss these provisions in any detail except to acknowledge that they exist and that they do offer basic assistance to families in need. The General Welfare Assistance programme offers short-term assistance and is administered under municipal auspices. The Family

---

26   Training and Staff Development Branch, Department of Social and Family Services, "Orientation Programme for Children's Aid Societies" (1971), p. 7. (Mimeographed.)

Benefits are intended for people who require help over a prolonged period of time and are administered by the Ministry of Community and Social Services. As in other parts of Canada, Ontario families receive also the federally-administered Family Allowances. The Ontario Housing Authority must also be mentioned since it provides housing to some low-income families. These are not specifically child welfare programmes but they do contribute to the well-being of children and thus have to be considered as cornerstones of any sound child welfare policy.

SUMMARY ASSESSMENT

It is apparent from the preceding cataloguing of major legislative provisions and private programmes that Ontario has quite an elaborate child welfare system, which should be able to deal with any of the many kinds of problems that can affect the well-being of children. They can be divided into two basic categories: those that are external to the child and outside the child's own behaviour and those that are related to the child's own condition, behaviour or interpersonal relationships.

Under the problems external to the child, the following conditions could be listed:

(1) neglect, abuse or exploitation of the child;
(2) physical or mental illness of parents;
(3) orphanhood or abandonment;
(4) severe parental/marital problems;
(5) unwed parents;
(6) financial need of family;
(7) inadequate housing.

The second category of problems relating to the child's own behaviour, condition or interpersonal relationships could include the following:

(8) emotional or behaviour problems of the child;
(9) child in conflict with the law;
(10) illness of the child;
(11) physical handicap of the child;
(12) mental retardation of the child;
(13) learning disabilities or problems.[27]

Clearly in Ontario an elaborate child welfare system has been evolved and developed. One could argue persuasively that the child welfare system has something to offer for every problem situation and that is exactly how the system seems to have evolved. A problem was recognized and in time some public or private provisions were developed to deal with it. When the next problem was identified, another provision or service was added. Still others followed. It was a piecemeal, problem-oriented approach that shaped the child welfare policies in Ontario. It resulted in a policy or a programme for every problem.

However, while it is useful to identify and classify problems and needs so it may be understood what one is dealing with, there are some inherent

27 Adapted from a scheme developed by R. Jeter, *Children's Problems and Services in Child Welfare Programmes* (Washington: U.S. Department of Health, Education and Welfare, 1963), p. 16.

shortcomings if one uses the problem approach for the formulation of policies and the organization of services. One tends to end up with a very fragmented and uneven system and that happened to child welfare in Ontario. It is a complex mosaic but the overall image lacks focus and balance. The mosaic was created over a long period of time by a variety of governmental departments and private organizations without the benefit of any overall design and seemingly without any effective communication among them.

There are at least four ministries of the Ontario government, many municipal governments and a great assortment of private organizations involved in the provision of child welfare services in the province. But there appears to be no one with a clear responsibility and corresponding authority for planning and co-ordination. Nor surprisingly, there does not appear to be any general plan or even a clear objective of what all the individual programmes are trying to accomplish.

While children can have problems, policies and programmes have to be designed for children and their families, and not for problems. First of all, problems tend to occur in clusters. For instance, a child may be showing delinquent behaviour, the parents may be having marital problems, and the whole family may be in financial difficulty. At the present time in Ontario, such a situation could require services provided by the Ministry of Correctional Services, by a private family agency and by a municipal welfare department. No one would be able to address the total needs of the family. The shortcomings of such a condition are obvious. The helping efforts are likely to be unco-ordinated and could even work at cross-purposes, thus diminishing the overall effectiveness of the services.

There are even more serious shortcomings in the problem-oriented approach, however. The programmes tend to be geared to children and families who are already seriously troubled. In those situations effective help is frequently very difficult, if not impossible, to provide. To be sure, there always will be a need for such programmes but they will never be able to make an appreciable dent in the incidence of child welfare problems or to keep up with the ever-growing need. Provisions are needed that would be geared more to the prevention of problems and to the assistance of well-functioning families and children to remain that way. Only such programmes can provide a hope that the rate of child welfare problems will start decreasing.

This brings us to another shortcoming of the present system. There are some very good legislative provisions, or privately organized programmes, but they are inadequately implemented or funded. One such example is the present Child Welfare Act. It contains a most impressive provision for offering preventative services. However, most of the Children's Aid Societies have been very slow in formulating suitable programmes and the provincial government has been even slower in providing funds for such programmes.

Another example of a similar situation is the Day Nurseries Act. The legislation has been considered by some as the best in Canada and yet the overall results are less than outstanding, primarily because of the inadequate allocation of funds.

If one more example is needed, the situation of the family service agencies can be cited. These private organizations, where they exist, generally provide high-quality service. However, most of them are starved for funds since the federated appeals, the major source of their revenue, have experienced difficulties reaching their objectives. Under the provisions of the Canada Assistance Plan, it is possible for the provinces to obtain some federal funds, on a matching basis, for such services. Yet Ontario has not chosen to take advantage of this provision even though the need is critical.

It is a well-recognized fact that social policies in most jurisdictions are the product of the interaction of the social, political and economic forces that operate in a given locality at a particular time. They also tend to reflect certain value premises and assumptions about man and society. These premises and assumptions are occasionally stated in explicit terms, but more often they can only be recognized implicitly by the actions taken. What kind of assumptions and premises does the Ontario child welfare system reflect?

This chapter began with a quotation from the United Nations Declaration of the Rights of the Child. Do the present provisions of the province reflect the value premises of that Declaration? The question can be reasonably answered that they do. It is apparent that Ontario has developed many provisions for the protection and benefit of its children. However, if one were to ask whether the province has achieved the state of well-being for its children that the Declaration implies, then it would also be reasonable to answer that it has not. It may be that such goals can only be striven for but never fully achieved. While every policy meets some needs, it also tends to create or expose some new needs which require additional measures.

However, the present child welfare policies appear to be based on some additional premises which may hinder a greater realization of the general objectives contained in the Declaration. This premise could be described as a belief that parents are essentially capable and responsible to meet the basic needs of their children and that the organized provisions need to come into play only when the parents are unable or unwilling to perform their natural function. This belief is reinforced by a dominant concept of parental rights which can be interfered with only in extreme situations. These factors would probably account for the problem orientation of the present provisions.

It is not intended to suggest here that parental rights should be disregarded. But they have to be balanced against children's rights. It also needs to be recognized that in our present society many parents receive very inadequate preparation for their child-rearing functions and many additional factors impinge on their capacity to function as effective parents. Child welfare policies need to reflect these realities much more than they presently do.

FUTURE DIRECTIONS

It was observed earlier that after a period of rapid expansion during the 1960s the Ontario child welfare services appeared to be going through a period of stock-taking and questioning of future directions. This questioning seems to be stimulated by the rising costs of existing programmes and by some doubts about their accomplishments. There is both a danger and an opportunity in such a situation. The danger is that the government could decide simply to hold the line or pull back on funding of existing child welfare programmes until it can be demonstrated that they really work. The opportunity could occur if the concern was used to re-think what is being done, what the strengths and weaknesses of the present programmes are and what changes should be made.

In the preceding discussion, some of the more obvious strengths and weaknesses of the existing programmes were identified. It would seem appropriate now to focus on what changes would likely improve the present system, or at least what should be the general thrust of the future child welfare policies of this province. However, it is not feasible within the scope of this paper to develop a detailed list of recommendations, and just an indication of the general directions will have to suffice.

The most pressing need seems to be to overcome the fragmentation in planning and in administering child welfare provisions.[28] This should be attempted at two levels. The first one is provincial and the other one is regional. At the provincial level, some division will have to be designated and charged with the responsibility for total planning and co-ordination of all policies pertaining to the well-being of children. The present Children's Bureau within the Ministry of Community and Social Services could possibly perform that function if its mandate was expanded to include the child welfare programmes operated under other ministries.

At the regional level, special boards should be formed that would be responsible for the development and co-ordination of all personal services to children and their families, regardless of the auspices. The new political and geographical units of the regional governments seem to be well-suited for this badly-needed function, if they are given the proper authority.

Once the appropriate planning and co-ordinating bodies have been established, coherent policy should be formulated that would take into account the present realities of family life which are at the core of all child welfare. Such policy should have a major thrust in the direction of assisting children and parents to cope with the pressures and uncertainties that impinge on them in our present society. It should facilitate well-functioning families to remain that way. It should be prevention-oriented rather than problem-oriented.

It is heartening to note that while this chapter was being written the province of Ontario announced a re-organization of the provincial services for children along some of the lines suggested here. Several major child welfare programmes operated by the Ministries of Correctional Services, Attorney General and Health were transferred to the Ministry of Community and Social Services where a new division for Children's Services was created and placed under the jurisdiction of a newly-established position of an associate deputy minister. The re-organization is intended to consoli-

---

28   Fragmentation of provisions was considered a serious problem across Canada by the Commission on Emotional and Learning Disabilities in Children, *One Million Children: The CELDIC Report* (Toronto: Leonard Crainfor, 1970).

date all services for children and youth in Ontario. It is hoped that this integration of child welfare, day nurseries, children's mental health, mental retardation and delinquency programmes will ensure improved methods for meeting the special needs of children. Certainly some time will be needed to assess the effectiveness of the July 1977 realignments.

BIBLIOGRAPHY

Bain, Ian. "The Role of J. J. Kelso in the Launching of the Child Welfare Movement in Ontario." Unpublished M.S.W. thesis, University of Toronto, School of Social Work, 1954.

Byles, John A. *Alienation, Deviance and Social Control: A Study of Adolescents in Metropolitan Toronto.* Toronto: Interim Research Project on Unreached Youth, 1969.

Canadian Council on Social Development. *Youth '71: An Inquiry into the Transient Youth and Opportunities for Youth Programmes in the Summer of 1971.* Ottawa: Canadian Council on Social Development, 1971.

_____. *A Right to Opportunity: A Report on Youth and Social Assistance.* Ottawa: Canadian Council on Social Development, 1972.

_____. *Day Care.* Ottawa: Canadian Council on Social Development, 1972.

Commission on Emotional and Learning Disabilities in Children. *One Million Children: The CELDIC Report.* Toronto: Leonard Crainfor, 1970.

Flint, Betty M. *The Child and the Institution: A Study of Deprivation and Recovery.* Toronto: University of Toronto Press, 1966.

Greenland, Cyril. *Child Abuse in Ontario.* Toronto: Ministry of Community and Social Services, 1973.

Hepworth, H. P. *Services for Abused and Battered Children.* Personal Social Services in Canada: A Review, 3. Ottawa: Canadian Council on Social Development, 1975.

Lamb, S., and Solomon, D. N. *The Social Behaviour Surrounding Children's Health Problems.* Toronto: Canadian Conference on Children, 1965.

Laycock, J. E. "Welfare and Prevention." *Ontario Association of Children's Aid Societies Journal* 11, no. 8 (October 1968): 1-3.

Minister's Advisory Committee on Adoption and Foster Care. *Report on Adoption and Foster Care.* Toronto: Ontario Department of Social and Family Services, 1970.

National Council of Welfare. *Poor Kids.* Ottawa: National Council of Welfare, 1975.

Nicholson, A., and Young, M. "Family Day Care." *Ontario Association of Children's Aid Societies Journal* 14, no. 4 (April 1971): 1-5.

Ontario Association of Children's Aid Societies. *1967 Conference Workshop Papers.* Toronto: Ontario Association of Children's Aid Societies, 1967.

_____. *Brief to the Task Force on Community and Social Services.* Toronto: Ontario Association of Children's Aid Societies, 1973.

Ontario, Government of. *Services for Children with Mental and Emotional Disorders.* Toronto: Department of Health, 1967.

Ontario Legislature's Select Committee on Youth. *Report.* Kingston: Hanson & Edgar, 1967.

Rae-Grant, Q., and Moffat, P. J. *Children in Canada: Residential Care.* Toronto: Canadian Mental Health Association, 1971.

Ramsey, P. "The Development of Child Welfare Legislation in Ontario." Unpublished M.S.W. thesis, University of Toronto, School of Social Work, 1949.

Rose, A. "The Community's Responsibility for Family Life." *Proceedings, Ontario Association of Children's Aid Societies, Annual Conference.* Toronto, 1970, pp. 51-61.

Social Planning Council of Metropolitan Toronto. *A Study of the Needs and Resources for Community-Supported Welfare, Health and Recreation Services in Metropolitan Toronto.* Toronto: Social Planning Council, 1963.
_____ . *Reaching the Unreached Youth.* Toronto: Social Planning Council, 1964.
Splane, Richard B. "The Welfare of Children." In *Social Welfare in Ontario 1791-1893*, pp. 214-77. Toronto: University of Toronto Press, 1965.
Steinhaver, P. D. "Crisis in Foster Care." *Ontario Association of Children's Aid Societies Journal* 13, no. 9 (November 1970): 9-14.
Stolk, Mary Van. *The Battered Child in Canada.* Toronto: McClelland & Stewart, 1972.
Tremblay, M. A. *The Social Bases of Maturity in Childhood.* Toronto: Canadian Conference on Children, 1965.
Urwick, Currie & Partners, Ltd. "Study of the Managerial Effectiveness of the CAS of Ontario." A report prepared for the Department of Social Family Services of the Province of Ontario, 1969.

Part III

Processes of Social Policy Formulation in Canada

In the first part of this book, we defined the concept of social policy. In the second part, we explored some of the many areas in which social policy is operant within our society. Now we must look at the processes by which social policies are formulated. The five studies in this section explore the various means by which social policy enters the arena of social legislation and the concomitant value orientations of the social and political groups involved.

Where does the responsibility for the implementation of appropriate social policy lie? Has it been left in the hands of our civil servants? Militant groups of citizens? Politicians? Trained professionals? How much do members of each of these groups contribute to our current policy-making? And how much of a role should they play in constructing current policies to solve modern Canadian social problems?

In this part, our authors describe the actual process of policy formulation and implementation. Since each writer comes to the topic from a different perspective, we are able to identify some of the values they bring to the process, thus enabling us to achieve a broader understanding of the divergent forces shaping social policy. The articles here raise some philosophical issues that are very much a part of any social policy discussion.

11

Social Policy-Making in the Government of Canada: Reflections of a Reformist Bureaucrat

RICHARD SPLANE

In an article discussing what he called the "professionalization of reform," Daniel Patrick Moynihan expressed the view that a major impetus for reform in the United States during the 1960s came from liberal-minded professionals working within the federal government. In his words, "the main pressure for a massive government assault on poverty developed within the Kennedy-Johnson administration among officials whose responsibilities were to think about just such matters."[1] Although there is no equally authoritative statement about the influence for reform within the federal bureaucracy in Canada, Andrew Armitage makes somewhat similar comments about this question in *Social Welfare in Canada: Ideals and Realities*. In discussing the distribution and use of power in Canada he states that "the elite corps of senior officials, aided by some of their provincial counterparts, provided an enduring and consistent force for social welfare reform."[2] He makes the further point that "the division of powers between federal and provincial governments increases the power and influence of the bureaucracy."[3]

1 Daniel Patrick Moynihan, "The Professionalization of Reform," *The Public Interest* 1 (Fall 1965): 9.
2 Andrew Armitage, *Social Welfare in Canada: Ideals and Realities* (Toronto: McClelland and Stewart Ltd., 1975), p. 68.
3 Ibid., p. 66.

These views about bureaucracy and reform, together with the relative lack of writing on the subject in Canada, suggests that there would be merit in directing the main focus of this chapter on the bureaucracy and on the proposition that elements within it have exerted an important influence for reform in the development of social policy in Canada. In view of the general orientation of this book there would also appear to be merit in two further delimitations in the scope of the chapter: having it deal primarily, though not wholly, with the welfare branches of the Department of National Health and Welfare, and placing considerable emphasis on the part played in it by social workers or those identified with the field of social welfare. Such an approach can accommodate a review of broader structures and processes affecting social policy, some comments on how those have changed since the establishment of the Department and an assessment of the prospects of social workers playing a significant role in the development of social policy in the future.

A further rationale for the focus of the chapter is that there has been some excellent writing on more general aspects of policy-making in Canada in a number of professional journals and a few books.[4]

This chapter is a frankly subjective exposition, made explicit in my use, at times, of the first person singular. I write (with due regard to the Official Secrets Act) as a former bureaucrat employed in the Department of National Health and Welfare from 1952 to 1972 and as an interested observer of the Department both before and after that time span. My career in the federal government, which followed experience in social welfare administration in Ontario, provided a good range of opportunities to observe and participate in the formulation and implementation of social policy. I worked initially in the Research and Statistics Division of the Department, nominally as an economist, though my graduate degrees were in Modern History and Social Work. I had a year as the Executive Assistant to the first Deputy Minister of Welfare, Dr. George Davidson, and for twelve years I was successively a director, director-general and assistant deputy minister. Those positions involved a considerable degree of responsibility for developing and implementing programmes that included Unemployment Assistance, the Canada Assistance Plan, the National Welfare Grants Programme, Family Planning and the Guaranteed Income Experiments Programme. I was involved in many interdepartmental activities concerned with social policy, particularly those associated with anti-poverty measures, and I spent some months on secondment to the Privy Council Office, in connection with the constitutional working paper, *Income Security and Social Services*. I saw something of Canadian involvement in international welfare, representing Canada on the UNICEF Board at meetings in New York and Bangkok, Thailand.

During a twenty-year period, I was associated with many officials who had a strong commitment to the advancement of social welfare (defined to include health) and who had been attracted to the federal public service in

---

4 The journals include those of long standing, notably *Canadian Public Administration* and the *Canadian Journal of Political Science* and the new quarterly, *Canadian Public Policy*. A number of the books appear in the reading list.

the expectation that they would have an opportunity to promote social welfare objectives in that setting. Those who worked in the welfare branches of the Department of National Health and Welfare were recruited more or less directly by Dr. Davidson and by Dr. Joseph Willard, the first Director of the Research and Statistics Division and the Deputy Minister of Welfare for twelve years. They were recruited from a number of backgrounds and disciplines, but persons with social work education and with experience in the field of social welfare predominated. Both Dr. Davidson and Dr. Willard had had previous experience in social welfare activities and identified sufficiently with professional social work to become members, under the "special circumstances clause" in the Canadian Association of Social Workers.

In referring in this chapter to a group of like-minded officials committed to social welfare advancement and reform, I need to make a number of qualifying statements about it. At no time was there a "group" in the organizational sense of that term. I am thus applying to a number of former colleagues, some still in the Department or in other departments, others widely scattered and some deceased who meet my ill-defined criteria of like-mindedness, commitment and involvement. Those to whom I would accord membership would not have regarded themselves as an "elite corps"; most would have found the term offensive. They included colleagues in both the health and the welfare branches of the Department; officials in other departments with social programmes, notably Indian and Northern Affairs, Manpower, Labour, Secretary of State and Veterans Affairs; officials in the Office of the Privy Council and even, though rarely, officials in the control departments and agencies—Finance, the Treasury Board and the Public Service Commission—which bodies, because of the use they made of their control of resources and the direction of their influence in the setting of priorities, we often regarded as our prime adversaries.

My credo, and the one I would ascribe in varying degrees to the other members of the group I have described as being committed to social welfare advancement and reform, was quite straightforward. Until about the mid-1960s it consisted almost wholly of a belief that, in the interests of all Canadians, and particularly of those least advantaged, a high priority should be given to the development of a comprehensive nation-wide social security system. The government of Canada had made a commitment to develop such a system, contingent upon certain specified forms of provincial collaboration, in the Green Book Proposals of 1945. It seemed quite appropriate, therefore, to those of us who were so inclined to promote by all suitable means a goal to which the government was committed internally by the 1945 proposals and externally through its membership in the United Nations and its endorsement of the 1948 Charter of Human Rights.

My perception of the structures and processes of the total Canadian political system was coloured by how they affected the attainment of that social welfare goal. Accordingly, the following review of a number of the political structures and processes—Parliament, the Cabinet and Cabinet committees, Ministers and their staffs, Deputy Ministers and the control agencies—reflects my views and biases, but I held some of them in common, I believe, with those in the group I have identified.

PARLIAMENT

We viewed Parliament with a mixture of exasperation and respect. Great debates in the House of Commons or the Senate on social policy issues are rare; many of the Members' questions requiring departmental answers seem trivial and the Members seldom make good use of the opportunity to probe into both policy and departmental administration during the annual review of spending estimates. But far more important than these weaknesses are what we regarded as its repeated affirmation of our own central conviction: that social welfare is a matter of prime national concern. A review of Hansard reveals the volume of questions directed, almost daily, to the Minister of National Health and Welfare, carrying the message that he bears a responsibility for these areas of vital human concern. Repeated replies to the effect that the issue in question falls within provincial jurisdiction fails to curb the flow.

More significant still is the consistent support the House of Commons has given to federal initiatives in social welfare. Even when some provinces —notably Quebec, but at times others, including Ontario and Alberta—were strongly resisting such initiatives, social welfare measures almost invariably received the support of members representing constituencies in all provinces. Parliament has not, that is, been a sounding board for the assertion of provincialism in social welfare.[5] Nor, with few exceptions, have Members of the Commons been the spokesmen for the go-slow-on-welfare positions of organizations like the Canadian Chamber of Commerce. Similarly, there has been little open support in Parliament (though there may well have been in the various party caucuses) for anti-welfare sentiments which sweep the country periodically and have recently been called the "welfare backlash." The position generally taken by the opposition to the social welfare measures presented by whatever government is in office is that their coverage is too narrow and their benefits are too small.

The approach by the Commons to social welfare has been affected by two aspects of the political process: the highly effective role of members of the New Democratic Party, notably Stanley Knowles, and the desire of the Liberal Party to nurture an image as the party of social welfare. The NDP's strong support for health insurance, pensions and the demogrant programmes of family allowances and old age security has consistently affected the mood of the Commons during social welfare debates. More substantively, it has influenced government policy in ways that are difficult to measure as well as in specific instances that have been documented, such as the NDP's impact on social welfare during periods of minority government.

The Liberal Party's image as the party of social welfare, sustained by its near monopoly of power since the mid-1930's, received some reinforce-

5   The Special Joint Committee of the Senate and of the House of Commons on the Constitution of Canada, which reported in 1972, seemed to support provincial priority in social

ment from an unexpected quarter, the Senate, as a result of the reports of two commissions chaired by Senator Croll respectively on aging and poverty. The rapid implementation of one of the recommendations of the former—that of a guaranteed income programme for the aged—proved to be a highly popular measure and made it possible for Liberal governments since 1966 to indicate their support of both the principle of the guaranteed income and its "appropriate" application.

Because of the apparent receptivity of the Commons to social welfare initiatives and with the Senate seen as capable of generating reports as useful as those on aging and poverty, those of us in the public service who were committed to strong social welfare programmes viewed Parliament favourably. The problem was getting the necessary policies developed within the government for presentation to Parliament.

INTERNAL STRUCTURES AND PROCESSES

The Cabinet is the ultimate locus of decision-making on policy and public servants are, except rarely, excluded from viewing its deliberations. The Cabinet, however, normally accepts recommendations that come from Cabinet committees, and in such committees officials do participate. And the life, death, or modification of departmental proposals is usually decided there. Social welfare proposals put forward by the Department of National Health and Welfare are dealt with by a Cabinet Committee on Social Policy and normally have to compete with other departments having social programmes for limited financial resources, the size of which have been pre-determined by the Planning and Priorities Committee.

The formal document in which proposals for new policies and programmes are put to Cabinet committees and then, if the proposals survive, to the Cabinet is known as a Memorandum to Cabinet. This supremely important document must present the case for the Department's recommendations in a half-dozen pages, though extensive appendices are normally attached elaborating the points made and providing supporting arguments and data. The success, within a Cabinet committee, of a submission to Cabinet will depend on a wide range of factors, some of which, like the planning and priorities guidelines, lie outside the decision-making authority of the committee. Within the committee, much depends on the Minister, including his skill in his relationships with his colleagues and his status in the Cabinet. Similarly, much hangs on the performance of Deputy Ministers and senior officials who are called upon to outline the programme, particularly its technical aspects. Around the table are their opposite numbers from other related departments and officials from the Privy Council Office, Treasury Board and the Department of Finance.

The relationships between these officials can bear crucially on the way a Cabinet document is dealt with and the decision that is reached on it. Officials of the Privy Council Office prepare the agendas and record the decisions of the Cabinet committees. They carry a co-ordinating role where

security, but there has been no evidence that its Report has affected the approach of Parliament.

policy issues affect, as is often the case, two or more departments. Officials of the Treasury Board and the Department of Finance have an appropriate concern about the short- and long-term cost implications and a responsibility to ensure that these are not misrepresented knowingly or by inadvertence. Individually, and sometimes collectively, officials from these agencies of control and direction hold views and convictions about policy issues no less intense and legitimate than those held by officials promoting social welfare programmes. During the preparation of a departmental submission to Cabinet, officials of the initiating department will formally, in interdepartmental committees, and informally, through various kinds of contacts, lay the groundwork for the submission and seek official support for it.

It has not been uncommon over the years for officials in the Department of Health and Welfare to encounter strong resistance from officials of the control agencies to their proposals for new social welfare initiatives. During the development of the Canada Assistance Plan, for example, there was prolonged and sometimes overt opposition from officials who opposed the measure for a variety of reasons. One was that it was a new federal-provincial shared cost programme. Such programmes had been opposed by a number of provinces, notably Quebec, with such force that the Liberal Party, while in opposition between 1957 and 1963 incorporated within its party platform an undertaking that any new shared cost programme that might be developed would permit a province to contract out of its provisions without financial loss. Another objection was that the Plan would, for the first time, share in the costs of welfare services and this was seen both as moving into a field of provincial jurisdiction and as constituting a precedent with unpredictable financial and other consequences.

Behind the submission to the Cabinet of a new, costly and complex measure like the Canada Assistance Plan, there could be many months and sometimes years between the departmental decision to seek approval of a new programme and the enactment of legislation bringing it into being. Much of the activity undertaken at the official level has elements of a military operation. The strategic objective of establishing a new programme is achieved only when the tactics of reducing or neutralizing the opposition and securing allies prove more successful than the counter tactics of the opposing officials. In the case of the Canada Assistance Plan, victory was achieved over formidable opposition when, as a culmination of prolonged and intense work at the official level, supporting forces in the anti-poverty programme of the Privy Council Office were brought into an alliance which also included provincial ministers and officials.

The extent to which policy is developed at the official level is directly affected by the degree of ministerial direction and the determination of a government to assert the role and responsibility of ministers individually and the Cabinet collectively in the formulation of policy. Because of the multiplicity of demands on his time and energy, however, a Minister tends, after a beginning period in a portfolio and after achieving certain initial policy goals, to be less active in policy development and more disposed to look to officials to propose and develop new initiatives. Ministers in minority governments, while having to generate policy actions that serve to keep the government in power, often have little energy beyond that required for day-to-day survival to devote to long-run or complex policy-making.

Much has been written about the determination of the majority government of Prime Minister Trudeau in 1968 to reduce the power of the bureaucracy within the programme departments and to strengthen the policy-making capability of Ministers and the Cabinet. This was to be done through a variety of means which included enlarging the office of the Prime Minister and the Privy Council Office, creating two Ministries of State to develop and co-ordinate policy in the fields of science and urban affairs, providing expanded personal staffs for Ministers and encouraging Ministers to develop white papers on policy issues in their area of responsibility.

The white papers, notably those on housing, Indians, taxation, unemployment insurance and income security did, in fact, result in an unprecedented degree of ministerial policy-making activity. The long-term impact of the white papers has yet to be assessed; the shorter-term effect was to damage the careers of some Ministers and to contribute to the near defeat of the Trudeau government in the election of 1972. But the white paper process did diminish the role of the bureaucracy in policy-making.

In part, this was because of the use by Ministers of persons brought in on special assignment or as part of the Ministers' staffs which, from 1968, were much larger than previously. The ministerial assistants tended to be young and idealistic, and to assume that, far from reformist, the bureaucracy was made up of persons interested in little beyond their own careers. Some officials found the incursions of ministerial aides into their programmes intolerable and left the public service. Other officials found it possible to establish constructive working relationships with the assistants and to profit from their points of view, their enthusiasm, their strategic location in the Minister's office and their network of relationships with their colleagues in other ministerial offices.

Illustrations of constructive relationships between the reformist bureaucrats who had joined the public service in the 1940s, 1950s and early 1960s and the new ministerial aides of 1968 could be cited in the welfare branches of Health and Welfare Canada. A number of the former, of whom I was one, had expected that the social security measures and other social programmes that had been enacted prior to 1968 would result in greater progress in reducing poverty and alienation than was evident from the then-available indicators. Accordingly, we were disposed to consider what additional means might assist in achieving our initial objectives and we found that some of the new ministerial assistants had useful insights into contemporary issues, notably those relating to participation and involvement. This, and some reciprocal appreciation on their part of our experience and motivation, provided a basis for collaboration in developing and presenting for ministerial approval measures designed to assist members of disadvantaged sectors of society in forming groups and organizations and otherwise gaining some power in matters affecting their social and economic needs and their human rights. The founding of welfare rights groups, the support of the Poor People's Conference, collaboration with other departments in programmes for transient youth, the promotion of the

Federal-Provincial Task Force on Alienation, the promotion of poverty law and community legal services, the reconstitution of the National Council of Welfare to place representatives of the disadvantaged in a strategic location for influencing policy-making, are examples of the work of this alliance of old and new reformist interests in the Department.

MINISTERS

The policy-making roles of officials were continuously affected by the approach of individual Ministers, itself affected by many factors, as well as by the stance at a particular time of the Cabinet on ministerial responsibility for policy-making.

Since the establishment of the Department in 1944, there have been seven Ministers—Brooke Claxton, Paul Martin, Waldo Montieth, Judy Lamarsh, Allan J. MacEachen, John Munro, and Marc Lalonde—all of whom, save Waldo Montieth, were members of Liberal governments. Unlike some provincial ministers who were regarded by the welfare field as being anti-welfare, all who have taken the federal portfolio have identified themselves with positive social welfare goals and have undertaken to extend the social security system toward the objective of comprehensive nation-wide coverage.

The degree to which each has succeeded during his or her years as Minister in securing the enactment of important social welfare measures depends on many factors, of which the Minister's zeal and desire to establish new programmes have not been the most important. They include, among others, the extent and consistency of support from within the political system, from the public and from special interest groups, the state of the economy and the state of federal-provincial relations. And, with special relevance to the focus of this chapter, the Minister's success depends on the capacity of the Deputy Minister and departmental officials to respond skillfully to the play of forces in assisting the Minister in all aspects of the complex process of policy formulation and implementation.

A Minister might be expected to find the basis for his policy positions in the platform of the party to which he belongs. And political party platforms have, in fact, been of considerable importance in bringing forward social policy issues and in the promotion of action on them. The platforms of the major parties, however, have been in substantial agreement on the need to extend the social security system. Even where, in particular general elections, discernible differences on social welfare could be identified, it would be difficult to determine whether they significantly affected the electoral outcome. Available evidence on how the voting public reacts to the record and posture of parties and governments on social welfare issues would probably support these kinds of hypotheses: that the Canadian electorate rewards governments which enact measures that provide improvements in social security coverage and benefits where those become or are expected to become immediately available; that it is rather indifferent to measures where benefits are deferred, such as those provided by the Canada Pension Plan; that it is ambivalent about social assistance which, while seen as vital in meeting the material needs of the poor, is also regarded both as being demeaning and as creating disincentives to work; that it is undecided about guaranteed income measures because, though viewed as eliminating some problems, they could result in swelling the ranks of the work-shy who are thought to be large in number and to be "ripping off" the existing programmes; that it is angered about weak administration which permits fraud and misuse; that it is not receptive, at a given time, to substantial increases in taxes for social security programmes funded from general revenues or to substantial increases in the premiums of the social insurance programmes.

If these observations are valid, it follows that a Minister of National Health and Welfare cannot look to the public in general for clear and sustained support for social welfare initiatives. Support does come from special groups seeking new or improved programmes. The aged have at times brought organized pressure to bear for increased benefits. Veterans' organizations have lobbied effectively over the years for their members. The blind have kept their needs before government, and the disabled mounted one remarkably effective campaign which led to the enactment, considerably earlier than would have otherwise been the case, of the Disabled Persons Act in 1954. In recent years measures for women and children, such as day-care and family planning, have been improved because of the *Report* of the Royal Commission on the Status of Women. The Commission and the machinery that has been established in and out of government to monitor progress in implementing its recommendations are products of a movement for improved rights for women, which is of increasing significance and potential.

Other groups seeking new or improved programmes to meet their needs have been less successful. This could be said of welfare rights groups notwithstanding the support they receive from government by way of grants and the forms of help and access extended by the National Council of Welfare.

A more easily recognizable factor affecting the prospects for ministerial initiatives in social welfare is economics, expressed in the rate of growth of the gross national product and more particularly in the perceived yield of federal taxes. Numerous examples could be cited of their on-off effect. The family allowance programme "could be afforded" in 1945 because of abundant revenues and declining war-related expenditures. The economic slow-down in the late 1950s and early 1960s limited Waldo Montieth's scope for implementing the "social justice" measures he aspired to introduce. John Munro was restricted to $150 million of new money around which to build his White Paper on Income Security for Canadians—a circumstance leading to his ill-fated, economy package, Family Income Security Plan. His successor, Marc Lalonde, profited from the astonishing yield of the new taxation measures and within a year could commit $1.4 billion to social security programmes.

Federal-provincial relations have similarly affected the timing and nature of the measures a Minister could submit to Parliament. As noted earlier, the Liberal governments in the 1960s felt bound by a party commitment to provide for contracting-out of new shared-cost programmes. This, they discovered, collided with the almost insuperable problems of treating provinces differentially in the funding of social programmes. The problems were dealt with, or rather deferred, by offering contracting-out to all provinces and, when only Quebec took advantage of it, placing the contracting-out privilege on an interim basis. Under the Established Programmes (Interim Arrangement) Act, the flow of funds to Quebec is channelled differently through tax arrangements and payments from the Department of Finance, but the province presents its claims to the Department of National Health and Welfare and carries out the same provisions in the sharing agreement as do all the other provinces.

The problems of shared-cost programmes are illustrative of others facing Ministers in which there is a combination of financial and constitutional issues. In the mid-1960s these were further complicated by the Quiet Revolution, most dramatically expressed in respect to social welfare programmes by Quebec's decision to establish the Quebec Pension Plan rather than to participate in the Canada Pension Plan. In the period 1968 to 1971, the federal-provincial constitutional review kept constitutional issues to the fore. The fact that the breakdown of the final meeting in Victoria in June 1971 was over social welfare powers is indicative of the difficulties facing Ministers seeking to proceed with social welfare measures. They proved insuperable during John Munro's last year as Minister. The situation changed dramatically, however, as a result of a meeting of provincial Ministers of Welfare in November 1972 which formally, if somewhat indirectly, acknowledged that close federal-provincial collaboration and strong federal leadership are essential for continued progress on social security. Marc Lalonde's skillful handling of the opportunity, through working out and including a federal-provincial strategy in his proposal for a five-year federal-provincial social security review contributed to the successful resumption of social security development in Canada. But ministerial skill and determination have not of themselves been able to remove the obstacles frequently presented by federal-provincial differences over financial and constitutional issues.

DEPUTY MINISTERS AND OFFICIALS

It is the responsibility of the Deputy Minister and, to varying degrees of departmental officials, to understand the factors and interplay of forces that alternatively place restrictions upon and create opportunities for ministerial initiatives.

From the establishment of the Department to July 1975 there were three Deputy Ministers: George Davidson from 1944 to 1959, Joseph Willard from 1960 to the end of 1972, and Albert Johnson from the beginning of 1973 to the end of June 1975. They are among Canada's most respected public officials. All have doctorates from Harvard, all have made their mark in a number of settings, each had a distinctive management style, and each made a distinctive impact on the Department. All have shown mastery in the art of government, including the art of working with Ministers in the formulation of policy.

George Davidson gave the welfare branches of the Department their initial form. Because of his previous experience in social policy and social administration at the provincial level (British Columbia), at the national level, in the voluntary sector, as Executive Director of the Canadian Welfare Council (now the Canadian Council on Social Development), and his concurrent experience in representing Canada in the Social Commission of the United Nations, he had a commanding grasp of social welfare policy. He sought to avoid complicated programmes requiring large administrative staffs and was himself the author of a number of the formulations on policy questions involved in the development of the demogrant programmes of family allowances and old age security and the social assistance measures for aged, blind, disabled and unemployed. With Brock Chisholm, the first Deputy Minister of Health, he established the Research and Statistics Division which for many years served both sides of the Department. With the encouragement of Dr. Davidson and under the direction of Dr. Willard, substantive policy proposals, as well as data, were generated within the Division and in general a sense of significant participation in the development of Canada's social security system resulted in high morale within it.

Joseph Willard's succession to the deputy ministership meant that there was little break in the continuity of administration. There was, however, a steady acceleration in work on policy and programme development. Officials were imbued with a sense of the importance of the work that had to be done, the magnitude of the obstacles that stood in the way of federal initiatives during the 1960s and the hope that with sufficient effort our commonly-held objectives could be achieved. Dr. Willard continued, as Deputy Minister, to use the Research and Statistics Division not only to collect and analyze data but to formulate policy proposals. He also encouraged the programme branches to regard policy formulation as a vital part of their responsibilities and the branches which I directed gave this the highest priority. In recruiting for administrators and consultants, we placed strong emphasis on a candidate's interest in policy development and on indicated capacity to promote it. If, as was often the case, they were social workers or had worked in the welfare field, they also brought a direct knowledge of the nature of social welfare problems, and of the impact on human lives of various forms of need or deprivation, together with a knowledge of the operation of social welfare programmes.

Dr. Willard was able to establish close relations with all provincial departments of welfare. The federal and provincial Deputy Ministers, programme administrators and advisors developed increasingly close communication links based on their shared recognition of unmet social welfare needs and an interest in finding workable solutions to common problems. Within the limits of the current stance of their governments, they accordingly sought to reduce federal-provincial problems standing in the way of social welfare development. In addition to contacts in an accelerating number of federal-provincial conferences, committees and task forces, many of the officials met as members of other bodies, such as the Public Welfare Division of the Canadian Welfare Council, the American Public Welfare Association and the Canadian Association of Social Workers. The impact on social welfare policy-making in Canada during the 1960s of these collegial relationships of like-minded officials is hard to estimate, but it was undoubtedly considerable.

The period during which Dr. Willard was Deputy Minister was one in which the forces for and against federal initiatives in social welfare were in a state of continuous turbulence. The attempt to develop a single social insurance programme to cover retirement, survivors and the disabled failed, and great efforts were required even to achieve transferability of coverage as between the Quebec and Canada Pension Plans. The forces for the breakup of the existing nation-wide social welfare system were strong, the forces opposing the establishment of new federal programmes often seemed overwhelming. The Ministers with whom he worked during the 1960s have testified to the wisdom of Dr. Willard's advice, the skill of his handling of federal-provincial and interdepartmental issues and his capacity to encourage and channel a strong performance from departmental officials. The magnitude of federal social welfare developments during those years can be credited, to a substantial degree, to the sustained and creative commitment to social welfare advancement by departmental officials and to Joseph Willard's direction.

The advent of Marc Lalonde as Minister in November 1972, followed soon after by the appointment of Albert Johnson, resulted in some inevitable discontinuity in departmental practices and relationships, but it also provided an opportunity for new approaches to social welfare issues. The Minister and the new Deputy Minister had previously worked together in a number of roles. They viewed the problems and potentialities of the situation facing the new minority government in a similar light and together formulated what became known as the Federal Provincial Social Security Review, first outlined in the speech from the throne and in Marc Lalonde's address in the Commons in January 1973. From then on and throughout the next two and one-half years, the welfare side of Health and Welfare Canada was preoccupied with the Social Security Review and the success of the welfare branches in formulating and implementing social policy can be largely assessed in terms of the success with which the Review has attained its objectives.

These were set out in the federal Working Paper on Income Security in Canada[6] (the Orange Paper) around which the Review has centred. The Orange Paper was presented in April 1973 to the first of a series of federal-provincial meetings of Ministers of Welfare. The purpose of the Review was described in the Paper as "the development by the federal and provincial governments of a new over-all approach to social security," and it proposed that this consist of a two-year developmental phase and a three-year implementation phase.

In the Orange Paper, the government addressed itself to the major problems, referred to earlier, that have affected the establishment of nation-wide social security programmes. It sought to gain wide public support through presenting its proposals within what it described as a comprehensive and logical framework which would seek to correct the known weaknesses in the existing system and to build on its strengths. It responded to the interest the public has shown in tangible action by containing substantial im-

6 Marc Lalonde, *Working Paper on Social Security in Canada* (Ottawa: Information Canada, 1973).

mediate benefits in the form of much higher Family Allowance payments. It proposed that the needs of the working poor—neglected under the existing system—be met with an income supplementation plan, but one that would be designed to avoid the perceived dangers of such a plan through having "built-in work incentives." It dealt with the concern about the effect of the proposals on the economy and on the taxpayer by indicating that the new measures to be proposed involved "implementation over time, within existing levels of taxation." And, of critical importance, it contained a new federal-provincial approach or strategy providing for provincial flexibility in setting the income support levels of new federal-provincial programmes subject to certain agreed conditions.

This approach was designed to avoid the constitutional problems which, as noted earlier, had presented such formidable obstacles throughout the 1960s and especially during the early 1970s.

The prospects for the success of the Review were enhanced by the support it appeared to have in Cabinet, by the buoyancy of federal revenues in 1972-73, and by the support given to the social security proposals in Parliament by the New Democratic Party, which held the balance of power until July 1974. And, with particular relevance to the capacity of the welfare branches to develop social policy, they were able to secure, from the control agencies, the resources of personnel, equipment and related services which they had not been able to secure earlier and the lack of which had severely limited departmental capacity to undertake the development of new policy. Scientific and professional personnel in the Income Security and Social Assistance Programme increased from 55 in September 1972 to 106 in the same month of 1974 and to 135 on March 31, 1975.[7] Those recruited, however, were almost exclusively persons with academic training deemed relevant to the work being undertaken on the quantitative aspects of the Social Security Review.

The Review was conducted by the federal and provincial Ministers of Welfare, who met six times during the period, by a Continuing Committee of Deputy Ministers and by working parties which developed data and formulated policy options in what the Orange Paper had referred to as the strategies by which the Review would pursue its objectives: an employment strategy, a social insurance strategy, an income supplementation strategy, a social and employment services strategy and a federal-provincial strategy.

The employment strategy involved collaboration with manpower departments and, after some months of work, the Review recommended and secured agreement on a proposal to establish some twenty developmental projects in the provinces directed to the improvement of the capacity of people to secure employment in the labour market and to develop employment for those whom the labour market does not employ. It will be perhaps two or three years before the findings of these experimental projects can be assessed for policy development. The Working Group on Social Services (the designation social and employment services having been discarded for a number of reasons) presented its report in 1974 after considerable work

7 Canada, *Estimates 1975-76* (Ottawa: Information Canada, 1975), pp. 16-48.

involving all provinces and a policy position on social services was agreed upon at the meeting of Ministers which concluded on May 1, 1975. The Working Party on Income Maintenance had the most complex issues to deal with and, notwithstanding the magnitude of the federal and provincial resources that were committed to it, was far from having completed its task by the end of the period.

The achievements of the Review to July 1975 are impressive. As outlined in the communique following the Ministers' meeting on May 1, 1975,[8] they include: the agreements reached between the federal government and most provinces covering developmental projects respecting the community employment strategy; the partial implementation of the social insurance strategy through improved benefits provided under the Canada and Quebec Pension Plans; the adoption of a social services strategy; agreement on the broad framework for a new guaranteed income system with separate income support and income supplementation components and on guidelines covering cost-sharing under the Canada Assistance Plan for an interim period. In addition, during the early stages of the Review, the enactment of the new Family Allowances measure and the "indexing" of benefits under federal programmes so that they escalate with the cost of living were of great significance. And in July 1975, Parliament enacted a Spouse Allowances programme to provide, on the basis of an income test, an allowance to spouses aged sixty to sixty-four of Old Age Security pensioners. This could be regarded as an increment in the evolving development of the income support component of the guaranteed income system.

Impressive as all this is, it falls well short of the optimistic assumption made in the Orange Paper that the policy formulation stage would be completed in "two years or less" and that implementation thereafter would be primarily a matter of phasing-in as financial resources became available. The May 1 communique made it clear that many complex issues had not been solved respecting the proposed guaranteed income system. These included the relationship between the income security system and the tax system, the harmonization of the social insurance programmes with the proposed new income system, as well as the basic characteristics of that system, notably the definition of income, the treatment of assets, the accounting period, the definition of the family unit, and the rate at which support and supplementation would be reduced as family income increased. Moreover, the Ministers were so far from agreement on the vital question of the delivery of the supplementation component of the guaranteed income system, including the level of government which would assume administrative responsibility, that they concluded "that it would be helpful for future discussions to have an independent evaluation of alternative delivery systems." They accordingly agreed "to commission a study to be considered at a future meeting of ministers."

A somewhat paradoxical aspect of the Review, in the light of the limited treatment of social services in the Orange Paper and the constitutional problems traditionally associated with social services, was the proposal

8   Canada, *Communique, Meeting of Federal and Provincial Ministers of Welfare, Ottawa, April 30 and May 1st 1975* (Ottawa: Health and Welfare Canada, 1975).

made by the Minister of National Health and Welfare and accepted by the Ministers of all provinces "for a sweeping change in the approach to the financing and development of social services in Canada." This well-conceived proposal, to take the form of a new federal social services bill to be placed before Parliament early in 1976, provided for federal sharing in half the costs of as wide a range of social services as are now covered under the Canada Assistance Plan but without its test of need or of the "likelihood of being in need." The new measure which provided for federal sharing in the cost of some services provided on a universal basis and some to which an income test is applied holds great promise for a new era of federal-provincial collaboration in the seriously neglected field of personal and community human services.

In assessing the accomplishments of the Review during its initial period, the surprising agreement reached on a social services measure compensates somewhat for the slower progress in policy formulation relating to the guaranteed income system and for the prolonged postponement of definitive action respecting community employment.

PROSPECTS FOR THE FUTURE

The future development of social policy on the welfare side of Health and Welfare Canada will be affected by many of the same factors that have been significant in recent years, together with some predictable and, doubtless, some unpredictable new ones. It may, however, be useful to speculate on future prospects for progressive social policy development and on the role that social workers may play in it.

It is likely that the Social Security Review will continue to be the vehicle for social policy action until 1978 and perhaps to the end of the decade. It is predictable that there will be no easy achievement of its remaining goals. The attack on shared-cost programmes following the federal budget of June 1975 suggests that the agreement of the Ministers of Welfare some weeks earlier on the new shared-cost social services measure may not be sufficiently binding on the eleven governments, and that it will not be readily accepted by all provinces if enacted. And something of the extent and complexity of the problems to be solved in attaining the goals of the community employment strategy can be discerned from the experience of the Opportunities for Youth Programme, the Local Initiatives Programme and the Work Activities Programme under the Canada Assistance Plan. They include formidable problems of securing public understanding and acceptance of a community employment programme even if it is well conceived and efficiently administered. The dimensions of the unsolved policy issues relating to a guaranteed income system have already been noted. One can predict that it will be several years, under the best of circumstances, before an income supplementation programme involving new legislation, as opposed to amendments to the Canada Assistance Plan, will be in operation.

The point of view from which this chapter is written suggests that the "best of circumstances," as it relates to all aspects of the Social Security Review, will need to include a quality of work by departmental officials during that period comparable to the highest level of performance achieved at any time since the early 1960s. By quality of work I have in mind work generated by a consistent commitment to social welfare reform and development and expressed through the whole range of activities touched on earlier that are required of departmental officials to ensure the success of ministerial initiatives in this complex and controversial field.

There are, however, a number of factors within the federal bureaucracy that are not conducive to the needed quality of work. I refer to the current policies in the public service which make it difficult for a person with an interest in social welfare reform and development to pursue a career which offers increasingly responsible involvement in policy formulation or in the administration of social welfare programmes at a senior level.

One of these factors, and the only one to be considered here, is the dominance in the public service of what are taken to be the imperatives of modern management. What I am referring to are the succession of endeavours that have been made by the Public Service Commission and the Treasury Board to increase the efficiency of the public service.[9] These have largely been based on models developed in business or engineering and have often resulted in highly inappropriate policies in departments like Health and Welfare where professional training and experience are essential for sound policy formulation and implementation. Under the prevailing approach, the development and operation of programmes, including the making of major policy decisions, is viewed as being the responsibility and prerogative of managers trained to employ the techniques of modern business management. The emphasis is on the deployment of resources related to the achievement of objectives. Since the latter are often defined simplistically and their attainment evaluated simplistically, the approach is proclaimed a success. Thereby, the dominant management philosophy of the control agencies is perpetuated.

At present the royal route to advancement in the bureaucracy is through the Career Assignment Programme, a programme for the selection and training of persons perceived to have management potential. Generalist rather than specialist interests are emphasized and frequent moves across departmental lines, with some experience in the Treasury Board or other other control agency, are stressed. Management skill and knowledge are distinguished from professional skill and knowledge and the manager is assumed to be able without undue difficulty to secure from professional, scientific or technical personnel the advice he needs for policy-making and programme administration. Persons in the professional categories of the public service now find it advisable to move from those categories and into programme management if they wish to progress to senior decision-making positions.

There are some strengths in the present system of training and deploying managers. It prevents ingrown departmentalism and gives to the new type of middle and senior managers a broad view of governmental operations and procedures. Its weakness—and it is a very grave weakness—is that it leads, particularly in Departments like Health and Welfare Canada, to super-

---

9   H. R. Laframboise, "Administrative Reform in the Federal Public Service: Signs of a Saturation Psychosis," *Canadian Public Administration* 14, no. 3 (1971): 303.

ficiality in policy formulation and decision-making. The cumulative effect of day-to-day decisions made by managers of programmes who lack an in-depth knowledge of the field in which they have been given responsibility can negate and all too often do negate the effect of sound policy formula-tion and good programme design. Ultimately, one must hope, the serious ill-effects of generalist management that were so clearly identified in British experience by the Fulton Commission[10] will be perceived in the public service of Canada and remedial action will be taken.

Until this occurs, however, account must be taken of the present policies on career prospects in the welfare branches of Health and Welfare Canada. The present situation is that persons with social work training wanting to enter the public service with a view to contributing to social welfare ad-vancement can elect to take positions in a professional category as consul-tants in the hope that they will be used constructively and that they will be able to make some impact on policy development and decision-making. Alternatively, they can seek to enter the programme management stream but that involves a diminution of professional identification, and even if they are successful in advancing to senior levels of management where new policy tends to be generated and day-to-day decision-making directly af-fects policy implementation, they can, because of the policy of inter-departmental transfers, only hope to have responsibility for social welfare programmes during part of their career.

What are the prospects for those now in the Department who have an identification with social work and the social welfare field to be employed optimally in policy development and programme management? There are now significantly fewer social workers in senior positions in the branches than there were three years ago. However, the branch which has responsi-bility for the social service component of the Canada Assistance Plan and will play the key role in the further policy development and implementation of the proposed social services legislation has, as its head, with the rank of Assistant Deputy Minister, a social worker, Brian Iverson. He has had exten-sive experience in both the public and voluntary sectors at the community, provincial, and national levels. Although his experience in the public ser-vice of Canada has been entirely within the welfare branches of Health and Welfare Canada this has not, thus far, been regarded as grounds for an enforced transfer.

The extent to which he and the experienced and committed officials in his branch will be used to the best advantage in policy development will, to a large extent, depend on the Deputy Minister, upon whom of course much else depends. The auguries are favourable: the fourth Deputy Minis-ter of National Welfare, who assumed responsibility on August 15, 1975, is Bruce Rawson. By profession a lawyer, Bruce Rawson has identified him-self with the social welfare field. As Chief Deputy Minister of the Alberta Department of Social Services and Community Health he has worked with non-professional and professional officials and takes a pragmatic ap-proach to the existing and potential performance of individual officials and

10 United Kingdom, *Committee on the Civil Service, 1966-68,* Vol. 1 (London: Her Majesty's Stationery Office, 1968), pp. 66-72.

categories of officials employed at a given time in his Department or required to meet its emerging needs. Such an approach gives promise that persons with social work training, social welfare experience and proven performance will again be appropriately recruited and used in the welfare branches. The Deputy Minister will require personnel with many types of training and experience. It will be important that among them there will be many whose identification with the values of the social welfare field gives them a self-renewing commitment to social welfare reform and development.

BIBLIOGRAPHY

Armitage, Andrew. *Social Welfare in Canada: Ideals and Realities*. Toronto: McClelland and Stewart Ltd., 1975.

Bryden, Kenneth. *Old Age Pensions and Policy Making in Canada*. Montreal: McGill-Queen's University Press, 1974.

Canada. *Communique, Meeting of Federal and Provincial Ministers of Welfare, Ottawa, April 30 and May 1st 1975*. Ottawa: Health and Welfare Canada, 1975.

————. *Estimates 1975-76*. Ottawa: Information Canada, 1975.

————. *Report of the Special Joint Committee of the Senate and of the House of Commons on the Constitution of Canada*. Ottawa: Information Canada, 1972.

Doern, G. Bruce, and Aucoin, Peter. *The Structures of Policy Making in Canada*. Toronto: The Macmillan Company, 1971.

Laframboise, H. R. "Administrative Reform in the Federal Public Service: Signs of a Saturation Psychosis." *Canadian Public Administration* 14, no. 3 (1971): 303-25.

Lalonde, Marc. *Working Paper on Social Security in Canada*. Ottawa: Information Canada, 1973.

Moynihan, Daniel Patrick. "The Professionalization of Reform." *The Public Interest* 1 (Fall 1965).

Simeon, Richard. *Federal-Provincial Diplomacy: The Making of Recent Policy in Canada*. Toronto: University of Toronto Press, 1972.

United Kingdom. *Committee on the Civil Service, 1966-68*. Vol. 1. London: Her Majesty's Stationery Office, 1968.

12

Citizen Participation and Social Policy

BRIAN WHARF

The purpose of this essay is to examine the contribution of citizen participation in the development and implementation of social policy. This ambitious task requires consideration of the following aspects of the subject:
- making explicit the normative positions which shape and guide the points developed in the essay;
- defining citizen participation and social policy; and
- reviewing the incomplete and scattered evidence regarding the experience accumulated to date on the involvement of citizens in social policy.

The essay is organized around the above points, each of which constitutes a major section. The final section briefly reviews some of the major dilemmas which have been identified in citizen participation, and attempts to form some tentative guidelines regarding citizen involvement in social policy.

GUIDING PRINCIPLES

A central theme in political science and philosophy in recent years has been the structures and processes of government: how citizens elect political officials, how these officials conduct themselves in office, and the influence of interest groups of various kinds on public decisions. This focus reflects a strong and widely-held view in Western societies that responsibility for conducting the affairs of society rests with the elected officials. Citizen responsibility is confined to participating in the election of officials and in a variety of interest groups, including political parties.

This theme has included examinations of not only who governs but the responsiveness of the political system. The voluminous literature, particularly in the U.S., on power structures at the local and national levels is divided into two conflicting schools of thought:[1] the *elitist position* which holds that power is concentrated in the hands of an elite few who strive to maintain and improve their power, and the *pluralist position* which argues that power is widely dispersed among differing groups and that on most issues a certain amount of "slack in the system"[2] allows groups whose interests are affected by proposed plans to organize and to wield effective influence on the eventual outcome. However, even studies of power structures have been primarily concerned with the influence of interest groups on elected officials.

Hence, the focus of concern has been on the political, governmental sphere. But the underlying assumption that publicly-elected officials governing, on behalf of the citizens they represent, exercise control over and are responsible for all aspects of life in society is increasingly being called into question. We may well be in the midst of a revival of the classical tradition in both practice and theory. The classical tradition in political philosophy centred on the nature of man and the division of responsibility between the individual and the state. It included a concern for the issues involved in returning to Athenian arrangements of participatory democracy. Indeed, it is patently obvious that many important decisions which affect people fall outside the boundaries of the political system. Certainly, the decisions regarding conditions of work are made by an elite few in industry and, though subject to bargaining between management and labour, are reached without government intervention. Pateman argues the case for participatory democracy as follows:

> The theory of participatory democracy is built around the central assertion that individuals and their institutions cannot be considered in isolation from one another. The existence of representative institutions at the national level is not sufficient for democracy: for maximum participation by all the people at that level socialization and social training for democracy must take place in other spheres in order that the necessary individual attitudes and psychosocial qualities can be developed. This development takes place through the process of participation itself.[3]

The above quotation reflects the guiding orientation of this essay. Citizen participation is not viewed here as being restricted to participation in representative government, but as being an essential feature in all significant aspects of society. As a normative position this essay takes as given that citizens have the right to participate in making decisions which affect them in their various roles of consumer, employee, and member of a politi-

---

1 Bonjean, Clark, and Lineberry, *Community Politics* (New York: Free Press, 1971), and T. Clark, *Community Structure and Decision Making* (San Francisco: Chandler Press, 1968).
2 Robert Dahl, *Who Governs* (New Haven: Yale University Press, 1961).
3 Carole Pateman, *Participation and Democratic Theory* (Cambridge: Cambridge University Press, 1970), p. 42.

cal state. Where size of numbers prohibits the direct participation of all affected, a representative system will be required, but here opportunities should be available to all to run for office and to participate in some way in the representative process. Where numbers allow for direct participation, as in small industry or small geographic areas, these "spaces" should be welcomed rather than seen as undesirable aberrations of the representative system.

Further, this essay argues that social programmes and organizations afford a unique opportunity for involving citizens, and that this opportunity, if seized, will serve to prepare citizens to participate in other areas of decision-making. The rationale for these positions is essentially pragmatic:

- People respect more those laws on which they have been consulted.
- People identify strongly with programmes they have helped to plan.
- People perform better in projects they have assisted in setting up.[4]

The rationale is, however, supported by a number of research studies. Blumberg claims that:

> There is hardly a study in the entire literature which fails to demonstrate that satisfaction in work is enhanced or that other generally acknowledged beneficial results accrue from a genuine increase in worker's decision making power. Such consistency of findings, I submit, is rare in social research.[5]

Before concluding this introductory section, it is necessary to draw attention to the differing interpretations of "citizen participation." Sherry Arnstein's article, "A Ladder of Citizen Participation," contains a useful breakdown of the various types of participation ranging from outright manipulation of citizens at one end of the continuum to citizen control at the other end. In view of the diverse forms of participation it is necessary to indicate the meaning of the term as used in this essay. Citizen participation is considered here to include citizen control where citizens have "full managerial power," delegated power to citizens for particular programmes and partnership arrangements where citizens can "negotiate and engage in trade-offs with traditional powerholders."[6] It excludes the five remaining rungs of Arnstein's ladder—placation, consultation, informing, therapy, and manipulation.

CITIZEN PARTICIPATION AND SOCIAL POLICY

The most troublesome aspect of this section consists of delineating, in sufficiently specific fashion, the boundaries and essential concerns of social policy. The salient characteristic of "policy" is the struggle involved in defining issues and in developing proposals for action. Policy constitutes a search for objectives; it does not refer to a settled, smooth course of decision-making which has agreed-on objectives as a starting point.

---

4 Francis Bregha, *Public Participation in Planning, Policy and Programme,* paper prepared for the Community Development Branch of the Ministry of Community and Social Services, Province of Ontario, n.d., p. 3.

5 P. Blumberg, *Industrial Democracy: The Sociology of Participation* (London: Constable Press, 1968), p. 123.

6 Sherry Arnstein, "A Ladder of Citizen Participation," *A.I.P. Journal* 35, no. 4 (July 1969): 217.

At a high level of abstraction social policy can be described as a continuing search to secure "the right ordering of relationships among men"[7] and with the process of resolving disputes among various groups in society as to what constitutes the right ordering of relationships. Obviously, the resolution of this vexing issue is heavily dependent on the objectives, values, and experiences of the key actors in power at any given time.

Social policies are then viewed here as being concerned with anticipating and resolving social problems, improving opportunities and enhancing the quality of life for all citizens. Because of these lofty aims and the complexities involved, social policies entail slippery philosophical and abstract considerations. And when policies attempt to alter the accepted social standards and to arrange opportunities and lifestyles in universal and egalitarian terms, enormous political and value-based difficulties must be overcome.

It is readily apparent that the above interpretation of social policy is highly prescriptive and loaded with particular values and priorities. It stands in marked contrast to existing values and priorities which are those of a competitive, acquisitive society dominated by concern for the unfettered workings of the market economy.

However, despite current commitments to free enterprise, to the work ethic, and to the myth of an equal society where all compete on even terms, social programmes have and are being developed. These programmes represent the flawed attempts to assist the casualties of the capitalist state, and to provide a measure of protection for all in such areas as health. They do not, in most instances, represent committed efforts to improve the lot of all individuals and families by such means as establishing public ownership of land, by equitably distributing income, and by providing for opportunity for participation in politics or other areas of life.

It needs to be added, however, that social programmes are of great significance, and that there are policy implications involved in planning and administering social programmes such as the resolution of competing priorities and conflicting values. This is particularly true in a federal state like Canada where first-level policy is typically enunciated in permissive legislation, and requires policy decisions at provincial and municipal levels.

Following the above arguments, it is submitted here that at the present time the primary responsibility for social policy, in effect the determination of the quality of life, rests with the federal government. Yet it is a responsibility that can be fulfilled only if it is widely shared, through the provision of information on the effect of current policies, and through encouraging participation in the discussion of proposed alternatives. Such participation is, however, bound to be limited by the complexities involved in the debate, by the difficulties of securing widespread participation at the federal level, and by the lack of competence and interest of many citizens.

Because of these difficulties and since the experience gained from the participation of workers in industry indicates that the ordinary citizen participates most effectively in low-level matters (in decisions which affect

7   A. MacBeath, "Can Social Policies Be Rationally Tested?" in L. T. Hobhouse Memorial Lecture (London: Oxford University Press, 1957).

him/her most immediately and directly),[8] one promising avenue for citizen participation is in the planning and administration of social programmes.

CITIZEN PARTICIPATION IN INTEREST GROUPS

The involvement of citizens in a wide variety of interest groups ranging from political parties, neighbourhood-based associations, recreational and athletic clubs to cultural and literary groups has long been a feature of Canadian society.

The participation of middle- and upper-class groups has been highly spontaneous and self-directed, made possible by the time available to these citizens, and by their confidence that by working together they can achieve common goals. In contrast, the involvement of disadvantaged groups has been secured in many instances through the direct help of government grants and by the assistance of professionals assigned to work with low-income groups from a variety of public and private agencies. Some indication of the support made available to these groups can be found from the Inventory of Demonstration Projects which summarized the financial grants awarded during 1969-1971 by the Welfare Grants Division of the Department of National Health and Welfare.[9] Of the forty-six projects funded during this period, nineteen were awarded to community groups seeking to develop a sense of identity and purpose and to take action on specific problems. In addition, many of the projects awarded to established agencies sought to reach out to disadvantaged groups.

The recent attempts by governments and by private agencies to support the involvement of disadvantaged groups in a variety of social programmes is, by no means, sufficient to overcome the handicaps these groups face in attempting to gain more resources. In the first place, if the groups resort to violent and even norm-violating strategies, such as sit-ins and protest marches, the public reaction is likely to be one of harsh criticism, resulting in demands to cut off the source of funds. Thus, for example, the grant of the Hamilton Welfare Rights Organization was discontinued when this group stirred up widespread complaints through their actions. And similar experiences were encountered by groups in the U.S. under that country's War on Poverty.

There are two points which should be emphasized in this discussion. First, consumer groups consisting of citizens in receipt of public assistance are regarded with intense suspicion by the majority of the working poor and the low-income groups in general. This segment of society unhesitatingly supports the work ethic and the principle of the individual's responsibility for himself and his family. Barely able to survive from their low wages derived from difficult and menial employment, they react with hostility to demands for improved financial assistance from the non-working poor. Rarely is this hostility directed at the "Corporate Welfare Bums" or those drawing exceedingly high salaries and enjoying lavish expense accounts. The low-income group is a divided group and this division is exploited to the

8 Pateman, *Participation and Democratic Theory.*
9 "Inventory of Demonstration Projects," unpublished paper prepared by the Welfare Grants Division of the Department of National Health and Welfare, Ottawa, 1971.

full by those who favour the existing values, institutions, and practices of our society.

Secondly, it is necessary to recognize the difference in goals, assumptions and strategies of "locality development" groups and "social action" groups.[10] The former tend to assume that the development of a cohesive neighbourhood association without significant conflicts is possible and desirable and that such an association will be able to negotiate effectively with such recognized bodies as city councils or even provincial governments. Further, these negotiations can be conducted in a highly consensual fashion and that, in essence, men of goodwill coming together to resolve differences will do so.

The social action groups make no such assumptions. Following Alinsky[11] they tend to assume that the subjugation of disadvantaged groups is purposeful and intended. Given this assumption and lacking resources other than numbers and a commitment to work for change, these groups eschew the consensual approach and attempt to bring about change by disturbing, disrupting, and confounding public bureaucracies. As already noted by the example of the Hamilton Welfare Rights Organization, social action groups face extreme difficulties in seeking and maintaining funds with which to operate.

Because of the public and governmental reaction to the disruptive tactics of social action groups, many professionals have sought through both direct advice and their writings to discourage the use of such tactics. Thus, a leading advocate planner in the U.S. asserts that urban planners, social workers and lawyers should aid poor people's groups "to reach increased levels of sophistication about what makes the city system, and subsystems, tick, to learn who and where the power leaders are and which levers to press to effect action and to incorporate such sophistication into concrete programmatic approaches."[12]

A contrary view is held by Frances Fox Piven and Richard Cloward who are widely credited with providing the strategies used by the Welfare Rights movement in the U.S. Piven claims that the type of educational process advocated above actually constitutes a disservice to poor people's groups.

> The irony is that the poor get the payroll and the rent money, in the first place, not because they have community organizations, but through mass disturbances. Mass disturbances sometimes produce important concessions as well; a $10 million welfare budget for example. That is not much, perhaps, but it is more than the poor have gotten until now, and it is much more than they are likely to get again soon, especially if they rely on their new community groups and professional advocates and on the paths of conventional organizations and influence.[13]

10 Jack Rothman, "Three Models of Community Organization Practice," in *Social Work Practice* (New York: Columbia University Press, 1968).
11 Saul Alinsky, *Reveille for Radicals* (New York: Random House, 1946), and *Rules for Radicals* (New York: Random House, 1971).
12 Sherry Armstein, "But Which Advocate Planner," *Social Policy* 1, no. 2 (July/August 1970): 33-34.
13 Frances Piven, "Rejoinder: Disruption is Still the Decisive Way," *Social Policy* 1, no. 2 (July/August 1970): 40-41. See also Eliot Krause, "Functions of a Bureaucratic Ideology:

In the writer's opinion both views are valid. Some poor people's groups will tend towards the ideology and the strategies of locality development. For example, newly-arrived immigrants living in ethnic neighbourhoods may be poor, but will aspire to, and will work in a committed fashion to, attain middle-class standards. For these groups the tactics of disruption would be abhorrent and unacceptable since these are aimed at altering the standards of the society they wish to join.

For other groups, social action strategies may constitute the most viable way of contending with a society which has degraded and humiliated them. Disruptions do provide a strong incentive for governments to examine issues, and to provide at least temporary solutions in order that they will not be embarrassed in the near future by subsequent challenges.

Hence, it seems vital that professionals working with poor people's groups take time to learn about their assumptions and attitudes and to devise strategies appropriate to these values. In addition, professionals have their own ideological positions, and should strive to match their ideologies with groups holding similar views.

Given the number and diversity of interest groups, it has proven impossible to conduct any continuous monitoring of their activities which would permit assessment of effectiveness. Evaluations have been undertaken on a case study basis of single organizations, and these tend to be partial and tentative in their conclusions. It does seem reasonable to argue that interest groups with representation from the respected and acceptable segments of society, with strong and committed members, with resources such as time and money, and with interests which are in tune with current societal values will indeed prosper. Neighbourhood-based associations may also do well in those areas where the interests of residents coincide on most important issues. Such associations may indeed increase in the future as a reaction against the anonymity of large metropolitan areas. However, as Barry Wellman has pointed out in a perceptive article, the residents of middle- and upper-income class areas are more likely, and are able, to seek out friends and associates on an interest rather than on a geographic basis.[14] Hence, locality development associations will probably continue to increase in areas where there is a high level of agreement on values and priorities.

The conclusions of Chris MacNiven, who was responsible for Volume 4 of the *Case Studies in Social Planning* sponsored by the Canadian Council on Social Development are relevant here. Volume 4 describes the development of planning under private and public auspices in Vancouver, and

'Citizen Participation,'" *Social Problems* 16, no. 2 (Fall 1968): 129-43. Krause's review of citizen participation in urban renewal and in community action programmes in the U.S. led him to conclude that the "target groups did not appear to have benefitted extensively when they did participate, and in many cases gained if they fought the proponent bureaucracy directly" (p. 142). Despite the conclusion, Krause also points out that "to refuse to participate and leave planning to the planners is to give the bureaucratic elite free rein" (p. 142). Participation can be successful only if the bureaucracy and the target group have similar aims and ideologies. Confrontation is a more effective strategy when objectives do not coincide.

14 Barry Wellman, "Who Needs Neighbourhoods," in *Citizen Participation Canada,* ed. James Draper (Toronto: New Press, 1971), pp. 282-87.

represents a careful and painstaking effort to evaluate the effect of locality development in Vancouver.

> In retrospect it is patently clear that the local area approach cannot resolve national social problems such as poverty and unemployment. Neither can it achieve an equitable distribution of resources and services with the metropolitan area of Vancouver. Thirdly, it cannot control the policies of either public or private agencies. But the local area approach can influence agencies to decentralize and to begin new services, it can develop new services, such as information centres and meals on wheels; it can serve as the focal point to fight against the unwanted intrusions such as highways being planned for the area. More importantly the local area approach in Vancouver has served as a training ground for citizens to begin to exercise some influence over the agencies providing service to local areas. Within the local area approach may be seen residents' first stirrings toward community control and an increased sense of self-responsibility and self-esteem.[15]

CITIZEN PARTICIPATION IN SOCIAL PROGRAMMES

This section of the essay attempts to review the experiences gained to date with citizen participation in the planning and administration of a variety of social programmes. Because of the variety of these programmes and the organizations operating them, a distinction is made between emerging-public and established-voluntary programmes.

Emerging-Public Programmes

Until very recently, social programmes operated under public auspices in Canada made little or no provision for citizen participation other than that of elected officials. In isolated instances advisory councils were developed. However, in the early 1970s two provinces—Quebec and British Columbia—restructured social service and health programmes and developed local and regional boards to manage the newly-integrated services. In the first rush of enthusiasm it seemed that for the first time provincial governments were prepared to delegate control of services, even though skeptics pointed out that both provinces retained final control of budgets. In addition, the bypassing of municipal governments was viewed with concern. One clear lesson from the U.S. War on Poverty was that to ignore City Hall was to court disaster.

Recent events have confirmed the concern of the skeptics. The election of a Social Credit government in B.C. in 1975 resulted in a policy which transformed existing resource boards into advisory councils and ruled out the development of new boards. In Quebec it appears that regional control is illusory and represents only a reflection of provincial policies.[16]

Innovative programmes have been underway in the U.S. for some time. Typically, these have taken the form of community controlled multi-service

---

15 Chris MacNiven, *Case Studies in Social Planning*, vol. 4: *Planning under Voluntary and Public Auspices in Vancouver* (Ottawa: Canadian Council on Social Development, July 1972), p. 103.

16 See David Woodsworth, "Power Redistribution in Canada," *Canadian Welfare* 52, no. 6 (January-February 1977): 13-16.

centres or corporations which have been added onto the existing programmes, rather than replacing them, as has occurred in Canada. The following paragraphs present a brief overview of the U.S. experience with citizen-controlled social programmes. These experiences are important in that they represent some of the first adventures with citizen control.

It should be noted first that the following material reviews only citizen control of social programmes, and does not attempt to examine the experiences of local control of schools or of economic corporations. Secondly, the difficulties and dilemmas involved in evaluating social programmes are immense. Typically, programmes are established with only vague and imprecise objectives, and criteria for determining whether these objectives are attained are not specified. Social programmes operate in extremely complex environments which confound attempts to relate effectiveness to any one set of variables. The experiences reviewed here are no exception to this state of affairs.

Howard Hallman's review of neighbourhood control of public programmes constitutes an ambitious effort to evaluate thirty centres which differed markedly in their aims and in the geographic areas in which they were located. His criteria consisted of feelings ("positive feelings of personal self-worth, identity, belonging, and self-pride . . . and negative feelings such as alienation, hopelessness, powerlessness and rage") and efficiency ("the accomplishment of the work at hand with the least expenditure of manpower and materials").[17] He acknowledges that "his judgments are, of course subjective, but they are based on direct observation conditioned by years of involvement with community programmes."[18] Unfortunately, Hallman neglects to mention how he tapped the feelings of those being served by the centres, or how he arrived at criteria for judging efficiency.

Hallman's conclusions are summed up in the following quotation:

> Various forms and styles of community control of public service programs are making significant differences in a number of cities. Unmistakably on the feelings side of my standards for judgment, significant results have been achieved. On the efficiency side a number of community corporations are performing well, and with one or two exceptions all those surveyed are doing no worse than related decentralized programs without resident control.[19]

A review conducted by Washnis reveals similar conclusions, and this study is of importance for its careful delineation of problems encountered in citizen control. Washnis believes that the most suitable form of community control is the partnership model where "city officials agree to pass down authority by ordinary charter or contract and generally retain authority to help select a portion of the governing board."[20] The partnership arrangement retains involvement by elected city officials, yet makes clear the authority vested in the neighbourhood for control of certain specified programmes.

17 Howard Hallman, *Neighbourhood Control of Public Programs* (New York: Praeger Publishers, 1970), p. 205.
18 Ibid., p. 210.
19 Ibid.
20 H. Washnis, *Municipal Decentralization and Neighbourhood Resources* (New York: Praeger Publishers, 1972), p. 10.

The dilemmas created by neighbourhood government are, of course, those faced in any large country with regional differences. While one can sympathize with the need for locally-elected and responsive governments, this often serves to divert attention from the equally pressing need to develop national policies and to arrange for the haves to contribute to the welfare of the have-nots. In view of this dilemma the partnership arrangement advocated by Washnis has considerable merit.

Another difficulty cited frequently by reviewers of community control experiences are conflicts between professionals and the citizen boards. In Canada one example of the conflict which can develop occurred at the Regina Community Health Clinic where the key professionals finally resigned because of the perceived intransigence of the citizen board. The issue is exceedingly complicated because citizens and professionals have differing perceptions of who should control what. From his review of relationships between these two groups in such settings as employee health services, youth clinics, and the local community service centres in Quebec, Peter New concluded that "professionals are most concerned with control over the clinical aspects of health delivery, and that most health professionals, especially physicians, do not really want to spend their time in dealing with the political problems of operating a community health centre."[21] Citizens interested in the quality of health care, by contrast, tend to want "total control over the political sphere and management of the health centre, and some participation in the clinical area, recognizing that some strictly medical routines are beyond their capabilities."[22] In addition, citizens want professionals to be involved in the political issues because they would bring clout and influence to the negotiations with elected officials.

Hence, in every aspect of the operation of services there is likely to be disagreement between citizens and professionals. In some multi-service centres in the U.S. bitter disagreements have occurred over salaries and the place of residence of professionals employed by the centres.

To counterbalance the above recitation of difficulties, the experience of one organization can be used as evidence that consumers and professionals can work together in a constructive fashion.[23] The National Council on Welfare, an advisory group to the Minister of National Health and Welfare, is composed of an equal number of the poor and professionals. Although the Council has no direct control over government policy or programmes, it has encountered and resolved a series of potentially divisive issues such as deciding on the right to publication of its reports, freedom to criticize government proposals where, in the opinion of members, criticism was warranted, and the issues it has selected to study. Such issues might well have produced enduring factions within the Council or indeed resulted in the dissolution of the Council.

21   Peter New, *Community Health Centres: Five Danger Signals*, a study prepared for the Report to the Committee on Community Health Centre Project, Anne Crichton, Coordinator (Ottawa: Information Canada, 1972).
22   Ibid.
23   Brian Wharf and Allan Halladay, *The Role of Advisory Councils in Forming Social Policies: A Case Study of the National Council of Welfare* (Hamilton, Ontario: McMaster University Press, 1974).

From the Council's experience, it seems that the key ingredients in developing cohesion and harmonious working relationships between the members include a conscious attempt to minimize roles and status differences in meetings, the opportunity for members to spend time together on a social basis, and the deliberate adoption by the Chairman and Director of the Council of a consensus approach to decision-making which allowed all members to contribute and which rejected the premature closure of contentious debates. The Council may well serve as a model for other groups with similar composition of members to emulate.

It should, however, be noted that candidates for membership were screened with some care, in order to ensure that those selected were committed to the objectives of this Council. In addition, in the early meetings, considerable attention was devoted to members getting to know each other.

CITIZEN PARTICIPATION IN ESTABLISHED PROGRAMMES

In contrast to public programmes, those operated under private auspices have had a long history of citizen involvement. Indeed, the benefits derived through participation of citizens has been one of the main arguments used by advocates of the voluntary sector to resist attempts to place all publicly-supported services under government administration. For example, the Ontario Association of Children's Aid Societies argues for the continuation of Children's Aid Societies on the following grounds:

> Children's Aid Societies have for 75 years been able to attract the most able and community minded people to their ranks. By this means, the society makes available for public service, the energies, talents and skills of people from many walks of life and different professions. At present there are 1,100 voluntary board members in Ontario, each of whom gives an untold number of hours per year in the service of the community.[24]

The voluntary agencies have, however, been criticized for their highly-selective involvement of citizens. It is difficult to make hard and fast generalizations since some agencies have undoubtedly striven to involve a wide variety of citizens—from professionals to consumers, and from high-, middle-, and low-income groups. Yet, the few studies which have been conducted into the composition of boards of directors of voluntary agencies confirm a widespread suspicion that these boards are indeed highly unrepresentative of both the area and the consumer served.[25]

The experience of the voluntary social welfare agencies parallels that of participation in voluntary associations and in political affairs. Citizens in the low socio-economic status do not participate as extensively as do citizens in middle and upper classes. The reasons are, of course, not difficult to

24 Ontario Association of Children's Aid Societies, "Brief to the Task Force on Community and Social Services" (unpublished, Toronto, 1973), p. 8.
25 See, for example, Hamilton and District Branch, Ontario Association of Professional Social Workers, "Study of Board Composition of Social Welfare Agencies in Hamilton and Area" (unpublished, 1972), and John McCready, "Lucky Who? The United Community Fund of Greater Toronto," in The City, Attacking Modern Myths, ed. Alan Powell (Toronto: McLelland and Stewart, 1972), pp. 163-75.

identify. They include childhood socialization experiences which tend to be authoritative and to provide little opportunity to participate in family decisions—a preoccupation with survival which leaves little time or energy for involvements outside the home and work experiences which reinforce the lessons learned in childhood and lead to apathy and alienation. "Economic underprivilege is linked to psychological underprivileges and engenders a lack of self-confidence which increases the unwillingness of the lower-class person to participate in many phases of our predominately middle-class culture."[26]

This point will be touched on again in the final section. It is sufficient here to register the often-noted criticism that a society which purports to be built around a representative democratic system while tolerating a high level of inequalities in opportunities to participate violates the very rationale of its existence.

SOME DILEMMAS IN CITIZEN PARTICIPATION

At the beginning of this essay the normative position was asserted that citizens in their various roles should have the right and the opportunity to participate in decisions which affect them. Dahl calls this the principle of affected interests. While he asserts that "it is not such a bad principle to begin with, it turns out to be a diffuse galaxy of uncountable possibilities,"[27] rather than providing explicit directions on the issue of who should participate. The problems raised by the principle of affected interests include: Whose interests are given primacy when diverse and conflicting interests are involved? For example, should consumer interests in social programmes be given ascendancy over the interests of the professionals and the contributors? Viewed differently, should national or local interests prevail in issues such as control of natural resources? Finally, the pragmatic issue of representative versus participatory democracy is encountered when a large number of people is affected.

Dahl's resolution of these puzzling questions is that the principle of affected interests has to be balanced with the principles of competence and of economy. He argues that consideration of these three principles will result in differing conclusions depending on the issue addressed and the circumstances surrounding the issue. The principle of economy is important because not all citizens have the time or the interest to participate in decision-making. The principle of competence should take precedence in those issues where highly-specialized considerations are involved. However, when these two principles cannot be shown to exercise compelling influence, the principle of affected interests should be dominant.

Dahl is correct in arguing for consideration of these three principles. Yet more is involved than the rational weighing of principles. In fact, as he has noted with respect to the principle of affected interests, all principles are less than explicit, and all are more subject to values and normative influences than to rationality. For example, if heavy reliance is placed on the

26 Genevieve Knupfer, "Portrait of the Underdog," in *Class, Status & Power,* ed. R. Bendix and S. M. Lipset (New York: Free Press, 1970), p. 66.
27 Robert Dahl, *After the Revolution* (New Haven: Yale University Press, 1970), p. 66.

principle of competence, as has happened in Western societies, a good deal of authority is vested in experts in medicine, urban affairs, social programmes and the like. But, as Thayer has pointed out, participatory democracy may achieve "cost avoidance."[28] By this he means that decisions reached through participation may avoid the delays and rejections, which are often the reception of unilateral decisions.

It should also be noted at this juncture that many competing interests conspire to interfere with sustained participation in political affairs or in social, health and educational programmes. Even where opportunities to participate exist, many choose to spend their time in recreational, intellectual or cultural pursuits. Oscar Wilde's quip that "the trouble with socialism is that it requires too many evenings" should not be lightly dismissed. The experience in many organizations which welcome participation has been that only a minority who have the time, the conviction that responsible membership requires participation, and the endurance to sit through lengthy and sometimes unproductive meetings do, in fact, participate in the decision-making process.

One powerful influence on participation is the relevance of the issue to the individual. When one's interests are threatened, interest and motivation increase dramatically, but, in the absence of such incentives, the temptation to indulge oneself in pleasurable pursuits more frequently than not outweighs the dictates of conscience to engage in responsible citizenship.

In many issues only a few people are directly affected and require the opportunity to participate in decision-making; hence, the issue of representative versus participatory democracy is not particularly troublesome. Since consumers of social programmes are much more directly affected by these programmes than other citizens, the principle of affected interests would award a significant share of the decision-making to consumers. But this pragmatic resolution raises another and equally serious problem. It is precisely because some people are more affected by important decisions in social policy than are the majority of citizens, and because these few possess the time and resources to develop arguments and to put pressure on policy-makers, that Canada and other societies remain unequal in opportunities and income. The principle of affected interests can, therefore, be used to support a position where only the affected participate. Nevertheless, since the existing state of affairs discriminates against the low-income and disadvantaged, priority must be given to increasing the participation of these groups. A beginning can be made by developing participatory democracy in areas where direct participation can occur. Pateman argues that:

> The argument of participatory theory of democracy is that participation in the alternative areas would enable the individual to better appreciate the connection between the public and private sectors. The ordinary man might still be more interested in things near home, but the existence of a participatory society would mean that he was better able to assess the performance of representatives at the national level, better equipped to make decisions of

28 Frederick Thayer, *Participation and Liberal Democratic Government* (Toronto: Queen's Printer, 1973).

national scope when the opportunities to do so arose and better able to weigh up the impact of decisions taken by national representatives on his own life and immediate surroundings.[29]

Pateman's argument has particular relevance for social programmes and ultimately for social policy. In the first place, while many social workers have sought to cloak their skills and techniques and helping processes in esoteric language and to emulate the traditional practices of other professionals, this social worker is convinced that the techniques of social work intervention and the objectives and limitations of social programmes are very amenable to explanation to the consumers of these programmes. In fact, their successful implementation requires it. Whether the intervention consists of supplying information, advocacy, services such as day-care, homemaker service or foster care, effective assistance demands that the consumer be engaged actively and fully in the process. Only if the consumer understands what is going on, only if he is seen as a worthwhile and important participant and only if there is a levelling rather than exaggeration of the roles between the professional and consumer will the intervention achieve its desired goals. Hence, in social programmes the principle of competence is not of overriding concern. (This is not to argue that professional social workers should not be competent. Nor should it be construed to mean that professional education is a waste of time. Social workers should be knowledgeable and well prepared for the demanding task of involving people in working out their problems and destiny.)

Secondly, a deliberate policy to foster involvement in the social services will provide useful learning opportunities for many persons who otherwise would not realize their potential to contribute to society. From this starting point, some exposed to the intricacies of programme planning and administration at the community and agency level may enlarge their scope of interest and become involved in broader policy issues. For example, some might expand their concerns from the relatively simple level of setting budgets for services to examining policies which result in higher rates to foster parents than to natural parents, and the implications of such a policy for preventive programmes. In time we might expect some serious consideration of the effects of social services on family structure. To the present such questions have been addressed only by a few politicians and civil servants. They desperately need the consideration of many citizens, as social services are costly and have both intended and unintended consequences upon individuals and families.

For this kind of examination to occur (and it needs to occur with equal urgency vis-à-vis medical care, housing, and education) it is necessary that citizens as members of community councils, of interest groups and of associations have access to federal and provincial proposals. At present, circulation of government proposals is severely limited; the *Working Paper on Social Security in Canada*[30] was available free of charge to anyone requesting it, but it was mailed directly only to agencies and professionals.

---

29 Pateman, *Participation and Democratic Theory*, p. 110.
30 Marc Lalonde, *Working Paper on Social Security in Canada* (Ottawa: Government of Canada, Department of National Health and Welfare, 1973).

Responses from a wide variety of citizen groups would be extremely valuable to federal policy-makers.

To conclude, it must be acknowledged that while this chapter has argued the case for citizen participation in the social services, the reality in 1977 appears to favour a return to strict provincial control. Participation will then be limited to involvement in the political process. And with Pateman and others, the position taken here is that such involvement is unduly restrictive, unnecessary and undesirable. For example, in British Columbia the currently-favoured policy positions are those which extol clear lines of accountability from workers in the field through regional directors, senior officials in Victoria, and culminating in the minister's office. Agencies, such as the Vancouver Resource Board, are seen as aberrations in an otherwise clear organizational structure. The view is clearly that effective and adequate programmes can be planned and managed within provincial departments and without assistance from outside. Yet equally clearly, we know that as organizations become larger and as control is centralized, there are inevitable problems of ensuring responsiveness to local community needs, of securing and maintaining the commitment of staff and of developing policies and vehicles to elicit opinions from outside on new and existing programmes. The most dramatic example of a closed organization which eventually became paranoid is, of course, the Nixon presidency. To offset and counter bureaucratic rigidities and tunnel-vision structures must be developed to involve many people with different points of view. Finally, the interest in the various applications of industrial democracy which are being tried in Europe and elsewhere and which seem to hold the promise of reducing conflict between labour and management may spill over into the public domain. In turn, experiments in participatory democracy in the work place may provide some incentives and support for citizens to assert their right to participate in planning and managing the social services.

13

Social Policy: The Role of the Governing Party

JOHN H. REDEKOP

INTRODUCTION

Government policies are usually distinguished from day-to-day decisions in that they are general in scope, they set parameters for future decisions, and they delineate long-range perspectives which generally reflect the ideological values of the political party in power. They are "deliberate coercion-statements attempting to set forth the purpose, the means, the subjects, and the objects of coercion."[1] Most government decisions, on the other hand, either have no significant policy content or, if they do, tend to reflect rather than create policies. Of course, some important decisions, such as the refusal to disallow Quebec's controversial language law, while not enunciated in policy terms, nevertheless serve as policies in their own right or at least constitute an important stage in policy formation. Social policies, in turn, are distinguished from other governmental policies in that they apply to domestic rather than foreign affairs and in that they deal with issues affecting broad, categoric segments of the population rather than corporations or individuals specifically named.

Social policies do not arise in a vacuum or by accident; they are the product of ongoing interaction involving individuals, groups, and agencies. In our Canadian system of responsible government the major role is played by the elected, collegial executive which we call the Cabinet. However,

---

1 Theodore Lowi, "Decision Making vs. Policy Making: Towards an Antidote for Technocracy," *Public Administration Review* 30, no. 3 (May/June 1970): 315.

since this group of leaders achieves Cabinet office only because of its leadership of the dominant political party, as selected by the electorate, and acts on behalf of that party, it is important that we ascertain the role played by the apparatus of the party and discover exactly how a party's policies and personnel affect the formation, enactment, and implementation of social policies in Canada.

Ideally, Canadian political parties holding government office relate to social policy in three general ways: they aggregate demands from all sectors of society, exercising a moderating but not a stalling influence; they provide able and informed decision-makers; and they offer continuing and consistent policy recommendations adopted at conventions or announced by leaders between conventions. Unfortunately, in actual practice the fulfillment of these basic functions is often neglected or compromised by short-term electoral expediency. As illustrated in preceding as well as subsequent chapters, political parties forming governments in Canada, at both provincial and national levels, have a spotty record according to all three criteria. The accomplishments of the two major parties, Liberals and Progressive Conservatives, in aggregating demands is at best only fair; witness the plight of Canada's native peoples, the great gaps in consumer legislation, and the increasingly impoverished state of the average senior citizen. Significantly, the New Democratic Party's record both as government and as opposition is relatively good in this regard, especially in British Columbia and Saskatchewan. With reference to the selection of competent leaders, all three parties in recent decades have done well at both national and provincial levels during their years in office.

Concerning the third area, that of policy formation, the record is uneven or worse, with the N.D.P. substantially ahead of the other two parties, but even it, as we shall see later, has frequently sacrificed its avowed principles as well as policy consistency to achieve success at the polls.

Since the Liberal Party has held office in Ottawa for all but six years during the more than four decades since 1935 and since most of Canada's national social policies were enacted during this long period of Liberal hegemony, we need to analyze it more closely. All political parties are bent on winning elections, but perhaps the Liberal Party, as the most pragmatic of Canada's three major parties, has been most willing to sacrifice ideology in order to gain voter approval. Indeed, some of its opponents have suggested that aside from sympathy for French Canada and support for multiculturalism and regional equalization, especially in Eastern Canada, it has no ideological commitment and that it is not interested in implementing any additional comprehensive social policies. Having established a minimum welfare state to cope with the most urgent social needs, the Liberal Party, some of these critics suggest, has decided against paying the political price of further reform in social policies and is committed to little more than a holding operation, perhaps even retrenchment, all the while scheming for continued electoral success and promising such usually minor ad hoc social policies as it thinks will help to bring about that continued success.

Historically, of course, the Liberal Party never was committed to fundamental social or economic change, but was more concerned with electoral, parliamentary, and judicial reform. Indeed, it is rather surprising that so pragmatic and elitist a party, looking mainly to victory at the polls, managed to provide Canadians with major national social policies covering family allowances, unemployment insurance, old age pensions, health insurance, general contributory pensions, and a host of other matters. One can argue, of course, that these social policies would have been enacted in Canada during the middle third of this century no matter which party held power and that the Liberals just happened to be in office when most of the prosperous countries adopted such policies. It is a fact that during its last year or so of office R. B. Bennett's Conservative government (1930-1935) did try to implement various social policies to counteract the effects of the Great Depression, but was thwarted by rulings of the Judicial Committee of the Privy Council in London as well as by some Canadian elites. It is also a fact that when the Conservatives under John Diefenbaker formed the government from 1957 to 1963 they did not reverse any Liberal social policies. Indeed, they expanded various programmes, utilizing the same arguments which the Liberals had used for decades. As far as Canadian social policy is concerned, we can describe the Diefenbaker interlude as continuing Liberal opportunism with a populist colouration. Significantly, at no time since the initiation of major social policy changes from the early thirties right down to the present has the Liberal Party, or the Conservative Party during its short-lived success, ever undertaken a thorough philosophical review of Canada's national social policies or explained the implementation of a specific social policy in terms of an integrated and inclusive national plan for social well-being. In any event, we can hardly overestimate either the significance of Liberal Party pre-eminence or the fact that its social policies were shaped more by the times than those policies shaped the times.

Awareness of the Liberal Party's basic orientation helps us to understand both its apologists and its critics. It also reminds us that perhaps the very limited impact which progressive activists in the party have on government social policy arises more from the party's stand on the desired degree of governmental interference in society and economy than from weakness in internal party communication or the inadequacy in demand aggregation. Thus, we see that the qualities and traits of the governing party greatly influence the way in which that party develops social policies. This close connection holds true whether we are talking about the Liberals in Ottawa, the equally elitist Progressive Conservatives in Ottawa, the N.D.P. in British Columbia, Saskatchewan, and Manitoba, or of any other provincial governments.

The development of social policy by a governing political party in Canada is affected by several other constraints besides party orientation. Any government assuming office inherits an array of continuing economic and other commitments. Under our system of social stability and continuity, virtually all of these social policies are customarily retained even if the new government opposed them while in opposition and campaigned on such a platform. Electorates have come to expect such policy retention. Therefore, unless a newly-elected government is prepared to raise taxes greatly or to redirect its priorities in public expenditure and weather the ensuing social disruptions and voter antagonism as major programmes are terminated, it will find that less than 10 per cent of national or provincial budgets are available for new ventures. There are additional problems. No matter what their political stripe, all national and most provincial governments are also subject to very strong, often contradictory, regional pressures, many of which rest on solid economic fact. Each government finds itself frustrated and hemmed in by these geographically-rooted regional differences and the concomitant regional rivalries and antagonisms. Consequently, at least at the national level, any major effort in social policy will inevitably trigger regional friction and alienation which, given the absence of a homogeneous Canadian political culture or value system, may quickly escalate into constitutional confrontation.

Resilient provincial autonomy further limits any national government's options in social policy. Ever since Confederation, when the provinces were given primary jurisdiction in the areas of hospital care, regulation of alcoholic beverages, property and civil rights, education, and welfare, the continual attempts of federal governments to establish national policies in many areas covered by these grants of power have generally been thwarted. It is, for better or worse, a fact of our national life that many crucial social policy issues lie principally in provincial jurisdictions. Thus, while more than 10 per cent of the national budget now goes into health care, most of it is channelled either through or to provincial governments. Using research grants, operating subsidies, and other devices, the national governing party may try to implement its policy priorities, but its hands are largely tied.

If the Canadian variety of centrifugal federalism greatly limits the governing party's social policy options, it also weakens the party itself. The same holds true for national opposition parties which have a national base. On paper the Progressive Conservative Party appears to be highly centralized, but in fact its Ottawa establishment, especially when in office, has had reasonably close ties at any one time with only one of its three main components: prairie populism, Bay Street Ontario conservatism, or Atlantic traditionalism. The Liberal Party, reflecting the perspective of its Quebec base, does not even make a claim to national homogeneity; the national party is essentially a loose federation of ten provincial organizations. Little wonder that its social policy proclamations tend to be vague generalities. The N.D.P. is the most decentralized party with the provincial parties functioning as autonomous entities. Should it ever form a national government, it would have very great difficulty, despite its supposedly common ideological commitment, in implementing its long-standing social policies. Since the N.D.P. until now has been in power only at the provincial level, the built-in conflicts have never surfaced fully.

The Liberal Party has been criticized for its continual social policy confrontations, especially between Prime Minister Trudeau and Quebec Premier Bourassa. But given the decentralization of Canada's political parties and the sometimes mutually reinforcing social, ethnic and other cleavages which fracture the Canadian body politic, such confrontation is inevitable, especially concerning Quebec, for any party in power at both national and provincial levels. The era of amiability between Prime Minister

Pearson and Quebec Premier Lesage in the early 1960s was atypical and was not the result of uniform Liberal policies but of major concessions concerning "opting out" and special status which Ottawa made to Quebec. These could not continue if Canada was to survive. The present Dominion-provincial tensions, despite all the ad hoc and permanent structures established to facilitate co-operation, will therefore in all likelihood continue as a major constraint on federal social policy options.

Several other aspects of the Canadian political situation warrant attention. For one thing, in many areas such as consumer protection, food stamp subsidies, school lunch programmes, special assistance to minority groups, etc., Canadian public expectations are greatly influenced by widespread media coverage of developments in the United States. These expectations evolve into pressures which provincial and national governments cannot ignore. Secondly, many of Canada's basic provincial and national social policies were launched before there were any political conventions, not to mention formal policy sessions, at which party spokesmen could articulate policies and gain media attention and presumably some measure of public support. Indeed, at the national level until the 1940s the non-parliamentary wings of the two major parties rarely concerned themselves with policy formulation of any kind. In both of these parties, as already suggested, the parliamentary wing, especially when forming the government, has no tradition of looking to the larger party for social policy directives. Having held office, it runs on its legislative record rather than on extra-parliamentary policy pronouncements. That may help to explain why it is that the longer a party is in office in Canada, for example the Liberal Party nationally, the less correlation there seems to be between social policy statements in party constitutions or election platforms and actual social policy legislation. While such a dichotomy is most obvious at the national level, it is also evident in most of the provinces.

Closely related to the above historical facts is the great extent to which social policy comes into existence by incrementalism. Rarely is a government party inclined and able to spell out and implement a totally new approach or programme. In most situations, because of financial constraints as well as the difficulty of bureaucratic redirection, it must be satisfied with making minor additions, deletions, or changes. Of course, since the two major parties both lack foundational policies in this area and since both are in general agreement concerning the appropriate degree of government regulation, proprietorship, income redistribution and other social policies, the two major parties now have no great debates on social policy. Both seem to be generally satisfied with the present situation. Therefore national elections are now won or lost more on the basis of personalities than on the basis of social or other policies. The burgeoning of television has accentuated that trend. (At the provincial level the situation in most of the provinces is similar but more complex because of the pre-eminence of the more ideological "third" parties.)

Acknowledging the above, John Meisel concludes that political parties, even when in office, have declined sharply as vehicles of policy formation and have been replaced by an increasingly powerful bureaucracy, by federal-provincial conferences, and by Task Forces and Royal Commissions.[2] In part he is right but if by government party we include the Cabinet, the Cabinet committees, the Prime Minister's Office, and other parliamentary structures more or less subordinate to party control, his assessment is misleading.[3] Indeed, the central thesis of this chapter is that despite all the problems of data acquisition and quantification the general situation is clear. The Prime Minister and Cabinet component of the governing party remains the dominant locus of social policy activity. This holds true, I suggest, whether we focus on the pre-parliamentary, parliamentary, or post-parliamentary phases of the social policy process, although it is especially evident in the last two.

THE PRE-PARLIAMENTARY PHASE

In the pre-parliamentary phase of social policy formation the governing party plays its most important role in the selection of a leader, a fact presumably not recognized by ardent advocates of membership-oriented policy conventions. This situation grows out of the fact that once he is chosen and becomes Prime Minister, or provincial Premier, the leader's value system is the single most important determinant of party policy and government action. Doubtless, his social policy inclinations play a major role as he appoints and fires Cabinet Ministers, establishes government priorities, controls the parliamentary schedule and agenda, speaks for the party, appoints senior party bureaucrats, and dominates election campaigns. Thus, when the Progressive Conservative Party chose John Diefenbaker as their national leader in 1956, they were also thereby authorizing more favourable social policies for Western Canada and for ethnic groups, they were endorsing greater class and regional income equalization, and they were opting for greater protection of civil rights, all of which social policies their leader instituted after becoming Prime Minister in 1957. Similarly, when in 1968 the Liberal Party selected Pierre Trudeau as leader and Prime Minister, they simultaneously opted for increased resistance to provincial fiscal demands, harsh suppression of violent separatism, an embargo against major new federal-provincial social welfare schemes, relaxation of divorce and drug laws, public subsidization of multiculturalism, and a massive campaign for bilingualism.[4]

While leadership selection is far and away the most important device a governing party has in influencing social policy, there are additional opportunities to influence the outcome. By various formal and informal means parties convey both supports and demands to their leaders in government. If they are active and efficient intermediaries they can partially bridge the gap between the legislative system and the political environment and thus

2   John Meisel, "Recent Changes in Canadian Parties," in *Party Politics in Canada*, ed. Hugh G. Thorburn, 2nd ed. (Scarborough: Prentice-Hall, 1967), pp. 33-54.

3   See the discussion in G. Bruce Doern, "The Development of Policy Organizations in the Executive Arena," in *The Structures of Policy-Making in Canada*, ed. G. Bruce Doern and Peter Aucoin (Toronto: Macmillan, 1971), pp. 57-58.

4   For a summary of Trudeau's views, see "Notes for Remarks by the Prime Minister at the Harrison Liberal Conference," Harrison Hot Springs, British Columbia, November 21, 1969, pp. 3-4. The document was distributed by the Office of the Prime Minister.

facilitate greater responsiveness on the part of those of their membership who form the Cabinet. This general pre-parliamentary liaison and input role takes on added importance in a system such as ours in which election results rarely communicate any specific social policy directives to the winners.[5] At least at the outset, Prime Minister Trudeau's regional desks played a significant role in this process.

In recent years all three major parties have articulated specific policy roles for the extra-parliamentary organizations but actual results remain very modest. Clause 6-B of the 1973 Constitution of the Liberal Party of Canada informs us that the Consultative Council, itself a large and unwieldy body not intended to meet between conventions, shall "guide the National Executive of the Liberal Party of Canada" in "the examination of important political issues." All evidence indicates that, at most, the summarized responses to the mailed questionnaires it uses serve as policy reinforcement rather than as sources of social or other policy. The constitution describes how questions may be referred to the Consultative Council, but there is no provision for direct policy input to the parliamentary wing nor any evidence that such input actually occurs. Section I of the party constitution asserts that "the basic policies of the Party shall be established by the Party assembled in policy conferences at least every two years." Even the additional requirement that the leader and the Party President shall report jointly, in writing, every six months "upon the action taken, the consideration given, the decisions made, and the reasoning therefore regarding resolutions passed at each convention" has not noticeably affected Cabinet dominance in policy determination and is increasingly ignored. The highlight of each policy convention continues to be the Prime Minister's stewardship report, his regaling of the party faithful, and his statement of policy intentions.

The much-praised Liberal Political Cabinet turns out to be only another vehicle for Cabinet dominance since the only lay member is the President of the Liberal Party and frequently he is an M.P. or a Senator. The current Party President is Senator Gildas Molgat. In any event this body plays no major role in social policy formulation. Significantly, the several social policy committees of the National Party report only to the National Executive and to each convention of the party. Committee concerns or viewpoints are rarely discernible in the legislative proposals of the parliamentary wing. An indication of the limited extent of actual convention power occurred in 1966 when the National Liberal Federation, in an attempt to promote income security in Western Canada, passed a resolution calling for a North American free trade area. Within a few days Prime Minister Pearson bluntly repudiated this proposal. His obvious embarrassment did not moderate his clear-cut rejection.[6] In 1968 Prime Minister Trudeau, ostensibly to broaden policy input, initiated the practice of appending relevant convention resolu-

5   For an analysis of the policy consequences of Canada's electoral system, see Alan Cairns, "The Electoral System and the Party System in Canada, 1921-1965," *Canadian Journal of Political Science/Revue canadienne de science politique* 1, no. 1 (March 1968): 55-80.

6   D. V. Smiley, "The National Party Leadership Convention in Canada: A Preliminary Analysis," *Canadian Journal of Political Science/Revue canadienne de science politique* 1, no. 4 (December 1968): 397.

tions to Cabinet documents. Ministers thus were at least made aware of discrepancies between party policy and Cabinet policy and some attempts were made at policy reconciliation. All available evidence indicates, however, that while conventions generate initiatives and ideas and stimulate discussion, they have no great influence in the final determination of party social policy as expressed by the parliamentary leaders of the Liberal Party.

A similar situation prevails in the Progressive Conservative Party.[7] The party's aim, as stated in Article 2 of the 1974 constitution, that "the state should be the servant of the people . . ." does not include the parallel notion that the elected members in the House of Commons should look to the larger party for direction. When John Diefenbaker was Prime Minister (1957-1963), it quickly became clear that he, perhaps more than any other Prime Minister, saw himself as servant—or leader—of all the people and not as an advocate of party-generated social policy. Even within the party he paid relatively little attention to organization attitudes. He dominated the party as Progressive Conservative leaders still do in that, for example, they appoint the party's Priority Committee, the Policy Advisory Committee, and, as is the case also in the Liberal Party, all senior headquarters and campaign officials.

The more democratically structured New Democratic Party grants a greater role to convention policy, but even there in provinces where the party has come to power the record is uneven. For example, the action of the Saskatchewan N.D.P. government in rejecting its party's convention proposal to have oil reserves developed by public rather than private corporations is a case in point. In British Columbia, concerning back-to-work labour legislation and the creation of a separate Department of Women's Affairs, Premier Barrett consistently opposed convention policy. And in earlier years the Douglas government in Saskatchewan repeatedly deemed it prudent to disregard certain convention decisions.[8] An early study of the C.C.F. national conventions, at a time when the party's general membership was more influential than in later years, illustrates the general practice. Of the sixty-nine policy resolutions proposed by "national leadership" at conventions between 1946 and 1952, 90 per cent were accepted while of the 390 proposed by local or area groups only 24 per cent were accepted.[9] Currently, Premiers Blakeney of Saskatchewan and Schreyer of Manitoba are experiencing similar problems. To the extent that the Liberals and Conservatives have even established formal procedures for local or regional policy inputs processed at national policy conventions—recent innovations for

---

7   "In 1947 the resolutions of the Liberal Federation were buried for three weeks before being given to the public, an interval which was presumably devoted to their revision and possible emasculation by the parliamentary members . . . . The Progressive-Conservative Association in 1947 passed resolutions which did not seem to be particularly startling . . . but they apparently caused consternation in Ottawa. For although the party had all the scope in these matters which comes from being in opposition, the resolutions were advanced with the astonishing proviso that there was no intention of committing the whole party membership to the Association's proposals." R. MacGregor Dawson, The Government of Canada, 3rd ed. (Toronto: University of Toronto Press, 1957), pp. 544-45.

8   Frederick C. Engelmann, "Membership Participation in Policy-Making in the C.C.F.," The Canadian Journal of Economics and Political Science 22 (1956): 171-72.

9   Ibid.

both parties—the policy influence of the parties' grass roots has been even less consequential.

One explanation for such widespread disregard of the non-parliamentary wing of the party in general, and of the party's grass roots in particular, concerning social policy formulation, is that the leaders of the two major parties and increasingly also of the N.D.P. have, by and large, seen their parties as vehicles to achieve power, not as sources of government policies once power has been attained or even of opposition parties' alternative policies. Time and again parliamentary party leaders have incurred the wrath of delegates in convention relishing the sweet taste of electoral success, by asserting that as they are now the government, they are not accountable to the party that worked for their election or even to the larger body of voters which elected them, but to society as a whole. Such Burkean logic generally does not sit well with the rank-and-file party activists who have worked long and sacrificially during hard-fought election campaigns. Of course, the situation is exacerbated further when pundits subsequently point out that in actual fact both national and provincial Canadian governments seem to be less concerned about public preferences concerning social policies or demonstrable long-term public benefits flowing from social policies than about shaping social policies to try to ensure their own short-term electoral success.

In all three parties, at both national and provincial levels, we find that extra-parliamentary party members and party organizations tend to follow rather than lead. Most convention resolutions on social policy never see the light of legislative day. But these policy statements may nevertheless serve a useful purpose. The two dominant parties are particularly adept at using social policies as means to win elections. The perennial Liberal promise to bring about national health insurance, which helped them win nine elections between 1921 and 1965, is a classic example.

Another route by which government political parties influence policy legislation involves the party caucus which meets weekly when Parliament is in session. Before a bill is introduced on the floor of the House, its general contents are outlined to caucus and members are usually given opportunity to react, often even in several subsequent meetings. Sentiments, wishes, and grievances are freely aired with the relevant Cabinet members paying close attention, especially if the government is in a minority position, but otherwise as well. Sometimes caucus reaction continues past the first reading stage and on occasion has brought about postponement or delayed further consideration of the measure. Thus, the controversial Drug Bill was continuously delayed from 1962 to 1968.[10] For more than a decade the Liberal caucus thwarted any government moves to abolish the death penalty by statute. More recently, the Liberal caucus successfully postponed parliamentary consideration of the Young Persons in Conflict with Law Bill.

Sometimes a caucus member serves as an undeclared public relations agent for a powerful interest group either because he shares its orientation,

10 See Robert J. Jackson and Michael M. Atkinson, *The Canadian Legislative System* (Toronto: Macmillan, 1974), pp. 36ff.

or because it wields much political clout in his constituency, or both. In such situations the government is especially inclined to try to accommodate the dissident member's objections. In recent years the much-expanded Prime Minister's Office has seen to it that caucus observations and dissenting views are given Cabinet consideration, particularly in several of the Cabinet committees which Prime Minister Trudeau created: Priorities and Planning, Science Policy, and Social Policy.

While the government caucus, especially in recent years, has helped shape social policy at both national and provincial levels, we must not overrate caucus power. In a majority government situation, Cabinet opinion normally prevails on all substantive issues.[11] The Cabinet not only decides what issues will be presented to Parliament but may also keep its own concerns off the caucus agenda. By not putting issues up for discussion, it avoids them. The desirability of admitting thousands of persecuted Ethiopians into Canada or of subsidizing beet sugar production in Ontario are recent cases in point. If needed, the Cabinet can always plead time pressures. Within the Cabinet, there is considerable log-rolling, that is, trading or exchanging support for particular issues in which Ministers are less concerned in return for support on those issues about which they feel strongly. Publicly, of course, Ministers are expected to maintain a united front which further enhances their status and power. This Cabinet dominance in policy determination, however, becomes fully evident only at the parliamentary phase.

THE PARLIAMENTARY PHASE

Once a social policy has been publicly enunciated in the Throne Speech or as a bill or White Paper, the manner in which the governing party relates to it changes. The extra-parliamentary wing plays little more than a public relations role during the parliamentary phase, at least in the usual course of events. All attention turns to the party leaders in the Cabinet who now assume full responsibility for both the contents of the measure as well as its successful passage through the legislative system. The locus of dialogue and confrontation shifts from an intra-party to an inter-party setting. However, despite all the rhetoric and verbal jousting, social policy is rarely determined on the floor of the House of Commons.[12] Normally it is only explained and defended.

Though, as we have already seen, the Cabinet plays an important role in the pre-parliamentary phase, its major impact on the country's social policies occurs during the parliamentary phase. Not only does it monopolize the initiation of social policy bills, at least those that have any hope of passing, and of all money bills, but it also determines the timing and sequence of introduction as well as the scheduling and duration of the debates.[13] Despite this great Cabinet power, however, most social policy

11   For a discussion presenting "senior officers of the central party organization" as having a "ubiquitous" influence, see ibid., p. 46.
12   The actual drafters sometimes have considerable input. See E. A. Driedger, "The Preparation of Legislation," Canadian Bar Review 31 (January 1953): 33-51.
13   Although the Canadian Parliament has had a closure rule since 1913, the Cabinet's power

developments come about as short-term measures, largely unplanned in terms of party philosophy, rather than as thoroughly analyzed policies based on continuing Cabinet study of philosophical values.

Since the life of the government depends on majority support in the House, Cabinet members continue to cultivate good will among government party backbenchers and involve them in the proceedings, but their main preoccupation is to make themselves and their policies look good, especially to the media people. The individual ministers carry much responsibility in this regard because only a Minister may carry forward departmental requests to the Cabinet or to the House and at present most social policy grows out of departmental evaluation of existing programmes. Moreover, only a Minister can defend departmental policies and actions.

As soon as government social policy has been announced, indeed sometimes prior to such announcements, the major pressure groups try to modify Cabinet thinking. Powerful and prominent organizations such as the Canadian Manufacturers Association, the Canadian Chamber of Commerce, the Canadian Labour Congress, the Canadian Medical Association, and the Canadian Council on Social Development regularly present written briefs and verbal arguments to Cabinet. Others, especially those directly associated with the clientele-oriented departments such as Indian Affairs, Multiculturalism, Agriculture, and Veterans Affairs, tend to plead their cases privately with the Minister involved. In order to strengthen their case these lobbyists commonly point to convention or election statements of the government party which support their arguments or stress the political, electoral, and general significance of the groups they represent. In the main, however, these presentations have very little demonstrable short-term effect. Presumably their arguments are weighed carefully in long-term policy planning, as they should be, for the requirements of an industrialized welfare state make the presentation of group interests an important adjunct to government activity.

One reason that group pressures or even extra-parliamentary government party intervention has little immediate impact at this stage is that governments tend to see each social policy measure as part of an interlocking legislative, electoral, and fiscal package. To grant one group special status, to raise taxes drastically and unexpectedly, or to favour one class or region at the expense of the other would throw askew the carefully balanced legislative policy package. Understandably, the Cabinet is very reluctant to drop a policy which it sees as part of a larger and necessary compromise. In addition, Cabinets normally resist pressures from their political party to grant it any obvious favours since if it appeared that partisan political consideration had a place in Cabinet deliberation, the legitimacy of related decisions would be seriously weakened. In addition, the government is loathe to backtrack publicly and must try to avoid antagonizing any substantial block of voters or openly defying any declared general party policies. At a time when the government is held accountable

has been considerably enhanced by the adoption, in 1969, of Standing Order 75. See C. E. S. Franks, "The Reform of Parliament," *Queen's Quarterly* 76, no. 1 (Spring 1969): 111-17, and R. J. Van Loon and M. S. Whittington, *The Canadian Political System: Environment, Structure and Process* (Toronto: McGraw-Hill, 1971).

for almost all facets of social well-being in a Canadian society fraught with deep cleavages, its social policy balancing act is not an easy one.

The most important individual at the parliamentary stage, as at the others, is the Prime Minister. Although, as we were powerfully reminded during the Diefenbaker years, he cannot exercise personal power in Parliament independent of Cabinet and caucus support, on substantive issues his personal wishes colour the entire proceedings. He and his close advisors in both the Prime Minister's Office, a coterie of political advisors and assistants, and the Privy Council Office, which is the legal arm of the Cabinet, must avoid party rifts, anticipate opposition arguments and strategy, evaluate each department's social policy aspirations in the light of other claims and of available funding, eliminate duplication and contradiction, and explain government actions to party followers in and out of Parliament. By his handling of the daily Question Period and in other ways, the Prime Minister also sets the general tone of Parliament, an important factor in terms of whether or not the opposition parties will allow social policy measures to proceed on schedule and in a form acceptable to the government.

At the parliamentary stage the government party backbencher usually plays no important, or at least public, role. Except in minority government situations the individual member's views are not of great consequence. The backbench agitation which brought about the creation of the Company of Young Canadians as a Canadian version of President Kennedy's highly popular Peace Corp was a notable exception. Provided that Cabinet members have discharged their caucus obligations well, the intrinsic cohesion characteristic of Canadian parliamentary parties will provide the needed backbench votes. The Party Whip looks after the details. In those infrequent situations when the government agrees to "take off the whips" and lets a bill's fate be decided by a conscience vote, each M.P. is, of course, free to vote as he sees fit. In recent decades the only major social policy issue, if we can call it that, which was thus decided was the restriction of capital punishment.

Perhaps the government should make greater use of its backbench strength in policy analysis, recommendation, formation, and defense. Even if the M.P.'s cannot match the expertise and experience found in the bureaucracy, they have the not-inconsequential advantage of being close to both the local party apparatus and the constituency grass roots. In recent decades governments at both national and provincial levels have increasingly relied on independent task forces and royal commissions, as well as on public opinion polls and a variety of departmental committees. It is high time that responsible parliamentarians be given greater responsibilities and greater prominence.

At first, the 1968 Pearson-Trudeau reforms dealing with the Commons Standing Committees held promise that such a trend was underway, but subsequent events have not sustained that hope. Maybe a vibrant and effective committee system is fundamentally incompatible with the Canadian political system based, as it is, on executive, i.e., Cabinet, dominance. Nonetheless, the Standing Committees, many having specific social policy interests, could be made to function much more effectively if they were smaller (so that members could develop expertise instead of rushing off to other committee assignments); if they had a more dignified setting instead of crowding around flimsy tables with "witnesses" sitting almost defiantly between them as equals if not superiors; if they were given more research staff, some of it allocated to the parties on a proportional basis, if they were given more time in which to meet; if easy and short-term membership substitution were discontinued; and if they were given authority to study issues and recommend measures for Cabinet consideration which they knew would in fact take place. Under the present arrangements, committee findings almost always come too late to have any bearing on the social policy being considered. Thus it is not surprising to find that more than half the Members of the Twenty-eighth Parliament believed that the committee system had no impact on policy formation.[14]

As we have seen, the parliamentary phase of social policy development includes important activities by individuals and groups, but perhaps the greatest significance of this phase lies in the fact that via parliamentary action the political parties, specifically the government party M.P.'s, grant legitimacy to executive actions. This legitimization covers not only the usual legislation but extends also the 6,000 or so Orders-in-Council which the government passes in Cabinet sessions each year and, retroactively, with debates and votes after the event, legitimizes quick government responses to disasters such as Hurricane Hazel or Arrow oil pollution as well as to F.L.Q. terrorism as Canada experienced it in 1970.

THE POST-PARLIAMENTARY PHASE

In the post-parliamentary phase, as in the parliamentary phase, the extra-parliamentary base of the government party plays only a minor role. Rank-and-file party members, but especially provincial and head office bureaucrats, suggest candidates for patronage positions, try to acquire social policy benefits for specific regions or groups, and may even attempt to influence government utilization of delegated legislative and executive authority. Their most important role at this stage, however, centres around their reaction to social policies which, to the extent that this response becomes feedback to the parliamentary wing, especially the Cabinet, serves as input for subsequent social policy revision or innovation.

While administrators and bureaucrats play a crucial role in this third phase, the Cabinet's role is also substantial. Most social policy statutes, at both national and provincial levels, require the government to develop detailed rules and regulations for the implementation of the general provisions. The bulk of these details are given legal status by Order-in-Council while some are issued simply as ministerial directives. In a more general sense the government retains ultimate control even at this last phase in that it may see fit to delay a programme either temporarily or indefinitely, it may provide certain kinds of additional benefits without specific parliamentary authorization, it may be less than zealous in enforcing legislation as has happened historically concerning immigration laws, and it may suspend any number of social policies by invoking emergency powers legislation or by simply suspending them.

14   Jackson and Atkinson, *Canadian Legislative System*, p. 183, fn. 3.

As a result of the passage of the Regulations Act of 1950 the Canadian government must now publish all rules and regulations arising from delegated legislative authority and table them in Parliament. Unfortunately, Parliament still does not undertake a full review of these documents nor has it seen fit to eliminate re-delegation of authority to lesser officials or to terminate the practice of including vague and sweeping clauses in enabling legislation. The Statutory Instruments Act of 1971 sought to terminate the most glaring abuses and the deficiencies concerning parliamentary surveillance of delegated legislation. It is still too early to tell whether the reforms will eliminate all of the major problems or whether the executive group in the parliamentary party will continue to exercise paramount influence on social policy at the implementation stage.

CONCLUSION

In our Canadian political system governments are elected to decide "who gets what, when, and how"[15] or, in other words, to bring about an authoritative allocation of values for an entire society.[16] In generating their programme of social policies they are influenced to a considerable degree, especially with reference to leadership selection, by the parties to which they owe allegiance. But they are probably influenced even more by their own personal preferences and by environmental constraints including pressure groups, other governments, existing commitments, social cleavages, scarce resources, electorate expectations, and bureaucratic power. Those observers who have judged environmental constraints to be paramount have suggested that Canada's national social policies are circumstantially determined. Given the long-term dominance of the pragmatic and reactive Liberal Party, such a description is partly true, but it is only partly true. Admittedly, social policy options are narrowed by environmental factors, but the governing party still makes major decisions concerning priorities, timing, and the very important details related to implementation.

At the national level in this complex situation we note the continuing dominance and pre-eminence of the Prime Minister. To a somewhat lesser extent similar first-minister domination exists in most provinces as well, no matter which party is in power. It seems to grow out of the need for fast and authoritative executive action and the requirements of television campaigning and television news coverage generally. Provided the first minister works with his Cabinet colleagues and respects both his party's commitment and parliamentary procedure, his pre-eminence need not be dysfunctional. After all, the Canadian system of responsible government implies Cabinet control over policy direction and within the Cabinet he ranks first, not just first among equals!

We have also seen that because of time constraints and policy cross-pressures, many long-term social policies develop virtually unplanned out of short-term contingencies. All too often governing parties make social

15 Harold Lasswell, *Politics: Who Gets What, When, How?* (New York: World Publishing Company, 1958).
16 David Easton, "An Approach to the Analysis of Political Systems," *World Politics* 9, no. 3 (April 1957): 383-400.

policies while focussing only on the next election. Existing party policy statements and even the promises made during the last election tend to be ignored. Maybe, as an antidote to hyperexpediency, and as one of many possible reforms,[17] our governments should follow the salutary, albeit potentially embarrassing, British custom of having non-partisan civil servants in the various ministries prepare documents for their Ministers showing precisely what party policy is and how party policy might be implemented. We might even go the British one better and have copies of such memoranda made available to media people.

As has been shown, governing parties, as parties, do play a significant role in social policy formation, legislation, and implementation in Canada. Maybe they should be more visible and more influential, but it is not at all clear that the rank-and-file members wish to assume a greater burden in the social policy process. They, and for that matter most of the public also, seem to be satisfied with their present level of effectiveness and the general Cabinet domination in pre-parliamentary, parliamentary, and post-parliamentary social policy phases. And while some of us may think that governing parties have been only moderately successful in transforming societal requests and needs into social policies, an analysis of the situation in other countries reminds us that our situation is comparatively favourable.

BIBLIOGRAPHY

Banks, M. A. "Privy Council, Cabinet, and Minister in Britain and Canada: A Story of Confusion." *Canadian Journal of Economics and Political Science* 31, no. 2 (May 1965): 193-205.

Bauer, R. A., and Gergen, K. J., eds. *The Study of Policy Formulation.* New York: The Free Press, 1968, especially pp. 1-27 and 149-80.

Blair, Ronald. "What Happens to Parliament?" In *Agenda: 1970*, pp. 217-40. Edited by T. Lloyd and J. McLeod. Toronto: University of Toronto Press, 1968.

Cairns, Alan. "The Electoral System and the Party System in Canada, 1921-1965." *Canadian Journal of Political Science/Revue canadienne de science politique* 1, no. 1 (March 1968): 55-80.

Cook, Terrence E., and Morgan, Patrick M., eds. *Participatory Democracy.* New York: Harper & Row, 1971.

Doern, G. Bruce. "The Development of Policy Organizations in the Executive Arena." In *The Structures of Policy-Making in Canada*, pp. 39-78. Edited by G. Bruce Doern and Peter Aucoin. Toronto: Macmillan Company of Canada, 1971.

_____. "Recent Changes in the Philosophy of Policy Making in Canada." *Canadian Journal of Political Science/Revue canadienne de science politique* 4, no. 2 (June 1971): 243-64.

_____, and Wilson, V. Seymour, eds. *Issues in Canadian Public Policy.* Toronto: Macmillan Company of Canada, 1974.

Driedger, E. A. "The Preparation of Legislation." *Canadian Bar Review* 31, no. 1 (January 1953): 33-51.

17 Thomas Hockin, "Reforming Canada's Parliament: The 1965 Reforms and Beyond," *University of Toronto Law Journal* 16, no. 2 (1966): 326-45; Pauline Jewett, "The Reform of Parliament," *Journal of Canadian Studies* 1 (1966): 1116; J. A. A. Lovink, "Who Wants Parliamentary Reform?" *Queen's Quarterly* 79, no. 4 (Winter 1972): 502-13; and J. A. A. Lovink, "Parliamentary Reform and Governmental Effectiveness," *Canadian Public Administration* 16, no. 1 (Spring 1973): 35-54.

Dror, Y. *Public Policy Making Re-examined*. San Francisco: Chandler Publishing Co., 1968.

Dupre, J. Stefan, et al. *Federalism and Policy Development*. Toronto: University of Toronto Press, 1973.

Easton, David. "An Approach to the Analysis of Political Systems." *World Politics* 9, no. 3 (April 1957): 383-400.

Engelmann, Frederick C. "Membership Participation in Policy-Making in the C.C.F." *The Canadian Journal of Economics and Political Science* 22, no. 2 (May 1956): 161-73.

———, and Schwartz, Mildred A. *Political Parties and Social Structure*. Toronto: Prentice-Hall, 1967.

Forsey, Eugene. "Comments." *Canadian Journal of Economics and Political Science* 31, no. 4 (November 1965): 575.

Franks, C. E. S. "The Reform of Parliament." *Queen's Quarterly* 76, no. 1 (Spring 1969): 111-17.

Fox, Paul W., ed. *Politics: Canada, Problems in Canadian Government*. 2nd ed. Toronto: McGraw-Hill, 1966, pp. 205-23.

Goffman, I. J. "Canadian Social Welfare Policy." In *Contemporary Canada*, pp. 191-224. Edited by R. H. Leach. Durham, N.C.: Duke University Press, 1967.

Halliday, W. E. D. "The Executive of the Government of Canada." *Canadian Public Administration* 2, no. 4 (December 1959): 229-41.

Hockin, Thomas. "Reforming Canada's Parliament: The 1965 Reforms and Beyond." *University of Toronto Law Journal* 16, no. 2 (1966): 326-45.

Huston, Lorne F. "The Flowers of Power: A Critique of OFY and LIP Programmes." *Our Generation* 8, no. 4 (October 1972): 52-61.

Jackson, Robert J., and Atkinson, Michael M. *The Canadian Legislative System*. Toronto: Macmillan Company of Canada, 1974.

Jantsch, Erich. "From Forecasting and Planning to Policy Sciences." *Policy Sciences* 1, no. 1 (Spring 1970): 31-47.

Jewett, Pauline. "The Reform of Parliament." *Journal of Canadian Studies* 1, no. 3 (November 1966): 11-16.

Lamontagne, M. "The Influence of the Politician." *Canadian Public Administration* 11, no. 3 (Fall 1968): 263-71.

Lasswell, Harold. *Politics: Who Gets What, When, How?* New York: World Publishing Company, 1958.

Lindblom, Charles E. *The Policy-Making Process*. Englewood Cliffs, N.J.: Prentice-Hall Inc., 1968.

Lloyd, Trevor. "Comments." *Canadian Journal of Economics and Political Science* 32, no. 1 (February 1968): 88-90.

Lovink, J. A. A. "Who Wants Parliamentary Reform?" *Queen's Quarterly* 79, no. 4 (Winter 1972): 502-13.

———. "Parliamentary Reform and Governmental Effectiveness." *Canadian Public Administration* 16, no. 1 (Spring 1973): 35-54.

Lowi, Theodore. "Decision Making vs. Policy Making: Towards an Antidote for Technocracy." *Public Administration Review* 30, no. 3 (May/June 1970): 314-25.

Meisel, John. "Recent Changes in Canadian Parties." In *Party Politics in Canada*, pp. 33-54. Edited by H. G. Thorburn. 2nd ed. Toronto: Prentice-Hall, 1967.

Robertson, R. G. "The Canadian Parliament and Cabinet in the Face of Modern Demands." *Canadian Public Administration* 11, no. 3 (Fall 1968): 272-79.

Rowan, M. "A Conceptual Framework for Government Policy-Making." *Canadian Public Administration* 13, no. 3 (Fall 1970): 277-96.

Salisbury, Robert H. "The Analysis of Public Policy: A Search for Theories and Roles." In *Political Science and Public Policy*, pp. 3-22. Edited by A. Ranney. Chicago: Markham Publishing Company, 1968.

Schindler, F. "The Prime Minister and the Cabinet." In *Apex of Power*, pp. 22-49. Edited by T. Hockin. Toronto: Prentice-Hall of Canada, 1971.

Simeon, Richard. *Federal-Provincial Diplomacy.* Toronto: University of Toronto Press, 1972.

Smiley, D. V. "The National Party Leadership Convention in Canada: A Preliminary Analysis." *Canadian Journal of Political Science/Revue canadienne de science politique* 1, no. 4 (December 1968): 373-97.

Smith, Denis. "President and Parliament: The Transformation of Parliamentary Government in Canada." In *The Canadian Political Process*, pp. 367-82. Edited by O. Kruhlak et al. Toronto: Holt, Rinehart and Winston, 1970.

Thorburn, H. G. "Parliament and Policy-Making: The Case of the Trans-Canada Pipeline." *Canadian Journal of Economics and Political Science* 23, no. 4 (November 1957): 516-31.

Ward, Norman. *The Public Purse.* Toronto: University of Toronto Press, 1962.

White, W. L., and Strick, J. C. *Policy, Politics and the Treasury Board in Canadian Government.* Don Mills, Ontario: Science Research Associates, 1971.

14

Party Politics and Social Policy: The Party in Opposition

MAX SALTSMAN

INTRODUCTION

The parliamentary opposition plays an important role in influencing social change and, although most of its methods are not always obvious, they are numerous and often effective.

There have been occasions, usually during minority governments, when the opposition was able to negotiate legislative changes by directly pressuring the government. But even during majority governments, the opposition has various means of influencing policy, not the least of which is the role of the opposition in creating and changing public opinion.

Public opinion enters directly into the political process during elections, but even between elections it has considerable and even crucial importance. Political parties have to maintain a constant vigilance with regard to changes in public attitudes for in many ways Parliament is one continuous election. A new election campaign begins as soon as the ballots for the old one have been counted. All parliamentary activity, by both government and opposition, is essentially preparation for the next test of electoral confidence.

The function of the opposition is usually defined as criticism and attack of the government. As Dawson and Ward put it, the opposition "wages perpetual war on the government, finding out its faults, picking its policies and proposals apart, offering substitutes and amendments, and lying in wait for any sign of weakness or dissension."[1] But victory in this war lies not in the immediate gratification of destruction, but in the results of the next election. What is crucial is not the effectiveness of heavy artillery in the House, but rather the appropriateness of the long-term electoral strategy.

Parliamentary debate consists of both government and opposition trying to demonstrate that the initiative for socially-beneficial legislation has come from their side of the House. While the members of all parties genuinely desire to improve their world, they must still face the next election, which makes it imperative to garner as much political credit as possible for the social legislation that has been achieved. It is not enough to do "good"; that "good" must also be highly visible.

Given our political structures, it is the opposition that usually has the better argument for policy initiation. The nature of being a government is to be beset by a continuous parade of problems arising out of past decisions. Although there are examples of governments initiating programmes on their own,[2] for the most part the duties of administration prevent much thought being given to innovation. It is here that the pushing and prodding of the opposition becomes important.

While this essay is primarily concerned with the role of the opposition in the formation of social policy, it is necessary to put the opposition in perspective by asking how opposition interests arise and how it is itself influenced while it is influencing the government.

HISTORICAL BACKGROUND

Political parties, in their modern form, emerged in Canada in the first two decades following Confederation. Loose coalitions of various religious, economic, and geographic interest groups had existed at least since the Act of Union, but true party discipline, both in Parliament and during elections, was a much later phenomenon. The complexity of the various religious and geographical cleavages, which Confederation increased rather than simplified, worked against the permanent unification of interest groups and the emergence of clearly ideological divisions.

The greatest obstacle to the emergence of parties was the pervasive assumption that the role of Parliament was not so much to decide the national destiny as to dispense patronage. The result was that many ridings sought to guarantee the free flow of funds to their area by electing independents or "ministerialists" who would support whichever group emerged as dominant enough to establish a ministry. With staggered elections many other ridings could afford the luxury of returning an official supporter of the government whose election was already secured. The system thus operated

---

1   R. MacGregor Dawson, The Government of Canada, 4th ed., rev. Norman Ward (Toronto: University of Toronto Press, 1966), p. 401.
2   Government initiation has been more obvious on the provincial level. The C.C.F. in Saskatchewan, Social Credit in Alberta, and, more recently, N.D.P. governments in three Western provinces have brought in extensive reform legislation, often in the face of strong federal government opposition. A strong ideological commitment, as opposed to a more pragmatic ethic, results in a far more innovative form of government. In fact, innovating on the provincial level has even influenced both sides of the House in Ottawa, as in the cases of hospital insurance and medicare.

to ensure that no significant opposition could emerge; the government would inevitably be supported by all but a tiny group of die-hard ideological opponents.

However much Sir John A. MacDonald might decry the existence of so many "loose fish" in Parliament, it was not the natural desire of any government for a more secure base in the House that spelled the doom of this system. What it took was the emergence of nationally contentious political issues such as tariffs, railways, and, most important of all, the Riel Rebellion. Even those might not have spelled the doom of the "ministerialist" had it not also been for two crucial electoral reforms: the secret ballot and simultaneous elections, first introduced in 1878.[3] Henceforth, elections would increasingly come to resemble plebiscites with the function of selecting a ruling party.[4] In the process, the power of the individual member declined, but the importance and function of the opposition was greatly enhanced.

While the party system became firmly established, dissatisfaction with it did not die out. It emerges most clearly in the prairie protest parties of the interwar period. In the programmes they advocated one finds demands for not only economic and social reform but also for electoral reform. More frequent elections and the ability of a constituency to recall its member were the most persistent of the proposals put forward in an effort to re-establish the more direct democracy that had been lost in the evolution of elections into plebiscites on parties.

But the clock could not be turned back. This type of electoral reform cut at the very heart of the Canadian political system as it had evolved since Confederation. In the end, an increased responsiveness of political parties to prairie problems was achieved, but this came through either the establishment of new parties or the effect of this establishment on the old parties.

The two-party system had failed to satisfy the emerging class consciousness of the urban worker and the growing regional and occupational awareness of the West, Quebec, and Northern Ontario. New parties, the Progressives, Social Credit, and the more durable C.C.F.-N.D.P., arose to represent those neglected collective interests, and with these new parties came an increasing advocacy of social change, social benefits, and income redistribution. The new parties thus became the conduits through which desires for social change could be channelled. By focussing and identifying interest in social change, they would play an instrumental role in many of the legislative reforms that were made.

But as much as these changes depended on the ideas coming from new political parties, social change also owes its growth and acceptance to the rapidly-increasing wealth of the post-war years and the concomitant increase in the revenues available to government for the distribution of those

---

3 Cf. Escott M. Reid, "The Rise of National Parties in Canada," in *Party Politics in Canada*, ed. Hugh G. Thorburn (Toronto: Prentice-Hall of Canada, 1963), pp. 14-21.

4 The same dynamic was at work in Britain, as David Butler and Donald Stokes have pointed out: "In the evolution of British democracy the parties were fostered as elite cadres by their ability to become objects of universal awareness. Party government is partially a tribute to the politicians' success in appealing for mass support in their parties' names" (*Political Change in Britain: The Evolution of Electoral Choice* [London: Macmillan, 1969], p. 19).

new surpluses. It was becomingly increasingly difficult to argue that we could not afford reform. Much of the social change also arose out of the need to hold Canada together; old age pensions and family allowances probably did more to keep Quebec in Confederation than any of the political exhortations for national unity and language rights.

In examining instances of where the opposition has been able to move the government toward its own point of view, one can seldom find any single clear reason for accommodation. With a minority government, the threat of defeat is a powerful weapon, but a weapon that can cut both ways. For the opposition to gain any benefit from defeating the government it must have public opinion on its side. Without public support, the opposition, rather than benefiting, is more likely to be punished by the voters for causing an election which, in the public's mind, was not justified by the issues involved.

The government understands this and assesses the degree to which it must give in to the opposition on the basis of where public opinion lies. Minority governments can thus often be as strong and stubborn as majority governments. If the government feels that it has public opinion on its side, it will, in fact, try to get itself defeated in the expectation of public support and, hopefully, a majority mandate.

This knowledge imposes a caution on the opposition as to how hard it can press on any given issue. It can also result in considerable embarrassment for an opposition that publicly calls for the defeat of the government while ensuring that enough of its members are out of the House for the confidence vote to be defeated. Instances of this kind are not lost on either the government or the press.

An opposition member in Canada, unlike an American Congressman, never has the satisfaction of seeing his name on a bill, regardless of how many years he may have been fighting for the contents of a piece of legislation. His pleasure comes instead from seeing those who had long been giving reasons why something could not be done now rise in the House, fresh from a conversion experience, to use his own arguments and often, because of the government's better bureaucratic talent, make an even more convincing case for something he had long advocated.

The individual member can also use Parliament's rules of procedure in his struggle for legislative change, using them to either obstruct or expedite the passage of a bill. In addition, a government's respect for individual opposition members may sometimes play a role in policy change, especially when the government is itself ambivalent on the issue involved. Like any institution, Parliament has its human side; considerations of friendship, altruism or animosity can often be as important as the requirements of order and efficiency.

The importance of such personal relationships will be illustrated in the examples of opposition influence that follow. To provide such examples requires a reliance on memoir material. To guard against distortions or lapses of memory, I have checked the details of each example with other participants. This can be a useful way to move beyond Hansard and trace the more subtle, personal relationships that leave no trace in the official record. The participant in the events may not have the detachment of later historians but his knowledge of the texture of behind-the-scenes bargaining and agreement adds an additional dimension to the record. The problem that has been repeatedly encountered, however, is that each of the participants consulted saw the events from a very personal perspective, often being unaware of many crucial aspects. The problem is thus to sift truth from misinterpretation, knowledge from invalid assumption, and to reconstruct the events in something of their true complexity.

The social policy that most clearly reflects the many pressures for change, as well as the different techniques open to the opposition, is old age security.[5] The archetypal case was in 1926 when Woodsworth and Heaps, holding the balance of power in the House of Commons, extracted a deal from Prime Minister Mackenzie King that brought in the first old age pension. Kenneth McNaught concludes that "in his interview with King at the beginning of the session, Woodsworth had secured the assurance not only of old age pensions but also the promise of amendments to the Immigration Act, the Naturalization Act, and the Criminal Code."[6]

This was one of the first of what was to be many examples of minority governments responding to opposition pressure. But since Parliament is really an ongoing election, the pressure on majority governments can sometimes be just as great. King's wartime diaries are replete with fears that he will lose his majority to the C.C.F. if his party fails to move with sufficient speed in the area of social security and human welfare policy.[7] King's budget of June 1944, which increased income tax exemptions, was specially designed to counteract C.C.F. influence.[8] King knew that without this measure a C.C.F. amendment to the budget might well pass, in which case "the C.C.F. would get the whole credit of being the Party that was really giving relief to the primary producers."[9]

We have another illustration of a Liberal majority government facing an election in 1957. The St. Laurent government had grown complacent after twenty-four years of unbroken Liberal rule and had reluctantly increased the old age pension by $6.00. The meagreness of the amount did them harm and earned Harris, the Minister of Finance, the historical obloquy of "six buck Harris." While there were many other issues in the election of 1957, old age pensions were certainly the most graphic example that Diefenbaker used to make his points against the government party.

Diefenbaker, elected with a minority, introduced a substantial old age pension change, raising pensions from $46.00 to $55.00 and, within a year, went to another election that gave him the greatest majority ever accorded a government—208 out of 265 seats. However, the Conservative hold did not

5 Cf. Kenneth Bryden, *Old Age Pensions and Policy-Making in Canada* (Montreal and London: McGill-Queen's University Press, 1974).
6 Kenneth McNaught, *A Prophet in Politics: A Biography of J. S. Woodsworth* (Toronto: University of Toronto Press, 1959), p. 220.
7 J. W. Pickersgill, *The Mackenzie King Record*, vol. 1: *1939-1944* (Chicago: University of Chicago Press, and Toronto: University of Toronto Press, 1960), pp. 547, 571, 598, and 601.
8 J. W. Pickersgill, *The Mackenzie King Record*, vol. 2, *1944-1945* (Toronto: University of Toronto Press, 1968), pp. 28-33.
9 Ibid., p. 30.

last long and with the defeat of the Conservatives in 1963 the Liberals were again faced with opposition demands for increases in the pension.

One of those occasions was on January 20, 1966 when John Diefenbaker moved an amendment to the Old Age Security Act that would have raised pensions from $75.00 to $100.00 a month. The N.D.P. supported the amendment. The minority Liberal government, under increasing pressure from both the opposition and public opinion, had to find some way of responding. The government's initial response was that it could not find the necessary money for such an increase.

While Allan MacEachern, then Minister of Health and Welfare, was defending this refusal in public, he was also fighting in Cabinet to convince his colleagues that the government needed to make a more substantial response. He wanted to avoid a defeat in the House and an election on the issue of government reluctance to increase pensions. No doubt the memory of the Liberal defeat in 1957 was there as a reminder of how potent a political football pensions could be.

MacEachern's department was then preparing a plan that would provide an increase in the amount paid to recipients of the old age pension, but which departed from the principle of universal benefits. It was to be a supplement programme based on a "means test" that had been semantically converted into something called a "needs test," so as to remove some of the odium attached to the world "means," a word open to all manner of puns.

MacEachern had been trying to get this plan through Cabinet, but without success. But with a government frightened by the pressure it was under, he seized the opportunity and pointed out to the Cabinet that the cost of a $30.00 supplement based on a "needs test" would cost the government much less than a $25.00 across-the-board increase in pensions.

Public opinion was increasingly supporting the opposition on the need to increase the old age pension. Unlike other social expenditures, like family allowances, unemployment insurance or welfare payments, which always divided public opinion, expenditures on old age pensions were always popular. Not everyone can see the rationale for family allowances and some people, despite all the evidence to the contrary, insist on viewing it as regressive encouragement for the poor to produce more children. Unemployment insurance expenditures also draw mixed reactions and welfare is, of course, always begrudged. Most voters do not anticipate having many children, being unemployed or being unemployable, but everyone, except perhaps the young, anticipates growing old and can thus see the merit in income security for their retirement years. Canadian politicians, especially in recent times, have therefore been particularly sensitive to the issue of old age pensions.

MacEachern won his point in the the Cabinet and was eager to announce his good news to the opposition, even to the extent of giving them a share of the credit. He sent a message to an N.D.P. member, saying that he had an important announcement to make, one that he was sure would please them, although he could not give the details. The message was relayed to the N.D.P. caucus, who worried that it might be a ruse to defuse an effective attack. The caucus insisted on knowing the details of the government's proposal and when that information was not given, continued their attack on the government.

MacEachern waited, then announced his new programme and rather than giving the N.D.P. credit, he lashed the opposition by insisting that the government was being more generous to the old age pensioners. MacEachern's proposal added $30.00 to the existing $75.00—$5.00 more than the opposition demand for $100.00. The generosity was, of course, selective, based as it was on a "needs test," but even without universality it gave substantial benefit to many pensioners.

In this case a government faction used the opposition to put through a programme they had not been able to obtain on their own; they were thus heavily dependent on opposition threats. In another case the government was again heavily dependent on one part of the opposition, not in the negative way of being threatened, but in a more positive way that the opposition party wanted the legislation as much, if not more, than did the government.

The passage of the Canada Pension Plan, introduced by Judy Lamarsh in 1964, depended heavily on the support of the N.D.P. opposition, particularly the N.D.P. expert and long-time advocate of better pensions, Stanley Knowles. When Judy Lamarsh spoke in defence of her bill, she compared her affection for the legislation with the love of a mother for her child.[10] The thought of Judy with maternal instincts was too much for an opposition wag who called out, "If Judy is the mother and Stanley is the father, what a baby that's going to be!"

While there was considerable public support for a contributory pension scheme, the C.P.P. was not without its enemies. The original government proposal for a C.P.P. had to be modified in many ways, particularly to accommodate the threat from Quebec to bring in its own plan. The confusion gave extra support to those opposed to the C.P.P. The Conservative opposition was supported by the insurance companies, business, and those of the public who had made provision for their retirement and saw the C.P.P. as just another scheme for redistributing income and imposing an extra tax on the better-off.

Under those circumstances, some opposition support was important, not only to sustain the minority government through the troubled passage of the bill, but also to add additional credibility and support for a contributory pension scheme. It is doubtful whether the C.P.P. would have been passed in the form it did and in the time it did without the N.D.P.

Sometimes an opposition idea can effect change by its innate reasonableness. A case in point was a Private Member's Bill, calling for the exclusion of Old Order Mennonites from the C.P.P. In this instance the private member was in the opposition, but it really would not have mattered if the member was on the government side, because all private members, if they have ideas, have to be considered in opposition to the government position.

10   Canada, House of Commons, *Hansard*, March 12, 1965, pp. 12297-98.

When the C.P.P. was first considered, the government had intended to exclude certain religious groups from the provisions of the Act, but changed its mind because of arguments from the N.D.P. that exclusions would weaken the universal principle of the C.P.P. and open the door for other exclusions that would undermine the success of the C.P.P.

The Private Member's Bill sought to amend the C.P.P. to allow the Old Order Mennonites to be exempt from its provisions, arguing that the Old Order Mennonites were a small group numbering about 800 families and their exclusion could not substantially affect the general coverage of the Act. Secondly, aside from the Mennonites, few groups could make the claim on religious grounds, particularly since the Old Order Mennonites had suggested a test of sincerity in which they were willing to make a contribution equivalent to the C.P.P. premium into some charitable fund, while foregoing all benefits from their contributions. Of particular importance was the argument that universality would be strengthened rather than weakened by allowing the opting-out in cases of genuine religious conscience, a principle recognized even in war-time.

The bill was first introduced in April 1969, and was reintroduced every year after that. The bill's sponsor[11] kept raising the issue with the government on every occasion open to him in the House and in Committee and found that considerable sympathy existed for the Old Order Mennonites. This sympathy was furthered by the sincere manner and arguments of the Mennonites themselves in their ongoing representations to the government. They argued that any kind of insurance scheme was destructive of the religious commitment they had with regard to the community's taking care of its own poor and aged members.[12]

But the government was reluctant to act on a matter of little public interest and that would be resisted by opposition members in both the P.C.s and N.D.P. Only when it became evident that some of the original opponents had accepted the merit of the amendment did the government include the exemption of the Mennonites in a package of amendments to the C.P.P. The only real opposition that remained was that of Jack Horner of the Conservative Party, and members of the opposition, including those in Horner's own party, contrived to get the bill passed quickly when Horner was out of the House.[13]

11 The first time I introduced this Private Member's Bill, I had considerable difficulty persuading anyone in the N.D.P. caucus to second the bill. In frustration, I finally went to John Diefenbaker, who agreed to second the bill if no one in the caucus would. But the thought of a Conservative seconding an N.D.P. bill proved to be enough of a threat to produce a seconder from the caucus.

12 In late 1972 a delegation of Old Order Mennonites presented their case directly to Herb Gray, then Minister of National Revenue, and John Munro, then Minister of National Health and Welfare. The arguments made by the Mennonites proved to be so reasonable that Gray and Munro issued a joint press release supporting their exemption.

13 Marc Lalonde introduced amendments to the Pension Act, including exemption for certain religious groups, in both the 1973 and the 1974 sessions of the Twenty-ninth Parliament. On the first occasion, Horner talked the bill to death; on the second he killed it with a flurry of amendments, criticizing members of his own party in the process. (Horner's concern in opposing the exemption was not the Mennonites but the Hutterites.) It was to take until 1975 for the exemption, now included in Bill C-22, to finally be passed. Horner was in the lobby of the House on that occasion but, recognizing the futility of fighting a majority government, he resisted temptation and decided he had better things to do.

However, the greatest victory for increased old age pensions came in the minority Parliament of 1972 in which the N.D.P. held the absolute balance of power. Unknown to the N.D.P. caucus, David Lewis, leader of the N.D.P., sent Stanley Knowles to Marc Lalonde, the Minister of National Health and Welfare, to negotiate a substantial increase in the old age security as a condition of continued N.D.P. support of the minority government. Lalonde at first refused to consider an across-the-board increase, preferring instead to increase the supplement to the old age security with the needs test criteria. Faced with an adamant Lewis and Knowles, the Minister not unhappily gave in and raised the universal old age security from $82.88 to $100.00. It was not the $125.00 that the N.D.P. had asked for, but it was nevertheless the greatest increase in the long history of the old age security.

Lalonde had recognized that as much as the government needed the N.D.P. support, the N.D.P. needed to show a victory of substance to the discontented and restless party hawks who had never reconciled themselves to supporting the minority Liberals.

Mutual need also provides an explanation for extension of the Veterans Land Act. In the Throne Speech debate of February 1974, Stanley Knowles raised the issue of extending the benefits available under the Veterans Land Act, due to expire at the end of March. But on March 7, Daniel J. MacDonald, the Minister of Veterans Affairs, expressed his hesitation about any such extension. This was followed on March 12 by a Conservative motion of non-confidence based on the Liberals' failure to extend the deadline. This motion was defeated by the combined votes of the Liberals and N.D.P.

While both the N.D.P. and Conservatives were in favour of the extension of the Veterans Land Act, another issue that had nothing to do with the Veterans Land Act was involved in the confidence vote. The Conservatives, reading the Gallup Polls, were convinced that they could sweep the country if they could engineer a defeat of the government. Their non-confidence motion on an issue such as the Veterans Land Act was designed to trap the N.D.P., holding the balance of power, into supporting a motion the N.D.P. was on record as favouring.

The N.D.P. had decided to support the minority Liberals for a time, in return for legislative concessions, and did not want to defeat the government at that point. Therefore, they argued that while they were in favour of the content of the motion, they were opposed to the consequences of voting for it. The N.D.P., therefore, had to suffer the embarrassment of their ambivalence.

Voting for the motion would not have extended the V.L.A.—it would only have precipitated an election, with only the implicit Conservative promise that, if they won the election, they would extend the V.L.A. as a matter of government policy.

But the message was quite clear to MacDonald. The N.D.P. had saved his government, albeit at a cost to the credibility of the N.D.P., and MacDonald had to take the N.D.P. off their petard in some way. Otherwise, the Conservatives would take another opportunity to repeat their embarrassing strategy and the N.D.P. hawks might prevail over the doves on the next test.

MacDonald responded by moving Bill C-17, extending the V.L.A. for one year, on March 28, admitting in the process that he had reviewed the situation on March 12, and overcame his previous objections. The bill was rapidly pushed through, being passed on March 31, 1974.

The opposition's influence in the changes in the Drug Patent Law resulted from the coming together of Public Service ideas, supported by political ambition in the government benches, opposition co-operation and a public sense of outrage.

For at least ten years before the introduction of government legislation to license the importation of drugs, the bureaucrats in the food and drug department had been pushing for some way to control the large drug companies.[14] Yet all their efforts had been stymied by the government's fear of moving against the drug industry, which maintained one of the most effective and powerful lobbies in Ottawa. But in 1966, a minority Liberal government, faced with N.D.P. demands for action against the high price of drugs, set up a special committee on drug costs and prices under the determined chairmanship of Dr. Harry Harley.

The committee met from June 1966 to February 1967 to consider one brief after another from the drug companies. This flurry of industry pressure even created a "cloak and dagger" atmosphere where lobbyists on both sides tried to avoid being seen in the Parliamentary Restaurant, only to keep running into each other in the Chateau Laurier where they had sought refuge from each other's scrutiny. Ultimately, the committee was able to force the industry to admit that its drug pricing system was based not on real costs but on a calculation of what the market would bear, and in its final report the committee recommended strong restrictions on industry practices.

In December of 1967, John Turner introduced Bill C-190, designed to increase competition and lower drug prices by establishing compulsory licenses for the import of prescription drugs. The government had finally been persuaded that public opinion was in a mood to support action against the industry. But opposition to the bill by the Conservatives and by some Liberal backbenchers held up its passage. As the Liberal leadership convention, and with it the end of the session, drew closer, the bill appeared doomed. Turner desperately wanted the bill passed as a demonstration of his progressiveness and thus as an aid to his own leadership ambitions. He sent his executive assistant to an N.D.P. member urging that party not to give up its fight on behalf of the bill. In response, the N.D.P. caucus decided to fight for a government commitment on the passage of the bill. When passage during that session proved impossible, a promise for the next session was demanded. That commitment was made on March 20, 1968, when Allan MacEachern promised the House that the bill would get early consideration after the recess.

That commitment was kept by the Liberals even though they were returned to the next Parliament with a majority. When the bill was finally

14 This was one of the rare instances of opposition contact with the bureaucracy. Bureaucrats are servants of the government, not of Parliament, and they only seek out members of opposition parties when their advice to the government goes far too long unheeded. And even this channel of dissent is declining in importance as bureaucrats tend more to leak news of their frustrations to the public directly via the media rather than privately to the opposition.

passed on March 28, 1969, the most powerful lobby in Ottawa had gone down to utter defeat.

In some situations the opposition may feel that it has no recourse except to obstruct or filibuster. Such tactics are a calculated risk, their success depending on the opposition's ability to rally public opinion to their side. If the opposition is in harmony with public opinion, the filibuster will continue, reinforced by newspaper support and public response via telephone or the mails. Members of both sides of the House will get a sense of the public mood in their constituencies. This "early warning system" may give such a clear response that even a majority government will have to respond or face the political consequences.

But if the opposition fails to attract public support for its filibuster, it may well be seen as a disruptive force, needlessly delaying other legislation. Then it would be the opposition that must proceed cautiously. On the other hand, it is also possible for public opinion to shift from one side to the other in the course of the debate. If the shift is away from the opposition, public opinion may provide as effective a limitation on debate as any closure rule at the government's disposal.

But stubbornness or conviction on the part of either parties or individual members may work against this dynamic of parliamentary responsiveness, as was the case with the Howard-Peters filibuster against the Senate's prerogative on divorce. Until the passage of the Canada Divorce Act in December 1967, applications for divorce went to the Senate as private bills. A committee of the Senate lubricously listened to the presentations of specialist lawyers, relishing the intimate details of real or contrived adultery, the principal grounds for divorce.

The Senate would pass the bills and send them to the Commons for concurrence. There they could only be considered during the Private Member's Hour, which imposed a one-hour limit on debate on any one day. With each member allowed twenty minutes to debate the bill, it only required two determined members, aided by either another speaker or by a few points of privilege or order, to talk out the bill and shelve it for another day.

Year after year Frank Howard and Arnold Peters used those tactics in an effort to draw attention to the dishonest, unfair and archaic way in which divorces were handled. At first, their position was widely supported for public opinion, it seemed, was well in advance of the government on liberalizing divorce laws. But as the backlog of divorce cases built up and created great personal problems for the divorce applicants, principle came into conflict with individual need and the public mood, particularly from those immediately affected, became bitter, even to the extent that the filibusterers were threatened with physical violence.

The government, too, found itself in an impossible and frustrating position. Even with 208 members, the Diefenbaker government found itself to be helpless in the face of two determined opposition members.[15] It was a

---

15 Government frustration with Peters and Howard is well illustrated in the frequent and bitter remarks made by Robert McCleave, the Parliamentary Assistant charged with expediting legislation during the Diefenbaker years. On one occasion he rose to denounce what he

standoff, but over a number of governments the Howard Peters filibuster was effective in overcoming government reluctance to move against a well-entrenched electoral minority opposed to any relaxation of divorce procedures.

Most observers now acknowledge that Trudeau's technocratic "Planning, Programming and Budgeting System" was a failure.[16] Instituted following the 1968 election, it was an attempt to copy McNamara's American methods of programming and setting priorities and timetables for legislation. But Parliament is not only an institution that operates on a combination of rules, public opinion, and personal relationships, it also turns out to be remarkably prone to accidents. It is hardly a setting designed for a well-ordered technocrat. Accidents can sometimes be very useful, particularly in providing time for a government to re-evaluate the benefits of a programme.

In the dying days of the Twenty-eighth Parliament the Liberals introduced Bill C-170, designed to set up a "Family Income Security" plan that would raise family allowance benefits on a selective basis. (Their experience with the needs test for the pension supplements was obviously influential here.) It was to be a Liberal showpiece in the upcoming election of 1972.

Many opposition members disliked the changes, seeing them as destructive of the principle of universality with regard to family allowances, but they could hardly afford to oppose a measure that would help the poor, even though public reaction to the bill was by no means clear. The result was that the bill was rapidly pushed through the House, getting second reading on March 24, and being introduced for third reading on June 29. With dissolution set for July 7, the government fully expected the passage of the bill, assuming that no member of the opposition would risk the political consequences of voting against assistance for the poor.

What they had failed to consider was the stubbornness of the Honourable Paul Hellyer, former Liberal Minister of National Defence and now sitting in isolation as an "Independent Liberal," having resigned from both Cabinet and caucus over a policy disagreement with the government. As third reading proceeded the government asked for the unanimous consent of the House to prolong debate for the July 7 sitting. The Senate was dutifully standing by to give its assent and the calling of a general election was just days away. When the Speaker called for consent, the lone voice of the Member for Trinity was heard to object and, under the rules of the House, the debate for that day had to be concluded. There was to be no other day for Bill C-170.

The House adjourned at the end of June, was later dissolved and a general election took place on October 30, 1972. Public opinion during the election had told the new members that if family allowances were to be raised, it would have to be on a universal basis. A new bill to raise family allowances on a universal basis was subsequently introduced and ap-

called "the most expensive garbage bilge this house has ever enjoyed . . ." (Canada, House of Commons, *Hansard*, June 14, 1960, p. 4921).

16   Cf. Thomas A. Hockin, ed., *Apex of Power: The Prime Minister and Political Leadership in Canada* (Scarborough: Prentice-Hall of Canada, 1971), pp. 127-45.

proved. A miscalculation in the House had proved itself more prescient of what the public wanted than 264 members.

Under our parliamentary system, it is clearly the government that has to be held responsible for both the good and the bad of a Parliament's record. Once the government decides to proceed in a certain way, its determination will seldom be changed by the opposition. Nevertheless, the parliamentary opposition has served to bring the present welfare state into an earlier existence through its influence of public opinion and the threat of defeat or destruction, through its use of the rules and its support of and friendship with reform elements and impatient souls in the government party, and through offers of co-operation and by sheer accidents or fortunate timing.

CONCLUSION

Over the past forty years, the opposition parties, supported by a real increase in the country's capacity for generosity, have profoundly changed their society. It has become one of the best societies that humanity has ever known. It provides greater freedom, security and comfort, and is more liberal, tolerant and open to ability than anything previous to it. For the first time in history we have a society where no one goes without food, shelter, education, medical attention, or security in old age. What is more important is that these benefits are no longer a function of work expended. Whatever indignities our society may be prepared to inflict on its members, starvation and exposure are not among them.

Yet it is hardly an ideal society. The gap between rich and poor has not significantly narrowed; rather than being true income redistribution, social benefits have largely come from an overall increase in wealth. Problems also remain in the prejudice that some groups experience, however subdued it may be.

Although a few people still refuse to accept the idea of a welfare state, the debate now is no longer on whether or not society has a responsibility to the poor and weak, but on the degree of support. With the exception of a few "cranks," everyone now supports medicare, hospital insurance, welfare, unemployment insurance, old age pensions, family allowance, income tax, and transfer payments from the better-off to the less-well-off—be it individuals or provinces. And some reformers have even called for the international extension of this principle, the transfer of wealth to the "have-not" countries.

Among leftists in both North America and Europe, it has become fashionable to see any kind of value consensus in society as repressive of free and natural human development. Thinkers such as Marcuse and Althusser are but the spearhead of a deep distrust of social agreement. Yet the value consensus on social legislation that we have arrived at in Canada is truly a worthy summation for the long efforts of many dedicated and thoughtful Canadians. If the role of the opposition is now more difficult, it is largely due to the substantial success of its efforts in this area.[17]

17 There are those who have a different explanation for the declining importance of the opposition. John Reid, for instance, presently Parliamentary Secretary for the Privy Council,

Because the opposition is so heavily dependent on the creation of public opinion to support its position, its future effectiveness is dependent on two main conditions. The first is a clearly-defined position around which the public can coalesce and the second is the ability to have its ideas relayed to the public through the news media.

The first is becoming increasingly difficult since most social problems are now receiving ameliorating consideration from governments at one level or another, and the debate now focusses not on the propriety of government involvement, but on the degree of such involvement. This makes for confusion in the public mind as to the existence of any sharp differences in policy amongst parties. If the opposition party becomes too innovative in their frustrating search for a discernible difference, they run the risk of turning off the public by the need to overstate in making their point. The Halcyon days of significant change may, therefore, be over, and we can expect little more than incremental changes: criticism and correction of what is now in place will replace significant innovation.

Moreover, the G.N.P., on which so much change is based, is no longer growing as quickly and may, in fact, start to decline, undercutting the ability of government to finance welfare programmes from automatically increasing tax revenues. New welfare programmes will have to be paid out of a real redistribution and levelling-off of income from those better-off to those less-well-off, something the majority will only accept with the greatest reluctance. It was one thing to improve the lot of the poor while everyone was getting a little richer; it is another to improve the lot of the poor by making the majority poorer. In another way even a small percentage increase on the substantial welfare programme now in place would represent large expenditures and only marginal personal benefits for the increasingly large number of people who now receive transfer payments of one kind or another.

Incrementalism is not the material out of which headlines are fashioned and the news media will, therefore, tend to focus more of its attention on the sensational and away from social welfare debate. It is much easier for the press to become excited about whether or not a new policy is being made than whether a few dollars' increase is being added to a programme already in existence.

The social legislation of the last fifty years was a response to what was perceived as structural and environmental evils. With the welfare state in place, problems such as alcoholism, juvenile delinquency, poverty, regional disparity, only mildly ameliorated by redistribution policy, now appear to be more personal and individual. This means that in the future, social change will be less a function of legislative action and more the result of the individual attention that only the psychologist and the social worker can provide.

While governments tend to effect social policy by incrementalism, the opposition must make visible leaps to accentuate its differences with the

sees a growing irrelevance not only of the opposition, but also of the whole Commons, where, he argues, antiquated procedures and an abysmal lack of expertise on the part of M.P.s have destroyed the ability to adequately respond to public needs (*Kitchener-Waterloo Record*, June 3, 1975, p. 13).

governing party. Those leaps are now becoming unlikely, and when this situation is joined with the reduction in the opposition's direct power, through rule changes designed to limit debate in the interest of expediting the greatly-enlarged volume of legislation, the proud record of the opposition in affecting social change can only diminish.

15

The Role of the Social Work Profession in Social Policy

FRANCIS J. TURNER

The purpose of this chapter is to examine the nature, extent, potential and limitations of the social work profession on Canadian social policy. It is proposed to deal with this question in a speculative rather than in an historical or empirical manner. Clearly, there would be advantages in pursuing an historical approach. To do so would give the reader an opportunity to examine and trace the changes and patterns in social policy activity over a fifty-year history. But important as such a task might be, the object of the book is more contemporary and forward-looking.

Just as clearly, an evaluative examination of the profession's effectiveness in the social policy field would be of critical importance. Interesting as such an approach would be, at this point I do not think we are in a position to do more than speculate on the nature and extent of our influence. We know all too well the process of developing, negotiating, and implementing social policy at any level is a highly-complex activity in which many significant variables are operating. Thus, most of what can be said at this time about our influence as a profession would be impressionistic only. At best a historian looking backward or a political scientist looking at current issues might be able to identify and differentially evaluate the influence of various factors including our own profession on a particular component of policy. But that is all. Hence, I have chosen to discuss the challenges facing the profession in its commitment to influence social policy and to identify some of the factors that appear to both enhance and limit our ability to operate in this process.

THE PROFESSION

The profession of social work as used in this chapter refers to the activities of those professional organizations that exist in Canada which represent or are seen by society as representing professional social work. This refers in particular to the Canadian Association of Social Work, the national professional social work organization. But in addition to this, the nature and function of the provincial social work organizations must be included. Although there are also organizations, such as the Canadian Association of Schools of Social Work, which speak for particular components of the profession, their activities in social policy will not be included.

Thus, the impact of individual social workers on social policy is not being considered although some comment will be made on this question. Nor will the impact on social policy of particular organizations, such as the Canadian Council of Social Development, be examined. This organization and others like it represent the social welfare viewpoint in a broad sense and certainly has been directly involved in social policy activities. But it does not purport to speak for the profession of social work as such, and thus it will not be included here.

SOCIAL POLICY AND THE PROFESSION

Obviously one of our assumptions is that social work as a professional system comes with an inherent responsibility to the analysis, development, and implementation of social policy. But this is not an assumption that would always have been gratuitously received by members of the profession. In fact, one of the criticisms that has been made of social work in its formal organizational identity is its failure to carry a significant role in the field of social policy.

Certainly in its professional origins, early social workers were committed to the improvement of services and resources to help individuals and families achieve a more satisfactory growth-enhancing lifestyle. Many, but not all, of the early social reformers came from the ranks of the developing profession. But in truth, from its very earliest days social work developed much more as a case-oriented profession rather than one of social reform of large systems.

Much, of course, has been made of the influence of casework in the profession and how this overinfluence was further reinforced by psychodynamic theory. Undoubtedly, one of the influences of this client-centred psychosocial understanding of man has been that much of the profession's interests, resources, and personnel were directed to the needs and problems of individuals, families, small groups, and communities. The emphasis has been on problem-solving rather than on social reform through improved social policy.

But it would be wrong to make this case too strong. If there is any factor that gives social work its unique identity it is the psychosocial view of man and his functioning. Thus, even when the profession was a case-centred one, there has always been, both institutionally and individually, a commitment by social work to the understanding and altering of man's significant environment. Included in this perception has been an understanding of the factors involved in bringing about improved resources, services, legislation, and social commitment for the benefit of persons in need. Hence, it would be incorrect to hold that the profession was not social-policy-oriented.

What can be concluded is that we have been naive and uneven in our social policy commitment. We have not given sufficient emphasis to the processes involved in changing social situations. We have not given sufficient concern to the analysis of current situations from the viewpoint of their social political-economic bases. We have clearly not given sufficient attention to the knowledge and skill required to develop expertise in the profession that could help us draw on our wealth of knowledge from clients about what improved policies are needed and how to achieve them.

At times, of course, within the profession the question has been debated that our proper professional role was the supervision of direct services to others; this has now passed. We are now in a phase of our history in which we have clearly recognized that we fail ourselves, our clients, and society if we are not engaged in the twofold thrust of direct service to clients and also to the ongoing research for improved social conditions and the political-economic base to sustain them that will prevent or alleviate psychosocial suffering.

Thus, as a profession we are now trying to catch up with our lack of proper attention to this policy role. Most of the comments that follow will reflect this idea that we have been stronger on enthusiasm and commitment than on the development and implementation of long-range goals with planned strategies for achieving them.

One of the mistakes frequently made about social policy considerations is to view the concept only from a macro-systems stance. In this regard the development of social policy is seen as the process that takes place in the large system arena dealing with such things as a province's activities in child welfare or the country's policies on housing.

Important as such issues are, it is incorrect to make them the total purview of social policy. If social policy is seen as the goals a person or group has for a particular human activity in relation to its commitments, resources and values, then in examining social policy from a social work position the activities, concerns, and issues of micro-systems must also be taken into account.[1]

There is a viewpoint still occasionally expressed that sees the profession's social policy activities in the micro-system as of little consequence, identifying the activities at the national level as of prime importance. Clearly, one of the strengths of social work commitment is that it turns equal attention to both large and small systems. Hence, it is the position of this paper that a small local branch of a professional organization, which seeks to alter a municipal government's policy around the transportation needs of elderly citizens, is just as involved in social policy activities as the national body responding to a green paper on immigration policies.

1 Francis J. Turner, "Social Policy and Social Welfare Services," *Public Welfare* 15, no. 2 (January 1970): 17.

THE C.A.S.W. AND SOCIAL POLICY

In discussing the role of the social work profession in social policy from a Canadian context, clearly a major point of departure is the Canadian Association of Social Work (C.A.S.W.). Examination of the organization's constitution indicates that a commitment to social policy is strongly supported. A similar examination of the Association's writings and activities of the past five years just as clearly indicates that this commitment has been operationalized in a variety of ways and over a wide spectrum of topics and issues.

As mentioned earlier, social work as a profession has not always included social policy as a major component of its activities. C.A.S.W., in its history, reflects this fact well. Dr. Elspeth Latimer has examined this historical question in her doctoral dissertation and subsequent writings.[2] It is evident from her work that the commitment of C.A.S.W. to social policy activities from its beginnings in 1926 has been uneven in quality and irregular in quantity. Although there has been an unevenness in our social policy activities, it would be incorrect to assume that they have been lacking. The number and diversity of such formal activities can be found in an important publication of the C.A.S.W., edited by Dogan D. Akman.[3] This publication lists some sixty reports, briefs, and position papers produced by the C.A.S.W. from 1937 to 1972 on a rich array of national topics and issues. However, regardless of our past, it is evident that our professional association has in recent years recognized and identified with a strong commitment to social policy activities and concerns and has strived to implement them.

In the remainder of this chapter the qualities and characteristics of the professional association that facilitate this commitment, that impede it, and that influence it will be examined.

In considering the social policy functions of a national organization, three principle roles can be identified. First, the C.A.S.W. should function as the formulator or initiator of social policy at a national level. By the very nature and structure of the organization, it is in a position to gather and make known attitudes, concerns, issues, and problems from all parts of the country. It can reflect all aspects of the profession, all forms of service delivery, all areas of professional concern, all modalities of practice, and thus develop positions and formulate proposals aimed at developing and modifying social policy. It can then use this knowledge to set short- and long-term policy objectives and strategies of implementation.

A secondary role in the social policy context is to serve as a feedback agency to the membership. This for a twofold objective: (1) it can keep the membership informed of social policy issues that are emerging either at a national or regional level that may have hitherto unrecognized implications

2 Elspeth Latimer, "Social Action Behaviour in the Canadian Association of Social Work from its Organizational Beginnings to the Modern Period" (unpublished Ph.D. dissertation, University of Toronto, 1972). Also, "Social Action in a Professional Social Work Association," *The Social Worker* 42, no. 1 (Spring 1974): 4-8.

3 Dogan D. Akman, ed., *Policy Statements and Public Positions of the Canadian Association of Social Workers* (St. Johns, Newfoundland: Memorial University, 1972).

for segments of the profession; (2) the C.A.S.W. can make use of the membership to exercise their individual and group influence in attempting to bring about sought-after policy changes. In the strategy of social policy development, having access to a national membership that can individually and collectively take action is indeed a powerful and critical resource when used appropriately.

The third general policy function of the C.A.S.W. is to be seen as a responder or agent of influence on social policy issues. Although we sometimes seem to presume that only our profession is in the business of social policy development and implementation, it is clear that many groups in society are involved in setting and seeking to achieve goals or objectives for all segments of particular societies. Our function as social workers is to constantly examine and appropriately respond to trends or aspects of emerging social policy in government or other national groups. Thus, the national organization such as the C.A.S.W. has a watchdog, responder, critical-observer function which, when skillfully utilized, can influence effectively the decision-making processes in the political arena at the national level.

The above three functions are, of course, objectives that are clearly differentially achieved by the C.A.S.W. in its current functioning. The extent to which we are effective in achieving these objectives, of course, depends on the extent of our commitment, the methods we utilize, and the resources available to us.

An examination of the C.A.S.W.'s activities in the last five years would show an unevenness but a focussed determination in the way we have pursued our social policy objectives. Clearly, the fact that we exist is an important factor. That is, having had a paid professional and support staff in Ottawa for many years has been an important component to our social policy role. There is no doubt that the executive directors whom we have had have demonstrated understanding and skill in making themselves known in government and in other national policy circles. In addition, each has kept abreast of emerging social policy issues, in making appropriate personal and written representations to members of the government and in general using personal contact to bring relevant viewpoints, ideas, and concerns to appropriate bodies.

In a similar way, the existence of a national body provides the machinery to prepare briefs, position papers, and engage in the data gathering and analysis necessary to the development and formulation of social policy positions. Especially in the last five years has this function been operative.

A related activity has been the use of the media as agents of influence. To an increasing extent, the C.A.S.W. has actively made use of regular press releases, television appearances, and press conferences in response to current issues and especially in response to planned or proposed government policy.

It can be concluded with assurance that the C.A.S.W. is by now a recognized and respected body in the nation's capital and is increasingly seen as a significant spokesman on social welfare matters. This, of course, increases our ability to influence social policy. An indicator of this increased position of influence is the growing number of occasions when the national office is approached by either members of government or senior civil servants to discuss matters of social policy content. A good example of this type of contact can be found in relation to the Green Paper on Immigration and its subsequent developments. As a result of the C.A.S.W.'s first response to the Green Paper and discussion with members of the Committee, the C.A.S.W. was invited to make a formal presentation to the government committee on immigration policy. In a related way the national office in both the person of the executive director and the national president has maintained an ongoing contact with the national Minister of Health and Welfare. The 1976 annual reports of both the national president and the executive director list a rich array of statements, briefs, and press releases made by the C.A.S.W. on social policy issues over the last year.

From the information viewpoint, the C.A.S.W. has been active and, I think, effective. One of the principle activities of the C.A.S.W. over the years has been the regular publication of the *Social Worker*, now in its forty-third volume, and a newer publication, *The Information Bulletin*, begun in 1971. An examination of both publications indicates that a significant amount of space has been given to issues of a social policy nature. The continued publication of these periodicals and the enhanced social policy thrust that can be identified in them serve a twofold role: (1) to keep our membership informed and oriented to emerging social policy questions, and (2) to build a public platform for the expression of views on social policy matters.

Active as we have been and continue to be in this area, it is difficult to assess how effective we have been. We know that our efforts have not been universally even and have been unevenly implemented; this is due to a variety of reasons.

Important and active as the national office has been in its efforts, there are inherent flaws in our structure, resources, and actions that must be identified to present the full picture. One of the most critical limitations for the area of social policy is our lack of resources. The C.A.S.W., in its present stage of development and format, continues to have serious financial problems. At best, it can support one professional position, the occasional part-time professional person and two or three administrative positions. With a staff this small, restricted finances, and a wide range of other responsibilities, inevitably the amount of resources that can be allotted to social policy issues is highly curtailed.

This overall resource limitation has clear negative consequences for our social policy activities. First, it drastically affects the quantity and quality of research effort that can be spared for the gathering of data, the formulation of briefs, position papers and presentations. In complex social policy questions, such as current concerns on housing or the guaranteed annual income, considerable amounts of time, money, and competence are required to analyze fully the sociological and political implications of various policies and strategies in emerging legislation and the socio-economic implications of the various alternatives. This we just cannot afford. Thus, we are placed in the position of responding to the work of others and developing brief impressionistic responses in which we use the data of other bodies

and form our opinions and positions with heavy reliance on our commitment and general "practice wisdom."

A related component of the expense issue is the necessity to spend much
of our meagre resources on the information dispersion role by which we
keep members informed and involved in relevant social policy issues. To
reduce this function in favour of more independent formulation of policy-
related matters could be disastrous to the identity and effectiveness of the
association.

There is a further inherent vulnerability in our potential ineffectiveness in
the social policy area related to our lack of resources. Since we are not in a
position to maintain a staff who can commit themselves fully to the examination, development and implementation of social policy issues, there
results a situation where we must depend on the interest and skills of a few
persons. Frequently, our resources require us to look to volunteers from the
Association to prepare position papers or responses or to await the unso-
licited action of others to gather material and prepare to take action. In such
situations the Association is in a position of having to accept uncritically the
position or views presented, since there is neither time nor personnel
available to give such independently originated questions more than a brief
review before making them public. This is not to disparage the importance
and effectiveness of volunteer activities in social policy issues. It is rather to
underscore that this is not always the most effective or efficient way of
functioning in the social policy arena. The expense and difficulty incurred
to assemble even the executive of the board of the C.A.S.W. is prohibitive,
thus again lessening the opportunity for policy formulation.

It follows from this that the executive directors of the C.A.S.W. have
emerged in the last few years as the official spokesmen for the professional
association. In acting in this way, they have limited opportunity to seek or
obtain support, direction, or approbation from the membership. Thus, in
attempting to evaluate the impact of C.A.S.W. activities in social policy
matters, there is an important prior question: To what extent have C.A.S.W.
positions reflected the Association, or only segments of it?

In his paper, Dr. Splane discusses some of the complexities of challenge
and frustration for a social worker practising at senior governmental levels
in social policy matters. These difficulties are further magnified when translated into the professional association, since the requisite resources are not
available.

A further result of our limited resources is that the C.A.S.W. is put in a
position of being a responder rather than an innovator in matters of social
policy. Being in a responder position or assuming a critical role is certainly
one of the functions of a professional association. But over and above that,
there is a further function to which we have committed ourselves—that of
being the leaders in the development and implementation of social policy in
both a short- and long-term manner. As has been implied, and as has been
indicated before, such innovative activities and projects are much more
complex than the responding role, important as it is. To this point it can be
noted that in the last five years the C.A.S.W. has not prepared any major
policy documents, even though we have been very active in the responding

critical role. It would be hoped that with the availability of further resources we could take a much more active and aggressive role as innovators and attempt to set the directions for emerging social policy.

Following from this, the point must also be made that there is an unevenness in the extent to which we function in the social policy arena. From a national viewpoint it is evident that there are many important and critical issues of current and emerging social policy, both in the general policy objectives of the Department of Health and Welfare and in secondary policy issues in other aspects of government policy.

A result of the complexity of our resource base is that there is an unevenness in the manner in which we can function in the responding critical role. Frequently, it happens that our ability to take appropriate action or to take any action related to policy questions is related to the timing of meetings of the executive of the Association or the availability of the executive director's time. Thus, it happens that many issues must be left untouched. Indeed, one of the criticisms of the Association both from within and from without has been related to the number of times in which it has not been possible for us to be visible or to be heard on important social policy matters.

This question of unevenness is further complicated by the fact that we have not developed an overall social policy platform of our own. No doubt, one could find some consistency in some of our writings and in some of our responses to social policy questions, but these reflect more the policies and interest of the concerned members of the Association rather than any carefully worked out profile of sound policy objectives.

In a more ideal situation, it would be hoped that our profession, through its national association, could develop and continually update both short- and long-range social policy objectives for the Association as well as to clearly map out strategies to implement them. But, as will be mentioned later, we do not appear to be at a point in our history where either structurally or conceptually we are able to move in such a direction.

It would be wrong to attribute all of the problems related to our social policy activities to a lack of resources in the Association. Many of our problems stem from the structure of the Association. An examination of the activities of the C.A.S.W. over the past five years would clearly show that much of our financial resources and much of our attention and concern have been given to organizational issues and the structure and future of the C.A.S.W.

Clearly, this is a phenomenon that has taken place in other professions and could be interpreted as a society-wide sociological realignment of the professions. Be that as it may, it is true that we have been so involved in our intraprofessional deliberations and struggles that little has been left to the discharge of our social policy mandate and responsibilities. This, in turn, has weakened our effectiveness and our credibility, and no doubt has lessened the support of our membership base.

At this point in time, the C.A.S.W. has just moved into a new structure —one that should permit a broad involvement in social policy. The new structure is in the form of a federation in which the various provincial and territorial professional associations become the members rather than our former individual membership base. This change will permit the C.A.S.W. to re-examine its position with regard to the social policy aspect of its professional responsibility. Certainly this new structure, the culmination of over a decade of discussion and struggle, should reduce, at least for the immediate future, the disproportionate amount of time and energy that has been devoted to what became known as "the federation issue." In operation, the new federation should provide a more efficient and effective way of developing national positions since the new board consists of members from each province and territory. It is hoped that the new C.A.S.W. will devote more of its effort to developing strategies and procedures which will permit the formulation of well researched, documented, and presented social policy position statements. It is also hoped that the national association can develop the earlier mentioned platforms that will give direction to our social policy activities. In establishing the new structure it was hoped that the federation, freed from many of its earlier administrative responsibilities to an individual membership base, would be able to contract for selective social policy statements, produce some of its own, and permit the staff national office to be more actively engaged in the fact-finding, observer, lobbying role.

As mentioned above, it is hoped that the new federation's board will set up a series of ongoing time-bound task forces with the responsibility of formulating and regularly updating position papers on a wide range of social policy questions related to a general policy commitment. This would help us move from the current situation where we are always answering in crisis rather than taking a more active leadership role.

Although the new federation has only been in existence for just over a year, already there are indications that some of these hopes may not be immediately forthcoming. There are still some internal struggles about the nature of the new federation. An even more critical problem that has emerged is the tremendously increased financial difficulties being faced by the provincial organizations. This, in turn, has greatly affected the ability of the provincial organizations to support the national body. At this point, the national body is faced with serious financial problems, and once again a large amount of time at both the executive and the staff level is being utilized in the ongoing negotiations with provincial bodies and the search for a more secure financial base.

It is clear that the move to a federation structure for the C.A.S.W. mirrors to some extent issues that are taking place in other sectors of the country. In the latter days of the planning for federation, much time and effort was devoted to sorting out the responsibilities of the national group in relation to the provincial groups. Just as the federal-provincial struggle continues to take place in Canada, so too is it taking place in the C.A.S.W. Important as is this discussion for the future of the C.A.S.W., it is a further factor that diverts the national body from its commitment to social policy. Certainly, it can be argued that there are elements of social policy involved in the very question of who speaks for the profession and how this is reflected in the emerging new structure for the Association. Nevertheless, these kinds of professionally oriented social policy issues are distinct from the targets of concern of our professional endeavours and of a second-order social policy nature.

Just as there are differences in viewpoint about the structure of the professional association, so too are there differences within the profession about some very basic issues. Several times in this paper it has been argued that a nationally based professional organization should attempt to develop a platform and a long-range commitment to a particular cluster of social policies. This viewpoint implies the ability of the profession to develop a consensus on selected policy issues. At this point, like other professions, it is clear that there would be a wide range of viewpoints on social policy issues with the result that we might not be able to get consensus on some matters. For example, the recent experience of the C.A.S.W. on the abortion referendum clearly indicated that there was far from a clear viewpoint on this issue. Thus, some of our endeavours to develop positions on social policy matters become weakened or diverted in attempting to find a viewpoint from which we can speak with the full support of the board.

Certainly, one of the issues that appears in much professional interaction relates to the macro-micro thrust of the profession. As has been mentioned, there is much ongoing social policy discussion in our literature that reflects a viewpoint that social policy always refers to issues related to the larger system. There are also social policy issues that are more related to smaller systems, such as neighbourhood agency policies, school policies, and municipal government policies which are more micro system in nature.

Some of the struggles as to where the profession should devote the majority of its interest and thrust revolve around this question of micro versus macro systems and once again dissipate our interest and energies in dealing with this important issue.

A further problem that affects our potential in the social policy arena relates to some uncertainties we still have about the nature of social policy practice. Without doubt, apart from a very small percentage of the profession, many members of the profession lack the requisite knowledge and skill to be effective in the social policy area. Undoubtedly, there has always been a strong commitment to bring about changes in social policy at all levels for the benefit of the individuals, groups, and families and communities that we serve. But there has been considerable naivety about how such changes are brought about. In our profession, we have lacked the requisite amount of expertise in this area of practice. Indeed, the question is still not settled whether there is a legitimate practice stream for the social policy person. Some schools of social work have moved into social policy concentrations, but as yet there is uncertainty as to where such persons may best practice and how they can best use their knowledge and skills in the profession. Thus, some of the efforts at bringing about change could well have been counter-productive through a lack of adequate understanding of the socio-economic political climate in which we are sometimes operating in our search for changed policies.

A concomitant factor to the above-mentioned uncertainty and lack of experience is that as yet we do not have many members of the profession who have equipped themselves either through training or experience to function effectively in the social policy arena. There are many signs that this is changing as an increasing number of students and graduates are showing increased interest in this area of practice. It is hoped that both the profession and its educational arm will respond to this interest by devoting increasing attention to this need.

In summary, the position of this paper is that the C.A.S.W. as the organized agency of the social work profession maintains a high commitment to social policy activities. It has been active and continues to be active in this area. However, it is severely limited in achieving its full potential and effectiveness for a range of sociological, economic, political, and conceptual reasons. One can be both critical and/or enthusiastic at what the C.A.S.W. has accomplished to date, depending on one's expectations of a profession and the priorities it should set. My own viewpoint reflects that of Dr. Latimer[4] that indeed we should not be surprised at some of the problems the C.A.S.W. has encountered, but indeed we should be surprised at the amount that it has been able to accomplish in this area in view of the many difficulties and limitations it has faced over its history.

THE PROVINCIAL ASSOCIATIONS OF SOCIAL WORK

As mentioned in the introduction, the existence and functioning of the ten provincial and one territorial associations of social workers in Canada must also be addressed in examining the social policy role of the profession of social work in Canada. In addressing this phenomenon, the focus will be on an overview of these structures rather than attempting an analysis of each association's strengths and weaknesses, success or failure, assets or limitations in a social policy role.

Even slight familiarity with the Canadian panorama suggests that these various associations will differ in size, degree of organization, and availability of resources. Obviously, a major factor in this variation relates to the differences in membership bases of each organization. This, in turn, affects its potential fiscal base.

This point is exemplified by the fact that three provinces have full-time paid staff, several others have part-time professional staff, while in other provinces the entire membership consists of fewer than fifty colleagues. Nevertheless, there are similarities in the social policy activities of these organizations. Much of what was said about the national office is applicable to the provincial scene with the understanding that the size of the professional cadre will result in some differences. Thus, the various provincial associations carry the threefold role of innovator of social policy, information carrier of social policy issues, and responder to social policy concerns. In discharging these roles the various professional associations are in a position to speak for the entire profession in that province or territory free of agency or departmental ties. In addition, they can gather data and convey information; they can also provide briefs and lead delegations, and finally, they can communicate viewpoints both to their own members and to the public.

4   Latimer, "Social Action Behaviour" and "Social Action in a Professional Social Work Association."

As with the national body, heavy use is made of written communications by various provincial associations. For example, several provincial associations publish regular newsletters that are increasingly approaching the form of a professional journal. These serve as important vehicles for the exchange of policy views, the dispersion of information, and the lobbying for support.

Like the national association, our provincial associations also suffer a serious lack of the personnel and financial resources necessary to meet the many demands on a contemporary professional association. Thus, as with the national organization, potential effect in matters of social policies is seriously curtailed.

In addition to the similarities with the national association, the provincial association's responsibility in professional matters is an area of difference. Because of the British North America Act, policy questions related to practising of professions are provincial matters. Thus, such things as registration, licensing and various controls of title membership, private practice, relationship to other professions, and competence are issues of direct responsibility and concern of the provincial association.

Although one might argue that these are not social policy concerns in the sense in which the term is used in social work, they are areas of importance. In spite of the many criticisms that professional associations are only self-serving, there is a basic value commitment to the improvement of standards for the general well-being of the public. Because of the many questions and challenges to professional bodies in recent years, much of the time, effort, and interest of provincial associations has been tied up in the work with government and agencies on these matters.

A facet of this interest is reflected in the increasing numbers of legal or quasi-legal processes around professional matters. Thus, some of our provincial associations have been involved in litigation revolving around such matters as competence, licensing, and ethical issues. Although from a case-by-case viewpoint, these are not social policy matters, the way in which such situations are settled does contribute to the development of social policy. There is an interesting secondary gain for the professional association in their pursuit of these professionally oriented matters that has a direct relationship to larger social policy issues.

Earlier it was mentioned that there have been some elements of naivety in the way we, as a profession, have pursued social policy goals. However, the experience of different provinces in litigation cases, in seeking to alter legislation, or in introducing and seeking approval for licensing or registration has been a tremendous learning experience for the profession and its professional associations. Already these experiences have been helpful to us in learning to be more efficient, effective, understanding, and sensitive to the body politic and how to both work it and work within it to achieve identified social goals.

In comparing professional provincial associations with the national association, several advantages possessed by the provincial associations can be identified which may result in the provincial being more active and effective than the national organization in social policy formulation and influence. First, the provincial association is not dealing with as heterogeneous a situation, either internally or in relation to social welfare, as does a national association. It is thus able to concentrate its energies in a more focussed way. It is able to relate more directly to the issues, developments, and social systems where social policy action would ordinarily be expected. Hence, the gathering of information is more easily done. In addition, access to the persons, bodies, and systems one is trying to influence is more available. It is also easier to maintain direct contact with members except, of course, in the very large provinces where distance and regional differences are almost as critical as on the national scene.

Obviously, throughout a country like Canada, provincial associations will vary in form. But it is this variation that permits these associations to develop structures that best suit the situation and, in turn, strengthen the potential impact of the association on those activities in which it elects to embark.

Within the given regional differences and national variations, the provincial association is frequently in a position to have immediate and direct impact on many social welfare issues. Often the association has easy and ready access to all levels and branches of government in a more personal way than is possible on the national level. They can be quickly and sensitively effective in influencing shifting and emerging social policy trends. The provincial association can also be more personally significant to its members, again because of distance, but also because the provincial associations are usually dealing with issues much more directly related to the day-to-day practice concerns of its members than is often the case on the national level.

This latter point appears to result in more membership support for social action issues at the provincial level than is found nationally. Certainly, in the provincial association there is the possibility of more informed opinion, of co-operation and participation in policy-related projects and activities. At the risk of generalizing in a situation as complex as this, I think it can be said that the various provincial associations of social workers have been involved in a wider range of social policy issues than has been possible at the national level. But this is impressionistic and to document it would require careful gathering and examining of data.

Another strength of the provincial association, I think, stems from the potentially closer relationship between members. The fact that the membership can know a significant part of itself in a personal way and also can more readily take group action reduces the possibility that a few persons or groups will have a disproportionate influence or be put in a position of speaking inappropriately on behalf of the entire body.

A further social policy strength of provincial organizations is the extent to which they can call upon individual members. Since much of our social policy activity is related to the body politic, it is important that we keep in close contact with those of our colleagues whose total practice activities are related to the development of social policy, such as colleagues who practise in various ministries of the government. At the provincial level it is possible for social workers in various government ministries to work together closely, and it is also possible for such people to be involved in the professional association, thus enhancing the communication process. Thus, the professional association can at times be quickly knowledgeable about developments in social policy issues and can have easy access to processes involved in the formulation and altering of social policy through various government commissions, procedures, and the emergence of new legislation.

One of the clear differences presently existing between the C.A.S.W. and its provincial counterparts is that in the former case the C.A.S.W. is a federation of provincial associations, while provincial associations are built on an individual membership structure. Thus, one no longer is an individual member of the C.A.S.W. but is an individual member of the provincial association and that association is the member of the C.A.S.W.

Already it can be seen that in the new federation structure there is a lack of identification with the C.A.S.W. by many individuals. Thus, to an increasing extent the C.A.S.W. must depend on the goodwill of the provincial associations in seeking direct access to the membership. To date, there has not been sufficient experience with this factor to state clearly the effect of it on social policy questions, but it certainly is a factor to be carefully watched in the future.

BRANCH ORGANIZATIONS

In considering the function of provincial associations, it is important that some consideration be given to the social policy role of the branch organization. In virtually all of the provincial associations, there are formal subdivisions of the organization. These branches assume a variety of formats, sizes, and structures, and undoubtedly represent a greater degree of heterogeneity than between the associations themselves. In addition, these branches vary over time since the structure changes considerably as the constituency changes or as the branch becomes identified with current high interest topics. Thus, the branch is limited in its social policy activities because of the lack of a permanent structure and almost total lack of anything but token resources.

But there may well be some advantages to this lack of structure. At the branch level there is the greater possibility of prompt, effective, informed social action activity than at a provincial or national level. This is because of the high degree of identification and proximity that usually exists between branch members and the broad social welfare community. I think this frequently results in a blurring of the social policy activities of the branch with the social policy activities of the constituent parts of the social welfare system. Thus, an agency's social policy goals and activities are frequently so close to the goals of the local branch that it would be difficult to sort out the precise boundaries.

A particular way in which a local branch of a professional association can be useful in social action issues is in the data-gathering process. This is especially true when individual case examples or other quantitative or qualitative data are required to build or strengthen a position, to underscore a viewpoint, or to heighten awareness. In such cases the branch, through its members, is able to tap directly practice experiences in a relevant, practical, and prompt manner.

Although a branch is often first drawn into a social policy situation through a particular local event or dramatic situation, it nevertheless can bring influence to bear at a provincial or, indeed, at a national level related to the local issue. This is often true if the branch is in a position to do a careful and fully documented analysis. Too often such events remain at the local level and, incorrectly, become hotly contested interpersonal struggles that in the long run have little impact on social policy either at the local or wider levels, except perhaps to further entrench commitment to outdated or harmful policies.

Implied in the above is the strong viewpoint that the local branch of professional associations can and do have a significant and effective role to play in social policy. As with our observation about the national and provincial associations, the limitations of the regional branches must also be pointed out.

Certainly, the very uneven structure of local branches, both in time and place, precludes their being effective in social action matters in anything but a sporadic or short-term manner. Occasionally, it has happened that branches have taken on particular projects related to local developments or situations in a particular setting on a time-extended basis and have effectively altered present and future policy. But again, it is the lack of time and resources and, indeed occasionally, of ability, that can and does minimize their effectiveness.

One further advantage of the local branch of a professional association is its ability to influence the political process through direct lobbying with either the provincial or the federal members within its boundaries. We are becoming more sophisticated in our use of the body politic and thus the associations have been much more active in recent years in making direct contact with individual members of government through individual member contacts.

Thus, well organized branches of a provincial association are in a particularly sensitive position to influence significantly social policy issues in their area. This stems from the ability to unite the competence of a group of members to achieve a particular goal. The particular strength of the branch is that usually there is closer identification with some of the policy issues so that there is both the intellectual commitment to social policy development as well as the emotional investment in matters close at hand.

Although the activities of the local branch become very blurred with the activities of members of agencies, there is no doubt that one of the important roles played by our profession in its history has been our ability to bring about changes in agency policy, in municipal policy, and in national policy through the activities of small groups of practitioners at the grass-roots level.

THE INDIVIDUAL PRACTITIONER

The essence of this paper has been to examine the social work profession in its organized system. Nevertheless, in a discussion of social policy some comment must be made on the role of the individual member of the profession.

If we maintain the broadly defined concept of social policy as the setting of goals of social transaction in institutions serving human needs, then it is obvious that the individual who is a practising social worker can play a significant role. Such a role can take a variety of shapes on a day-to-day basis. For example, social workers can use their perceptions and observations about agency policy as viewed through their practice experiences as the basis for changing policy through both the formal and informal agency systems.

I think social work education of recent years has been able to instill into new graduates the conviction that they are able to influence the policies of the settings in which they work, and indeed have a responsibility to do so. Also, it is clear that agencies and helping systems are responsive to the need for ongoing evaluation of policies in the light of changing current demands. Such a responsiveness makes it more possible for individuals to influence policy change than was possible a few years ago.

Few, if any, social workers who are committed to their practice field and the individual, group, and community needs of their clients have not included in their practice activities efforts to alter and improve the objectives that underpin the services they offer. Sometimes these efforts have resulted in dramatic changes for some groups of clients through attitude changes or the development of new resources. At times, the efforts have resulted in slow and almost imperceptible shifts in attitudes and later of policy. These efforts can range from the senior civil servant at the national level striving to change policies and services for native peoples to the caseworker in a family agency striving to get support for commitments to service for a small group of single-parent families. Clearly, the whole process of the intricate network of social policy development that has resulted in our present spectrum of services has been influenced by the accumulated practice wisdom of our colleagues. Frequently, they are unaware that their involvement is the process of social policy development, but would only see themselves as carrying out their professional responsibility by expressing concern based on unimpeachable practice wisdom.

SUMMARY

In reviewing the above paper, it is obvious that the majority of it rests on assumptions and gratuitously asserted conclusions that could not stand the challenge of anyone who asked, "What is our evidence that social work has in fact influenced policy in a particular way and has not followed trends, rather than set them?" It is this type of challenge that makes it difficult to discuss the adequacy or lack thereof of our social policy activities. I am sure that throughout our whole profession's history we could find some who would claim credit for all social policies related to our field and others who decry our lack of interest, ability, and effectiveness. Where one emerges in this debate is partially influenced by one's attitude about the current social situation and the speed with which one hopes for or demands that change take place. This issue is particularly relevant at this time with the heavy emphasis on accountability and evaluation. On all sides we are required to demonstrate that what we are trying to do is important as well as showing that we are achieving what we are trying to do. Obviously, research into the effectiveness of social policy activities is difficult because of the myriad of influences both known and unknown that go into the decision-making processes involved in any change of objectives for social programmes, be they political or sociological. As in most fields of human endeavour, it is extremely difficult to utilize classical experimental models to develop and test hypotheses about the effectiveness or non-effectiveness of various professional strategies aimed at modifying policy. It is even more difficult to move into the area of attempting to assess the effectiveness of the policies themselves because of the strong component of value orientations in the setting and ordering of priorities of objectives, especially those related to the psycho-social well-being of man.

But even if we cannot at this time demonstrate in a statistically significant way that particular efforts resulted in particular outcomes, the emphasis on accountability has compelled us as a profession to move into our social policy activities from a "cause" base to a "function" base. We have also learned that we must not only establish strategies to achieve goals, but also that we must do a periodic re-assessment both of the goals and of the differential effectiveness of the strategies we employ. This stress on skill as well as commitment to social policy is of particular relevance to our professional organizations.

Thus, there is a strong responsibility for our organizations to act as both leader and resource in aiding individuals to make the most effective use of various techniques and procedures to achieve established goals. One way of discharging this responsibility would be for the various levels of the professional organizations to become clearing houses, data information centres, and consultants in social policy matters within their various capabilities and resources. We are now, and have long been, engaged in social policy formulation. The challenge of yet unmet societal demands is that we unite our commitment to change social policy with a commitment to improve our ability to assess the outcome of our actions.

CONCLUSION

The profession of social work emerged from an organized and common commitment to the twofold thrust of the provision of direct services and to the seeking and implementation of effective social policies. We have never ceased to be active in continuing our commitment to achieve socially desirable policies, services, and resources. Whether our activities in this area have been sufficient, well directed, effective, or relevant is a value question as well as a methodological challenge to which we must address ourselves. If we have learned anything it must be that commitment to a cause or to an activity is not sufficient. For us in the decade of the seventies to discharge adequately this long-standing commitment in the social policy field requires that we divert an increasingly large amount of our time, energy, resources, and personnel to constantly make use of our accumulated wisdom, our knowledge of intervention, our skills in intersystemic functioning, and our position in society to seek to develop, modify, and achieve the social policies to which we aspire for our clients and for our country.

Part IV

Social Policy Evaluation

Our final section explores the "measuring sticks" that might be used to assess the effectiveness of existing or planned implementation of social policy. Both the practical and theoretical implications of evaluative research are presented, as well as a strategy for viewing the evaluation itself.

The article stands by itself to emphasize the importance of giving a hard look (if not a purely scientific one) at social policy proposals—and to suggest to students just how they might go about doing this.

16

The Faith of the Evaluator: Issues in Evaluation of Social Welfare Policies, Programmes, and Services

MAURICE KELLY

In a situation where rising expectations confront limited resources available for the development of human services, decision-makers are looking for guidance to the social sciences. However, the scientists tend to find that

> evaluative research is an activity surrounded by serious obstacles. Satisfied with informal and impressionistic approaches to evaluation, policy-makers are often reluctant to make the investment needed to obtain verifiable data on the effects of their programs. Evaluative researchers are typically confronted with problems of measurement and design, which greatly restrict their ability to reach unambiguous conclusions. Abrasive relations with practitioners and clients can add to the evaluator's difficulties in obtaining information. Evaluative research is often addressed to a distressingly narrow range of issues, and results not fully or widely disclosed. At the same time, policy-makers often ignore highly pertinent findings of evaluative research. Little wonder that many social scientists regard evaluative research as a dubious enterprise.[1]

The present chapter aims to explore, within a Canadian context, some of the issues which emerge to test the "faith of the evaluator" as he seeks to use his skills in settings ranging from government department to local social service agency.

1 F. Caro, "Evaluation Research: An Overview," in *Readings in Evaluation Research*, ed. F. Caro (New York: Russell Sage Foundation, 1971), pp. 27-28.

RATIONALISM

In light of current commitment to goal-oriented rationality in policy and programme development, government interventions should supposedly be guided by clear identification of goals to be achieved, by logical specification of the means for achieving these goals, and by subsequent assessment of the degree of success achieved in meeting the goals. The motive is to reduce reliance upon the shifting interplay of various pressure groups in determining policy, the delicate balancing of interests through the political process, acting because "it seems like a good idea," in favour of an ethos of efficiency and effectiveness that enables "optimal deployment" of scarce resources to achieve "socially desirable" aims. Social decision-making should proceed from scientifically-gathered evidence rather than depending on faith or fad. The particular function of evaluation, then, is to acquire objective information to serve as a basis for selecting among alternative policies and programmes.

Commitment to this approach in North America over the past decade or so is but the latest round in the ongoing dialectic between rationalism and anti-intellectualism that has dominated Western intellectual history for centuries.[2] The tantalizing dream of "reform," of bridging the gap between what "is" and what "ought to be" through the power of reason aided by scientific inquiry, has clashed with understandings of men and society that questioned the validity of these hopes: philosophies variously identified as "scepticism," "romanticism," and the like.

Modern faith in progress, in the possibility of planned change for universal human betterment, in the primacy of reason in determining human behaviour, stemming from the eighteenth-century Enlightenment, may be contrasted with a contrary model of man in society which argues for the important influence of emotions, drives, and prejudices, whether consciously held or otherwise, in determing human behaviour. Freud, for one, saw reason as but the tip of the iceberg. Consequently, it would be unrealistic to rely on this faculty as a sure guide to problem solution. The sociologist Pareto would go further in arguing that there is an underlying equilibrium in society which is constantly being disturbed but constantly renewed *despite* the activities of planners and intellectuals. Rational, planned intervention is dangerous, as it may produce unpredictable, undesired effects. The ingrained habits of the human race are more useful to survival than the logic of reformers. The role of government, said the British writer Bagehot, is to enable discussion, hence to postpone action on seemingly serious problems, and so to allow time for the healing work of nature.

A contemporary anti-rationalist in the social welfare field argues that the practice of counselling, psycho-therapy, and the like are basically nonscientific, and may be successful precisely because they are so. Justification of personal therapy should not rest on measures of client change:

> The lurking and undeclared faith of the counsellor is that the concern which prompts him to act will overflow into the act, and will never completely fail if it

2   C. Brinton, *Ideas and Men* (New York: Prentice-Hall, 1950).

is sufficiently steeped in a person-to-person relationship between worker and helped. Neither failure nor success need be recognized by third parties . . . .[3]

It is in the context of these intellectual and social currents that the contemporary thrust toward systematic evaluation of welfare policies, programmes and services may appropriately be understood. Manifestations of the thrust are numerous and well known. One thinks of programme control mechanisms such as Planned Program Budgeting Systems (P.P.B.S.) and Program Evaluation Review Techniques (P.E.R.T.), of the emergence of the "value-free" technocrat in government, and of the current explosion of books and articles on evaluation strategies and methodology. The seeming triumph of rationalism, however, is often frustrated. Programme and policy evaluations are technically difficult to conduct in the face of administrator resistance; the findings are not always acted on; the waste and self-deception tend to continue unhindered.

EVALUATION AND POLICY-MAKING

"Evaluation" is intended here to refer to all of those systematic activities which purport to assess the state or functioning of a segment of society, whether or not the assessment has been preceded by some form of planned intervention, and whether or not this assessment is expressed in quantitative form. This definition is broader than that of Suchman, "the determination . . . of the result . . . attained by some activity . . . designed to accomplish some valued goals or objectives,"[14] inasmuch as some form of objective determination of the actual state of affairs with respect to a supposed social problem area *prior* to intervention is—in theory—an essential aspect of social planning, and hence is included here.

Two major types of issues may be distinguished with reference to the evaluation of social welfare policies, programmes, and services: issues of a methodological nature, and issues related to the "politics" or "strategies" of evaluation. Methodological questions know no frontiers, and are already well treated in the growing United States literature in this field. The focus here, rather, is on political/strategic questions, drawing particularly on the limited Canadian material on hand: what factors influence or determine the relationship between evaluative research activities and policy and programme decision-making structures?

Social policy design and implementation is often conceived as an essentially linear progression from goals through policies to programme to consequences. Research inputs may be required at various points in this continuum, as indicated in the following diagram. The present paper aims to describe these "input-points" and to identify contingent factors that tend to distort the supposedly linear research-policy relationship at each level.

3   P. Halmos, *The Faith of the Counsellors* (London: Constable, 1966), pp. 149-50.
4   E. Suchman, *Evaluation Research* (New York: Russell Sage Foundation, 1968), pp. 21-32.

A MODEL OF THE RELATIONSHIP BETWEEN EVALUATIVE RESEARCH AND
POLICY/PROGRAMME DEVELOPMENT

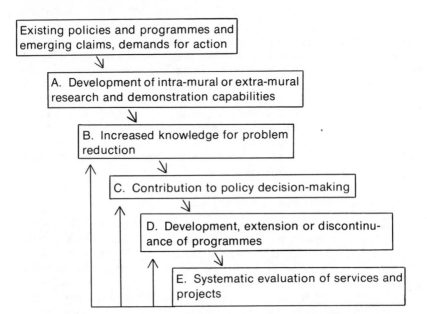

A. Development of Research and Demonstration Capabilities

Government response to emerging, and often competing, claims upon the public exchequer, and to demands for "action," is typically to develop pools of technical expertise, both within and outside the public service. Experts can be expected to provide detailed information and practical wisdom concerning specific topics of interest upon demand. They may also be called upon to generate new knowledge in support of both long-range and short-term planning and policy development through the development of various research and demonstration activities. Such activities may consist of systematic, if routine, monitoring and data collection, or of various types of empirical enquiry.

Various methods are used to structure and/or facilitate the production of empirical data and analysis by federal and provincial government departments. Here we briefly consider apparent merits and disadvantages of: (1) full-time intra-departmental research branches; (2) contract research to external experts; (3) research institutes/units affiliated with one government department or with a single large programme; and (4) directed external grants programmes.

(1) Most of the federal departments have now established in-house policy planning and/or research branches, with the aim of providing analytical and informational back-up for policy decision-making. A typical statement of objectives:

The Policy Planning Branch develops urban policies for the federal government. Using analytical information from many sources and information flowing to and from various levels of government, citizens, and other sources, it will:
– develop federal urban policy objectives;
– suggest how such objectives might be most effectively attained;
– systematically evaluate federal activities to see whether they are consistent with real urban priorities in Canada. . . .

    The Research Branch . . . will attempt to accelerate understanding of urban systems in Canada . . . concentrate on analyzing the not well understood but nonetheless real interdependence between such major elements as transportation, land use . . . ; conduct its own extensive research work. . . . [The] findings will be translated into models capable of being tested, so that the consequences of alternative policies can be tried out before significant new policies are proposed. . . .[5]

(Other research activities planned by this Department included an external research programme and an information and data systems division.)

    Characteristically, however, the in-house research branch encounters a variety of hazards. It may become overoccupied with non-research activities, such as contributing to the Minister's speeches, answering public inquiries, and drafting Cabinet documents. There may be difficulty in retaining qualified staff, or in reserving blocks of staff time to meet unpredictable demands emanating from higher levels of the system. Evaluative-type activities, in particular, may require considerable lead time to mount and complete, whereas the demand for answers to specific pressing questions is usually immediate. A further limitation is that considerations of inter- and intra-departmental rivalries frequently influence the nature of assignments to a research branch. Sometimes an implicit aim of upholding the prestige, and hence relative influence, of the particular administrative unit becomes as important as the production of information for outside use. Factors such as these may limit the capacity of in-house research units to conduct more than relatively routine data-gathering activities, despite the lofty initial statements of purpose.

    (2) The use of the research contract is a well-recognized method used by government departments and branches to accomplish discrete tasks in relatively short time periods. Such tasks appear to lend themselves to precise definition more frequently at the programme and project level, for example, in the form of project evaluation studies. In favour of the contract approach is the relatively high degree of control which it provides to the administrator or policy-maker, although the pace of varying demands within the department sometimes tends to make the resulting reports irrelevant. "Front burner" concerns rapidly become displaced by other, yet more pressing, substantive issues, and the reports do not get the attention which they often merit.

    One difficulty is that the senior administrators themselves often do not know what the problem is, and consequently may have considerable trouble in communicating their informational needs to researchers. Thus, a

5 Canada, Ministry of State for Urban Affairs, *A Living Place* (Ottawa, n.d.).

question may arise in the course of intra-departmental discussion as to the relative contribution being made to the needs of certain disadvantaged groups by a given group of voluntary organizations. As the question is important in determining the department's future posture toward these organizations, particularly as they may later seek direct financial support, the decision may be made to contract for an independent study. With some difficulty, a social scientist is located who is not only willing and able to conduct a study upon short notice, but also appears to be knowledgeable with reference to the methodological and political issues involved. The question is then asked, "What is it, exactly, that you want to know?" Even an exploratory study requires a reasonably clear focus, and only to instruct the researcher to "assess the impact" of the respective entities is manifestly inadequate. "Assess the impact" in terms of what? However, the policy-maker is really only looking for clues; basically he seeks a global impression of the activities of the organization and is often fuzzy as to the actual criteria of effectiveness which may be relevant in the particular case.

(3) The affiliated research institute has theoretical advantages over the in-house research branch for developing and retaining technical expertise, for pursuing a selected research "mission" and mounting appropriate large-scale policy research projects, and for sustaining varying degrees of objectivity concerning the findings of such projects. In Canada we may point to the research units attached to the New Start programmes (Nova Scotia, Saskatchewan), which sought to conceptualize the nature of poverty and other characteristics of their target groups as well as to devise evaluation methodologies for their particular programmes. The former Human Resources Research Council (Alberta) was similar in its objective of mounting and/or funding studies on a wide range of actual and anticipated social problems at the provincial level.

A number of shortcomings to this approach to the promotion of policy research have been suggested, notably the relatively high costs ($100,000 per year for core expenses would probably be a modest figure), and the difficulties of maintaining relevance of the research endeavour to informational needs of decision-makers. (Indeed, the administration of such research units tends to become a subspecialty of its own.)[6]

(4) A few government departments and agencies are beginning to seek the advantage of concentrated thrusts of inquiry into designated areas, while avoiding the heavy costs, through the use of mission-oriented external grants programmes. Current examples are the Federal Department of Indian and Northern Affairs, the Central Mortgage and Housing Corporation, and the Canadian Council of Urban and Regional Research (which, however, could probably be described as quasi-autonomous in relation to government). Key areas of concern ("missions") are identified periodically by the respective officials (and/or by advisory councils), research grants applications in these areas are solicited from the academic community, and

6   R. Wiener and J. Bayley, "The Administration and Evaluation of Research Units and Projects," *British Journal of Sociology* 22 (1971): 193-99.

subsequently research findings are received. Varying arrangements or requirements are made for dissemination of the final reports, including provision of supplementary assistance for publication.

Whatever structure is used, a recurring problem is that research and demonstration activities of all kinds tend to be supported and/or contracted for which have no potential for immediate or even long-range pay-off. "Just gathering dust on the library shelf" is a common complaint. We observe the

> proliferation of research addressed to vague questions; the multiplications of inquiries about clear, but trivial questions; and the subsidy of research in which the question and the answers may be clear, but where no policy is at hand to respond to the finds. Since no one with the power to act knows why the questions were asked, or necessarily agrees with the reasons for their having been asked, there is no one to act upon the answers.[7]

Even mission-oriented grants programmes appear not to have solved this problem. One writer suggests that a test of relevance be applied before funding any study intended to be addressed to current policy concerns. The researcher should be asked to imagine the possible outcomes of his proposed inquiry, then to "consider the difficult and important question of what difference each of these potential outcomes will make with regard to the problem under consideration." How would validation or rejection of the given hypothesis, for example, affect policy considerations? If this question could not be answered satisfactorily, the inquiry should not be undertaken.[8]

A preliminary conclusion is that government can be successful in recruiting technical experts from a wide range of disciplines to feed information and advice into the internal decision-making streams; however, the development of mechanisms to generate and actually use new empirical evaluation data appears as yet to be only partly successful.

B. Increased Knowledge for Problem-Reduction

The generating of knowledge relevant to practical problems at hand is normally assumed to increase problem-reduction capability and hence to provide useful guides for action. This assumption presupposes that the information can provide answers to the "right kinds" of questions.

At least two levels of impact of evaluative information upon policy-making can be specified: (a) assessment of a current situation, as a basis for planning new policies and programmes; and (b) assessment of the extent to which a given policy or programme is meeting its objectives, as a basis for reaching decisions concerning its future development.

(a) "Assessment of the current situation" refers to disciplined inquiry into attitudes or other factors seemingly associated with social behaviour

---

7 I. Nettler, "Knowing and Doing," paper presented to the Conference on Social Science Research and Social Policy, Human Resources Research Council, Edmonton, February 1971.

8 D. Larsen, "Research and Policy: Creative Opportunities and Practical Constraints," paper presented to the Conference on Social Science Research and Social Policy, Human Resources Research Council, Edmonton, February 1971.

deemed problematic (whether as putative causes or effects). It is assumed that the study of the various factors will provide a definitive basis for policy recommendations. As one example, federal response to the drug abuse issue was to establish a Commission of Inquiry (the Ledain Commission), which through research and sounding of opinion was to arrive at a definitive and defensible policy on the question. This proved to be a time-consuming effort, in which deeply-held values (prejudices?) combined with the difficulty of obtaining hard data to produce what might be considered as an equivocal result. Part of the problem in such situations is that "When social scientists are asked to measure consequences in terms of badly conceptualized or hard-to-measure 'effects' of one among many highly inter-related 'causes,' all of which operate (if at all) over long periods of time, they tend to discover that there is no relationship or at best a weak or contingent one."[9]

The use of Royal Commissions and the like may, however, often serve the latent function of justifying inactivity—hopefully until the problem loses its initial urgency, and compromises at the political level become feasible. Recent proposals regarding the use of marijuana appear to reflect this process. The contribution made by the Commission's research activities *per se* is hard to determine at this time.

(b)　Assessment of the extent to which a policy or programme is meeting its objectives obviously presupposes clear formulation of such objectives; however, decisions to establish government programmes characteristically result from compromise, from concealment of differing goals through vagueness, from a general need to reconcile divergent interests both within and outside of government while offending as few groups as possible. In the absence of a clear, definable set of objectives to be achieved, there can be no explicit set of criteria laid down for programme evaluation (in the sense of outcome or "impact"). The problem is well illustrated in an evaluation report on the Opportunities for Youth programme, where the characteristic ambiguities of political thinking were quite evident. Study of background documents from this $57.2 million programme (as of 1971) indicated three major goals that were sought to be achieved simultaneously through creation of the programme:

(i)　provide summer jobs for students and thereby significantly reduce their unemployment levels;

(ii)　provide students with opportunities for participation in "meaningful" activities, and thereby reduce the likelihood of social unrest during the summer months; and

(iii)　promote national unity.[10]

We observe that these objectives are likely to be mutually incompatible (for example, to maximize student placement in jobs—of any kind—may conflict with the provision of "meaningful" experiences). Further, such objectives may defy operational definition (for example, what are meant

9　Ibid.
10　Canada, Department of the Secretary of State, *Report of the Evaluation Task Force to the Secretary of State: Opportunities for Youth '71* (Ottawa, 1972).

precisely by "participation," "meaningful," and "national unity"?). Such questions are not purely academic, inasmuch as programme goals-should serve to guide not only outcome studies, but also the selection and rejection of project applications. In the absence of clear guidelines, rule of thumb, subjective, and seemingly arbitrary criteria had often to be used by programme officials in winnowing through the many thousands of often excellent proposals submitted annually by expectant students across the country.

Vague statements of programme objectives make for difficulties in generating the type of evaluative information needed by policy-makers faced with important practical questions, such as, for example, "Should Opportunities for Youth be continued, amended, or discontinued?" In this type of situation, the social scientists would say, almost any type of programme can be justified.

C. Contribution to Policy Decision-making

It is normally assumed that increased problem-solving capability, in the form of information appropriately derived and transmitted, will become a major input into policy decision-making. The ethos of goal-directed rationality virtually presupposes that decisions regarding deployment of resources (inauguration, amendment, or cessation of programmes and projects) be made according to scientific criteria.

> The basic rationale for evaluation is that it provides information for action. The primary justification is that it contributes to the rationalization of decision-making. Although it serves such other functions as knowledge-building and theory testing, unless it gains serious hearing when programme decisions are made, it fails in its major purpose.[11]

And yet, such is frequently not the case. Experience reveals that

> The development of policy is typically not a straight question and answer, challenge and response operation, but a much more iterative, drawn-out and interactive process—where, for example, answers sometimes precede questions. It would be nice if policy problems invariably manifested themselves clearly through internal and external information media and through parliament, which decision-makers converted into well formulated question, and if research people then came up with firm answers capable of immediate policy application. Unfortunately it rarely happens that way. The problem may not have been accurately identified in the first instance, the question may be vaguely formulated and the research people may disagree with the question, both because they think it is the wrong question and because in any case their data and techniques only permit them to answer properly some other question.

In fact, "The results of formal research in the social sciences are only one of a number of major informational streams flowing into the decision-making process, the relationship between the various streams being in some degree competitive."[12]

11 D. L. McQueen, "The Modes of Feeding Research into Policy," paper presented to the Conference on Social Science Research and Social Policy, Human Resources Research Council, Edmonton, February 1971.
12 Ibid.

Experience indicates that empirical inquiry may often follow, rather than precede, policy decision-making. A case in point was the major decision taken in 1970 to establish a national Family Planning programme. This decision was taken in response to the prompting of various interest groups, but without benefit of empirical data concerning Canadian fertility patterns that might have helped to define population groups in particular need of information, contraceptive devices, and the like, or data concerning the expressed wishes of such groups. Subsequently, a non-directed external grants programme was established for research, demonstration, training, and direct service, funded in 1974-75 at $1,750,000. Judging by falling birth rates across the country, however, it would appear that the great majority of Canadians already were able to limit their fertility; consequently, it seems that this "shot-gun" approach was really needed only to avoid any hint that a national population policy was being developed. (What might be the greater problem, moreover—the relatively high cost to lower-income families of commercially-available contraceptive devices—has apparently yet to be investigated systematically or even commented on officially.) This national programme, then, well exemplifies the frequent situation where political need and "seat-of-the-pants" reasoning form the major inputs into policy-making, rather than the results of preliminary empirical study.

As another example, consider the Seebohm Committee which was established to gather evidence on the need for social services in England, and to formulate recommendations to the the government for the strengthening of these services. It has been noted[13] that this Committee failed to undertake systematic research—especially as to the opinion of service users—despite the strong previous recommendation to this effect by the Younghusband Committee. This failure to conduct adequate empirical inquiries may have been partly necessitated by the time frame involved; however, it is interesting that the British government was willing to act on the ensuing report without benefit of such data.

Moreover, research findings which purport to assess the present situation with respect to a given social problem may, in some instances, be rejected. A current example (again) is the federal government's unwillingness to fully legalize the use of marijuana despite the lack of clear evidence (to date, at least) that such use is genuinely injurious to individual health. This unwillingness reflects a pragmatic political understanding of the temper of our times which goes beyond the researcher's horizons.

The contribution of research (particularly empirical studies) to policy-making is strongly affected also by existing patterns of communication within the system. Clearly, it is insufficient for the committed researcher merely to present his report to the decision-makers and gracefully withdraw; indeed, it is now being argued that the process whereby findings can be communicated in ways most likely to produce appropriate changes in habits and attitudes should itself become the subject of research. It has been suggested that "research utilization [is] a psychosocial process in-

---

13 P. Townsend, "The Objectives of the New Local Social Service," in *The Fifth Social Service: A Critical Analysis of the Seebohm Proposals* (London: Fabian Society, 1970), pp. 7-22.

volving a dynamic interaction of specific systems which behave at least in a partially predictable manner."[14] Five specific steps may be identified in the utilization process (results dissemination, information reception, conceptual comprehension, psycho-social acceptance, and internalized assimilation) and each could warrant investigation. There is an apparent need for *ongoing* communication between researchers and practitioner/ policy-makers, and for training in research utilization for both groups. Specific problems in communication may arise because:

(i) The written report may be badly written, with poor arrangement of the material, with excessive use of jargon words, and with lack of discussion of implications in terms relevant to the concerns of the programme being evaluated. Some writers recommend, with respect to the latter point, that final reports not be based solely on the researchers' analysis of the data. Persons at all levels of management should be asked to help the researchers to interpret the findings and to provide the focus which they need. In this way the interpretations emerging from the data become those of the officials and staff rather than of the researchers exclusively. Consequently, the findings should be more likely to have a constructive impact.[15]

(ii) Occasionally, differences in intellectual orientation (e.g., differing definitions of problems) impede effective communication of research results. A case can probably be made for the desirability of establishing the position of liaison person to play a go-between role. Two models come to mind here. We think of the successful "ag-rep" whom farmers come to trust as a result of the valid technical advice which he has given them over the years. Alternatively, we may consider the liaison person as a travelling salesman who seeks to "sell" new research and demonstration findings to service agencies for them to implement. In either case, the aim would be to develop the kind of interpersonal trust that facilitates teaching and learning. This person would be neither a researcher nor a policy-maker, but he has learned to get along well with both.

In general, there appears to be little evidence that Canadian social science research has yet had an important impact on the development of social policy. A similar conclusion was reached regarding the relationship between economic research and economic policy,[16] and in view of the superior theory and data bases of the latter discipline, the argument should certainly hold in the case of other social sciences. The potential influence of evaluative findings, in particular, upon social welfare policy decisions may be limited by competition from other informational streams, by broader political considerations, and by barriers to effective communication of findings from researchers to policy-makers.

14 G. Goldin et al., *The Utilization of Rehabilitation Research*, Monograph No. 6 (Boston: Northeastern University, 1969).
15 F. Mann and R. Likert, "The Need for Research on the Communication of Research Results," in *Readings in Evaluation Research*, ed. F. Caro (New York: Russell Sage Foundation, 1971), pp. 143-51, and E. Suchman, "Action for What? A Critique of Evaluative Research," in *Evaluating Social Action Programs*, ed. C. Weiss (Boston: Allyn & Bacon, 1972), pp. 52-84.
16 D. Slater, "Economic Policy and Economic Research in Canada since 1950," *Queen's Quarterly* 74, no. 1 (1967): 1-20.

D. Development/Extension/Discontinuance of Programmes

The influence of evaluation research findings upon policy may be expected to find expression in decisions to develop, extend, or discontinue specific programmes. In theory, given a consensus regarding policy goals, and following upon objective determination of optimally-efficient and/or effective means of achieving these goals, implementation of policy decisions in terms of goal-related programme activities should easily follow. However, such is frequently not the case—whether for technical or for political reasons.

Apart from methodological difficulties inherent in attempting to assess the impacts of a whole programme, the typical aforementioned absence of clear programme goals frequently necessitates reliance on subjective approaches. Such approaches are criticized as tending to reflect the pre-existing biases of the evaluator, buttressed perhaps by opinions of selected informants. (This criticism is particularly salient in the case of evaluation reports prepared by external research contractors: who would knowingly bite the hand that feeds?).

Personal observation suggests that weakness in definition of programme objectives is a common characteristic of Canadian federal external grants programmes in particular. Apart from the minority of "directed" research programmes, such as those described previously, it is rare to find, whether in the official programme manuals or in statements by the respective programme officers, genuinely clear perceptions of programme goals presented in operational terms. Perhaps in consequence, there tends to be continued rumination among officials about defining "priorities" as a basis for selection of types of projects to be funded. This matter of priorities is not a problem in the context of a purely laissez-faire approach: "We'll fund virtually anything that appears to be feasible and methodologically sound." However, when concerns emerge for greater programme "impact," a more focussed approach comes to be required—a requirement difficult to satisfy in the absence of clear goal statements to start with.

In fact, it may be quite unrealistic to effect adequate assessments of programme impact, in the sense defined here. With some possible exceptions, tacit Canadian policy objectives in establishing "demonstration" self-help programmes, for example, were not really the testing of theories, or the production and dissemination of new knowledge for improving social service delivery and facilitating citizen-participation; rather, one important aim seems to have been to head off social dissent by harnessing the energies of "indigenous" leaders in a variety of self-selected social development activities (see Opportunities for Youth objectives above, for example). Hopefully, these activities would also prove to be socially useful; however, the motivation to assess such usefulness has come more recently, as part of what appears to be a conservative reaction against the "participation" ethos of the late sixties.

At the "political" level of programme evaluation, a number of factors come into play. A frequent observation, for example, is the failure of programme administrators to devote sufficient supplies of personnel and money to the tasks of self-assessment—whether this be in the form of management information systems, or in terms of project funding policies that permit and require adequate evaluative procedures to be followed. An extensive American study concluded (as of 1970):

> The most impressive finding about the evaluation of social programs in the federal government is that substantial work in this field has been almost non-existent. Few significant studies have been undertaken. Most of those carried out have been poorly conceived . . . .[17]

Additionally, the saliency of research into programme outcomes or effectiveness may be exposed to a process that Weiss has called "politicization." She notes the pressure on evaluators, from both the operating agency and perhaps also the government funding body, "to vindicate the program" and sometimes to make unwarranted leaps from data to recommendations. Findings that show no effect tend to be ignored or criticized on methodological grounds. The evaluation process itself may be abandoned, rather than allowing it to endanger the life of a particular programme. Due to the financial implications that hang increasingly upon project and programme evaluations, the possibilities for valid and useful studies of this type become more difficult.[18]

E. Evaluation of Individual Social Welfare Services and Projects

Here we are concerned with evaluation of individual services and projects administered or funded by government programmes or voluntary organizations. For this purpose it is helpful to distinguish demonstration projects from established services, in view of the particular methodological problems posed by evaluation of the former type of activity. There has been a considerable thrust in Canada (as also in the U.S.A.) over the past decade or so toward the encouragement of citizen involvement in the creation, operation, and encouragement of various welfare-related projects through the mechanism of external grant programmes.[19]

Many of the anticipated benefits and the problems associated with formal evaluative studies which were detailed above in relation to policy development and programmes apply equally at the level of these individual services and projects. One writer summarizes the benefits to be anticipated in relation to evaluations of the former American Community Action Projects as: (a) accounting to government for the uses made of public funds; (b) feeding back findings from the projects for use in policy development/planning; (c) disseminating results to promote their use by other authorities; (d) contributing to theory in the sense that projects represented tests of implicit if not explicit theories about people in society and

17   J. Wholey et al., *Federal Evaluation Policy* (Washington: The Urban Institute, 1970).

18   C. Weiss, "The Politicization of Evaluative Research," *Journal of Social Issues* 26, no. 4 (1970): 57-68.

19   Within the Department of National Health and Welfare, for example, the following external grants programmes were budgeted in total at approximately $20 million for the fiscal year 1974-75: Family Planning, National Welfare Grants, New Horizons, Non-Medical Use of Drugs. See Canada, Department of Finance, *Estimates for the Fiscal Year 1974-75* (Ottawa, 1973). This figure included grants to established organizations for research, training, and the like; however, it is probable that one-half of this figure was devoted to citizen action projects *per se.*

the possibilities of change. This idealistic research perspective (published in 1964, just as the American "War on Poverty" was getting under way) has a naive quality today, in the light of the many problems encountered by the Community Action Projects in seeking to achieve and to demonstrate some impact on intractable social problems. These difficulties have been described at length in the literature; however, it is useful to summarize them here and to add what Canadian impressions may be available in the public domain.

Inasmuch as the various citizen self-help programmes, and the projects funded under these programmes, have been intended to be short-lived, to serve perhaps as sparkplugs for activities that would hopefully find other sources of funding in due course, it has been natural to employ the evaluational rhetoric of "demonstration." In the case of the National Welfare Grants programme, for example, demonstration project applicants are expected to phrase their objectives in terms of "demonstrating new means" of delivering a specific service or of "testing a new method" of helping certain disadvantaged groups to help themselves with respect to exercising rights, acquiring resources, and the like. Where constitutionally-defined jurisdictional boundaries may be infringed on, as in the case of welfare and health projects, the short-term demonstration concept is a particularly useful rubric for justifying federal involvement. However, output of scientifically adequate evaluations of Canadian self-help projects has been low. For example, we appear to know—in a formal sense—little more now than we did ten years ago about the conditions under which planned change activities by citizen self-help groups are likely to be successful.

"ELITIST" AND "DEMOCRATIC" PLANNING

The elitist planning model implicitly underlying this paper may be contrasted with democratic models which envisage a maximum of popular participation in the formulation of policies and the evaluation of programmes and projects. Technical discourse among social scientists and administrators or officials is seen in the ideology of participation to be less relevant than the concerted expression of citizen sentiment on issues of public concern. Where the drive to promote social change clashes with canons of scientific inquiry, the latter may have to be sacrificed.

As a case in point, the absence of strictly measured, or measurable, project outcomes may be lauded, rather than condemned. Some evaluators who are particularly sympathetic to the needs and aspirations of socially alienated peoples argue for assessments of external grants projects which are based upon an essentially subjective understanding of the respective situations. Techniques of participant observation and interviews with key informants, supplemented by conceptual analysis, seek to draw out the meaning of the project activities to the persons involved as they themselves see it. The choice of variables to be observed in this view is ultimately a political process (as, indeed, is the choice of the evaluator). The familiar argument that measurement taps only micro-level phenomena, or "trivia," is also advanced. A refinement of this viewpoint sees the research process itself as a community development technique: either the findings are considered to be less important to the community than the activities which produced them, or the findings are deemed to be of primary importance to the self-development of the people under study rather than to the needs of the funding body. In either case, it is argued, a raising of social consciousness is—or ought to be—the true aim of evaluative studies of citizen groups. At the very least, the true role of project and programme evaluation should be to enable citizens to maintain a watchdog role over government departments (rather than, in effect, vice versa).

Arguments such as these do not command support among professionals and administrators committed to a rationalist stance toward planning, due to the strong possibility of subjective bias in research reports of this type. Consequently, proponents of greater citizen involvement, who point to the lack of structured machinery for facilitating participation of minority and self-help groups in the policy process, are hampered in gaining acceptance for their views by the unacceptability to the orthodox planners of their techniques. Badly needed now are methods to generate and channel public sentiment on key issues in ways that satisfy the current rationalist-scientific ethos.

Beginnings are seen in the work of social reformers, such as Ralph Nader, who seek to influence policy through the impact of their objective research findings upon the general public. This approach may satisfy the technical criteria of evaluative research; however, the true aim of the reformers is to promote change through confrontation of divergent interest groups, rather than to pursue the consensus route implicitly favoured by the majority of researchers.

TECHNICAL PROBLEMS OF EVALUATING DEMONSTRATION PROJECTS, IN SUMMARY

A number of general technical problems inherent, from a government perspective, in evaluating demonstration or other citizen self-help projects can be summarized:

(a) The *de facto* objectives are typically imprecise, or they may change frequently during the life of the project, with the result that satisfactory goal-attainment criteria are extremely difficult to identify;

(b) The nature of the project or service itself may be vague, and may differ considerably from the "paper" description which originally secured the funding;

(c) It is generally impossible to use the classical "control" or "comparison" group to assess impact;

(d) In any event, the evaluator is—more often than not—called in toward the end of the life of the project in response to the funder's demands. He has, therefore, to rely primarily on retrospective data and subjective impressions of a variety of informants upon which to base his report;

(e) Frequently, the "data" is in any case incomplete even with respect to project activities undertaken, the numbers and the characteristics of those persons served, and the like, before even considering how to measure outcomes;

(f) Potential role strains between evaluator and project director may be averted by the director using the evaluator as a kind of consultant. This may be at considerable risk, however, to the latter's capacity subsequently to produce an objective report for the use of the funding body.

EVALUATION OF ESTABLISHED SOCIAL SERVICES

By comparison with demonstration or self-help projects, evaluation of established social services, while frequently difficult, tends at least to be more feasible. Here, ongoing service goals are often found to have stabilized and to be capable of fairly clear definition. It may be possible to persuade the staff to implement and adhere to methodologically respectable research designs and data-gathering techniques. It may be feasible to secure at least some "hard" measurements. There may be hope that the findings can and will find expression in organizational changes.[20]

Role strains between evaluator and professional practitioner may, however, be unavoidable. The practitioner fears exposure of real or imaginary inadequacies, and he may also anticipate threats to his professional convictions and to his personal commitments to a given programme, if he takes the evaluation reports seriously.[21] Again, the need for interpreter or liaison person may be indicated.

When evaluation reports on agency projects and programmes fail to show desired changes in terms of expected outcome, a variety of responses may come into play. A fairly common pattern among social welfare practitioners has been to ignore negative findings altogether. Proceeding from the anti-intellectual stance described above, these practitioners have often preferred to continue in their reliance on faith and confidence in the old ways. Alternatively, they may place strong reliance on an emergent method of practice which is ideologically acceptable, but without seeing any need for empirical verification. Briar[22] commented that Virginia Satir's family therapy, for example, had come to enjoy strong, unquestioning professional and funding support without any adequate evaluative confirmation of its value ever having been published (as of 1971). The recent emergence, however, of a more sophisticated response pattern among social work professionals is reflected in attempts to meet the negative research findings head-on, for example, in responsible criticism of validity or reliability of studies (e.g., MacDonald's assessment[23] of the report "Girls at Vocational High"[24]).

---

20 For one example among a number of Canadian studies that could be cited, see G. Speers and M. Kelly, "A Behavioural Approach to Preventtion in Child Welfare," *The Social Worker* 42, no. 1 (Spring 1974): 64-74. The favourable outcomes reported in this pilot project evaluation study contributed to legitimation of the project within the agency's ongoing programme.

21 H. Rodman and R. Kolodny, "Organizational Strains in the Researcher-Practitioner Relationship," *Human Organization* 23 (1964): 171-82.

22 Scott Briar, "Family Services and Casework," in *Research in the Social Services*, ed. H. Maas (New York: N.A.S.W., 1971), p. 115.

23 M. MacDonald, "Reunion at Vocational High: An Analysis of Girls at Vocational High: An Experiment in Social Work Intervention," *Social Service Review* 40, no. 2 (June 1966): 175-89.

24 H. J. Meyer, E. F. Borgatta, and W. C. Jones, *Girls at Vocational High: An Experiment in Social Work Intervention* (New York: Russell Sage, 1965).

SYSTEM MODEL EVALUATIONS

Outcomes or goal-attainment evaluation—i.e., studies that seek to determine the degree to which service or programme objectives have been achieved, through comparison of before and after measures of various aspects of client functioning or attitudes—may fail, as noted above, because the service or programme objectives had never been clearly articulated. Alternatively, this type of evaluation may fail owing to insensitivity of the measures themselves or because the time span over which measures were taken was too small realistically to allow much change to have occurred. In either case, the narrow focus upon outcomes cannot encompass either other goals being sought by the organization or the internal dynamics of the situation which could be contributing differentially to the doubtful results. Consequently, a broader evaluation model may be deemed more appropriate and more useful to administrators and planners.

Of particular interest in this context is the system model, which focusses on four essential tasks of any organization: "the achievement of goals and sub-goals; the effective coordination of organizational sub-units; the acquisition and maintenance of necessary resources; and the adaptation of the organization to the environment and to its own internal demands."[25]

Through the use of information feedback mechanisms,

> the effect of the actions of the sub-units within the system are reported and compared . . . the system model approach is designed to yield information about the various components of an organization as it implements the program being evaluated. [Also] by evaluating several units carrying out the same program, *relative* effectiveness can be compared from one unit to another . . . .[26]

A particular project may largely have failed in terms of goal achievement, yet in other terms have been successful—for example, in stimulating staff morale to undertake new experiments, in promoting better public understanding of the needs of certain disadvantaged groups, and even in the sense that its poor outcome may nevertheless have been superior to that of competing programmes.

OTHER VIEWS

It could be argued, however, that much current thinking in this field reflects a simplistic understanding, both of the processes of policy development and of the limitations of social scientific knowledge and method. New models of the interrelationship between science and policy are needed to help researchers develop feasible goals, while assuring that public decision-making can become at least one step removed from purely *ad hoc* responsiveness.

Implicit in most local area social planning studies of recent years, for example, has been an assumption that through systematic study, clarifica-

---

25 H. Schulberg and F. Baker, "Program Evaluation Models and the Implementation of Research Findings," *American Journal of Public Health* 58, no. 7 (1968): 1248-55.

26 N. Carter and B. Wharf, *Evaluating Social Development Programs* (Ottawa: Canadian Council on Social Development, 1973). Also see P. Levinson, "Evaluation of Social Welfare Programs, Two Research Models," *Welfare in Review* 4 (1966): 5-12.

tion of confused thinking, and patient negotiation, it is possible to develop a rational and comprehensive social services structure characterized by a minimum of fragmentation, duplication, and inefficiency. However, the inability of planning bodies to achieve much impact in this field may require us to rethink our homeostatic conceptions regarding ideal delivery models:

> For instance, we would have to recognize the accelerating mismatch between peoples' needs and the institutions set up to meet them, the need to live with and adapt to unstable arrangements and to seek to reduce uncertainty through approaching larger functional fields other than specific services and to design and manage transformation of services through a variety of network roles.[27]

Another writer argues that policy-making in the real world does not start with clearly formulated social goals, only "norms." There are no distinct steps of model-building and hypothesis-formulation leading to data-gathering and analysis, and thence to policy-making and implementation.[28] (Rather, one might imagine a spiral progress in which goals and programmes are constantly amended in the light of experience, and hence evaluative procedures and criteria change accordingly.) "In [today's] dynamic context of ill-structured problems, the notion of evaluation is completely changed. The difference between ends and means, between blueprints and little steps, between policy objectives and the social technology which is set up to pursue them, is blurred . . . .[29]

It may be argued that "the [organizational] learning process triggered by dynamic monitoring [of the system] will lead to 'better' results than those achievable by administrative rules of thumb."[30] However, "as we have very little theory of the overall system and practically no overall apparatus for collecting, processing and feeding back information and since no good feedback apparatus exists between analysis and problem-formulation in social policy, there is no hope that the present haphazard and ad hoc practices will soon disappear."[31]

In the short run, at least, social scientists will apparently have to rely on personal involvement as consultants to policy-makers if their expertise and research knowledge is to have impact at the level of government.

CONCLUSION

Another chapter of our intellectual history is being written as the dialectic of reason and scepticism continues. We cannot tell whether the rationalist swing of the pendulum has yet reached its outermost limit. Clearly, the

---

27 W. M. Nicholls, "Achieving that Well-Ordered Network of Services," review of *Case Studies in Social Planning* (Ottawa: C.C.S.D., 1971-), in *Canadian Welfare* 49, no. 1 (January-February 1973): 25.

28 G. Paquet, "Social Science Research as an Evaluative Instrument for Social Policy," paper presented to the Conference on Social Science Research and Social Policy, Human Resources Research Council, Edmonton, February 1971.

29 Ibid.

30 Ibid.

31 K. E. Boulding, *A Primer on Social Dynamics* (New York: Free Press, 1970), cited in Paquet, "Social Science Research as an Evaluative Instrument for Social Policy."

planners would not have it so, and researchers are still dazzled by the potential contribution of their methods to policy development:

> [T]here is a strong argument for emphasizing evaluative research in social programming. This country spends enormous amounts for social services programs (including health and education). At the same time the effectiveness of many of these programs is seriously questioned. Increases in program costs tend to be much more conspicuous than improvements in the quality of services. If it is agreed that social programs whould be strengthened and that improvement is most likely to come about through the use of rational methods, it is clear that the evaluation role is vital. Because the results of social programs are often not obvious, the methods of empirical research are needed to obtain precise information on program effectiveness.[32]

Such is the "faith of the evaluators." It may be a misdirected faith. Politicians tend to listen first to various interest groups, and as consumer groups of all types strengthen in coherence and numbers, their preferences and their perceptions of the adequacy of programmes and services may gain increasing influence over the formulation of social welfare policy. A more realistic role for evaluators might be to reduce uncertainty through seeking to specify the trade-offs associated with alternative political decisions, thereby allowing the decision-makers to apply their preferences and values more surely.

Hopefully (and this has been beyond the scope of this paper), such a role would also help to discourage tendencies to be wasteful on the part of programme administrators. We can merely note here that failure to specify both clear goals and evaluative criteria, combined with pressure—inherent in the structure of the public administration process itself—to spend all of the money allocated to that programme, may result in serious mismanagement of public funds. Recent allegations (December 1977) concerning federal grants to Alberta Indian bands under a small business incentive programme could be a case in point.

BIBLIOGRAPHY

Boulding, K. E. *A Primer on Social Dynamics.* New York: Free Press, 1970.

Briar, Scott. "Family Services and Casework." In *Research in the Social Services.* Edited by H. Maas. New York: N.A.S.W., 1971.

Brinton, C. *Ideas and Men.* New York: Prentice-Hall, 1950.

Brooks, M. "The Community Action Program as a Setting for Applied Research." *Journal of Social Issues* 21, no. 1 (1965): 29-40.

Canada. Department of Finance. *Estimates for the Fiscal Year 1974-75.* Ottawa, 1973.

_____. Department of the Secretary of State. *Report of the Evaluation Task Force to the Secretary of State: Opportunities for Youth '71.* Ottawa, 1972.

_____. Ministry of State for Urban Affairs. *A Living Place.* Ottawa, n.d.

Caro, F. "Evaluation Research: An Overview." In *Readings in Evaluation Research.* Edited by F. Caro. New York: Russell Sage Foundation, 1971.

Carter, N., and Wharf, B. *Evaluating Social Development Programs.* Ottawa: Canadian Council on Social Development, 1973.

Goldin, G., et al. *The Utilization of Rehabilitation Research.* Monograph No. 6. Boston: Northeastern University, 1969.

32 Caro, "Evaluation Research," pp. 27-28.

Halmos, P. *The Faith of the Counsellors.* London: Constable, 1966.

Larsen, D. "Research and Policy: Creative Opportunities and Practical Constraints." Paper presented to the Conference on Social Science Research and Social Policy, Human Resources Research Council, Edmonton, February 1971.

Levinson, P. "Evaluation of Social Welfare Programs, Two Research Models." *Welfare in Review* 4 (1966): 5-12.

Lithwick, N. H. *Urban Canada: Problems and Prospects.* Ottawa: Central Mortgage & Housing Corporation, 1970.

M. MacDonald. "Reunion at Vocational High: An Analysis of Girls at Vocational High: An Experiment in Social Work Intervention." *Social Service Review* 40, no. 2 (June 1966): 175-89.

McQueen, D. L. "The Modes of Feeding Research into Policy." Paper presented to the Conference on Social Science Research and Social Policy, Human Resources Research Council, Edmonton, February 1971.

Mann, F., and Likert, R. "The Need for Research on the Communication of Research Results." In *Readings in Evaluation Research*, pp. 143-51. Edited by F. Caro. New York: Russell Sage Foundation, 1971.

Meyer, H. J.; Borgatta, E. F.; and Jones, W. C. *Girls at Vocational High: An Experiment in Social Work Intervention.* New York: Russell Sage, 1965.

Nettler, I. "Knowing and Doing." Paper presented to the Conference on Social Science Research and Social Policy, Human Resources Research Council, Edmonton, February 1971.

Nicholls, W. M. "Achieving that Well-Ordered Network of Services." Review of *Case Studies in Social Planning* (Ottawa: C.C.S.D., 1971-). *Canadian Welfare* 49, no. 1 (January-February 1973): 25.

Paquet, G. "Social Science Research as an Evaluative Instrument for Social Policy." Paper presented to the Conference on Social Science Research and Social Policy, Human Resources Research Council, Edmonton, February 1971.

Rodman, H., and Kolodny, R. "Organizational Strains in the Researcher-Practitioner Relationship." *Human Organization* 23 (1964): 171-82.

Schulberg, H., and Baker, F. "Program Evaluation Models and the Implementation of Research Findings." *American Journal of Public Health* 58, no. 7 (1968): 1248-55.

Slater, D. "Economic Policy and Economic Research in Canada since 1950." *Queen's Quarterly* 74, no. 1 (1967): 1-20.

Speers, G., and Kelly, M. "A Behavioural Approach to Prevention in Child Welfare." *The Social Worker* 42, no. 1 (Spring 1974): 64-74.

Suchman, E. *Evaluation Research.* New York: Russell Sage Foundation, 1968.

———. "Action for What? A Critique of Evaluative Research." In *Evaluating Social Action Programs*, pp. 52-84. Edited by C. Weiss. Boston: Allyn & Bacon, 1972.

Townsend, P. "The Objectives of the New Local Social Service." In *The Fifth Social Service: A Critical Analysis of the Seebohm Proposals.* London: Fabian Society, 1970.

Wiener, R., and Bayley, J. "The Administration and Evaluation of Research Units and Projects." *British Journal of Sociology* 22 (1971: 193-99.

Weiss, C. "The Politicization of Evaluative Research." *Journal of Social Issues* 26, no. 4 (1970): 57-68.

Wholey, J., et al. *Federal Evaluation Policy.* Washington: The Urban Institute, 1970.

Index

Headings are arranged alphabetically word by word; subheadings likewise alphabetically by the first noun occurring in phrases.